"Wasteing my Substance by Riotous living"

New-England Runaways, 1778-1783

Compiled by
Joseph Lee Boyle

Copyright © 2022 by
Joseph Lee Boyle

All Rights Reserved.

Published for Clearfield Company by
Genealogical Publishing Company
Baltimore, Maryland
2022

ISBN 9780806359472

INTRODUCTION

The majority of the individuals in this compilation are runaway servants, slaves, and apprentices, both men and women, military deserters, with horse thieves, counterfeiters, burglars, jail breakers, an occasional murderer, pirates, traitors to the American cause, and other lowlifes are represented, as well as numerous supposedly errant spouses. Some of the alleged crimes were vague such as Evan Jones who was "suspected to be unfriendly to the United States of America." Others would not now be considered jailable such as Rhode Islander Jonathan Green who was sought in 1778 for the "crime of getting a girl with child," and Patrick Reiley, "confined for blaspheming against the Holy Ghost."

Tracking an individual by name may often lead to a dead end as multiple names were commonly used by miscreants, and middle names were not often used at this time. Elijah Austin Smith was committed to Worcester jail for breaking into a shop, "but he has gone by several other Names, such as Pumroy, James Lines, Elijah Wood, James Potter, &c" An ad in another paper for the same individual gives the names Elijah Smith, Elijah Austin, Elijah Pomroy, James Lynds, alias Elijah Wood, &c. And, of course, none of those names may have been his real one. Some of the multiple names that appear are likely due to spelling or pronunciation errors.

When ads are published in different newspapers or even in the same paper on different dates, discrepancies in the ads sometimes appear. If the variations are substantial, the separate ads are included. The reader should be prepared for phonetic spellings of people they are interested in, such as Read/Reed that appear in this volume, and Jonson/Johnston/Johnson is always a challenge. In a few cases letters or numerals were indistinct and thus appear in brackets.

Some of the runaways were skilled workers. Butchers, bakers, coopers, carpenters, joiners, farriers, shoemakers and taylors (tailors) are represented. Skills of others might today be rare today such as that of a paper maker and shoe maker. Others such as wire drawer, soap boiler and worsted comber no longer exist.

Ads were sometimes so delayed that the culprits were probably long gone. In August 1783, William Burns posted an ad dated the previous November for Ebenezer Pinkham. In March 1778, James Sheffield advertised for apprentice Asa Crandal who had left the previous August, offering only one shilling reward. Mary Brown left her husband on January 9, 1779, but her husband did not advertise for her until the following January.

Some ads are for sailors who deserted, most are civilian, a few are Royal and Continental Navies. Ads for privateers and privateering are mentioned indicating skills at sailing in the wars of the period. For most military deserters from New

England during the American Revolution, the reader is directed to this author's two volume set *"He Loves a Good Deal of Rum": Military Desertions During the American Revolution, 1775-1783*, published by Clearfield Company in 2009.

It is impossible to know how many runaways there really were. No newspapers were published in Delaware for the entire period covered. What are now the states of Maine and Vermont did not exist as separate colonies. Vermont did not have a newspaper until 1783, and Maine had none for this period. After the British occupied New York City in 1776, ads from the rebel states were rare.

Also printed handbills were often circulated, and some masters may have only advertised with them. Given that so many of the servants appear to be scapegraces, one wonders why their masters spent money to advertise for them, let alone pay a reward for their return. Masters were likely to ignore those who left for a few days of dissipation, particularly planters during the agricultural slow season.

Some masters may have not wanted to pay the cost of the ads. Those masters whose servants absconded from more remote parts of America may not have bothered to advertise them. Subscribers who waited lengthy periods to advertise must have greatly reduced the chance of capturing the rogue. Several ads seem to have been intended to let the runaway know how little the master thought of them as very low rewards were posted. In 1783 Stephen Bean offered only "one Spanish petatoe" for returning apprentice John Gilman. Amos Culver advertised for "small and weakly" apprentice boy Asa Larabee, and offered only one shilling as a reward.

Some of the people are well described, many not at all. Some identifying marks were obvious. Easy to recognize would have been a Negro named Warwick who ran away from Ebenezer Craft, described as "about 5 Feet 6 Inches high, about 18 Years of Age, has the Guinea Marks on his Forehead, Cheeks and Chin, and Holes through the Sides of his Nose."

A number of ads were by men for their allegedly errant wives. Jonathan Soule reported that wife Mary had behaved "in a very indecent Manner...has made sundry Attempts to take away my Life, by stabbing me with Knives and Forks, beating me with the Distaff, Tongs, and Hammer; scratching and biting me very inhumanly...." One wonders why he further complained she had left him. In 1779 Isaac Brown reported that Jane "hath allowed herself in repeating threats of revenge on my person, even in murder, and to destroy my house by fire, and hath attempted to put in execution her revenge—embezzled my goods, and run me in debt." John Robie had forbidden any credit to his eloped wife Naomi in 1775, he rescinded the ban in 1777, but in 1778 again advertised against her.

Other men claimed their wives were unfaithful. John Phillips of Gloucester claimed his appropriately named wife Desire "hath also violated her Marriage Covenant, by cohabiting with another Man." Remembrance Filey claimed Anna Cryrena, his wife "hath had unlawful concern with another man, while I have been absent...about ten months in the army, by which means she is now pregnant," and he intended "to take lawful measures to get rid on her as soon as may be."

Several wives countered the statements of their spouses. In 1779 Daniel Rogers advertised his wife Hannah as "eloped from my bed and board" and forbade "all persons from entertaining or trusting her on my account, for I will pay no debts for her after this date." The following week Hannah rebutted him with a long reply to

his "unjust aspersion" and that she suffered from a consumption and he had neglected her, and was "cruelly accused by a pitiless and unjust husband of having eloped from him."

A sad case was Charity Welch who filed for her marriage to be dissolved as her husband Benjamin about seven years ago, "left her destitute of any Support, went to Sea, entered on Board a British Man of War, and has continued with the Enemy ever Since." She claimed he had married in England and had a child there. A more amusing incident is that of Samuel/Anne Smith who inlisted in the Continental Army at Springfield in 1782. "After many enquiries and a very *minute* examination, this adventurer (altho artfully dressed in mans apparrel) was discovered to be of the female sex; and soon conducted to goal." She was also a horse thief and "acted the man so perfectly well through the whole she might probably have passed, had not the want of a beard, and the redundance of some other matters led to a detection."

Some complicated relationships appear. Gideon Leavenworth advertised as a runaway Negro man Lively who "says he is free by inlisting into the Continental Army, and hath a Copy of a Pass from General Gates." In 1783 William Rice advertised that he would not be responsible "for any Bargains, Contracts, or Negotiations" of Esther, "a young Woman, whom People call my Wife, because a few Years since the marriage Ceremmony was imposed upon us in a fiarcical Manner contrary to both our Inclinations."

The previous two volumes of this series introduced the "notorious Burglarian," named John Brown, who had been sentenced to death for his various crimes noted as early as 1770. In 1780 he was trying to escape another crime and drowned. This work also includes individuals with New England connections who did not run away from those colonies. Negro Peter ran away from "Dutchess" county New York but was at "Deerfield about the first of June last, and proposed going down

Connecticut to look for work." Apprentice Joseph Chase ran away from Philadelphia but "has the New England dialect, being born at Boston."

This compilation lists all individuals mentioned. If an individual is listed with more than one name, all the names appear in the index. Titles are not listed unless no first name appears for the subject. While some of the Negroes and Indians are listed as slaves, many are not, so they may have been paid servants. People of mixed or uncertain racial status such as Phoebe "Half Indian and Half Negro" are listed under both races, as is Pero who appears in an ad as a Mustee or Mulatto. Even in the eighteenth-century racial descriptions were difficult. Joseph Raynolds advertisers for his Negro man named PERO" who "went off with a couple of Mulatto fellows, or at least they looked like such." Those designated as "Mustees" are listed separately when of unspecified mixed races.

The legal status of most of the non-white individuals rarely is given. While many would have been slaves, some such as James who ran away from James Boies were not, specifically "not a Slave but was bound for a Number of Years, and has almost two Years to serve." Sixteen year old Dinah "a Molatto Wench" was advertised as being an absent apprentice.

I have retained the original spelling, punctuation, and capitalization of the ads. Illegible words or letters are in brackets. Sometimes the ads in different papers are very similar and only the ad which occurs first in time is included, with references to the later ones. Minor differences in the advertisements are considered to be capitalization, spellings such as trousers/trowsers and 7/seven. If the ads are substantially different, each appears at the time it is first run. The majority are advertised in only one paper, some in two or more. Names can be spelled multiple ways such as Michael Murrey/Murry, George Monro/Munro, and William Berry/Barry. Big differences are sometimes found. The accuracy of some of the publications can be questioned. In 1778 James Burdick broke jail and appears as being "about six feet eight inches high." Possible but most unlikely.

Newspapers Consulted:

It should be noted that none of these newspapers had a complete run for the period. Also the names of some changed as time progressed. There were no newspapers published in Delaware for the entire period, and New York was in enemy hands until November 1783. Newspapers from south of Maryland were not consulted.

The American Gazette or the Constitutional Journal,
The American Journal And General Advertiser,
The Boston Evening-Post,
The Boston-Gazette, And The Country Journal,
The Connecticut Courant,
The Connecticut Gazette; And The Universal Intelligencer,
The Connecticut Journal, And The New-Haven Post Boy, 1780
The Continental Journal, And Weekly Advertiser,
The Essex Gazette,
The Essex Journal And New-Hampshire Packet,
The Essex Journal; Or The New-Hampshire Packet, And The Weekly Advertiser,
The Exeter Journal,
The Freeman's Journal, Or The North American Intelligence,
The Independent Chronicle and the Universal Advertiser,
The Independent Ledger, and the American Advertiser,
The Maryland Gazette,
The Massachusetts Gazette,
The Massachusetts Spy Or, Thomas's Boston Journal,
The New-Jersey Gazette,
The New-England Chronicle: Or, The Essex Gazette,
The New-Hampshire Gazette, And General Advertiser,
The Newport Mercury,
The New-York Gazette; and the Weekly Mercury,
The New-York Journal; or, The General Advertiser,
The Norwich Packet or, The Chronicle of Freedom,
The Pennsylvania Gazette,
The Pennsylvania Ledger
The Pennsylvania Packet
The Providence Gazette; And Country Journal,
Rivington's New-York Gazetteer,
The Salem Gazette,
The Royal Pennsylvania Gazette,
Thomas's Massachusetts Spy Or, American Oracle of Liberty,
The Vermont Journal and the Universal Advertiser.

1778

Ran-away from the subscriber about six weeks ago, a Servant Boy named George Swane, about 14 years of age. Whoever will take up and secure said boy, shall have ONE dollar reward.
          JOSEPH STEBBINS.   *Springfield, Dec.* 15.
The Continental Journal, And Weekly Advertiser, January 1, 1778; January 8, 1778.

WHereas Patience,
the Wife of the Subscriber, hath left his Bed and Board, refusing to return; he hereby forbids all Persons to credit her on his Account, as he will not pay any Debts of her contracting from the Date hereof.
          HOSEA BENNETT.   Scituate, December 27, 1777.
The Providence Gazette; And Country Journal, January 3, 1778; January 10, 1778.

TWENTY DOLLARS Reward.
RUNAWAY from the Subscriber, on the 19th of October last, an Apprentice Lad named *Anthony Willett Carpenter*, by Trade a Taylor, about 19 Years old, and about 5 Feet 5 Inches high, of a light Complexion and light Hair, pretty thick set. Whoever will take up and return said Lad to his Master, shall have Twenty Dollars Reward.
          EZRA FORD.   New-Haven, January 3. 1778.
The Connecticut Journal, January 7, 1778; February 4, 1778.

North Fairfield, December 17 A. D. 1777.
WHEREAS my Wife Elizabeth has eloped from my Bed and Board:—These are to forbid any Body's trusting her upon my Account, as I will pay no Debts of her contracting from the above Date.
          NEHEMIAH BLECKMEN.
The Connecticut Journal, January 7, 1778.

RUN away from me the subscriber, a Negro Man named ROBERT; said negro is about 5 feet 5 inches high well set, is of a yellowish cast, talks good English; had on when he went away, a light-colored coat and breeches, with yellow mettle buttons, yarn stockings; carried off with him, a suit of gray homespun, besides what he had on. Any person who shall take up said negro, and secure him in goal, or otherwise, shall receive a reward of 15 DOLLARS, and all charges
          paid, by   JOHN PARKER.
                    Georgetown, December 14, 1777.

The Independent Chronicle and the Universal Advertiser, January 8, 1778; January 15, 1778.

RAN away from the subscriber, last Tuesday, a Negro Woman, named Silence, about 22 Years of Age. Whoever will take up said Negro, and return her to any Goal, shall have Four Dollars Reward, and all necessary Charges paid by me, ALDEN BASS.
    N. B. All Persons are cautioned against harbouring or concealing her, as they wou'd avoid the Penalty of the Law. Any Person inclining to purchase said Negro, may have her, at a reasonable Price, by applying to said Bass.
    The Independent Chronicle and the Universal Advertiser, January 15, 1778; January 22, 1778; January 29, 1778.

ALL *persons that are indebted to or have any demands on the Estate of Thomas Mullins of Leominster, Blacksmith who is absconded and gone from his usual place of abode, and believed to be gone over to our enemies for protection are desired to bring them in to the subscriber at or before the first day of March next,*
    THOMAS STEARNS, Agent.
    Leominster, January 7, 1778.
    The Massachusetts Spy Or, American Oracle of Liberty, January 15, 1778.

WHEREAS I the subscriber did in the Exeter news-papers insert an advertisement bearing date march 3d, 1777, therein for reasons mentioned, did forbid all harbouring Hannah my wife or trusting her on my account the difference being amicably settled of certain conditions known to sundry persons then present; I do from this date make void what was contained in said advertisement relating to her being trusted on my account, and inform all persons that from this date she shall have the same privileges as though she had not been advertised.
    MOSES HILLS.
    Chester, New-Hampshire, December 19, 1777.
The Massachusetts Spy Or, American Oracle of Liberty, January 15, 1778; January 22, 1778; February 5, 1778; February 12, 1778. See *The Massachusetts Spy Or, American Oracle of Liberty*, April 16, 1778.

    FORTY DOLLARS REWARD.
RAN away the 14th Inst. William Naler, born in England, 19 Years old, speaks broad, 5 Feet 2 inches high, well set; had on when he left his master a Tow Shirt, Red-Baize Jacket, new Cloth Ash colour'd Breeches, (rather too small) white Yarn Stockings.—Stole and carried away one good Serge

brown Coat, Silver wash'd Buttons, on large Man's Loom Homespun Gown, one good Beaver Hatt, two white jackets, one Pair striped Woolen Trowsers, and one Pair white Yarn Stockings.—
Whoever will take up said Thief, and bring him to the Printer hereof, shall have FORTY DOLLARS Reward,
   paid by ROBERT PIERPONT.
              Boston, January 17, 1778.
The Boston Gazette, and Country Journal, January 19, 1778; February 2, 1778.

MADE his escape on the night of the 10th instant, one SIMON STEVENS, about 5 feet 11 inches high, and about 40 years old; he was an officer in the King's service last war, and said he was born in New-Hampshire, and has been in this present war; he intended when he ran away, to have gone on to Long-Island, but got cast-away on Gulls-Island:—He had on a light coloured surtout, a white spotted jacket, a pair tow trousers, a pair brown stockings, a checked woollen shirt, and an old hat; he took off with him, two Negroes.—Whoever will take up said STEVENS, and deliver him to me, or secure him in any of the public jails, shall receive TEN DOLLARS reward, and necessary charges,
   paid by NOBLE HINMAN.
         New-London, January 19, 1778.
The Norwich Packet and the Connecticut, Massachusetts, New-Hampshire, and Rhode-Island Weekly Advertiser, January 19, 1778; January 26, 1778; February 9, 1778.

BRoke gaol, at S. Kingstown, on the 19th of January, Christopher Fowler, of N. Kingstown, 5 feet 9 inches high, of a light complexion, has light hair, and a red scar on his cheek: Had on when he went away a blue great coat, a blue jacket, and light coloured stockings. Whoever secures said Fowler in any gaol within the United States, shall have Ten Dollars reward, and all necessary charges,
   paid by SAMUEL MUMFORD, Gaoler.
The Providence Gazette; And Country Journal, January 31, 1778; February 7, 1778; February 14, 1778; February 21, 1778.

        STOP THIEVES!
CAME to the house of the subscriber, on the 25th of January 1778, one JAMES HAMILTON, about 5 feet and an half high, well sett, black short curled hair, black eye brows, light blue eyes, can read and write well; had on when he went away, a white out-side jacket, with one button on each sleeve, at the wrist, a pair white breeches, much wore, a pair blue and white stockings, his left thumb (upper joint) put out, so that he can slip it in or out.

Likewise, one PATRICK BRIAN, about 6 feet high, a sprightly well limbed man, short strait brown hair, light blue eyes, speaks broad: had on when he went away, a green coat faced with red, and yellow buttons, a white coarse linen shirt, a pair white cloth breeches, almost new, a pair blue and white clouded stockings, a good felt hat, with a metal button thereon: Both these fellows were Irishmen, said to desert from the 22d regiment on Rhode-Island the 6th day of September last, and had passes from Governor Cook at Providence, to go into the country to get work; they tarried with me till Friday the 30th ult. (after dinner) then went off without paying for their board, and carried off one white Holland shirt and sundry other things, to the value of 22 or 23 dollars.—Whoever will take up said villains, and bring them to Norwich or New-London jail, so that justice may be done them, shall have SIX DOLLARS reward, and all necessary charges
     paid by me EBENEZER GROVER.
Norwich, February 2, 1778.
The Norwich Packet and the Connecticut, Massachusetts, New-Hampshire, and Rhode-Island Weekly Advertiser, February 2, 1778; February 16, 1778; February 23, 1778.

     TWENTY DOLLARS REWAD. [*sic*]
RUN away from the subscriber about two months past, a negro boy named YORK, about 5 feet 7 inches high, of a very black complexion, had a scar like a burn near one of his eyes; it is supposed he is gone to old Lebanon, to one Mr. Tisdell's the place where he was bought. Whoever shall secure or bring the said Negro to the subscriber, shall receive the above reward and all reasonable charges paid,
    by STEPHEN TUTTLE. Albany, Jan. 13 1778.
 The Connecticut Courant, and Hartford Weekly Intelligencer, February 3, 1778.

RUN away from the subscriber in Haddam, on the 30th of November last, a negro man servant named London, about 34 years of age, about 5 feet 7 inches, is subject to the phthisick, had on and carried with him, a blue duffel surcoat, buckskin breeches, a blue plain cloth coat, a blue broad cloth waistcoat, trimmed with mettle buttons, a blue calamanco coat, a light brown cut velvet waistcoat, a brown coat and waistcoat, linnen and cotton, trimmed with mettle buttons, a good beaver hat, a pair of striped trowsers, two woolen and one holland shirts, sundry pair of stockings, a pair of small silver knee buckles, marked with S: V. a pair of silver plated shoe buckles. Whoever will take up said negro, and bring him to me, or secure him so that I may have him again, shall have three Dollars reward, and all necessary
    charges paid, by ELEAZER MAY.
        Haddam, January 7th, 1778.

N. B. All persons are forbid harbouring said negro.
The Connecticut Gazette; and the Universal Intelligencer, February 13, 1778.

WHEREAS my Wife Elizabeth, (Daughter of James Niles of Charlestown, State of Rhode-Island) has behaved in a loose disorderly Manner, and left my Bed and Board, and refuseth to return and cohabit with me; and after trying every reasonable Expedient to bring her to a Sense of her Duty, without any Effect, I am reduced to the Necessity of taking this Method in order to secure my Interest, by preventing her running me in Debt. I do therefore hereby forbid any Person or Persons trusting her on my Account, for no Debt contracted by her after this Date will be paid by me. I also forbid any Person entertaining or her the said Elizabeth. Witness my Hand,

his
JAMES—I—Freeman,
Mark.

GROTON, 22d Jan. 1778.
The Connecticut Gazette; and the Universal Intelligencer, February 1 3, 1778.

Goshen (in Litchfield County) Jan. 31. 1778.

RANAWAY from said Goshen on the night after the 25th of January instant, two persons, both Irishman, one named *Peter Golden*, about 23 years old, light complexion, about 5 feet 8 inches high, short hair; had on and carried with him an old felt hat, grey coat, vest, and breeches, pair of grey woolen stockings, pair of white ditto, pair of white thread ditto, striped Holland shirt, black velvet stock, square copper shoe buckles. The other *John May*, he belonged to the 40th regiment is about 28 years old, and carried with him a felt hat, light brown surtout bound with white, grey coat lined with brown tammy, black home made vest & breeches, pair of black woolen stockings, two pair of blue and white ditto, on pair white thread ditto, two pair of shoes, pewter shoe buckles, silver knee buckles, striped Holland shirt, two white linnen shirts. It is supposed the said prisoners are endeavoring to escape to the enemy, as they had parted with most if not all their regimentals before they went off. Whoever will secure said prisoners and send them to Hartford to the care of Ezekiel Williams, Esq; commissary of prisoners, or to the subscriber at said Goshen, shall be well rewarded.

EBEN'R MORTON.

The Connecticut Journal, February 18, 1778.

RAN-away from the Subscriber in New-London, about six months ago, an apprentice Boy named George Ledyard, about 17 years old, large of his age, wore his own hair of a light colour, light complection, a blacksmith by

trade. Whoever will return him to me in New-London shall have one Dollar reward.   Eliakim Perry.   Feb. 10, 1778.
The Connecticut Gazette; and the Universal Intelligencer, February 20, 1778; March 6, 1778; March 13, 1778.

RAN away from the Subscriber, living in Albany, a Negro Man, named POMPEY LARKIN, 19 Years and 10 days old, late the property of Francis Moor, Baker, of Cambridge, an arch, knowing, deceitful Negro. Whoever will take up said Negro, and deliver him to Major John White, Quarter-Master to General Nixon's Brigade, at the American Coffee-House in State-Street, or secure him in any Goal, within 60 Miles of Boston, and give Major White notice thereof, shall be entitled to the sum of Four Pounds, and all necessary Charges,
          paid by   NEAL SHAW.
N. B. Twenty Pounds will be paid to any one, that will bring him to said Shaw, in Albany.
The Independent Chronicle and the Universal Advertiser, February 26, 1778; March 5, 1778; March 12, 1778.

RAN away from the Subscriber, on the evening of the [ ] instant, an apprentice boy, named SAMUEL BANCROFT, about 18 years of age, five feet six inches high, light complection, short nut brown hair. Whoever will take up and return said boy to his master, shall receive one Dollar, reward, and all persons are forbid to harbour or conceal him at their peril.
             THOMAS BAIRD, Jun.   Worcester, Feb. 26th 1778.
The Massachusetts Spy Or American Oracle of Liberty, March 5, 1778; March 19, 1778.

RAN-AWAY from the subscriber, an apprentice boy named Daniel Bostwick, about four feet nine inches high, of a light complexion, yellow hair; had on and took with him, a mixt coulored blue and white coat and jacket, one light coulered coat and jacket, and sourtout coat, a pair of blue breeches, mixed coloured trowsers, two check woolen shirts one check linnen ditto, one felt hat; said boy is fifteen years of age.—Whoever will take up said boy and return him to me the subscriber, shall have six pence reward, paid by me,
             ABIJAH JONES.   Salsbury, Feb. 25, 1778.
The Connecticut Courant, And Hartford Weekly Intelligencer, March 10, 1778.

One Hundred Pounds Reward.
BROKE out of the Goal in Exeter, in the State of New Hampshire in the night of the 28th ult. by way of the Vault, Col. STEPHEN HOLLAND,

convicted of counterfeiting the State's Currency, &c. &c.—He is a well looking Man—light Complexion—middle aged—fleshy—pitted with the Small-Pox—about five Feet eight Inches high—and wears a Wig—It is supposed that he will make for the Enemy—Whoever will take him up and return him, or secure him in any Goal of the UNITED STATES, shall be intitled to the above Reward, and all necessary Charges paid.
                    NICHOLAS GILMAN.
One of the Council of Safety of said State.   Exeter, March 2d, 1778.
The Exeter Journal, or, New Hampshire Gazette, March 3, 1778; March 10, 1778; March 17, 1778; *The Freeman's Journal, or New-Hampshire Gazette*, March 10, 1778. See *The Boston-Gazette, And Country Journal*, May 5, 1777.

RAN away from the Subscriber, sometime in August last, an apprentice Boy, named Asa Crandal: This is therefore to forbid all Masters of Vessels, or any other Persons employing, harbouring, or any wise detaining said Apprentice from my Service; and whoever will return him to me in New-London, shall have one Shilling Reward.
                    James Sheffield.
The Connecticut Gazette; And The Universal Intelligencer, March 13, 1778; March 20, 1778; April 3, 1778. See *The Connecticut Gazette; And The Universal Intelligencer*, August 22, 1777.

BROKE out of the County Goal in New-London the Night following the 4th of March Inst. one THOMAS ROGERS of New-London Great Neck, he is pretty small of Stature, long black Hair and dark Eyes. Whoever will take up said Rogers and secure him so that I may have him again, shall have TWENTY DOLLARS Reward, and all necessary Charges
                paid by   EPHRAIM MINER, Goaler.
                                      New-London, March 5, 1778.
The Connecticut Gazette; And The Universal Intelligencer, March 6, 1778; March 13, 1778; March 20, 1778; April 3, 1778.

BROKE out of the Goal in New-London, the Night following the 11th Day of March Inst. one WILLIAM HOWARD, of this Town, about 32 Years old, about 5 Feet 10 Inches high, tawny Complexion, dark Eyes and Hair. Whoever will take up said Howard and return or secure him so that I can have him again shall have TEN DOLLARS Reward and all necessary Charges, paid by
            EPHRAIM MINER, Goaler.   New-London, March 12, 1778.
The Connecticut Gazette; and the Universal Intelligencer, March 13, 1778; March 20, 1778; April 3, 1778.

RAN-away from the Subscribers in Stonington, sometime last Summer, an apprentice Boy named Daniel Saunders, jun. about 20 Years old. All Persons are hereby forbid to harbour, conceal, or any Way entertain my said Apprentice on Penalty of the Law; and whoever returns him to the Subscriber in Stonington, shall have one Shilling Reward.
    George Sheffield, jun. Stonington, Mar. 9, 1778.
The Connecticut Gazette; And The Universal Intelligencer, March 13, 1778; March 20, 1778; April 3, 1778.

RUN away from the subscriber on the 2d Inst. an apprentice boy about 14 years of age, named Nathan Smith, well set, fair complexion, had on a striped flannel jacket, flowered serge waistcoat, crimson broad cloth breeches and white yarn stockings. Whoever will return him to the subscriber in Groton, shall have two Dollars reward,
    paid by THOMAS AVERY. Groton, March 12, 1778.
The Connecticut Gazette; And The Universal Intelligencer, March 13, 1778; March 20, 1778; April 3, 1778; April 10, 1778. See *The Connecticut Gazette; And The Universal Intelligencer*, November 8, 1776.

BROKE goal in Northampton and escaped the last evening, the following prisoners viz. Jeremiah Rogers late of Colchester or Milford or Lebanon in Connecticut a well set fellow about five feet nine inches high twenty six years old; he was committed for theft, had on a blue coat; also James Burdick late of Lainsborough about six feet eight inches [*sic*] high, dark complexioned about 27 years old, also James Reynolds near six feet in heighth, 22 years old the two last were taken at Bennington.
 It is hope the friends to the happiness of their country will exert themselves, if they have opportunity to apprehend and secure the said persons, so that they may be brought to justice for which they shall be rewarded.
    JOSEPH COOK, Goaler, Northampton, March 14, 1778.
The Connecticut Courant, And Hartford Weekly Intelligencer, March 17, 1778.

BROKE out of the County Goal in New-London the Night following the 19th of March Inst. two Prisoners, one named JAMES HOLT, a smallish Man, pretty much Pock-broken, lightish Complexion and Eyes; the other named JAMES DAVENPORT, short and thick set, light Complexion and Eyes, and dark Hair, both belonging to said New-London. Whoever will take up said Prisoners and return them or secure them so that I can have them again shall have TEN DOLLARS Reward, and all necessary Charges

paid by EPHRAIM MINER, Goaler.
New-London, March 20, 1778.
The Connecticut Gazette; And The Universal Intelligencer, March 20, 1778; March 27, 1778; April 3, 1778.

ABsconded from my service, on Tuesday morning the 17th instant (thro' the instigation of evil-minded persons) Relief Thurber, son of the late Samuel Thurber, shipwright, deceased: He is a short, thick-set boy, about 10 years of age, much pitted with the small-pox, and generally known in this town.

Whoever will return him to me, within 20 days from the date hereof, shall be paid two dollars reward. Any person who shall be guilty of secreting him, may depend on being prosecuted, by me,
JONATHAN ARNOLD. Providence, March 20, 1778.
The Providence Gazette; And Country Journal, March 21, 1778; March 28, 1778; April 4, 1778; April 11, 1778.

RAN away last Tuesday morning, from the subscriber living in Front-street, between Arch and Race streets, an apprentice boy named JOSEPH CHASE; he is about fourteen years of age, stout made, and has the New England dialect, being born at Boston. He had on when he ran away, a blue coat and jacket, coarse short, and pepper and salt coloured beeches. He is a deserter from Washington's army, about which he is very fond of talking. Whoever brings him to his master, shall have SIXPENCE reward, and the sweepings of the shop board.
HUGH M'CONNAL. March 2.
The Pennsylvania Evening Post, March 23, 1778.

TAKEN up as a Runaway, a Molatto Boy, about 13 Years old, has short, black, strait Hair; he says he formerly belonged to one William Rose, of Branford. His Master is desired to take him away, and pay Charges to the Subscriber, Innholder in Milford, near New Haven Bounds of the Road.
JOSIAH PARDY. Milford, March 24, 1778.
N. B. He has no Pass or Money, and but very indifferently clothed; says he is inlisted in the Army.
The Connecticut Journal, And The New-Haven Post Boy, March 25, 1778; April 1, 1778; April 8, 1778.

ON the 18th Instant the House of the Subscriber was broken open, & stolen from thence one new light coloured broad-cloth Coat, full trim'd, with the same coloured Shaloon, save Part of the Sleeves, with white Tammy, and with mohair Buttons, short Cuffs, and large Buttons on them; a Vest of the

same, the Back lined with white tow Cloth, one striped blue and white Cotton Vest with Sleeves, one Pair of white Home made Fustian Breeches, one check'd woolen Shirt, four and four, one striped black purple and white Calico Gown; one Coverlid, with large Checks black & white; one Sheet, one Pillow Case. The Thief, without doubt, is John Burk, an Irishman, broken spoken, near 5 Feet 6 inches high, had on a light colour'd Coat with yellow Facing, green Vest and Breeches, he belongs to Col. Hazen's Regiment. Whoever will take up and secure the Thief or Thieves, with the above Articles, so that the Owner may have them again, shall have Five Dollars Reward, and all necessary charges paid
    Caleb Clark.   North Haven, March 25.
The Connecticut Journal, And The New-Haven Post Boy, March 25, 1778; April 8, 1778.

ON the Night on the 23 Instant the following Persons broke out and made their Escape from the Gaol in New Haven, viz. JEREMIAH CONNEL, an Irishman, about 5 Feet 6 Inches high, thick set, has a red Face and white Eyes, an Inhabitant of New-Haven; also one PELATIAH TURNER, of Hartford, of a middlng Stature, thin Vissage, and poorly Clothed; they were both taken up an committed on suspicion of traiterous Practices against this and the other States. Whoever shall take up and secure them in any Gaol in Connecticut, shall receive Two Dollars Reward for each.
    STEPHEN MUNSON, Gaoler.
The Connecticut Journal, And The New-Haven Post Boy, March 25, 1778; April 1, 1778; April 8, 1778.

RUN way from the Subscriber in Groton on the 30th of January last, one Phebe Perkins, alias Morgan, 17 Years old, middling Stature, has a down Look, brown Hair and dark Eyes, wore away a brown Gown and Wine coloured Quilt. Whoever will take up said Runaway and return her to me, shall have Six Pence Reward.
    JOSEPH STANTON.   Groton, March 20, 1778.
The Connecticut Gazette; And The Universal Intelligencer, March 27, 1778; April 3, 1778.

        Sandwich, February 26, 1778.
This Day were committed to the Goal of the County, Melatiah Bourn, Isaac Knowles, Seth Perry, John Jennings, Abiel Ellis, and Prince Tupper, all Inhabitants of this Town, for refusing to take the Oath of Allegiance to this State. As they have always been high Tories, the loss of these Inhabitants is not much regretted by this Town. These, with Lemuel Bourn, Samuel Perry, Thos. Perry, Stephen Perry, Sam. Perry, jun. other Inhabitants of this Town, who voluntarily went to our Enemy at Rhode

Island last Fall, making 14 in the whole, we expect will soon be augmented to about double that Number from among us, who will refuse to take the Oath; when we have got rid of them, the Town will be pretty well purged.
The Boston-Gazette, And Country Journal, April 6, 1778.

WHEREAS Mary, the Wife of me the Subscriber has without just cause denied my Bed & board, this is therefore to forbid all person harbouring or trusting her on my account, as I am determined not to pay any debts she may contract after the date hereof.
    James Cochran, 3d.   Pembrook, March 27th, 1778.
The Exeter Journal, or, New Hampshire Gazette, April 7, 1778.

Run-away from the Subscriber, the latter End of January last, a Molatto Wench about 16 Years old, named DINAH, thick and large. All Persons are hereby forbid to harbour said Apprentice [sic] on Penalty of the Law; and whoever returns her to the Subscriber in Pomfret shall have Nine Pence Reward.
    Samuel Sumner.   Pomfret, Mar. 25, 1778.
The Connecticut Gazette; and the Universal Intelligencer, April 10, 1778; April 17, 1778; May 1, 1778.

MADE his escape from Windsor, one Stuart Mason a British prisoner, he is about 23 years of age small of Stature, fair complexion, a large scar under his chin.—Whoever will bring said fellow to the Goal in Hartford shall have a handsome reward and necessary charges
    paid by EZEK. WILLIAMS Com. Prisoners.
 N. B. As sundry other of the prisoners particularly two of the Stages, taken last year on Long Island have also ran away; it is hoped that all friends of their country will keep a good look out for all such fellows travelling without a pass.
The Connecticut Courant, And The Weekly Intelligencer, April 14, 1778.

BROKE out and made their escape from Fairfield goal, on the night of the 3d instant, the following persons, viz. *David Washburn, Seth Seeley, Uriah Hair, William Allen, Abel Skidder, Matthew Sherman, Samuel Denton,* and *Patrick Reiley*; the seven first born in this country, and confined for traiterous practices against this and the other States; the latter, Reiley, confined for blaspheming against the Holy Ghost, born in Ireland. Whoever shall take up and secure them in any goal in this State, shall receive Thirty Two Dollars Reward, or Four Dollars for each,
    from ISAAC HUBBILL, Goaler.
                Fairfield, April 4 1778.

The Connecticut Journal, April 15, 1778; April 21, 1778; May 6, 1778.

Confined in New Haven Goal, a transient Person by the Name of *Evan Jones*, committed by the Authority of Durham, suspected to be unfriendly to the United States of America. Found on said Jones about 14 Yards of white Flannel, about 8 Yards of ash colour'd Flannel. Any person claiming said Cloth and proving his Property, and paying Charge, may have it again be enquiring at the Goal.
The Connecticut Journal, April 15, 1778; April 21, 1778.

Whereas *Hannah* my wife, refuses to live with me, and has gone from me, I therefore forbid any person to trust her on my account, as I will not pay any thing for her after the date hereof.
    Jonathan Lincon,   Abington, April 10, 1778.
The Continental Journal, And Weekly Advertiser, April 16, 1778; April 23, 1778.

WHEREAS I the Subscriber did in an Exeter News-Paper insert an Advertisement dated March 3d 1776, [sic] forbidding all persons harbouring or trusting of Hannah my Wife, then expected the difference was amicably settled known to sundry persons then present, I did make void in a Worcester Paper, what was in the first paper relating to her being trusted on my account; but she still absents herself, and refuses to come to live with me, I do again forbid per parents and all persons from harbouring said Hannah my wife any longer, upon the penalty of the law, and I do forbid her parents and all persons, from trusting her on my account, for I will not pay any debt of her contracting from the date hereof. Notwithstanding if she will return and live with me peaceably I will receive her and use her well.
    MOSES HILLS.   Chester, (New-Hampshire) March 21, 1778.
The Massachusetts Spy Or, Am\\erican Oracle of Liberty, April 16, 1778. See *The Massachusetts Spy Or, American Oracle of Liberty,* January 15, 1778.

WHereas my Negro Man, named JEFFERY, hath absented himself from me without Leave: I do hereby forbid any Person or Persons entertaining or employing him, in any Manner, as they will answer it at their Peril.
    EDWARD SEARL.   Cranston, April 25.
The Providence Gazette; And Country Journal, April 25, 1778; May 2, 1778.

THE subscriber informs the public, that his son, Benjamin Commins, a minor, is non compos mentis, and incapable of acting for himself; all recruiting officers are therefore notified not in inlist him, as will not answer for the service in any respect. Said Benjamin has been already inlisted oftener than once, and having trifled away the bounty, the officer or the public has lost it, as he would not pass muster.
    JOSEPH COMMINS.   Coventry, April 21, 1778.
The Providence Gazette; And Country Journal, April 25, 1778.

WHereas Desire Phillips, the Wife of me the Subscriber, hath in my Absence, while in the Army as a Soldier, in Defence of my Country, run me in Debt, and greatly wasted and squandered my Estate, although I left her a Sufficiency to subsist on; and hath also violated her Marriage Covenant, by cohabiting with another Man: I therefore forewarn and forbid all Persons whatever to trade with or trust her on my Account, as I am determined to pay no Debts of her contracting from the Date hereof.
    JOHN PHILLIPS,   Gloucester, April 17.
The Providence Gazette; And Country Journal, April 25, 1778; May 2, 1778.

MY wife Sabarah having forsaken my bed and board, I forbid all persons to trust her on my account, as I not pay any debts she may contract from the date hereof.
    SETH BASSET.   Killingly, April 15, 1778.
The Providence Gazette; And Country Journal, April 25, 1778; May 2, 1778.

WHoever will apprehend one *John Christopher Zedericks*, a Thief, about 36 Years of Age, about 5 Feet 6 Inches high, light Hair, bald Head; & much Pock-mark'd, and will bring him to the Subscriber, shall have Twenty Dollars Reward, and all necessary Charges
   paid by EDMUND G. WELDS.
              Roxbury, April 25th, 1778.
 N. B. He had on a light-coloured Cloth shirt Coat, and wore a Cap, and had white Overalls instead of Breeches.
The Boston-Gazette, and Country Journal, April 27, 1778; May 11, 1778.

NEW-LONDON, April 10.
 At the Superior Court held at Norwich, last Week, Elisha Fox of the North-Parish in this Town, was convicted of attempting to join the Enemy, and for that Purpose going to Long-Island, was sentenced to two Years Imprisonment, and to pay a fine of £. 20. Benjamin Fitch, a Lad, was also

convicted of the same Crime, and sentenced to two Months Imprisonment and to pay £. 5.
The Connecticut Journal, April 21, 1778.

RUNAWAY on or about the 22d day of January last, from his Master, James Folsom, in the State of New-Hampshire, Barber, an Apprentice Boy named Thomas Jackson, about 16 years old light complexion, and light hair: Whoever will take up said Runaway, and convey him to his said Master, shall have two dollars reward; and all persons are hereby cautioned against harbouring or concealing said apprentice, as they would avoid the penalty of the Law. Exeter, April 2th, 1778.
The Exeter Journal, or, New Hampshire Gazette, April 28, 1778.

RAN-AWAY from the subscriber, on Sunday the 26th inst. the following persons, viz. ISAAC KETCHUM, who was taken from the west end of Long-Island some time ago: He is of middle stature, about 50 years of age, dark complexion, dark hair and eyes, the eyelid of the left eye hanging almost over the same, walks stooping, and has a down look: Had on a greyish coat and vest, leather breeches, and a white felt hat. GEORGE SNYDER, a German, who was taken prisoner; he is about six feet high, and had on a red coat faced with blue. Whoever secures said persons, shall have Ten Dollars for each.
   JOHN BARNEY, junr.   Norwich, April 27, 1778.
The Norwich Packet, April 27, 1778. See *The Norwich Packet*, May 4, 1778.

WHEREAS MELE, my Wife, has behaved in a very indecent Manner, refusing to live with me, and has left my Bed and Board. I therefore hereby forewarn all Person not to harbour her, or to carry her to Long Island; and I also forbid any Person trusting her on my account, for I shall pay no Debts of her contracting after this Date.
   John Anturny.   East-Haddam, April 23, 1778.
The Connecticut Gazette; And The Universal Intelligencer, May 1, 1778.

BROKE out of the State Goal in Boston, on the Night of the 23d Instant, John McLothling, of New-Boston, in the State of New-Hampshire; he is about 5 Feet 8 Inches high, has short black Hair, pale Face'd; had on green Plush Cloath, and an old brown Surtout. Whoever will apprehend the said McLothling, and bring him to the State Goal in Boston, shall have *Twenty Dollars* Reward, and all necessary Charges
   paid by J. OTIS, Dep. Goaler,   Boston, April 28.

The Boston-Gazette, and Country Journal, May 4, 1778; May 11, 1778; May 23, 1778.

FORTY DOLLARS REWARD.

RAN-AWAY from Norwich Goal, on Sunday the 26th inst. the following persons, viz. ISAAC KETCHAM, who was taken from the west end of Long-Island some time ago: He is of middle stature, about 50 years of age, dark complexion, dark hair and eyes, the eyelid of the left eye hanging almost over the same, walks stooping, and has a down look: Had on a greyish coat and vest, leather breeches, and a white felt hat. GEORGE SNYDER, a German, who was taken prisoner, at the northward last year by Gen. Arnold's army, and has been on parole in this town for some months past; he is full six feet high, well set, about twenty-five years of age, light complexion, light coloured hair, talks bad English, and is pitted with the small-pox: Had on a red regimental coat faced with blue, the buttons on the same marked 2[ ], a brown jacket, leather breeches, and an old felt hat.—Went off at the same time, PATRICK KELLY, an Irishman, who was brought a prisoner from the State of New-York in October last, and was permitted to stay in this town on his parole for a few months, then to return to the said State:—Said KELLY is about 34 years of age, 5 feet 7 inches high, red face and redish hair, light blue eyes, well made; had on a dark brown coat and vest, buck-skin breeches, white shirt, and two pair of worsted stockings, one pair white the other dark grey, walks remarkable strait, is very fond of snuff, and the produce of the West-Indies. Whoever will take up any of the above persons, and return them to the subscriber, or confine them in any goal in this State, shall have FOUR POUNDS reward for each.

JOHN BARNEY, junr. Gaoler.   Norwich, April 27, 1778.

The Norwich Packet, May 4, 1778; May 11, 1778; May 18, 1778. See *The Norwich Packet*, April 27, 1778.

STOLEN out of the stable of Philemon Sanford of Goshen, in Litchfield County, the night after the 20th of April instant, a MARE, 13 hands and a half high, ten years old, of a bay colour, large black mane, lying on the right side, with a black tail, good carriage, a good pace and trot, shod before toe cork'd, a white spot under the saddle; she has a remarkable bunch of a considerable bigness on the inside of each hind foot near the huff.—Also at the same time stolen from Jonathan Wadhams of said Goshen, a good hunting saddle, with a cloth housen of a lightish colour, green fringe. The thief is supposed to be a transient fellow, who came to Goshen about six months ago, calling his named Daniel Foreman, about 21 years old, well set, pretty fleshy, rather taller than middling, short, straight light brown hair, has of late usually worn white jacket and breeches, a blue coat faced

with white in the regimental mode, he being a soldier of that lately received 100. for inlisting into the Continental army, as also a white blanket surtout. Whoever will secure and return said Mare shall have Five Dollars Reward, and Two Dollars for said Saddle, and all necessary charges for securing said Thief, in any of the public goals, so that he may be brought to justice, paid by, JONATHAN WADHAM, PHILEMON SANFORD.
Goshen, April 21, 1778.
WHEREAS the above named David Foreman is returned to me as an inlisted soldier in the Continental army; and hath neglected to obey my orders to prepare for marching to join said army:—I apprehend him to have deserted said service. Whoever therefore will apprehend said Deserter, and return him to me in Litchfield, in Connecticut, or secure him in any Continental goal, and notify me, shall have Ten Dollars Reward, and reasonable charges paid by.
BAZALEEL BEEBE, Recruiting officer of the 6th brigade of the Continental Military.   Litchfield, April 21, 1778.
The Connecticut Journal, May 6, 1778; May 13, 1778; *The Connecticut Courant, and the Weekly Intelligencer*, May 26, 1778. Minor differences between the papers. The *Courant* spells the deserters last name as Furnam in one place, and Farnam in another, and Beebe's first name appears as Bezaleel in the *Courant*.

WHEREAS MARY, my lawful Wife, has behaved in a very indecent Manner, refusing a virtuous Compliance with the Apostle's Injunction to Wives; but on the contrary has made sundry Attempts to take away my Life, by stabbing me with Knives and Forks, beating me with the Distaff, Tongs, and Hammer; scratching and biting me very inhumanly; and has now eloped from Bed and Board, and refuses to cohabit with me: I therefore forbid all Persons harbouring or trusting her on my Account, for I will not pay any Debt of her contracting after this Date. And she has privately conveyed away a Number of valuable Articles of my Houshold [*sic*] Furniture, I also forbid any Person whatsoever concealing any such Articles on Penalty of the Law.
JONATHAN SOULE.   Pomfret, April 25, 1778.
The Connecticut Gazette; And The Universal Intelligencer, May 8, 1778; May 15, 1778; May 22, 1778.

ON Thursday Night last, broke out of Barnstable Goal, one Seth Perry, of Sandwich, in the County of Barnstable. He was committed for refusing to take the Oath of Allegiance to this State. He has since his Commitment been informed against as one concerned in a dangerous Plot and Conspiracy against these States, and of spreading counterfeit Money among the People, brought from our common Enemy; and on several Examination since the

Information, and by his own Confession, there is no Doubt but he is guilty of Part, if not the whole.—Whoever will apprehend the said Seth Perry, and confine him in any of the Goals in this State, shall receive FIFTY DOLLARS REWARD, and all necessary Charges

paid, by   ENOCH HALLET, Sheriff.

Yarmouth, April 25, 1778.

N. B. It is suspected he is gone to Nantucket, the Vineyard, or Kennebeck.

The Boston-Gazette, And Country Journal, May 11, 1778; May 18, 1778; May 25, 1778.

RUNAWAY from the subscriber, a Negro woman, named Hannah, about 19 years old, country born, had on when she went away a striped tow and linnen gown an old red shag short cloak, a linen and woolen peticoat, and a striped tow apron. Whoever will take up said Negro and deliver her to the subscriber on the middle parish of Killingly or secure her and send me word shall have 4 dollars reward and all necessary charges

paid, by   NATH'L PACKARD.

N. B. All persons are forewarned not to harbour or conceal said servant.

The Connecticut Courant, and the Weekly Intelligencer, May 12, 1778.

Whare as Hanah my Wife Refus es to Leve with me & has Left my hovs & by ye help of my Enemis & hor frinds talken Bds and provisn ovt of ye hove stolk of ye farm thare fore I for bid any Parson troosin hor on my a Covnt for I will not Pay any thing fer hor I Likewise for bid any Parson to har bor my cartel shepe or hoggs

John sheilds   monson April ye 2 1778

The Connecticut Courant, and the Weekly Intelligencer, May 12, 1778. Spelling as shown. See *The Connecticut Courant, and the Weekly Intelligencer,* May 26, 1778.

WHEREAS a certain Rachel Page, did in the Month of November past, come into the Town of Wallingford, and dwell in the House where the Subscriber then lived, and pretended herself to be Rachel Wells, Widow of a Son of Colonel Wells, and lately fled from Long Island, fearing the British Troops; being a Person of the best Character, in the most effluent Circumstances, and her Conduct being wholly unexceptionable to all Appearances, the Subscriber was unfortunately induced to marry her, when soon after his Marriage, he found her to be a Dweller of North Branford, a Person infamous of her Character, having been publicly convicted of Theft, the Mother of a bastard Child, and a profane Swearer, with many other Crimes disagreeable to mention, and then fled from Branford, her Conduct being such she could not longer dwell there, and soon after her Marriage having thrown off all Pretences to Goodness and Virtue, and it being impossible for the Subscriber in any Way to live with her, and fearing her ruining her Interest as well as destroying his Happiness, he is obliged to take this disagreeable Method publicly to expose her fraudulent Conduct: And I the Subscriber do hereby forewarn all Persons not to trust said Rachel any Thing upon an Account, as I will pay no Debts or her contracting after this Date.

OBADIAH MUNSON.   New Haven, May 11th, 1778.
The Connecticut Journal, May 13, 1778; May 27, 1778.

Ranaway Saturday the 9th Inst.

A Negro Man named Caesar, from his Master Sam. Wallis of Rye—35 Years of Age—Five Feet and a half high; had on when he went away a blue Kersey Coat, grey homespun Breeches and grey Stockings.—Whoever takes up said Negro and returns him to his Master shall have Twenty Dollars Reward.

The Freeman's Journal, Or New-Hampshire Gazette, May 12, 1778; May 19, 1778.

RAN-AWAY from me the subscriber, a NEGRO MAN named FORTUNE, about 50 years of age, talks very broken English; had on when he went away, a grey coat and jacket, and leather breeches. Whoever will take up said run-away, and return him to his master at Reading, shall be handsomely rewarded, and all necessary charges

paid by me,   NATHAN PARKER.

The Continental Journal, And Weekly Advertiser, May 14, 1778; May 21, 1778; June 4, 1778.

TWENTY DOLLARS REWARD.

STOLEN from the Subscriber in Richmond, on the 20th of April Currant, a sorrel coloured HORSE, natural Pacer, has one white hind Foot, his Back very crooked, is about 14 Hands and 2 or 3 Inches high; one Saddle almost new, Saddle-Cloth check'd blue and white bound with yellow; Saddle Bags middling large, some soil'd; Bridle almost new. The Thief is supposed to be a Man about 30 Years old, of midling Stature, dark Complection, strait black Hair, says he is a Dutchman, talks thick and broken English, calls his Name JOHN RAY, (the Place of his Abode unknown) had on a light coloured Surtout somewhat wore, lappell'd Jacket of a brown Colour clouded white, under Jacket striped blue and white Flannel, the Stripes go round him, old Leather Breeches very much soiled, Stockings blue Yarn ribb'd, old Shoes and Shoe-Strings, is very apt of boast of his Silver Money. Whoever will take up said Thief & Horse, and the other Articles described to be stolen, shall be entitled to the above Reward, or fifteen

Dollars for either the Thief or Horse and other Articles, they securing the said Thief so that he may be brought to Justice, and the Horse and other Articles so that I may have them again. Necessary Charges to be
paid by   THOMAS KINYON, Son of DAVID.
Richmond, (State of Rhode-Island) 22d April, 1778.
The Connecticut Gazette; And the Universal Intelligencer, May 15, 1778; May 22, 1778; May 29, 1778. See *The Providence Gazette And Country Journal*, May 30, 1778.

HEAD QUARTERS Boston, May 20, 1778.
ESCAPED last night from the
Main-Guard, THOMAS HARRISON, alias STEEL, alias WILLIAMS, alias many other names, under sentence of death—He is a man of middling stature; had both his ears crop'd, black hair, which hangs pin'd over them, and turns back on his forehead, on which is a scar where he was formerly branded, black eyes, light complexion, something pock-broken, and about thirty years of age. It is supposed that he is secreted somewhere in town.
Whoever will apprehend said HARRISON, &c. and return him to the Main-Guard, shall have the thanks of the General, and ONE HUNDRED DOLLARS Reward. By order of Major General Heath,
DANIEL LYMAN, A. D. C.
☞ *The several Printers of the Public Papers are desired to insert the above.*
The Continental Journal, And Weekly Advertiser, May 21, 1778; May 30, 1778.

PROVIDENCE, May 8th, 1778.
LAST Night made his Escape from the Provost Guard, in Town, MICHAEL MANLEY, a Deserter from Col. Alden's Regiment of the Massachusetts-State, he lately belonged to Gen. Burgoyne's Army, had on when he made his Escape, a light colour'd Grey Coat, very ragged, is about 5 Feet 10 Inches high, has short black curl'd Hair, light Complexion, black Eyes, and is mark'd with the Small-Pox: 'Tis supposed he'll attempt to join the Enemy on some Part of the Continent. Any Person that will return said Deserter to Providence, shall have THIRTY DOLLARS Reward, and all necessary Charges paid, by applying to Col. PECK, Adjutant-General of the Army in the State of Rhode-Island.
The Connecticut Gazette; And The Universal Intelligencer, May 22, 1778; May 29, 1778; *The Providence Gazette; And Country Journal*, May 23, 1778; *The Connecticut Courant, and Hartford Weekly Intelligencer*, May 26, 1778. Minor differences between the papers.

WHereas HANNAH, Wife of the Subscriber, has behaved in a very indecent Manner: This is therefore to warn People from trusting her on my Account, as I will not pay any Debt of her contracting after this Date.
    DANIEL CULVER.   New-London, May 20, 1778.
The Connecticut Gazette; And The Universal Intelligencer, May 22, 1778; June 5, 1778.

RUNAWAY from the subscriber on the night of the 10th instant a molatto slave about 34 years of age, about 5 feet and 9 inches high a well set fellow black hair tied up, wore away a pair of pumps that had been soald, and a pair of plated buckles had a good caster hat and a poor felt hat a check'd flannel shirt and one of linnen, had a coat and jacket of mix'd cloth a dark brown, and a pair of breeches of the same, said fellow has had the small pox. Whoever will take up and secure said slave or return him to the subscriber shall have ten dollars reward and all necessary charges
    paid, by MOSES COMSTOCK.
                   Norwalk, May 17, 1778.
The Connecticut Courant, and Hartford Weekly Intelligencer, May 26, 1778.

RUN away from Simsbury on the 6th instant, a British soldier, named John Bates, belonging to the 24th regiment, about 5 feet 6 inches high, thick-set well-shaped, had a large scar on his left cheek, wore and took with him a felt hat, brown coat red waistcoat with regimental Buttons, leather breeches, white stockings, two checkt linnen shirts. Whoever will secure said run away in any prison and give information or bring him to Hartford, shall have 5 dollars reward and all necessary charges
    paid, by Ez'l. Williams, Dep. Com. Pris. May 15, 1778.
The Connecticut Courant, and the Weekly Intelligencer, May 26, 1778.

WHEREAS Hannah my wife refuses to live with me and has left my house, and by the help of my enemies and her friends taken beds and provision out of the house, and stock off the farm. Therefore, I forbid any person trusting her on my account for I will not pay any thing for her I likewise forbid any person to harbour my cattle sheep or hogs.
    JOHN SHIELDS.   Munson, April 2, 1778.
The Connecticut Courant, And The Weekly Intelligencer, May 26, 1778. See *The Connecticut Courant, And The Weekly Intelligencer*, May 12, 1778.

STolen from the Subscriber, about the 20th of ult. a bright sorrel gelding Horse, 5 Years old, 14 Hands and 3 Inches high, has one white hind foot

with some white in his Face, a natural Pacer. And a Saddle, almost new, with a blue and white checked Saddle Cloth, a Pair of Saddle Bags, and a Bridle. The Thief is supposed to be one John Ray, a Dutchman; he is of midling Stature, has long black Hair, is about 38 Years of Age, and talks very broken: Had on a light coloured Surtout Coat somewhat worn, a dark brown outside Jacket, blue and white striped Flannel under Jacket, old Leather Breeches, blue Yarn Stockings, and old Shoes. Whoever will take up said Thief, and secure him so that the Horse, &c. may be recovered, and the Thief brought to Justice shall have Twenty Dollars Reward, and all necessary Charges, or for the Thief or Horse alone Fifteen Dollars,
   paid by THOMAS Kinyon,
    of Richmond, in the State of Rhode-Island.
The Providence Gazette And Country Journal, May 30, 1778; June 6, 1778. See *The Connecticut Gazette; And the Universal Intelligencer*, May 15, 1778.

RAN away on the Night of the 18th of May last, a Negro Boy, named POMP, about 14 Years of Age; had on a green Coat, Cuffs and Cape turn'd up with Red, a Buff Waistcoat, and White Breeches. He has a small Scar in his Forehead. Whoever will bring him to the Subscriber, shall have THIRTY DOLLARS Reward, and all necessary Charges paid by me,
   EDMUND FOWLE. *Watertown, June* 1st, 1778.
The Boston-Gazette, And Country Journal, June 1, 1778.

WHEREAS Eunice, wife of the subscriber, has behaved in a very indecent manner:—This is to therefore to warn all persons from trusting her on my account, as I will not pay any debt of her contracting after this date.
   JOHN OLNEY WATERMAN. Norwich, June 1, 1778.
The Norwich Packet, June 1, 1778; June 8, 1778.

           Woodbury, May 10, 1778.
ON the Night after the 5th Instant was taken out of the Dwelling House of *Joseph Hurlburt*, in Woodbury, aforesaid, Thirty-six Pounds in Cash, one blue and white Flannel Jacket, one black and blue double breasted Ditto, one white woolen Sheet, one checkt Shirt, one Frock. It is supposed one Roger Blasdel, a Continental Soldier, took the above Articles and Cash. He is about 30 Years of Age, 5 Feet 10 Inches high, something round shoulder'd, very much pitted with the Small-Pox, he has short black curl'd Hair; had on a brown lappell'd Coat somewhat worn, a Pair of linen Overhalls, and a new felt Hat with a white Lining. Whoever shall take up said Thief and secure him so that the Owner receives the above Articles, shall have Ten Dollars Reward therefor, and all necessary Charges
   paid by me, JOSEPH HURLBURT.

The Connecticut Journal, June 3, 1778; June 10, 1778.

RUN away the 26th of May, inst. one John Tom an Irishman belonging to the 21st British regiment, taken at the Northward in September last by trade a Blacksmith, had on when he went away a short blanket coat, striped vest, tow cloth trowsers, about 5 feet 6 inches high, light complexion, 21 years of age fore teeth rotten. Whoever will take up said runaway, and secure him in any goal or return him to the subscriber, shall have 5 dollars reward and all necessary charges
paid, by Ez'l. WILLIAMS Dep. Commiss. Prisoners.
Hartford, June 2, 1778.
The Connecticut Courant, and the Weekly Intelligencer, June 9, 1778..

RAN away from Samuel Lee, in Manchester, on the 9th Day of June, 1778, a Negro Man named CAESAR, about five Feet and a Half high. He had on a new uniform Homespun Coat, his other Cloathing not known, was born in New-England, and when he pretended to stand upright, his Knees bends forward. EIGHT DOLLARS Reward will be given to any Person, that shall take up, and secure said Negro in any of the Goals of the Thirteen United States of America, bring or send him to his said Master, and all other necessary Charges.

The Independent Chronicle and the Universal Advertiser, June 11, 1778. See *The Independent Chronicle and the Universal Advertiser,* December 25, 1777, and *The Independent Chronicle and the Universal Advertiser,* July 30, 1778.

RAN away from me the Subscriber, on the 4th Day of May Instant, a Negro Girl named VENUS, in the 19th Year of her Age. All Persons are hereby cautioned and forbid against harbouring, concealing or employing said Negro, as they would avoid the Penalty of the Law.
EPHRAIM FULLER.   Middleton, May 28, 1778.
The Independent Chronicle and the Universal Advertiser, June 11, 1778.

IN the month of May last, some evil minded person or persons broke open several locks and doors, and stole from the subscribers, and other persons, sundry articles. On the 31st of the same month discovered was made of a stranger in the woods, and upon further search a cave was found, and the said stranger apprehended, who proved to be one Arthur Thrusher, of Rehoboth; he confessed that he had stolen several articles from the subscribers, and had lived in the woods three weeks. On the first of June he made his escape, before he could be brought to justice, and left behind him several articles, which it is supposed were stolen, viz. a gun, one blanket, a

piece of woollen cloth, marked W. I., one liver-coloured coat, two shirts, two pillow cases, &c. The said Thrusher is about 18 or 19 years of age, 5 feet 4 inches high, and has strait black hair. Whoever will apprehend him, and deliver him to the subscribers, shall have twenty dollars reward.
     NEHEMIAH CARPENTER, JOSEPH HEWES, jun.
N. B. The above mentioned articles will be sold after the 1st day of July, if the thief should not be found nor the owners appear.
                   Wrentham, June 10, 1778.
The Providence Gazette; And Country Journal, June 13, 1778; June 27, 1778; July 4, 1778.

WHereas Joana, the wife of me the subscriber, hath in my absence with the army, violated her marriage covenant, by cohabiting with other men: I therefore forbid all persons whatever trading with or trusting her on my account, as I am determined not to pay any debts or her contracting from the date hereof.
    JOSEPH SPRINGER.   Tiverton Camp, June 7, 1778.
The Providence Gazette; And Country Journal, June 13, 1778.

WHEREAS Percilla Martin wife of me the subscriber hath lately eloped from me contrary to my will. I hereby forbid all persons trusting her on my account, as I will not pay no debt contracted by her after this date.
    JOSEPH MARTIN.   Stafford, June 13, 1778.
The Connecticut Courant, And The Weekly Intelligencer, June 16, 1778; June 23, 1778; June 30, 1778. See *The Independent Chronicle and the Universal Advertiser*, December 3, 1778.

RAN away from the Subscriber in Lyme, on Tuesday Night last, a Negro Man named TOM, about 23 Years old, about six Feet high, well set, can read and write, and is supposed to have a forged Pass, took a Fiddle and Fife with him on which he plays; carried away between 3 & 4 suits of Cloathing, among which was a grey Jacket and Breeches, a red belt Jacket, a snuff coloured Ditto, a blue & white linen Coat, &c. Whoever will take up said Negro and return him to me in Lyme, shall have Forty Dollars Reward and necessary charges, but if taken on Long-Island, One Hundred Dollars Reward will be given, and necessary charges,
    by ELISHA LAY.   June 18, 1778.
The Connecticut Gazette; And the Universal Intelligencer, June 19, 1778; July 3, 1778.

ESCAPED from the Goal in New-London, on Friday Evening last, a certain *JOHN AMES*, who was in Goal upon an Execution, also in Custody for a Breach of the Peace: his Abode for some Time past was at the House of

Broadhurst Bacon in Lyme, he is of midling Stature, has very light coloured Eyes, and has been in the Army. Whoever will take up said John, and return him to New-London County Goal, shall receive twenty Dollars Reward,
from EPHRAIM MINER, Goaler.

New-London, June 13, 1778.
The Connecticut Gazette; And the Universal Intelligencer, June 19, 1778; July 3, 1778.

WHEREAS my Wife Abigail Bradford continues to behave herself in a very indecent Manner, refusing to return to my Family, notwithstanding the most earnest Solicitations thereon. I do therefore strictly forbid all Persons trusting her on my Account, as I will not pay any Debt by her contracted until she shall return to her Duty.
WILLIAM BRADFORD.

Dated at Canterbury, June 8, 1778.
The Connecticut Gazette; And the Universal Intelligencer, June 26, 1778; July 3, 1778. See *The Connecticut Gazette; And The Universal Intelligencer*, August 23, 1776, and *The Connecticut Gazette; And the Universal Intelligencer*, July 24, 1778.

RUN-away from the subscriber the 18th of June instant, a Negro man named DICK; had on a light coloured woolen coat, vest and breeches, a pair of blue grey stockings a felt hat 37 or 38 years old, 5 feet 3 inches high Whoever will take up said Negro and return him to the subscriber shall have twenty dollars reward and all necessary charges
paid, by AARON WHITE.   Middletown, June 21 1778.
The Connecticut Courant, And The Weekly Intelligencer, June 30, 1778.

RUNAWAY from the subscriber in Derby on the night of the 27th of instant June, a NEGRO MAN, named PETER, about five feet and eight inches high, about forty five years old; had on when he when away a redish jacket, a pair of leather breeches and tow trowsers, shoes with strings, a pair of blue stockings, and a tow frock. Whosoever shall take up said Negro Man, and deliver him so that he may be had, shall have Ten Dollars reward, and all necessary charges
paid by me,   NATHAN SMITH.   Derby, June 30, 1778.
The Connecticut Journal, July 1, 1778; July 8, 1778; July 15, 1778.

RANAWAY from the Sloop Revenge, Capt. Conkling, on the 27th ult. two Negro Men taken in a British Prize, also a Negro owned by Capt. Bulkley of Wethersfield, named SAM, about 5 Feet 10 Inches high; all poorly cloth'd. Whoever will return them on Board said Sloop, lying in New

London, shall be well rewarded. Also ranaway at the same Time, a likely Negro Man named LONDON, owned by Picket Latimer, in New-London about 24 Years old, 5 Feet 8 or 10 Inches high, had good Cloathing, among which is a blue Coat faced with Buff, is a good Cook and Barber, one of his Toes on the Right Foot has a Corn, which has crook'd it. Whoever will return him to his Master shall have FORTY DOLLARS Reward, and all necessary Charges.
New-London, July 1, 1778.
The Connecticut Gazette; And the Universal Intelligencer, July 3, 1778; July 24, 1778. See *The Providence Gazette; And Country Journal*, July 4, 1778, for London.

RUN away from the subscriber, the 16th of March last, one Jonathan Green, formerly belonging to Coventry, in the state of R. Island, and taken by a special warrant by me, for the crime of getting a girl with child in said Coventry. Said Green is of a middling size, of a light complexion, has light hair, winks very quick, has blue eyes, and stammers in his speech; had on a brown surtout, a light short coat, a striped jacket, and leather breeches. Whoever will take up said Greene, and return him to me the subscriber, shall have fifty dollars reward, and all necessary charges,
paid by me, EPHRAIM WARREN, jun.
Killingly, July 1, 1778.
The Providence Gazette; And Country Journal, July 4, 1778; July 11, 1778; July 18, 1778; July 25, 1778.

RUN away from the subscriber, the 19th of June, a Negro fellow, named London, 6 feet high, well set, and is a barber by trade; took with him a blue coat faced with buff, a nankeen ditto, 3 white shirts, 2 flannel ditto, and several other articles. Whoever takes up and secures said Negro, so that his master may have him again, shall have a handsome reward, and all charges
paid by PICKET LATEMORE.
New-London, July 1, 1778.
The Providence Gazette; And Country Journal, July 4, 1778; July 11, 1778; July 18, 1778; July 25, 1778. See *The Connecticut Gazette; And the Universal Intelligencer*, July 3, 1778, which spells the name as Latimer.

RUNAWAY the night after the 14th instant a negro man named Dick about 24 years old, about five feet high not thickset has a scar on his left arm above his elbow, cut by an ax, had a blue coat a brown millcolour'd one and old one two vests, one bever hat cut in fashion two pair of leather breeches and other cloaths. Whoever will take up said negro and return him to me, shall have ten dollars reward, and all necessary charges paid.

MARTIN KERUM.   Nobletown, June 15, 1778.
The Connecticut Courant, And The Weekly Intelligencer, July 7, 1778; July 14, 1778.

RAN away from his Mistress, at Franklin, on the 11th of June, at Night, a Negro Man, named CAESAR, about 5 Feet 5 or 6 Inches high, about 55 Years old; had on a Straw Hat, red and straw colour'd, bound with blue, a red worsted Cap, a black and white mixt Coat, with large plate Buttons; carried with him, two Jackets and two Pair of Stockings, one Pair of Shoes, tapt, two striped Wollen Shirts, a blue Duffel Gown, and two Pair of Breeches. Whoever will take up said Negro, and bring him to his Mistress, at Franklin, shall have 3 Dollars Reward, and all necessary Charges,
paid by me, ABIGAIL POND.   Franklin, June 13, 1778.

N. B. All Masters of Vessels are forbid carrying him off; all Officers from Inlisting him, and all Farmers from employing him; or any Person having any Dealings with him, on their Peril.
The Independent Chronicle and the Universal Advertiser, July 9, 1778; July 16, 1778.

WHEREAS, my Wife Sarah, has eloped from my Bed and Board and has refused to live with me, and as she has greatly run me in Debt, this is therefore to caution any Person from harbouring of trusting her as I am determined not to pay one Farthing she may contract, after this Date.
BENEJAH SMITH.   CHESTERFIELD, June 20, 1778.
The Independent Chronicle and the Universal Advertiser, July 9, 1778.

RAN away from his Master, at Franklin, the 11th of June, at Night, a Negro Man, named QUONSO, about 40 Years old, a trim well-built Fellow, talks very broken, and stammers and opens his Mouth very wide when he talks. He wore away a Felt Hat, and carried away 5 Shirts, 3 Pair of Breeches, 1 Pair of striped Trowsers, 5 Pair of Stockings, a mixt black and blue Great-Coat 3 Jackets, and a Pair of Pumps tapt. Whoever will take up said Negro, and bring him to his Master, at Franklin, shall have 10 Dollars Reward, and all necessary Charges,
paid by me,   ASA WHITING.   Franklin, June 13 1778.

N. B. All Masters of Vessels are forbid carrying him off; all Officers from inlisting him; and all Farmers from employing him; or any Person having any Dealings with him, at their Peril.
The Independent Chronicle and the Universal Advertiser, July 9, 1778; July 16, 1778.

TWENTY DOLLARS REWARD.

RAN-AWAY from the subscriber, the evening after the 5th instant, A NEGRO WOMAN named ZILPHA, about 25 years of age, of a middling stature, something slim, one of her fore teeth gone: She went away with one CRISMAN, a Negro man belonging to Mr. Stephen Bingham of Andover, in Hebron, in the county of Hartford, and carried with her the following valuable articles, viz. One brown Camblet Gown, almost new; 1 black Tammy ditto; 1 blue and white figured Stuff, ditto; 1 dark coloured Callico ditto, almost new; 1 light coloured Callico ditto, partly worn; 1 striped Linen ditto, almost new; 1 black Calimanco quilt, almost new; 1 flowered Lawn Apron; 1 red Broad cloth Cloak, almost new; 1 brown Camblet Riding-Hood, partly worn; 1 black Sattin Bonnet, almost new; with a variety of other articles, consisting of Caps, Handkerchiefs, Shoes, Stockings, Ribbands &c. &c. &c.—Whoever will take up said Run-away, and return her to me the subscriber, shall have the above reward for their trouble, paid by DAVID BARBER.
Hebron, July 13, 1778.
The Norwich Packet, July 13, 1778; July 20, 1778; July 27, 1778; August 3, 1778; August 10, 1778.

WENT away the 28th of June last, from the subscriber, two Dutch prisoners, one named JOHN FISHER, a pretty large clumsey fellow, the other HENRY DORIOUS, middling stature. They had on new oznaburghs shirts and trowsers, and carried away two buff coloured waistcoats, and two red ones; they are of fair complexion, brown hair, and about 25 years old. Whoever will give notice of them, either to the Printer or to me, shall be rewarded for their pains.
THOMAS LEGATE.   Leominster, July 13th, 1778.
The Massachusetts Spy: Or, American Oracle of Liberty, July 16, 1778; July 23, 1778; July 23, 1778; August 6, 1778.

BROKE out last Night and made their Escape from the Goal in Concord, *Edward Heyward,* 30 Years old, about six feet high, light complexion, brown hair, bald headed: *Richard King,* 26 Years old, 5 feet 6 inches high, light complexion, very light blue eyes; both speak broken English, and both belonging to the state Troops of Convention, and were committed to said Goal for Robbery. Whoever will apprehend said *Heyward* and *King,* and commit them to safe keeping in any of the Goals of the United States, and give Information thereof, shall receive TEN DOLLARS Reward for each or either of them, and all necessary Charges
paid by   JAMES PRESCOTT, Sheriff.
The Boston Gazette, And Country Journal, July 20, 1778; July 27, 1778; August 3, 1778.

RAN away from the Subscriber on Monday last, an Apprentice Boy named GILBERT WOODWARD, but calls himself GILBERT THOMAS, 15 Years old, had with him a streaked Shirt and Jacket, and a butternut Jacket, has short dark Hair & light Eyes. Whoever will return him to me shall have 2s. Reward, I forbid all Persons harbouring or carrying him off, on Penalty of the Law.

     ASA PARK.   Preston, July 8, 1778.

The Connecticut Gazette; And The Universal Intelligencer, July 24, 1778.

     To the candid and impartial PUBLICK.

WHEREAS my Husband, Mr. Wm. BRADFORD, of Canterbury, has twice advertised me as being guilty of unreasonably departing from his Family, and refusing to return, notwithstanding his most earnest Solicitations thereto; I now think myself in Duty bound for the Vindication of my own Conduct, to give a short Narrative of the Reason of my leaving Mr. Bradford as I have: As to my first withdraw, which was in the Month of April 1776, I went to Norwich only on a Visit to my Children and other Friends, with a Design to tarry about a Week or ten days, and then to return, but before that Time, I was surprised to see my Name advertised in the Connecticut Gazette, in as hard and opprobrious Language as a hard Master could have advertised a runaway Negro, not only forbidding any one to trust me, but forbidding all Persons harbouring or entertaining of me; but these Matters, and the cruel Treatment which I had before received from Mr. Bradford, was fully heard and adjudicated by three Gentlemen mutually chosen to assist and advise me under our Difficulties in the Month of January last, and [full h   ]ing them Gentlemen were so far convinced of the reasonableness of my Complaints, that they advised and ordered that Mr. Bradford should relinquish all my Interest which I had before my Intermarriage with him, and put it over into the Hands of my Son, for my Sole use and Benefit; so that if Mr. Bradford should not treat me with more Kindness for the future than he had done before, I might take what was my own and live in a separate State; to which Mr. Bradford readily agreed, and executed the proper Writings accordingly; and on his then solemnly promising before them Gentlemen and others, for the future to treat me with all possible Kindness, and never again to speak an angry or hard Word to me, I consented to make another Tryal to live with him, resolving to do every Thing as far as was in me to please him and keep him in his perfect good Humour, but I soon found myself an unwelcome Guest in the Family; and that evil and Nabal-like Spirit, which is so natural in Mr. Bradford, began again to trouble him, and I felt the bad Effects of it; he called me many hard Names, charged me with Stealing, threatened me with a Horse Whip, and then in a very angry austere Manner looked up every Thing in

the House from me, even the most common Necessaries of Life, and at length his Pleasure was to sleep alone (which by the way was no Mortification to me) and for more than a Week before I left the House, I was every Night bolted up fast in my Bed Room like a Prisoner in a close Goal, and there obliged to remain till Mr. Bradford or some of the rest of the Family pleased to give me Enlargement, which was generally so late in the Morning to make my Confinement very disagreeable. I at length one Sunday Morning made my Escape at the Bed Room Window, and went round to the Kitchen Door, but found it locked against me, I attempted to enter by the Window, but was pushed back by one of the Family with such Violence, that I was much hurt by the Means; I begged to come in to get my Clothes to go to Meeting, but was denied, and obliged to go to a kind Neighbour's for Shelter. I suffered a second Affront of the like Kind, but was determined to beware of a third; the second Time I was so shut out of the House, I went immediately to my Son at Norwich, got him to send for my Things, which Mr. Bradford honestly delivered up according to the former Advice and Agreement; and I have taken Lodging with a kind Friend, where I live in Peace and free from the cruel Hands of Tyranny. I hope my unhappy Lot will be a warning to others, and excite the Compassion of all candid Christian Friends to whom I submit the Case of
their humble Servant. ABIGAIL BRADFORD.

The Connecticut Gazette; And the Universal Intelligencer, July 24, 1778. See *The Connecticut Gazette; And The Universal Intelligencer*, August 23, 1776, and *The Connecticut Gazette; And the Universal Intelligencer*, June 26, 1778.

Twenty Dollars Reward.

RANAWAY last Night, from his Master Henry Talpey of Old-York, a likely Negro Man named BOB, about twenty Years old—He had on a Homespun Coat and Jacket, Breeches, &c. He carried away several Things of Cloathing done up in a Bundle. Whoever takes up said Negro, is desire to put him in Goal, and give Notice, so as his Master may have him again shall receive the above Reward, and all necessary Charges,
per me, HENRY TALPEY.

N. B. All Masters of Vessels and others, are hereby caution'd from concealing or carrying off said Negro, as the would avoid the penalty of the Law. Old-York, July 20, 1778.

The New-Hampshire Gazette; or, State Journal, and General Advertiser, July 28, 1778; August 5, 1778.

RAN away from SAMUEL LEE, of *Manchester*, on the Night of the 26th of *July* instant, three Negroes, one a Negro Man, named CAESAR, about 30 Years old, when he pretends to stand upright, his Knees bend forward; and a likely fat Negro Woman, 31 Years old, Wife to the above Negro Man; they carried off a Male Child, about 6 Months old; had on, and carried away with them, all their Cloathing. Whoever will take up said Negroes, and return them to their Master, or commit them to Goal, and inform me thereof, shall have TEN DOLLARS Reward, and all necessary Charges,

paid by SAMUEL LEE. *Manchester, July* 28, 1778.

The Independent Chronicle and the Universal Advertiser, July 30, 1778; August 6, 1778; August 13, 1778. See *The Independent Chronicle and the Universal Advertiser*, June 11, 1778, and *The Independent Chronicle and the Universal Advertiser*, December 25, 1777.

RAN-away from Mr. Lawrence, of Cambridge, the beginning of July inst. a Negro Man, named PRINCE, aged about 25 Years, and about 5 feet 9 inches high, remarkable thin Legs. Whoever apprehends and brings the said Prince to *Abraham Watson*, Esq; at Cambridge, shall receive THIRTY DOLLARS Reward, and all reasonable Charges paid.

The Boston-Gazette, And Country Journal, August 3, 1778; August 10, 1778; August 17, 1778.

TWENTY DOLLARS REWARD.

RAN away from his Master a Negro Man about thirty Years of Age, a likely strait limb'd Fellow, about 5 Feet 6 or 8 inches high. Had on when he went away a strip'd home-spun Jacket, and a Pair of strip'd Overalls, and carried with him a variety of other Cloathing.—Twenty Dollars and all necessary Charges shall be paid to any Person who shall take up said Negro and bring him to his Master,

SAMUEL WHITEWELL. Boston, August 6, 1778.

N. B. All masters of Vessels and others, are forbid concealing or carrying off said Negro as they would avoid the Penalties of the Law.

The Continental Journal, And Weekly Advertiser, August 6, 1778; August 13, 1778; August 20, 1778.

Whereas Ann, the Wife of the Subscriber, hath, during his long Captivity with the Enemy, made great Waste of his Property, and otherwise conducted herself in a very unbecoming Manner. I therefore forbid all Persons crediting her on my Account, as I shall not pay any Debts of her contracting from the Date hereof.

THOMAS WESCOTT. Providence, August 6, 1778.

The Providence Gazette; And Country Journal, August 8, 1778.

RUN away from this town, Nathan Marston, indebted to Mrs. Elizabeth Ingalls twenty-four pounds. Any person that will give information, so that he may be brought to justice, shall receive Ten Dollars reward, and all necessary charges paid by me,
    ELIZABETH INGALLS.   Salem, July 25, 1778.
N. B. Said runaway is six feet high, dark complexion; had on when he walked off, long tow trowsers, no stockings nor shoes.
 The Boston-Gazette, And Country Journal, August 10, 1778; August 17, 1778; August 24, 1778.

TWENTY DOLLARS Reward.

RAN away from his master a Negro man named PRINCE, about twenty three years of age, a likely strait limb'd fellow, about five feet seven inches high; he carried away some jackets, two shirts, three pair of breeches, &c.—Twenty dollars and all necessary charges shall be paid to any person who shall take up said Negro and bring him to his master. All masters of vessels and others, are forbid concealing or carrying off said Negro, as they would avoid the penalties of the law.
    JAMES CLARKSON.
 Portsmouth, New-Hampshire, August 10th, 1778.
 The Continental Journal, And Weekly Advertiser, August 13, 1778; August 20, 1778; August 27, 1778.

MADE his escape from the gaol in this town, on Tuesday evening last, the noted PHINEAS FAIRBANKS, an American born, and who was imprisoned for being inimical to the glorious cause of Liberty: Had on when he made his escape, a white under jacket, a short red broad cloth Coat, a snuff coloured pair breeches, white shirt, brown thread Stockings, is a person of a dark complexion, has long black hair, five feet ten inches high, and is about thirty-five years old.—Whoever will take up said Fairbanks, and convey him to me at Norwich, or confine him in any of the gaols in this State, shall have TEN DOLLARS reward, and all necessary charges, paid by
   JOHN BARNEY, jun. Gaoler. *Norwich, August* 17, 1778.
 The Norwich Packet, August 17, 1778; August 24, 1778; August 31, 1778; September 7, 1778; September 14, 1778; September 21, 1778; September 28, 1778.

THIRTY DOLLARS REWARD.

THE night after the 12th inst. the shop of me the subscriber was broke open, and the following articles taken out, viz. 2 pieces of light brown homespun; 4 yards nankeen; 5 yards striped linen; and over coats cloth cut

out for a boy; several garments made up; upwards of 100 sticks of twist, a quantity of Buttons of various sizes and colours, with sundry other articles. Whoever will take up and secure the thief and goods and inform the subscriber hereof, shall be entitled to thirty dollars reward and all necessary charges paid by their friend and sufferer.
       NATHANIEL CORNWELL.
N. B. The thief is supposed to be one Taylor by name and occupation, an old countryman, has lost his right eye.
              Worthington, Aug. 13, 1778.
The Connecticut Courant, and Hartford Weekly Intelligencer, August 18, 1778; September 1, 1778.

WHEREAS Seth Mitchell of Bridgewater
has been represented to be a person non-compos mentis, and not of capacity to take care of himself and his estate, to the Hon. Joseph Cushing, Judge of Probate for the county of Plymouth—and his honor having appointed the subscriber guardian to me the said Seth Michell—This is therefore to forbid all persons trading or dealing with him the said Seth Mitchell, in any way or manner whatever, as no bargain or contract made with him will be deemed as valid, and no debts contracted by him will be paid.
    JOSEPH GANNET. *Bridgewater,* August 17, 1778.
The Continental Journal, And Weekly Advertiser, August 20, 1778; August 27, 1778.

THIRTY DOLLARS REWARD.
RAN AWAY from the Subscriber in Colchester, the Night following the 18th instant a Negro man named GUINEA, 33 Years of Age, 6 Feet high, well built, wore away an old Castor hat, a claret coloured Coat, striped Vest, Leather Breeches, white Holland or striped Tow Shirt. Whoever will take up said Runaway and give Information, or return him to the Subscriber in Colchester, shall be entitled to the above Reward and all necessary Charges paid by   JOSHUA BULKLEY.
N. B. All Masters of Vessels are forbid harbouring said Negro.
            Colchester, 19th August, 1778.
The Connecticut Gazette; And The Universal Intelligencer, August 21, 1778; August 28, 1778; September 4, 1778. See *The Norwich Packet*, August 24, 1778.

RAN away from the Subscriber, in Groton, on the 7th of October last, a Negro Man Slave named Timothy Titus, very light complexion, about 24 or 25 years old, 6 Feet 1 or 2 inches high, and extremely well built, has a scar on the back of his left hand near his wrist. Whoever will return him to the

Subscriber in Groton, or secure him so that he may be had, shall receive Thirty Dollars reward,

   paid by Abel Franklin.   Groton, Aug. 7, 1778.

The Connecticut Gazette; And The Universal Intelligencer, August 21, 1778; August 28, 1778.

THIRTY DOLLARS REWARD.

RUN AWAY from the Subscriber in Colchester, the night following the 18th instant a Negro man named GUINEA, thirty three years of age, six feet high, well built, speaks good English and is capable to tell a good story to support his cause; wore away an old castor hat, a claret coloured coat, striped vest, leather breeches, white Holland or striped tow shirt.—Whoever will take up said Negro and give information, or return him to his Master in Colchester, shall be entitled to the above reward and all necessary charges

   paid by JOSHUA BULKLEY.

N. B. All Masters of vessels are forbid harbouring said Negro.

            Colchester, August 24, 1778.

The Norwich Packet, August 24, 1778; August 31, 1778; September 14, 1778. See *The Connecticut Gazette; And The Universal Intelligencer*, August 21, 1778.

                August 18. 1778.

TEN DOLLARS REWARD.

RUN away from the subscriber, living in New-Hartford, Litchfield county, the night following the 16th inst. a negro man, named Neptune, 24 years of age about 5 feet 7 inches high, well set, something pock broken, has scars on his knees, the toes of each foot almost gone, part of two toes grow together on one foot, and speaks good English. Had on when he went away a strip'd woollen shirt, linen frock and trowsers, and a light-hoseman's [*sic*] hat with No. 62 on it. Whoever will take up said negro, and secure him so that his master may have him again shall receive the above reward, and all necessary charges,

   paid by ABRAHAM PETTIBONE.

The Connecticut Courant, And Hartford Weekly Intelligencer, August 25, 1778; September 8, 1778.

WHEREAS Joanna Nickols, wife of me the subscriber, hath lately eloped from me, contrary to my will. I hereby forbid all persons trusting her on my account, as I will not pay any debt contracted by her after this date.

   JONATHAN NICKOLS. Sheffield, July 23. 1778.

The Connecticut Courant, and Hartford Weekly Intelligencer, August 25, 1778.

RAN away from the Subscriber, on Sunday Night last, a tall, likely NEGRO-MAN, named JAMES, had on a lightish coloured Coat, and brown Jacket, green Breeches, white Linnen Shirt, white Cotton Stockings, speaks very good English, is a Paper-Maker by Trade. Whoever will take up said Negro, and secure him any of the Goals of this or the neighbouring States, or return him to the Subscriber, shall be paid TEN POUNDS, and all Charges.

JAMES BOIES.   MILTON, August 25, 1778.

N. B. He is not a Slave but was bound for a Number of Years, and has almost two Years to serve.

The Independent Chronicle and the Universal Advertiser, September 3, 1778.

Boston, Sept. 7, 1778.

RAN away from the Subscriber the 27th August, a Negro Girl Servant, named PHILLIS, about Twenty Three Years of Age, She is very Black, has a Scar in her Face, speaks good English very Quick. Whoever shall take up said Servant, and Return her to the Subscriber, shall receive Thirty Dollars Reward, and all Charges paid by their humble Servant.

HENRY HOWELL WILLIAMS.

N. B. All Persons whatsoever are forbidden Harbouring or Secreting, the said Servant, upon Penalty of the Law.

The Boston-Gazette, And Country Journal, September 7, 1778; September 14, 1778; September 28, 1778.

MADE his escape from the gaol in this town, on the evening of the 4th instant, one JOHN SMITH, who was taken up as a suspected person to the cause of America: Had on when he went off, a striped woollen shirt, a red jacket without sleeves, a pair tow trowsers, and is about 50 or 60 years of age.—Whoever will take up said SMITH, and return him to me, shall be well rewarded for their trouble.

JOHN BARNEY, jun. Gaoler.   Norwich, September 7, 1778.

The Norwich Packet, September 7, 1778; September 21, 1778.

One Hundred Dollars Reward.

STOLEN from the subscriber, living in Suffield, about eighty or ninety pounds Continental bills. The thief calls his name James Briges, but will likely change it, says he deserted out of Boston just before it was shut up, and has since been in the American army: Had on when he went away, a gray colour'd Coat, Buckskin Breeches check shirt, blue Stockings, felt hat, is about 5 feet 10 inches high, much pock broken, something stocky speaks broad, walks grand, is an Irishman, and understands combing wool. Whoever will take up said thief and money, so at the owner may have the

money and secure the thief in any of the goals, or bring him to Suffield in Connecticut, in Hartford county shall receive the above reward or for the thief only shall receive 60 dollars, and all necessary charges
paid by me, AARON HALLADAY.
The Connecticut Courant, and Hartford Weekly Intelligencer, September 8, 1778.

TEN DOLLARS REWARD.

RUN AWAY from his master, last night, a Negro Man, named JUBE, about 28 years old, six feet high, has a large under lip, redish eyes, speaks good English, keeps his knees near together when he walks, runs his shoes on sole side, and makes use of much tobacco. Had on or took with him a blue serge coat and jacket a brown home-spun waistcoat, lined with black and white, breeches of the same, a brown jacket with a belt, one check'd linen shirt, one Holland ditto, one pair strip'd linen trowsers, one pair blue stockings one pair black ditto, a black hat and straw ditto: He has some hard money with him: It is supposed he will endeavour to get to the enemy. Whoever will take up said Negro and return him to his master, shall have the above reward, and charges
paid by GEORGE SMITH.   Hartford Sept. 4, 1778.
The Connecticut Courant, And Hartford Weekly Intelligencer, September 8, 1778.

THIRTY FIVE DOLLARS REWARD.

MADE their escape from Hartford, on the 1st of September, 1778, the following prisoners, viz. Nicholas Philips, a Dutchman, about 50 years of age, dark complexion, about five feet eight inches high. Had on a white short woollen jacket, and trowsers made out of an old blanket. Also, Nicholas Philips, jun. and John Philips, sons to OLD NICK; about the same height and complexion: Had on each an old green coat. Also, John Crookstone, a tall, slim fellow, and black eyes: Had on a short green jacket with yellow lining, almost new, and white linen overhauls. Also, John Chambers a Dutchman, and Nathan Smith, both of middle stature, and dressed in like manner as Crookstone. Likewise, William Sutherland, a Scotch man, about 40 years of age, a short, thick set fellow: Had on a short green coat faced with red and linen overhauls. Whoever will take up said prisoners, and return them to Hartford gaol, shall be entitled to the above reward, or five dollars for each, and necessary charges,
paid by EZEKIEL WILLIAMS,
Deputy Commissary of Prisoners.
The Connecticut Courant, And Hartford Weekly Intelligencer, September 8, 1778; September 22, 1778.

STOLEN, on the 3d Inst. a black Mare, 14 Hands high, 8 Years old, her hind Feet white, has a small Star in her Forehead, and a few white Hairs intermixed on her Buttocks, trots and paces. Also a russet Saddle, with large flowerd Staple-Nails, a Nail lost from on the left Side before, the Pad worn out. Said Mare was doubtless stolen by a Man who calls his Name Johnston, about six Feet high, well set, of a sandy Complexion, has an impudent Air, and often talks of being in Battles. Whoever shall secure the Mare, so that I may have her again, together with the Thief, shall have Twenty Dollars Reward, and for the Mare Fifteen Dollars,
    paid by SAMUEL DANIELSON.
     Killingly, August 31, 1778.
The Providence Gazette; And Country Journal, September 12, 1778.

RUN AWAY from me the subscriber an indented servant girl named Thebe. Any person that will apprehend said run-away, shall receive thirteen pence half penny, and reasonable charges; said girl lately lived with Mr. Woolsey at Danbury.
    JOHN LLOYD, jun.   Hartford, August 5. 1778.
The Connecticut Courant, and the Weekly Intelligencer, September 15, 1778; September 22, 1778.

WHEREAS, Elizabeth Goodrich, my wife, hath lately eloped from me, contrary to my will. I hereby forbid all persons trusting her on my account, as I will not pay any debts contracted by her after that date.
    BENJAMIN GOODRICH. Hancock, July 9, 1778.
The Connecticut Courant, and the Weekly Intelligencer, September 22, 1778; October 27, 1778.

RANAWAY from me the Subscriber the 14th Instant, a NEGRO MAN named *Prince*, about twenty four years of age. Had on when he went away blue Breeches, a good Hatt, white Stockings, and a light colour'd Coat, speaks good English, and plays on a Violin, limps on his left Leg. Whoever shall take up said Negro, and secure him in any of the States Goals, shall have Ten Dollars Reward, & all necessary charges paid, giving me timely Notice.
    JOSEPH PATTINSON *of Newington,* *Sept.* 16, 1778.
The New-Hampshire Gazette; or, State Journal, and General Advertiser, September 22, 1778; September 29, 1778; October 6, 1778.

DESERTED from my Company in Col. Meigs's Regiment, *Isaiah Blakslee* and *Jesse Tharp*, some Time in July last, Blakslee is about 28 Years of Age, about 5 Feet 9 or 10 Inches high, of a dark Complexion, with black Hair and grey Eyes, is rather slim built, and carries his head a little forward; had on when he went away, a brown Jacket, a check'd linen Shirt and Trowsers. Tharp is about 26 or 27 Years of Age, about 5 Feet 6 or 7 Inches high, of a light Complexion, has light brown Hair and grey Eyes, a wide Mouth and broad fore Teeth, some of which stand out rather farther than the Rest, one of his Ankles is larger than the other, and his Foot turns a little inwards, occasioned by a Cut he received in his Ankle in his Youth; he had on when he went away a butternut colour'd Jacket, white linen Shirt and Trowsers. Whoever shall take up said Deserters, and secure them in any of the Goals in these States, or bring them to me, shall have Twenty Dollars Reward, and all necessary Charges paid, and for either of them Ten Dollars, by me

    JOSEPH MANSFIELD, Capt.   White Plains, August 16, 1778.

The Connecticut Journal, September 23, 1778; September 30, 1778.

RUnaway from the Subscriber at Wethersfield, the 15th of Instant September, a Negro Boy named Nirum, about 17 Years of Age, about 5 Feet 6 Inches high, thick Lips, talks very good English, born in the Country, had on a brown Jacket, felt Hat, tow cloth Trowsers, no Stockings. Said Negro was taken up in Guilford, and made his Escape from thence on Sunday last. If any Person will take up said Negro, and send him to me, or secure him and send me Word, shall have Ten Dollars Reward, and all necessary Charges paid by me,

    WAIT ROBBINS.   Wethersfield, 21st September, 1778.

The Connecticut Journal, September 23, 1778; September 30, 1778; October 7, 1778.

RUN away from the subscriber, on the 26th of August, an apprentice boy, named Potter Wight, about 12 years of age, has black eyes and black hair: Had on when he went away a white shirt, striped breeches and a felt hat. Whoever will return the said boy, shall have one dollar reward, paid by his master, in Johnston.   JOSEPH FISK, jun.

The Providence Gazette; And Country Journal, September 26, 1778; October 3, 1778.

BROKE GOAL, and made his Escape, in this Town, on the Night of the 16th Instant, one JOHN M'GOTH, about 25 Years of Age, born in Ireland, about 5 Feet 2 or 3 Inches high, considerably pock-marked, had on a short red Coat—He had a Woman with him whom he called his Wife.—Whoever will return him to the Subscriber, shall have 20 Dollars Reward.

    JOSEPH OTIS, Dep. Goal-Keeper.

The Independent Chronicle and the Universal Advertiser, October 1, 1778.

ABsconded from his master's service, James Gardner, an indented Indian servant, about 17 years of age: Had on when he went off, a grey coatee, the sleeves and cape yellow, cloth coloured breeches, and a beaver hat; he had on shoes or stockings. 'Tis supposed he is gone towards Boston. Whoever will return said servant to his master, the subscriber, shall have Ten Dollars reward, and all necessary charges,
paid by   WILLIAM BOWEN.
N. B. All persons are forbid harbouring or carrying off said servant.
Providence, Oct. 8.
The Providence Gazette; And Country Journal, October 10, 1778; October 17, 1778.

WHereas about a Year ago, by a public Advertisement, I forewarned all Persons from trusting my Wife Polly on my Account; I do now in the same public Manner revoke my said Order and Declaration.
JOHN COOPER.
The Providence Gazette; And Country Journal, October 10, 1778; October 17, 1778. See *The Providence Gazette And Country Journal*, September 13, 1777.

WHEREAS Abagail, the wife of me the Subscriber, hath eloped from me contrary to my will. I therefore forbid all persons trusting her on my account, as I will not pay any debt contracted by her after this date.
DAVID ALLIN.   Petersham, August 23, 1778.
The Connecticut Courant, and Hartford Weekly Intelligencer, October 13, 1778; October 27, 1778.

WHEREAS TITUS a molato slave, hath
left my business, under pretence of being free. This is to warn all persons not to trade or imploy him, as they will avoid the penalty of the law.
HENRY LEE.   Barre. Sept. 28. 1778.
The Connecticut Courant, and Hartford Weekly Intelligencer, October 20, 1778; October 27, 1778.

Whereas Naomi, wife of me the
Subscriber, has eloped from me, and strolls from house to house. This is to caution all persons against trusting her on my account, as I am determined to pay no debt of her contracting from the date hereof.
JOHN ROBIE.   Chester, October 5th, 1778.
The New-Hampshire Gazette; or, State Journal, and General Advertiser, October 13, 1778; October 20, 1778; November 4, 1778. See *The Essex Journal Or, New-Hampshire Packet*, August 18, 1775,

and *The Freeman's Journal, Or New-Hampshire Gazette,* July 19, 1777,

Ten Dollars Reward.

RANAWAY from Daniel Tilton of Exeter, on Thursday last, a Negro Servant named Cato, 19 Years old, about five Feet 8 or 9 Inches high, and slim, speaks tolerable plain, had on when he went away, an old Felt Hat, check Linnen Shirt, a pair of coarse strip'd Tow and Linnen Trowsers, a red half thick Waist coat, and a blue outside Jacket very ragged; without either Shoe or Stocking. Whoever will take up said Negro, and carry him to me the Subscriber, shall have the above Reward, and all necessary charges
    paid by DANIEL TILTON. Exeter, October 6th, 1778.
The New-Hampshire Gazette; or, State Journal\, and General Advertiser, October 13, 1778; October 20, 1778.

Whereas *Lucy,* the wife of me the
subscriber, has eloped from my bed and board; and as I am in danger of being run into debt by the said Lucy, this is to warn all persons from harbouring or trusting her upon my account for the future, as I will not pay one farthing therefor.
    DAVID WYMAN.   Marlborough, October 13.
The Continental Journal, And Weekly Advertiser, October 15, 1778; October 22, 1778; November 5, 1778.

RAN-AWAY on Saturday last from
me the subscriber, a Negro Fellow named PRINCE, about 18 years old, had on when he went away, a pair of canvas trowsers, a blue jacket, an English round wool hat, about 5 feet 9 inches high, a handsome well built fellow—he went off with a 4 oar'd lapt boat, with two spread sails, he has been us'd to the sea—it is suspected that he is gone towards Salem or Marblehead.—Whoever will secure said Negro and the boat, and give information to John Forbes, at Mr. John Coburn's in State-Street, shall have a reward of 100 Dollars, and all necessary charges
    paid by JOHN FORBES.
The Continental Journal, And Weekly Advertiser, October 15, 1778.

A person that calls himself *John Taylor,*
took from me the Subscriber on the 30th of September, a bay MARE, 8 years old, a very small white spot in her forehead, a new russet saddle, a bridle, a blue great coat, the cape serge of the lighter blue and different sort of cloth, and has not yet return'd; he is a of a short stature, black strait hair, light or rather gray eyes, speaks Dutch or Irish, he often boasts of his wealth, frequently shows his money in Gold Guineas in a long green purse.

Whoever shall take up and secure said Thief, or give information so that I may have my Mare and Goods shall be well rewarded and all necessary charges paid by me
    ASA ROCKWOOD.   *Holliston, October* 2.
The Continental Journal, And Weekly Advertiser, October 15, 1778; October 22, 1778; November 5, 1778.

        Stolen on Friday night last, from me
the subscriber, a blue Broad-Cloth Coat and Jacket, with white buttons, one pair of striped trowsers, one felt hat, one red and white silk handkerchief, one cotton ditto, one pair of open work silver buckles, one pair of sheepskin breeches, and one two shirt; supposed to be stolen by a negro man who passes by the name of Jo Fisher, alias Sampson, alias Sambo, is very black, about five feet six inches high, speaks broken English, also French, Dutch, and many other languages, and is supposed to be about 36 years of age, has been a privateering out of New-London and Rhode-Island.—Whoever will take up said negro and confine him in some goal in this State, and send word to the subscriber, shall be handsomely rewarded by
    WILLIAM DRAPER.   Dedham, Oct. 12.
The Continental Journal, And Weekly Advertiser, October 15, 1778; October 22, 1778; November 5, 1778.

        TWENTY DOLLARS REWARD.
RAN-away from the Subscriber in Lancaster, on Friday the 9th Inst. a Negro Boy named CAESER, 14 years of Age, about five Feet one Inch high: Had on when he went away, a light colour'd Coat and Jacket, short white linnen Trowsers, a round straw Hatt; supposed to be in or near Boston. Whoever will take up and secure said Negro, so that he may be returned shall have the above Reward and all necessary Charges
      paid by AARON SAWYER,   *Lancaster, Oct* 15th.
  N. B. All Masters of Vessels and others, are hereby cautioned from Harboring or Concealing said Negro, under penalty of the Law.
  The Independent Ledger, and the American Advertiser, October 19, 1778; October 26, 1778; November 2, 1778.

RAN-away, on the first Instant, from his Master, JOHN WHITE, of Billerica, a Negro Fellow, named SAMBO, is about 5 Feet 5 Inches high, bow-leged, well set, had on when he went away, a brown cloath-coloured Broad Cloth Coat, a striped home-spun Jacket, a pair of Leather-Breeches, a Cotton and Linnin Shirt, an old Beaver-Hat; carryed with him a blue and white striped Cotton and Linnin Shirt.—Whoever will take up said Negro and secure him in Goal, or otherwise, so that his Master shall have him again, shall have Ten Dollars, and all necessary Charges.

The Independent Chronicle and the Universal Advertiser, October 22, 1778. See *The Boston-Gazette, And Country Journal,* May 26, 1777.

A Certain person who called himself Thomas Thompson, alias William Wilmarth, hired two horses and a chaise of the subscriber, in Boston, on the 12th of October inst. since which he has sold one horse and the chaise in Providence ; the other horse is missing with the saddle and bridle. A reward of one hundred and fifty dollars is hereby offered to any person who will apprehend and secure said Thompson, with the missing horse, or fifty dollars for the horse, saddle and bridle only. Said Thompson is a short, well set man, has the appearance of a gentleman, and says he deserted from the English on account of killing his captain in a duel.

John Magner. Boston, October 22, 1778.

N. B. the above-mentioned horse is black, has a strip [*sic*] in his forehead, and some sore spots under his saddle ; he is about 8 years old, near 13 hands high, trots and canters, and has white legs.

The Providence Gazette; and Country Journal, October 24, 1778; November 7, 1778.

RUN away from the ship Munificence transport, Thomas Elding, master, an apprentice named ABRAHAM SPRINGER, a native of New-England; had on when he went away, a large light coloured upper jacket, a pair of long trowsers, a large round hat, his own short light coloured hair, about 16 years of age, 5 feet 2 inches high, smooth faced, and brown complexion. Also run away from the same ship, an apprentice named JAMES YOUNG, about 15 years of age, smooth faced, brown complexion, had on when he went away, an old red jacket, a pair of long trowsers, and an old cock'd hat, about 4 feet 10 or 11 inches high. Whoever will give such information as may enable the master of the above ship to get them back to the ship, shall have ONE GUINEA Reward for each of them.

All persons are cautioned not to harbour them at their peril.

The Royal Gazette, October 24, 1778; October 28, 1778. See *The Royal Gazette,* November 7, 1778, for Springer.

SIX DOLLARS REWARD.

WHEREAS Peleg Winslow and George Wires, were convicted before the special court at Westminster, the 30th day of September last for beating, wounding, and abusing the wife of William Wiman, in a very inhuman manner; in consequence of which they were committed to goal in said Westminster, and on the evening of the same day made their escape, supposed to have been assisted by some evil-minded person or persons. Said Winslow is about 5 feet and 10 inches high, light complexion, light

short hair, a mole on his left cheek, of an insolent air, and about 50 years of age. Said Wires is a slim built fellow, light complexion, about 23 years of age. Whoever shall apprehend said Prisoners and secure them, or either of them, in any of the goals within this State, or any of the United States, or deliver them in the subscriber at Windsor, shall receive thirty dollars for each of them, and all necessary charges
paid, by   JOHN BENJAMIN, Sheriff.
State of Vermont, Windsor. Oct. 5. 1778.
N. B. All masters of vessels are forbid at their peril, harbouring or carrying off said prisoners.
The Connecticut Courant, and the Weekly Intelligencer, October 27, 1778; November 3, 1778.

WHEREAS my wife ELIZABETH has without any just cause or provocation, eloped from my bed and board, and carried off great part of me household stuff, and had declared she will never live with me again, and I am apprehensive will run me in debt. These are therefore to warn all persons from trading, trusting, harbouring or entertaining her on my account, as I will pay no debt contracted by her after this date.
JEDDIAH LEE.   Willington, October 19, 1778.
The Connecticut Courant, and the Weekly Intelligencer, October 27, 1778; November 3, 1778.

WHEREAS Phebe Brown my
wife has lately left me, and is running me in Debt. These are therefor to warn all Persons not to trust her on my account for I am determined not to pay any Debt she shall hereafter contract on my account; and hereby warn all Persons against harbouring her on any account, as they may expect to suffer the consequences to me
JOSEPH BROWN.   Kensington October 22, 1778.
The New-Hampshire Gazette; or, State Journal, and General Advertiser, October 27, 1778.

Two Hundred Dollars Reward.
BROKE Goal, in Worcester, on
Friday evening the 23d instant, NATHAN DAVIS, formerly of Ware, in the country of Hampshire, six feet high, short black curled hair, light complection, about 40 years old, had on when he broke goal, a checked shirt and trowsers, a coloured close-bodied coat and waistcoat, and a small brimed old hat. WILLIAM MOSMAN, late of Lancaster in the county of Worcester, five feet, 10 inches high, light Hair cut short, sandy complection, about 35 years of age, had on when broke goal, a white shirt, red coat and waistcoat, old black plush breeches, without any hat. Whoever

will take up and secure said Davis and Mossman, shall receive 100 dollars reward for each, and all necessary charges
    paid by Wm. GREENLEAF, sheriff.
                  Worcester, Oct. 15, 1778.
Thomas's Massachusetts Spy Or, American Oracle Of Liberty, October 28, 1778; November 5, 1778. See *Thomas's Massachusetts Spy Or, American Oracle Of Liberty,* July 22, 1779, for Mosman.

        Whereas *Mary* the wife of me the
subscriber, has eloped from me: These are therefore to caution all persons whatsoever not to trust her on my account, for I will not pay one farthing for any debt that she may contract after the date hereof.
    JONATHAN SMITH.   Roxbury, Oct. 28.
The Continental Journal, And Weekly Advertiser, October 29, 1778; November 5, 1778; November 12, 1778.

BROKE Goal, and made his Escape, in the Town, on Tuesday, the 20th instant, one *Thomas Moore,* a Sailor, about 28 Years of Age, born in England, about 5 Feet 6 Inches high, had on a red out-side Jacket, and striped Trowsers. He was committed to Goal for Debt, and for deserting from the Continental Ship Alliance. Whoever will return him to the Subscriber, shall have 20 DOLLARS Reward.
    JOSEPH OTIS, Deputy-Goal-Keeper.
                 Boston, October 28, 1778.
The Independent Chronicle and the Universal Advertiser, November 5, 1778.

RUN away from the general hospital in Providence, the 19th instant, the following prisoners of war, taken by the French fleet under the Count D'Estaing.

  Joshua Chadwick, mate, about 27 years of age, of a fair complexion, has light eyes, and is pitted with the small-pox: Had on a light blue coat, knit pattern jacket, and white breeches, and carried with him a blue sea jacket.

  James Nesfield, seaman, about 20 years of age, born in Barbados, of a dark complexion, is pitted with the small pox, and has short black hair: Had on a blue sea jacket, seamed with white, grey woollen trowsers, and a round felt hat, and carried with him an old brown jacket.

  James Kemp, seaman, about 19 years of age, of a fair complexion, and has light short curled hair: Had on a round hat, cloth coloured jacket, and sea trowsers.

Whoever will apprehend the above-mentioned persons, or either of them, and secure them in any public goal, so that they made be had for exchange, shall receive a generous reward, and all necessary charges, paid by   JEREMIAH HILL, Com. of Prisoners
Providence, Oct. 26, 1778.   State of R. Island.
The Providence Gazette; and Country Journal, November 7, 1778; November 14, 1778; November 21, 1778.

ABSENTED himself from his Master's service, William Smith, apprentice unto Thomas Eldding, Master of the Munificence, transport, late in the evening of the 5th of November, had on when he went away, a short double-breasted red jacket, a large blue outside one, long canvas trowsers, silver round womens buckles, and small bound round hat, dark complexion, short hair, long visage, and is a native of South Shields, was late in the watch and clock-making business. It is earnestly requested not Watch-Maker, or other person will employ or harbour him, or they will answer the same at their peril.

Absented at the same time, Abraham Springer, a native of New-England, about 16 years old, his head lately shaved, had on when he went away, an inside flannel jacket, a soldier's red cap on his head, dark brown stockings, and white cloth officers breeches.
The Royal Gazette, November 7, 1778, November 11, 1778. See *The Royal Gazette*, October 24, 1778, for Springer.

DEserted from my Company, one William Money, a Negro, belonging to the Town of Walpole, and hired for said Town for the Term of eight Months. He is about 24 Years of Age, and about 5 Feet 6 Inches high.—Also one Joseph Hunt, some Time in August, on his Way from Dorchester to Peeks-Kill; he is about 20 to 25 Years of Age, and about 5 Feet 10 Inches high, a stout well-built Fellow; he is supposed to have returned back to Dorchester again. Whoever will take up said Deserters, and bring them to Camp, at West-Point, shall receive TEN DOLLARS Reward for each.
JOHN ELLIS, Capt.   West-Point, October 20, 1778.
The Boston-Gazette, And Country Journal, November 9, 1778; November 16, 1778; November 23, 1778.

TWENTY DOLLARS REWARD.
RUN away from the subscriber, an indented servant mulatto boy, named *Obadiah*, 16 years of age, about 5 feet 4 or 5 inches high, of a slender make; had on when he went away, a brown linsey Woolsey jacket, a tow shirt, and old pair of two trowsers, a pair of old shoes and stockings, and

took with him a rifle frock. 'Tis supposed he went to New-Milford with an intention of inlisting in Col. Meigs's regiment which lay at that place. Whoever will take up and secure said servant, so that his master may have him again, shall receive the above reward, and all other reasonable charges
paid by   JOHN GRENELL. Fairfield, October 22, 1778.
The Connecticut Journal, November 11, 1778; November 18, 1778; November 25, 1778.

Two Hundred Dollars Reward.
Broke out of *Barnstable* goal, on last Tuesday night, SAMUEL PROCTER, later of *Philadelphia*—was committed on a suit commenced against him by MATHIAS HALSTED, of the State of *New-Jersey*, merchant—Said PROCTER is about 24 years of age, 5 feet 8 inches high, light complexion, short hair, very slim,—was born in *Boston*—appears like a gentleman, and has been in the mercantile business—Whoever shall take up and secure said SAMUEL PROCTER, in any goal in this State, and give information to the subscriber, shall receive the above reward, and all necessary charges
paid by   ENOCH HALLET, Sheriff.
Barnstable, Nov. 14, 1779.
The Continental Journal, And Weekly Advertiser, November 19, 1778; November 27, 1778; December 3, 1778. See *The Boston-Gazette, And Country Journal,* June 14, 1779.

RAN away from the subscribers, in Stonington, on the 10th inst. two Negro men servants,—one named Cyrus, the other named Jehu,—Cyrus is about 23 years old, about 6 feet high, well set and stoops, has a large scar on one cheek, carried with him a brown fustian and a dark linen coat, a linen and black jacket, a strip'd swan skin ditto, two pair shoes, two felt hats, and two pair mix'd coloured breeches. Jehu is about 5 feet 6 inches high, thick set, strait built, has lost one eye, carried away a soldier coat with steel buttons on the pocket flaps and plated ones before, two strip'd flannel jackets, a felt hat, blue sarge breeches, with trowsers over them, and silver plated buckles in his shoes. Whoever will take up and return said servants to us in Stonington, or secure them in goal and inform us thereof, shall have FORTY DOLLARS for both, or TWENTY DOLLARS for either of them,
paid by   JOHN WILLIAMS, ELIHU CHAMPLIN.
Stonington. November 25. 1778.
The Connecticut Gazette; And The Universal Intelligencer, November 27, 1778; December 4, 1778; December 11, 1778; December 18, 1778; December 25, 1778.

WHEREAS SARAH my wife has for a long time absented herself from me, and behaving very unbecoming, especially in being more free than is

customary, with such persons as are easily deluded by the fair sex. (The snake presented the apple, and she partook of the forbidden fruit.) This therefore is to forbid any person harbouring of her, or trusting her on my account, as I will not pay one debt contracted by her after this date.
     BENJAMIN WAIT.   Granville, Nov. 9, 1778.
The Connecticut Courant, and Hartford Weekly Intelligencer, November 24, 1778.

WILLIAM CALWILL, a British Prisoner, hired of me the Subscriber, on Saturday the 13th of November, one Horse and one Mare; the Horse was about 5 & ¼ hands high, and of a red colour, with a yellow mane and a short square tail, *also* a white spot in his forehead, trots and canters well; the Mare was of a black colour, and about 14 hands high; the Mare was for his servant to ride on, the Horse and Mare had on each a good saddle & bridle, the smallest and neatest saddle was on the Horse. Said Caldwill is a likely genteel fellow, had on when he went away, a light colour'd coat and a pair of royal ribb'd breeches, he wore a cockade in his hat, and a hanger by his side: he was taken in a sloop of war by a privateer out of Marblehead; said Calwill is a headstrong fellow, and very generous in company. Whoever will take up and secure said Calwill, the Horse, Bridle and Saddle, so that I the Subscriber shall have them all again, shall have One Hundred & Fifty Dollars Reward, or Fifty Dollars only, for the Horse.
    Paid by me DAVID PARKER.
The Boston-Gazette, And Country Journal, November 30, 1778; December 7, 1778; December 14, 1778.

      One Hundred Dollars Reward.
RUN AWAY from the Subscriber, of Beekman's precinct, in Dutchess County, the 23d inst. a certain GEORGE CARY, a resident of Plainfield, in Connecticut, a likely, fresh, hearty looking young man, 22 or 23 years o age, about five feet, seven or eight inches high detected for passing counterfeit Continental Thirty Dollar Bills. Whoever will secure him in any of the jail in the United States, shall be entitled to the above reward, and all necessary charges
     paid by PETER NOXON, Constable. November 24, 1778.
The Connecticut Courant, and the Weekly Intelligencer, December 1, 1778. See *The Independent Chronicle And The Universal Intelligencer*, May 2, 1777, and *The Freeman's Journal, Or New-Hampshire Gazette*, May 8, 1777.

      Whereas *Precillia*, the Wife
of me the Subscriber, has eloped from my Bed and Board, and now resides in the Town of *Lunenburgh*, in the State of *Massachusetts Bay*—This is

therefore to forbid Persons from trusting her on my Account, as I will not pay one Farthing that she may contract, after the Date hereof.
          JOSEPH MARTIN.
Stafford, State of Connecticut, November 30*th,* 1778.
The Independent Chronicle and the Universal Advertiser, December 3, 1778; December 10, 1778; December 17, 1778. See *The Connecticut Courant, And The Weekly Intelligencer,* June 23, 1778.

Stolen, on Tuesday last, by a Frenchman who called himself Anthony, two gowns; one of them a dark striped patch, somewhat worn; the other a new light blue crape. The thief is a thick set fellow, wore a light brown jacket, and a blue ribbon round his neck. It is supposed he went towards New-London. Whoever returns the above articles to the subscriber, shall be handsomely rewarded; and if offered for sale, it is requested they may be stopped, with the thief.
          LEWIS THOMAS.   Providence, Dec. 3, 1778.
The Providence Gazette; And Country Journal, December 5, 1778; December 12, 1778; December 19, 1778; December 26, 1778; January 2, 1779.

BROKE Goal last Thursday Night, one James McKenzie, about 5 Feet 6 Inches high, with short brown Hair. Whoever apprehends, and with bring said McKenzie to the Goal in Boston, shall receive TWENTY DOLLARS Reward, and all reasonable Charges,
          paid by   JOSEPH OTIS, Goaler.
The Boston-Gazette, And Country Journal, December 7, 1778; December 14, 1779; December 21, 1778.

RAN away from the schooner Katy, on the second instant, a Negro man named Peter, about 54 years old, about 5 feet 4 inches high, speaks no English; had on a whitish coat, very much greas'd; has lost most of his teeth, an ugly-looking fellow. Also ran way from the same schooner, on the fourth instant, another Negro, named Nero, a very likely fellow, about 15 years old, about 4 feet [*sic*] 6 inches high, speaks all French; had on a blanket-coat, with a cap which turn'd over his head, and a woolen cap under it, Duck breeches, white thread stockings and have very long feet for his stature. Whoever will take up said runaways, and convey them on board said schooner, lying at Pitt's Wharf, or to the Printer hereof, shall have ten Dollards [*sic*] reward for each or either of them, and all necessary charges
          paid by   Capt. Jarreau, Master of said schooner.
    N. B. All masters of vessels and others, are hereby cautioned against harbouring or concealing said runaways on penalty of the law.

The Boston-Gazette, And Country Journal, December 7, 1778; December 14, 1778; December 21, 1778.

WHEREAS Mary, Wife of the Subscriber, has behaved in a very indecent Manner, and wholly refuses to bed and board with me: This is therefore to warn all Persons not to trust her on my Account, as I will not pay any Debt of her contracting after this Date.
ALEXANDER PHELPES.   Lyme, December 2, 1778.

The Connecticut Gazette; And The Universal Intelligencer, December 11, 1778.

Whereas *Relief,* the Wife of

me the Subscriber, refuses to cohabit with me, this may certify, that I will not discharge any Debt contracted by me after the Date hereof.
OLIVER PACKARD.   BRIDGWATER, December 7, 1778,

The Independent Chronicle and the Universal Advertiser, December 17, 1778; December 31, 1778. See *The Independent Chronicle and the Universal Advertiser,* July 1, 1779.

RAN away from his Master Henry Howell Williams, living on Noddle's Island, on Thursday Night 10th instant, a Negro Fellow, named YORK, about 21 Years of Age, 5 feet 6 inches high, remarkable for a very pleasant Countenance and plausible Tongue. Had on when he went away, a short blue Coat, a buff Jacket, and black plush Breeches, with white Stockings, and large silver Buckles in his Shoes. Whoever shall discover and secure said Negro, so that his Master may receive him again, shall be intitled to TEN DOLLARS Reward, and all reasonable Charges
paid by   H. HOWELL WILLIAMS.

It is supposed he intends making a Cruise. The Officers of Ships of War and Privateers are requested, should he apply to enter on board either of their Ships, to secure him. And all Masters of Vessels, either Armed or Merchant Ships, are cautioned against carrying him off as they would avoid the Penalty of the Law for so doing.

The Boston-Gazette, And Country Journal, December 14, 1778.

WHEREAS a Person who called himself by the Name of John Gale, (Son of John Gale, of New-York, whose Widow kept the Sign of the Blue-Anchor there; but afterwards married one Mr. Pike, Mariner and with him, 'tis suppos'd removed to Philadelphia,) died at the House of the Subscriber in Middle-Street, Boston, on the 19th ult.—These are therefore to give Notice to all to whom it may concern, That on proper Application to him, they may be informed of the Particulars of the Deceased's Effects.
ALEXr. McLEAD.   Boston, Dec. 19, 1778.

The Boston Gazette, and Country Journal, December 21, 1778; January 4, 1779.

THIS may purpose to notify all Persons that shall have the Pleasure to read the same, that is to wit, that the Wife of Mr. David Frost of Cambridge, hath privately conveyed or concealed herself away; any Person that shall let me know where she it, shall be entitled to receive Ten Dollars Reward, and all necessary Charges paid; and I do hereby forbid all Persons from entertaining her, as they shall be punished to the severity of the Law.
        As Witness my Hand.   DAVID FROST.
                                          Cambridge, Dec. 17, 1778.
The Boston Gazette, and Country Journal, December 21, 1778.

TEN DOLLARS REWARD.

ABSENTED himself, suspected with a design to run away, on Saturday the 13th inst. a negro fellow named CATO, he is about 21 years of age, of a yellowish complexion, was brought from the Island of Jamaica about six years ago, all which time, until a month past here, he has resided with his master at Rhode-Island. He was born in Guinea, of the Chamba nation, and has his country marks on his cheeks, talks English enough to be well understood, branded on one of his shoulders P. E. and wore a dark coloured surtout coat, the rest of his dress not remembered. Whoever apprehends and brings him to Captain Laird's Office, in Hanover Square, shall receive the above reward, but whoever conceals or harbours him after this public notice shall be prosecuted.
The Royal Gazette, December 23, 1778.

BROKE out of the County Goal in New-London, the Night after the 21st instant, Noble Hinman, confined for passing counterfeit Money; of a fresh Countenance, pitted with the Small-Pox, long Chin, middling Stature, full breasted, pretty much of a Talkative, legs and feet something remarkable. Whoever will take up said Hinman and confine him in any public Goal, shall have Fifty Dollars Reward, and necessary Charges.
        EPH. MINER, Goaler.   New-London, Dec. 23, 1778.
The Connecticut Gazette; And The Universal Intelligencer, December 25, 1778.

1779

WHereas Eunice, the wife of the subscriber, hath behaved in a very indecent manner, and hath made much disturbance in my house and family, and also used many threatening words: This is therefore to warn all persons

not to trust her on my account, as I will not pay any debts of her contracting after the date hereof. THOMAS KINNE.
                     Worthington (Massachusetts-Bay), January 7, 1779.
The Providence Gazette; And Country Journal, January 9, 1779; January 16, 1779.

WHereas Lovice, the wife of the subscriber, hath forsaken my bed and board, carrying off my goods without my consent or knowledge, and hath behaved herself out of all character as a wife: I therefore forbid all persons to trust her on my account, as I will not pay one farthing of her contracting after the date hereof.
         BENJAMIN SMITH.   Providence, Jan. 30, 1779.
The Providence Gazette; And Country Journal, January 30, 1779.

                     Six pence Reward.
RANAWAY from me the Subscriber, on the night of the first instant, an indented Apprentice, named *Jonathan Edwards*. Whoever will take up said Runaway, and return him to me, shall have the above Reward, and all necessary Charges paid by me,
         JOHN MORRILL.   Kingston, January 26, 1778. [*sic*]
The New-Hampshire Gazette; or, State Journal, and General Advertiser, February 2, 1779; February 16, 1779.

                 Whereas *Isabel*, the wife of
me the subscriber, has refused to live with me: This is, therefore, to forbid all persons from trusting her on my account, as, I will not pay one farthing she may contract from the date hereof.
         JOSEPH HAILE.   *Wrentham, January* 29, 1779.
The Independent Chronicle and the Universal Advertiser, February 4, 1779.

                                     HARTFORD Feb. 6 1779.
MADE their escape from the Goal in this Place, the following Prisoners, viz. NATHANIEL AKERLY, a Tory, belonging to the State of New-York, a stout thick set fellow, light complexion, grey eyes and brown hair. JOHN BAKER, of Woodbury, midling stature, black hair, dark complexion, and dark eyes. AARON OLMSTEAD, of New-Milford, a tall strait fellow, light coloured hair, light grey eyes, and fair countenance. JOEL MURRAY of New-Milford, rather tall thin lanthron jaw'd fellow, dark brown hair and strait built. THOMAS SMITH of Middletown, a young man, small of stature, long dark brown hair, and grey eyes. BLNATHAN BURTS, [*sic*] a native of Long Island, a slim meagre starv'd looking scoundrel—All the above described fellows are tories. BENJAMIN SEAGER, of Hartford, a

tall strait fellow, short sandy hair, white eyes, a large scar on his upper lip. PETER GANTER, of New-York state, tall stout fellow, black hair and blue eyes; the two last committed for theft. Whoever will apprehend either of the above prisoners, and return them to this, or secure them in any other goal, within this or the neighboring states, and inform the subscriber, shall be entitled to a reward of Twenty Dollars, and all necessary charges
paid, by   BARZ. HUDSON, Goaler.

The Connecticut Courant, and Hartford Weekly Intelligencer, February 9, 1779.

RAN-away from the Subscriber on the 3d inst. a Negro fellow named SIMON, about 24 Years of Age, well set, 5 feet 9 inches high, a little lame in one ancle; had on when he went away a grey homespun outside Jacket, a striped flannel under Waistcoat and Trowsers. Whoever shall take up said Negro and bring him to the Subscriber or to Thomas Lloyd Halsey, in Dedham, shall receive Thirty Dollars reward, and all necessary Charges,
paid by JOSEPH WHIPPLE.

Smithfield, Feb. 10, 1779.

N. B. All Masters of Vessels and others are hereby forbid harbouring, concealing, or carrying off said Negro.

The Boston-Gazette, And Country Journal, February 15, 1779; February 22, 1779; March 1, 1779.

RANAWAY from the Subscriber in Lebanon on the 25th instant, a Negro Boy named NEWPORT, about 17 Years old, small of his Age, well set and strait lim'd, one of his Eyes is much less than the other; had on when he went away, a dark coloured buff Coat, and old striped Jacket, an old felt Hat, a pair of old leather Breeches, mixt black and white Stockings, a pair old Shoes, brass Buckles, carried nothing with him but what he wore away. Whoever will take up said Runaway and return him to me the Subscriber in Lebanon, or secure him in Goal and inform me thereof, shall have Twenty
Dollars Reward.   DAN THROOP.

The Connecticut Gazette; And The Universal Intelligencer, February 19, 1779; February 26, 1779. See *The Connecticut Gazette; And The Universal Intelligencer*, May 3, 1776.

WHEREAS Elizabeth the Wife of me the Subscriber, has Run me in Debt while I was at Sea, Wasteing my Substance by Riotous living, and as I am in Danger of being further Run in Debt by the said Elizabeth, this is to warn all Persons from harbouring or Trusting her on my Account for the future, as I will not Pay one Farthing from this Date.
his

STEPHEN X MORSE,
Mark. SALEM, Feb. 1779.
The Boston-Gazette, And Country Journal, February 22, 1779; March 8, 1779.

PROVIDENCE, *February* 19 1779.
ESCAPED from the main guard in this town, about nine o'clock in the evening of the 18th instant, a certain WILLIAM CROSSING, who says he is a Captain in Whitman's corps of tory refugees; and JOSEPH CASWELL, of said Crossing's company, who were captured at Seconnet. CROSSING is about 40 years old, 5 feet 9 inches high, has a light complexion, light blue eyes, short hair, is marked with the small-pox, and is a man of great activity; was dressed in a brown velvet coat, red waistcoat and breeches, and a furr cap. CASWELL, is about 40 years old, 5 feet 7 or 8 inches high, full fac'd, well set, very dark complexion'd, has a remarkable black bushy beard, wears his hair short, and was clothed with a blue coat and waistcoat, and dark brown breeches.—Whoever will apprehend and secure the abovementioned villains, shall receive Two Hundred Dollars Reward or One Hundred Dollars for either of them.
Published by order the honorable Major Gen. Sullivan.
WILLIAM PECK, Adj. Gen. I. R. I.
The Norwich Packet, February 22, 1779; March 1, 1779; March 8, 1779; *The Connecticut Gazette; And The Universal Advertiser*, February 26, 1779; March 5, 1779.

WHereas Mary, the wife of me the subscriber, hath absented herself from my bed and board, and behaved in a very indecent, cruel and unlawful manner, and carried away my property without my consent, and I fear will endeavour to run me in debt; I do hereby strictly forbid all persons to trust her on my account, as I will pay no debt of her contracting from the date hereof. JOSIAH FULLER.
North-Providence, Feb. 23, 1779.
The Providence Gazette; And Country Journal, February 27, 1769; March 6, 1779; March 13, 1769; March 20, 1769.

WHEREAS Isabella, the Wife of the Subscriber, hath eloped from her Bed and Board, this is to forewarn all Persons from harbouring, entertaining or crediting said Isabella, as I hereby declare I will not pay one Farthing of any Debt of her contracting on my Account. As Witness by Hand this 1st Day of March, 1779. DANIEL COLLINS.
The Boston-Gazette, And Country Journal, March 1, 1779; March 8, 1779; March 15, 1779; March 22, 1779.

TWENTY DOLLARS REWARD.

RUN away from the subscriber in October last, a Negro Wench named ZIL, about 15 years old, small of her age, pretends she is free, the last she has been heard of she was going to Lenox. Whoever will return her to her master shall receive the above reward; or if any person will send word or inform her master so that he can get her again, shall be well rewarded for their trouble.
    REUBEN HOPKINS.   Sharon, January 25, 1779.
The Connecticut Courant, and Hartford Weekly Intelligencer, March 2, 1779; March 9, 1779.

FOUR HUNDRED DOLLARS REWARD.

RUN away from his bail one Nathan Stark, of Lebanon, in the State of Connecticut, on the 23d day of January 1779, is about 50 years old, midling stature, has a large red nose; and we the subscribers being bound in a bond of two thousand pounds for said Stark's appearance at court promise that whosoever will bring the said Nathan Stark to us or either of us, in Norwich, shall have the above reward.
    GEORGE HARRIS. JONATHAN GARDNER.
    ELIJAH LAMPHEAR.   February 16, 1779.
The Connecticut Courant, and Hartford Weekly Intelligencer, March 2, 1779; March 9, 1779; March 16, 1779.

WHEREAS my Negro man, named NAT, has taken undue liberties by trading and running me in debt; this is therefore to forbid all persons harbouring or trusting him on my account, as I will not pay any debt of his contracting from the date hereof.
    PHILIP LOGEE.   Smithfield, March 2, 1779.
The Providence Gazette And Country Journal, March 6, 1779; March 13, 1779; March 20, 1779; March 27, 1779.

WHEREAS MARTHA, the wife of me the subscriber, has eloped from my bed and board. These are therefore to forbid all persons crediting her on my account, as I will not pay any debt or contract she may make hereafter.
    DAVID ALLEN, jun. East-Windsor, February, 26. 1779.
The Connecticut Courant, and Hartford Weekly Intelligencer, March 9, 1779; March 16, 1779; March 23, 1779.

RUN-away from Captain Charles Handy, sometime in the month of September last, an active negro man named MOSES, about five feet six inches high, born in Rhode-Island, it is supposed that he is either lurking about this city or gone a privateering. Whoever apprehends the said negro

man, and will deliver him to Coupland and Tench, No. 7. Water-street, shall receive Two Half Johannes Reward.
The Royal Gazette, March 10, 1779; March 13, 1779; March 17, 1779; March 20, 1779.

BROKE out of Boston goal a Negro Man, named Hampshire Dean, about 5 feet 10 inches high, had on a short white jacket and trousers, white mill'd cap, slim built. Whoever will take up said Negro, and deliver him to JOSEPH OTIS, goal-keeper, shall have TWENTY DOLLARS Reward.
The Continental Journal, And Weekly Advertiser, March 11, 1779; March 18, 1779; March 25, 1779.

BOSTON, March 11.
At the Honourable Superior Court held in this town last week, the following prisoners convicted of the several crimes of which they were charged, and sentenced as follows, viz.—Isaac Taft, convicted of fraudulent practices, sentenced to pay a fine of 30 l. for the use of the government and people of this State, stand publicly in the pillory the space of one hour, recognize for his good behaviour for 12 months, in the sum of 200 l. with two sureties in the sum of 100 l. each, pay costs of prosecution, and stand committed till sentence is performed.

Simon Baxter, convicted of uttering and passing counterfeit bills, knowing them to be counterfeit, sentenced to pay a fine of 90 l. for the use of the State, pay treble damages to the person injured, suffer six months imprisonment, sit one hour on the Gallows with a rope about his neck, pay costs of prosecution, and stand committed till sentence is performed.

John Bowen, convicted to theft, sentenced that he receive 20 stripes on his naked back at the public whipping-post pay three times the value of the goods stolen, and stand committed till sentence is performed.

James Dennis, convicted of theft, sentenced to pay treble damages, that he receive 20 stripes on his naked back at the public whipping-post, pat costs, and stand committed till sentence is performed.

Agreeable to the sentence of the Hon. Superior Court, Simon Baxter, was last Friday set upon the public gallows—He was afterwards remanded to prison, there to suffer the remainder of the decree of Court, affix'd to his attrocious crime.
The Independent Chronicle and the Universal Advertiser, March 11, 1779. See *The Massachusetts Spy Or, Thomas's Boston Journal*, July 1, 1779, *The Independent Chronicle and the Universal Advertiser*, July 29, 1779, and *The Boston Gazette, And The Country Journal*, November 1, 1779, for Taft.

NEW-LONDON, March 5.
Last Thursday was brought into Stonington, a sloop called the Refugee, laden with wood and wheat, being one of the fleet which passed the harbour the day before for Newport. On board the sloop were two sons of Col. Gilbert of Freetown, a noted tory. On Friday they were brought to this town and committed to gaol. It is said these young Gilberts lately piloted a party of the enemy from Newport to Warren.
The Massachusetts Spy Or, Thomas's Boston Journal, March 11, 1779.

WHEREAS Mehitabel, the wife of the subscriber, being disordered in her mind and goes about from place to place: This is to warn all persons from harboring or trusting her on my account, as I will not pay any debt of her contracting after this date.
                 SAMUEL BLACKMAN.   Hebron, January 17, 1779.
The Connecticut Courant, and Hartford Weekly Intelligencer, March 16, 1779; March 23, 1779.

RUNAWAY from the Subscriber in Ripton, a Negro Fellow named *Lively*, about 32 Years old, has remarkable red Eyes, which were burnt when he was small, is about 5 Feet 10 inches high, round shouldered, is a Fiddler, and says he is free by inlisting into the Continental Army, and hath a Copy of a Pass from General Gates: it is supposed he is in Greenfield or Danbury. Whoever will take up said Negro, and secure him, and send me Word, or return him to me in Ripton, shall have 30 Dollars Reward, and all reasonable Charges paid,
                by GIDEON LEAVENWORTH.   Ripton, March 9 1779.
The Connecticut Journal, March 17, 1779; March 31, 1779; April 7, 1779.

WHEREAS Lois, the reputed Wife of Eliakim Hide, of Stratford, in the County of Fairfield, being in a disorder'd state of Mind, has behaved extremely ill, & is endeavouring to run him in Debt: These are therefore to forewarn, and to give full Notice to all Persons whatsoever, not to entertain, nor to credit the said Louis, in any Manner, on Account of the said Eliakim, as he will not pay any Debt, or be answerable for any Contract by her made or enter'd into after the Date hereof. Dated in Stratford,
              this 8th Day of February, 1779.   ELIAKIM HIDE.
The Connecticut Journal, March 17, 1779.

              Ran-away from their masters, on Sunday
last, an apprentice Boy named Nathaniel Proctor, aged 20 years, of small stature, had on a blue suit of cloaths with white metal buttons, and white

stockings.—Also, a NEGRO-MAN named Caesar, belonging to James Boice of Milton, and George Clark of Dorchester, he is of small stature, has very crooked [   ], (which have lately been scalded) and blubber lips.—Also, a BOY named James Cox, belonging to Hugh McLean of Milton.—If the above described will return to their duty, they shall be forgiven, if not, any person who shall apprehend them and convey them to their Masters, or the Printer hereof, shall receive TWENTY DOLLARS as a reward or each.

⁂ All masters of vessels, and others, are hereby cautioned against concealing or carrying them off, if they mean to avoid the penalty of the law.

As they belong to the paper-mills in Milton and Dorchester, their being apprehended will be of great service to the public.

JAMES BOICE, GEORGE CLARK, HUGH McLEAN.

Dorchester, March 18.

The Continental Journal, And Weekly Advertiser, March 18, 1779.

RUN-away from the subscriber in Woodbury, a Negro Man, about 23 years of age, very black and trim built, a small head and flat nose and pitted on the nose with the small pox; he is about 5 feet 9 or 10 inches high; took away with him a butternut coloured great coat, a strait bodied coat and over halls of the same colour, the coat has yellow buttons and a yellow button on his hat; a large quantity of other cloaths of all sorts. Whoever will take up said Negro and confine him or deliver him to me, shall have One Hundred Dollars Reward.

OBADIAH WHEELER.   April 7, 1779. [*sic*]

The Connecticut Courant, And The Weekly Intelligencer, March 30, 1779; April 20, 1779; May 4, 1779. See *The Independent Chronicle and the Universal Advertiser*, April 15, 1779, and *The Connecticut Gazette; And The Universal Intelligencer*, April 15, 1779.

STOP THIEF!

ON the 22d day of March last, was stolen from the house of Mr. Peirce, innkeeper in Mansfield, a BAY HORSE, SADDLE and BRIDLE; the Horse about nine years old, paces and trots, well made and in good order, about fourteen hands high. Stolen by one Martin a Frenchman, who is acquainted with the business of waiting and tending stables, &c. he is pitted with the small pox, about five feet ten inches high, dark brown hair, pale fac'd jail looking fellow, speaks very little English. Whoever will apprehend and confine the thief, and secure the horse, that the right owner may have him, shall have ONE HUNDRED DOLLARS REWARD, and necessary charges, paid by   JOHN VIOLENE.

Wethersfield, April 9, 1779. [*sic*]

The Connecticut Courant, And The Weekly Intelligencer, March 30, 1779.

STOLEN from the Stable of Mr. GIDEON ARNOLD, in Warwick, last Tuesday Evening, a dark sorrel Horse, in good Order, shod all round, and had on when stolen, a Saddle and Bridle. Said Horse in Six Years old, Fourteen Hands and Three Inches high, is a natural Trotter, and has a Star in his Forehead.

The supposed Thief is between Twenty and Thirty Years of Age, of a middling Stature, well built, wears his own Hair, and had on a blue Coat, faced with White, a ruffled Shirt, &c. Whoever will take up said Horse and Thief, and deliver them to the Subscriber in Warwick, shall receive Sixty Dollars Reward, and necessary Charges, or Thirty for the Horse only.
    CHARLES HOLDEN.   Warwick, April 1.
The American Journal and General Advertiser, April 1, 1779.

WHereas Sarah, the Wife of
me the subscriber, has Eloped from me, and refuses to live with me: This is to forbid any person crediting her on my Account, as I will not pay any Debts of her contracting from the Date hereof.
    Caleb Hutchings.   Kittery, April 6, 1778.
The New-Hampshire Gazette; or, State Journal, and General Advertiser, April 6, 1779; April 13, 1779; April 27, 1779.

RAN-AWAY from the Subscriber, a Negro Man, named CATO, formerly owned by Mr. John Manley. He is about 5 Feet 8 Inches high, and is scarified in the Face: Had on when he went away a Cloth coloured Jacket, and striped Woolen Waistcoat and Trowsers, a Castor Macaroni Hat, and a striped Flannel Shirt: He took with him a Linen Coat, Jacket and Breeches, a white Shirt, two Pair of white Cotton Stockings, and a Cloth coloured Great Coat, in a Bundle. Whoever will apprehend said Runaway shall receive Thirty Dollars Reward, and all necessary Charges.
    PHILIP TABOR,   Dartmouth, April 6, 1779.
The American Journal And General Advertiser, April 8, 1779; April 15, 1779; April 22, 1779; April 29, 1779.

BROKE out of the pubic Goal in Norwich, on the Night after the 6th Instant, one —— Forsythe, convicted of Horse-stealing, and sentenced to Newgate Prison in Simsbury; also Noble Hillman, convicted of passing Counterfeit Continental Currency. Whoever will apprehend the above Persons and return them to the Custody of the Goal-keeper in Norwich, shall have Two Hundred Dollars Reward, or One Dollars for each, and necessary Charges paid by

MOSES CLEVELAND, Goaler.   Norwich, April 7th, 1779.
The Connecticut Gazette; And The Universal Intelligencer, April 8, 1779.

RAN away from the subscriber in Lyme, on the 4th instant, a negro man servant named PEROW, about 30 years old, had on a Scotch cap, outside waistcoat of brown full'd cloth, stript trousers, woollen, &c. speaks broken English, seemingly very good humour'd; carried with him considerable Cash, among it some hard money, a pair large silver shoe buckles, the ends of part of his toes have been froze off, smoaks tobacco in an iron pipe which he carried with him. Whoever takes up said negro and returns him to me or secures him and gives me notice so that I can have him, shall have Twenty Dollars reward, and all necessary charges
    paid by William Brockway. Lyme, 12 March 1779.
The Connecticut Gazette; And The Universal Intelligencer, April 8, 1779; April 15, 1779; April 22, 1779.

WHEREAS Jeremiah Glover, an Indented Apprentice, hath a long time past deserted, and now absences himself from his Master's service, this is to caution all persons from harbouring, concealing or dealing with said servant, as they would avoid the penalty of the Law provided in such cases.
    NATHANIEL BARRELL.   York, April 13.
The New-Hampshire Gazette; or, State Journal, and General Advertiser, April 13, 1779; April 20, 1779; April 27, 1779; May 4, 1779; May 11, 1779.

RAN away from the Subscriber at Woodbury in this State, a Negro Man named POMP, 23 Years old, 5 Feet 9 or 10 Inches high, well built, very black, small round Head, flat Nose, talks good English, and is a little pitted on the Nose with the Small Pox; carried away with him, a Butternut colour'd Great Coat, streight bodied Coat with yellow Buttons and Overhauls, with a yellow Button on his Hat, and a Quantity of other Clothes. Whoever will take up said Negro and give Notice thereof, shall have one Hundred Dollars Reward, paid by
    OBADIAH WHEELER. *Woodbury, April 8*, 1779.
The Connecticut Gazette; And The Universal Intelligencer, April 15, 1779; April 22, 1779; April 29, 1779. See *The Independent Chronicle and the Universal Advertiser*, April 15, 1779, and *The Connecticut Courant, And The Weekly Intelligencer*, March 30, 1779.

RAN away from the Subscriber, in Woodbury, State of Connecticut, a Negro Man named POMP, about 23 Years old, 9 or 10 Inches high, a trim built Fellow and very black, a small round Nose, a little pitted with the

small Pox on his Nose; had a Butter-nut coloured great Coat, and Overhalls of the same Colour; a yellow Button on his Hat, and had with him a Number of other Clothes; talks good English; is about 5 Feet 9 or 10 Inches high. Whoever will take up said Negro, and return him to me, shall have one Hundred Dollars Reward, paid by me,
      OBADIAH WHEELER. *Woodbury, April* 8, 1779.
The Independent Chronicle and the Universal Advertiser, April 15, 1779; April 22, 1779. See *The Connecticut Courant, And The Weekly Intelligencer*, March 30, 1779, and *The Connecticut Gazette; And The Universal Intelligencer*, April 15, 1779.

      Whereas SARAH my Wife, hath
eloped from me, embezzled and made way with my substance wherever she could find it, and has otherways behaved as a wife should not do to her husband—This is therefore to caution, and forbid the public having any dealings, or crediting her on my account, as I will not pay any debt she may contract, or abide by any bargain, or agreement she may make, from the date hereof; being determined to have nothing more to do with her.
    JAMES MULVANY. *Newbury-Port, April* 23d. 1779.
The Independent Ledger, and the American Advertiser, April 26, 1779; May 3, 1779; May 17, 1779.

RUN away from the subscriber the 10th of March last an apprentice boy named Daniel M'Collom, about 13 years old, small of his age, has black hair and eyes, had on when he went away an old felt hat bound with red and yellow ferret, a brown jacket, and striped flannel one under it, check'd linnen shirt, long trowsers, blueish stockings, old shoes, and square brass buckles. Whoever will take up said apprentice and return him to me, in New-London, on Jordon Plain, shall have Six Dollars reward,
    paid by JAMES CULVER.   *April* 26, 1779.
N. B. All persons are forbid harbouring said boy on penalty of the law.
The Connecticut Gazette; And The Universal Intelligencer, April 29, 1779; May 5, 1779; May 12, 1779.

RAN away from me the Subscriber, the 21st ult. *Catherine Cassada*, a servant Girl, about 16 Years old. Whoever will take up said Runaway, and return her to me, shall receive SIX PENCE reward. And all Persons are cautioned against harbouring said Servant, as they would prevent Trouble.
    MOSES WHEELER.   *Rowley, April* 6, 1779.
The Independent Chronicle and the Universal Advertiser, April 29, 1779; May 13, 1779.

WHEREAS ZILPAH, the wife of me
the Subscriber, has (with doing her utmost to ruin my character,) eloped from
my bed and board. This is therefore to forbid all persons trusting her on my
account, as I will not pay any debt she contracts after this date.
REUBEN SMITH. Rupert, April 7, 1779.
The Connecticut Courant, And The Weekly Intelligencer, May 4,
1779; May 11, 1779.

WHEREAS HANNAH, the wife of
me the Subscriber, hath by her late conduct rendered it necessary, for me to
forbid all persons crediting her on my account. I do therefore hereby forbid
all persons trusting her on my account, as I will not pay any debt of her
contracting after this date.
SAMUEL ALLEN. Suffield, April 26, 1779.
The Connecticut Courant, And The Weekly Intelligencer, May 4,
1779; May 11, 1779.

RAN away from the Subscriber in Pomfret, the 2d. Inst, a Negro Man named
WARWICK, 5 Feet 10 Inches high, 25 Years old, very Talkative, slim built,
very Active, and carried with him a Quantity of Cloaths of his own and some
others.—Whoever will secure him so that his Master may have him again
shall have Fifty Dollars Reward, & necessary Charges,
paid by Nath'l Pearse. May 4, 1779.
The Connecticut Gazette; And The Universal Intelligencer, May 5,
1779; May 13, 1779; May 27, 1779.

RAN away from the subscriber in Exeter, in the State of Rhode-Island, a
negro man servant named Prince, had on when he went away a mill'd
coloured worsted serge coat and breeches, a striped flannel jacket, and had
with him a grey coat of full'd cloth, is about 6 feet high, pretends to be of a
religious turn and a great exhorter. Whoever will take up said negro and
return him to the subscriber in Exeter, shall have Ten Dollars reward, and all
necessary charges, paid by
JEFFERY CHAMPLIN. Groton, April 15, 1779.
The Connecticut Gazette; And The Universal Intelligencer, May 5,
1779; May 13, 1779; May 20, 1779; May 27, 1779.

WHEREAS Abagail the wife of
me the subscriber, has for a considerable time past separated herself from me,
without any reasonable cause, and as I have reason to fear that she will by
her contracts (if not prevented) run me in debt, and subject me to other
disadvantages, I hereby warn and forbid all person to treat her on my account,
for I will not pay any debt of her contracting after the date hereof.

JOHN DANIELS. Grafton, May 5th, 1779.
Thomas's Massachusetts Spy Or, American Oracle Of Liberty, May 7, 1779; May 13, 1779; May 20, 1779; May 27, 1779. See *Thomas's Massachusetts Spy Or, American Oracle Of Liberty,* May 13, 1779.

FIVE HUNDRED DOLLARS REWARD.

BROKE out of the County Goal in Boston, on Saturday Night the 8th inst. JOHN JONES, who was committed by the Hon. Council, as an Enemy to the State; he is about 36 Years Old, about 5 Feet 7 Inches high, of a very Dark Complexion, Black Eyes, short Black Hair, and of a Guilty Countenance, he had on a Blue Coat and a pair of Black Velvet Breeches. Whoever will apprehend the said JONES, and Convey him to the Goal in Boston, shall be Intitled to *Five Hundred Dollars*
from Wm. GREENLEAF, Sheriff.

The Boston-Gazette, And Country Journal, May 10, 1779; May 24, 1779, *The Independent Ledger, and the American Advertiser,* May 10, 1779; May 17, 1779; May 24, 1779; May 31, 1779; June 7, 1779; June 14, 1779, and *The Independent Chronicle and the Universal Advertiser,* May 20, 1779. Minor differences between the papers. The *Ledger* and *Chronicle* have "*Boston, May* 10, 1779." at the bottom of the ad and the Greenleaf's first name as William.

EIGHTY DOLLARS REWARD.
Whereas a certain RICHARD
WRIGHT, did on Friday last, hire of the Subscriber, to ride to *Danvers,* a large dark bay Mare, about 5 Years old, with a blaze in her face, and has a short main and brush tail, trots and paces genteelly, and had on a new blue Saddle and Briddle with a cross-barr'd Saddle-cloth: And as said WRIGHT has not yet thought proper to make his appearance; this is therefore to desire him to return with the Mare immediately; or if any person will be kind enough to forward him, or secure him in any of the Continental Goals, so that he may be brought to justice, and the Mare recovered again, they shall receive the above reward of EIGHT DOLLARS, and all necessary charges; or if the Mare only is recovered, a Reward of FIFTY DOLLARS and charges, will be
paid by MARY BANISTER.

N. B. Said WRIGHT sometimes called himself HOWARD, is about forty years old, wears short brown curled hair, is bald-headed and round-shouldered, and has a long chin: Had on a dark-colored French coat, and a close-bodied Broad-cloth coat, near the same color, with a darn upon one of the shoulders, black everlasting Breeches, and grey seemed stockings, with open work'd flower'd Shoe-Buckles in his shoes—As he was seen going towards *Boston* on Saturday inst. it would be esteemed a particular favor, if

a look-out would be kept there; but in an especial manner by such Gentlemen who are any wise concerned in trade or Sea-faring Business, as said WRIGHT has already sold shares, under pretence of going in Capt. HOBB'S Privateer.   *Salem,* April 28. 1779.
   The Independent Ledger, and the American Advertiser, May 10, 1779; May 17, 1779; May 24, 1779.

RANAWAY last Sunday from his Master Capt. Samuel Langdon, of Portsmouth, a Negro Man named Ceaser, about 30 Years of Age, thick set short Fellow, very fond of Singing, had on a grey homespun Pea Jacket, striped Wastecoat, Leather Breeches—Whoever takes up said Negro, and conveys him to his Master, shall receive Twenty Dollars Reward, and necessary Charges
                   by SAM. LANGDON.   Portsmouth, May 11, 1779.
   The New Hampshire Gazette, Or State Journal And General Advertiser, May 11, 1779; May 18, 1779. See *The Exeter Journal, or The New-Hampshire Gazette and Tuesday's General Advertiser,* May 18, 1779, and *The New-Hampshire Gazette, And Historical Chronicle,* April 30, 1781.

STOLEN from the subscriber on the night following the 5th inst. a dark colour'd home made bearskin great-coat, with a cape of the same, and a small brown cotton cape over it, with mohair basket buttons, one pair of home made gray worsted stockings, and a check'd linnen shirt, none of them worn but little, supposed to be taken by one John Davis a noted soap boiler. Whoever will return the articles and secure the thief, shall have Twenty Dollars reward, and all necessary charges.
              JEDEDIAH SAFFORD.   Norwich May 9, 1779.
   The Connecticut Gazette; And The Universal Intelligencer, May 13, 1779; May 20, 1779.

                   WHEREAS John Daniels hath
Published me the Subscriber, in last week's paper, that I had absented from him without any real cause; which is an absolute falshood. I leave it to the impartial reader to judge; for he hath frequently visited a whore for above twenty years, which I think is a sufficient cause; and as he forbids any person trusting me on his account, his caution is good, but needless, for I daresay nobody would have trusted me upon his account for two years past, had I tried his credit. Therefore I forbid any person or persons trusting the said JOHN DANIELS upon my account, for I do declare there shall not one farthing of my estate go to pay any debt which he shall contract from the date hereof.

ABIGAIL ROCKWOOD, alias DANIELS.
Grafton, May 10, 1779.
Thomas's Massachusetts Spy Or, American Oracle Of Liberty, May 13, 1779; May 20, 1779; May 27, 1779. See *Thomas's Massachusetts Spy Or, American Oracle Of Liberty,* May 7, 1779.

RANAWAY from me the Subscriber, last Sunday, a Negro Man, thirty Years of Age, about five Feet high, a thick-set Fellow, Tawney Complexion; had on when he went away, a good Hat, Grey Coat & jacket, Woollen Shirt, Moose Skin Breeches, blue Stockings. Whoever will take up said Negro, and confine him in any of the Goals in the United States, and send me word, shall have FIFTY DOLLARS REWARD, and all necessary Charges paid, by me, SAMUEL LANGDON.
Portsmouth, May 11, 1779.
The Exeter Journal, or The New-Hampshire Gazette and Tuesday's General Advertiser, May 18, 1779. See *The New Hampshire Gazette, Or State Journal And General Advertiser,* May 11, 1779, and *The New-Hampshire Gazette, And Historical Chronicle,* April 30, 1781.

RAN away from the subscriber the 16th inst. an apprentice boy named William Maxson, about 14 years old, wore away a brown full'd jacket a check'd shirt, a pair striped linen trowsers, a pair blue yarn stockings, a pair new shoes, and a felt hat, half worn. Whoever will take up and return him to the subscriber, shall have Six Pence reward.
PIERPONT BACON.   Colchester, May 18, 1779.
N. B. All Persons are forbid harbouring said boy on penalty of the law.
The Connecticut Gazette; And The Universal Intelligencer, May 20, 1779; May 27, 1779; June 3, 1779.

WHereas named TEMPERANCE, the wife of me the subscriber, hath eloped from my bed and board; this is to forbid any person trusting her on my account, as I will not pay any debts of her contracting after the date hereof.   ROGER COREY.   Tiverton, May 27, 1779.
The American Journal And General Advertiser, May 27, 1779; June 3, 1779; June 10, 1779.

THIRTY DOLLARS Reward.
RAN away from the Subscriber the Night following the 9th Instant, a Negro Man Servant, named named SI, about 24 Years of Age, 5 Feet 7 or 8 Inches high, well built, wore away a russet Jacket with scarlet Cape and Cuffs, Breeches of the same, a striped flannel Shirt, and took with him a striped tow and linnen Ditto, yarn Stockings and felt Hat, is very much addicted to swearing. Whoever will return said Negro to the Subscriber in Voluntown,

or secure him in any Goal of the United States, shall receive the above Reward, and necessary Charges
    paid by JOHN DORRANCE.   Voluntown, May 15 1779.
    N. B. All Masters of Vessels are hereby forbid harbouring or carrying off said Negro.
The Connecticut Gazette; And The Universal Intelligencer, May 27, 1779; June 3, 1779; June 10, 1779. Advertiser's name appears as DORRAMCE in the second ad.

    WHEREAS *Jane*, the wife of the subscriber, hath allowed herself in repeating threats of revenge on my person, even in murder, and to destroy my house by fire, and hath attempted to put in execution her revenge—embezzled my goods, and run me in debt. This is to give notice to all persons, not to credit her on my account, for I hereby declare I will not pay one farthing of any debt she may contract from the date hereof; as witness my hand.
    ISAAC BROWN.   May 24, 1779.
The Continental Journal, And Weekly Advertiser, May 27, 1779; June 3, 1779; June 10, 1779.

    Whereas the subscriber, on December last, publicly refused to discharge any debts contracted by named RELIEF, his wife; he hereby revokes and disannouls the same, and stands obliged, in every respect, as though no such publication had been made.
    OLIVER PACKARD.   Bridgwater, June 20, 1779.
The Independent Chronicle and the Universal Advertiser, July 1, 1779. See *The Independent Chronicle and the Universal Advertiser*, December 17, 1778.

STOLEN, at sundry times, out of my wife's drawers, by Rebecca Boham, a Negro woman, a calico curtain, containing two yards and an half, one holland shirt, two yards black tammy, one cotton and linen tester, containing four yards, one black homespun cloth, one hair thread mittens, some skeins cotton yarn, and a double sheet of fine linen, containing eleven yards, which I brought from Scotland, 1750, and kept for two winding sheets for my wife and myself.—Any person that will bring back the same, or inform me of them, as I can recover all the above articles, shall have TWENTY DOLLARS Reward,
    paid by   ROBERT CLELAND.
    N. B. The said Rebecca had a hut on the Indian land, which they pulled down for her honesty to them.
    New-London, (North-Parish) June 11, 1779.
The Norwich Packet, June 1, 1779; June 15, 1779; June 22, 1779.

Three Hundred Dollars Reward.
RUNAWAY from the Subscriber, on the Night of the 30th Instant, two NEGROES, a MAN and WENCH; the Man 25 Years of Age, thick-set, and well built, low spoken, speaks as if his Mouth was fill'd with Wool. A down cast Look, and most commonly shews his Teeth. The Wench 20 Years of Age, lately belonged to Mr. Foot of Cheshire, short and thick set, and this Country born, a large Foot, and treads her Shoes sideways. They carried considerable Provision with them, which makes it most probable they will travel a Nights, and lie still a Days. It is supposed they have gone with a Design to get to Long Island, or on board some Privateer. All Masters of Vessels are forbid taking them on board. Whoever shall return them to me, shall receive the above reward.
    EDWARD HINMAN.   Woodbury, May 31, 1779.
The Connecticut Journal, June 2, 1779; June 16, 1779; June 23, 1779. See *The Connecticut Courant, And The Weekly Intelligencer,* June 8, 1779.

DESERTED from on Board the Ship Oliver Cromwell, the following Persons, viz *Jedidiah Norton, of Middletown; Samuel Thrasher, of Ditto; Joseph Carter,* of *Plainfield; Anthony Francis,* a Portugese, swarthy Complexion, his Hair tied behind; *Peleg Sanford,* of *Rhode-Island; James Richards,* a Native of *Boston,* taken on Board the *Sheriah* Privateer, out of New-York, and voluntarily entered on Board, light complexion, sandy bushy Hair, about 5 Feet 8 Inches high, 24 or 25 Years old, stocky well built, had on when he went away a blue out side Jacket, white flannel lining, round felt Hat, and long Ticklinburg Trowsers. Trowsers. Whoever will take up the above Persons, or any of them, and deliver them to the Commanding Officer at New-London, shall receive Fifty Dollars Reward, and all necessary Charges
   paid by NATH'l SHAW, Agent for the State.
The Connecticut Gazette; And The Universal Intelligencer, June 3, 1779; June 10, 1779.

FIFTY DOLLARS REWARD.
Ran-away from the subscriber, in the Night of the 31st of May, a NEGRO MAN, named BANDON, about 21 Years of Age, five feet ten inches high, smooth faced, speaks broken English, carried with him a light colored cloth jacket, and a red under one without sleeves, also a red and white flower'd calico, and a red and white gingham ditto with sleeves, a pair of leather breeches, a pair of white linen ditto, two white Shirts, two cambrick and one black Stock, white Stockings, two Pair of Shoes, one Pair new, two old hatts, one of them newly dress'd, silver knee and stock buckles.—Whoever shall take up said negro and convey him to me, at Roxbury, or to Capt. Job

Prince in Boston, shall receive the above reward, and all necessary charges paid; and all masters of vessels, and others, are forbid harbouring or carrying said Negro off, as they would avoid the penalty of the Law.
    DANIEL McCARTHY.   Roxbury, June 1, 1779.

The Continental Journal, And Weekly Advertiser, June 3, 1779; June 10, 1779; June 17, 1779; June 24, 1779; *The Independent Chronicle and the Universal Advertiser*, June 3, 1779; June 10, 1779; June 17, 1779. Minor differences between the papers. See *The Boston-Gazette, And Country Journal*, February 24, 1777, and *The Boston-Gazette, And Country Journal*, June 14, 1779.

FORTY DOLLARS REWARD.

BROKE out of the Custody of the Subscriber, on Thursday 27th of May—a Prisoner who was found guilty of Burglary, aged about 20 Years, and about 5 Feet 6 Inches high, had on a pale blue Coat, white Breeches and Stockings, with short black Hair, who calls his Name *William Whittey*. Any Person who shall take up said Villain, and secure him on some Goal, or return him to me, shall receive the above Reward.
    CALEB HAWARD, Constable. Stoughton, May 28, 1779.

The Independent Chronicle and the Universal Advertiser, June 3, 1779; June 10, 1779.

RAN away from the Subscriber, a Negro Man, named Cato; he sometimes calls himself Cato Mawny, and at other Times Cato Brown; about 5 Feet 10 Inches high, well set; had on when he went away, a striped blue and white Flannel Jacket, a Pair of white woollen Trowsers, a white Tow Shirt, and a new Felt Hat. Whoever will take up said Negro, and confine him in Hartford Gaol, shall receive Three Hundred Dollars Reward, or Three Hundred and Fifty Dollars if delivered at my House at Stephentown.
    NATHAN BROCKWAY.

The Providence Gazette; And Country Journal, June 5, 1779; June 19, 1779.

THREE HUNDRED DOLLARS REWARD.

LAST night ran away from the subscriber, a Negro man and Negro girl, the man about 25 years old, thick, well built, speaks low, and shews his teeth when he speaks, has a down look, this country born, his name is BUD, the girls name is NABBY, a short thick set full faced girl, about 20 years old, low spoken, a subtle crafty creature; it is most likely their design is to get on board some privateer, and its probably the girl may be dress'd in mens cloaths; the man is about 5 feet 8 inches high, both well cloathed. Whoever shall take them up and return them to me, or give such notice of their being secured, as I can obtain them, shall have the above reward of three hundred dollars, two hundred for the man only, or one hundred for the girl only, and reasonable charges

paid, by EDWARD HINMAN. Woodbury, May 31, 1779.

FIFTY dollars reward will be given to any one who will return to the subscriber in Woodbury, a Negro girl named LETTICE, about 24 years of age, trim built and speaks good English; who it is supposed went away with the above Negroes.

EPHRAIM HINMAN.

The Connecticut Courant, And The Weekly Intelligencer, June 8, 1779; June 15, 1779; June 22, 1779. See *The Connecticut Journal, And The New-Haven Post Boy,* June 2, 1779.

Pomfret, January 25. [*sic*] 1779.

STOLEN this day from the door of Caleb Grosvenor, in Ashford, a Horse, Saddle and Bridle. Said horse is about 16 hands high, of a dark sorrel or rather a chestnut colour, with a white snip on his nose, a small mane and foretop, carries his tail very high, trots and canters, a strait gant [*sic*] built horse; a russet saddle, green housing with a green fringe and curb bridle. The thief is a man of about 25 years of age, dark complexion, short black hair, small of stature; had on a light mixt coloured double breasted surtout with brass buttons, leather spatterdashes with brass hooks and eyes, with a small round bound hat. Whoever will take up said horse and thief and return them to the subscriber at Pomfret, shall have a reward of four hundred dollars, and for the horse only two hundred and fifty dollars and all reasonable charges

paid, by   JOSEPH GROSVENOR.

Said horse is 5 or 6 years old this spring.

The Connecticut Courant, And The Weekly Intelligencer, June 8, 1779; June 15, 1779; June 22, 1779.

WHEREAS, my Apprentice

Benjamin Barton, near 18 years of age, light complexion, slim, about 5 feet 6 inches high, absented himself from my service on the 4th of May last, and has not returned. Whoever will take up said apprentice and return him to me, shall receive twenty dollars reward. If said Benjamin will return to me, without further trouble, he shall be kindly received.

DAVID BALDWIN.   Leicester, June 7, 1779.

N. B. All persons are hereby cautioned against concealing or harbouring said apprentice, as they would avoid the penalty of the law.

The Massachusetts Spy Or, Thomas's Boston Journal, June 10, 1779; June 17, 1779; July 1, 1779. See *The Massachusetts Spy Or, Thomas's Boston Journal,* July 1, 1779.

TWO HUNDRED DOLLARS REWARD.

RAN away from the Subscriber in the Night of the 31st of May, a Negro Man, named BANDON, about 21 Years of Age, smooth-faced, speaks broken English: Carried with him a light-coloured Cloth Jacket, a red under ditto, without Sleeves, a Pair of Leather Breeches, a Pair of white Linnen ditto, 2 white Shirts, 1 Check ditto, 2 Cambrick and 1 black Stocks, white Stockings, blue Yarn ditto, 1 Hatt, newly dress'd, 1 Pair new Shoes, Silver Knee and Stock Buckles, and sundry other Cloaths.

Whoever shall take up said Negro, and convey him to me, at Roxbury, or to Capt. Job Prince, in Boston, or will give Information where he is, so that his Master may have him again, shall receive the above Reward, and all necessary Charges paid: And all Masters of Vessels and others, are forbid to carry said Negro off, as they would avoid the Penalty of the Law.

DANIEL McCARTHY.   Roxbury, June 1, 1779.

The Boston-Gazette, And Country Journal, June 14, 1779; June 21, 1779; June 28, 1779. See *The Boston-Gazette, And Country Journal*, February 24, 1777, and *The Continental Journal, And Weekly Advertiser*, June 3, 1779.

FIVE HUNDRED DOLLARS REWARD,

BROKE OUT OF Barnstable Goal on Saturday Night last, SAMUEL PROCTER and JOHN CHASE, the said Procter is a sprightly Man of about 25 Years of Age; Chase is a dark Complexion, stout Man, of about 45 Years of Age; it is supposed they are either bound to Boston or Rhode island, and have parted since they left Goal: Whoever will take up and bring them to Goal, shall be intitled to the above Reward, or to 250 Dollars for either of them.

ENOCH HALLET, Sheriff.   YARMOUTH, June 7th, 1779.

The Boston-Gazette, And Country Journal, June 14, 1779; June 21, 1779; June 28, 1779. See *The Continental Journal, And Weekly Advertiser*, November 19, 1778, for Procter.

FIFTY DOLLARS REWARD.

Ran-away from the Subscriber,

in the night of the 10th June, a Negro Man named POMP, about 20 years of age, talks good English, a scar under his eye: Had on a snuff coloured short Coat, a pea green Jacket, white Breeches, or Trousers, with a Blanket and other Cloaths. Whoever shall take up said Negro, and convey him to me in *Boston*, shall receive the above Reward.—All Masters of Vessels and others, are forbid to harbor or carry off said Negro, without giving me Notice, if they would avoid the Penalty of the Law.

SAMUEL SELLON.   *Boston, June* 14, 1779.

The Independent Ledger, and the American Advertiser, June 14, 1779; June 21, 1779; June 28, 1779.

WHEREAS Sarah the wife of me the subscriber, hath for some time past, absented herself from my bed and board: These are therefore to forbid any person or persons trusting her on my account, for I will not pay any debts of her contracting, after the date hereof.
                JOHN ABBE.   Enfield, May 26, 1779.
The Connecticut Courant, And The Weekly Intelligencer, June 15, 1779; June 22, 1779.

WHEREAS MERRIUM wife of the Subscriber, has been induced and instigated by advice of wicked evil minded persons, to elope from my bed and board, and it is apprehended that she may endeavour to run me in debt. This is to forbid any person or persons trusting her on my account, as I will pay no debt of her contracting after this date. Also all persons are hereby forewarned against harbouring the said Merrium, on Penalty of the law.
                LEMUEL LADD.   Coventry, June 9, 1779.
The Connecticut Courant, And The Weekly Intelligencer, June 15, 1779; June 22, 1779.

THIRTY DOLLARS REWARD.
LOST on the road between Reading and Fairfield, on the 10th instant, a pair of SADDLE BAGS, containing one black Taffety Gown, one black silk Apron, and one cambrick one, one pair black silk Gloves, one black gauze Handkerchief, and two cambrick do, two pair Stockings, one Shift, one lawn and three other caps. Said Saddle Bags were seen to be taken up by a footman, who immediately fled into the woods, and carried them of. Said man is about six feet high, dark complexion, black hair; had on a green coat and trowsers; pretended to be a deserter from the British army.—Whoever will take up and secure the above described man, and good, and inform the subscriber, shall be entitled to the above reward or 10 dollars for the goods only.   SARAH FORD.   Newtown, June 11, 1779.
The Connecticut Courant, And The Weekly Intelligencer, June 22, 1779; June 29, 1779. See *The Connecticut Journal,* June 23, 1779.

LOST on the 10th Instant in North Fairfield, a Pair of Saddle-Bags, containing one black Taffety Gown, one black silk Apron, do. Cambrick, two Cambrick Handkerchiefs, do one black Gauze, one Shift, one lawn lace Cap, do. three others, two Pair Stockings, one pillow-Case, one Towel, three linen checkt Handkerchiefs: seen to be carried off by a tall slim Fellow, with a green Jacket, brown Overhalls, speaks bad English. If any

Person will secure the Fellow, and Things or above Articles without him, shall have Twenty Dollars Reward, & reasonable Charges paid by the Subscriber living in New-Town.
    SARAH FORD.   June 11, 1779.
The Connecticut Journal, June 23, 1779; July 9, 1779. See *The Connecticut Courant, And The Weekly Intelligencer*, June 22, 1779.

       Whereas *Peggy,* the Wife of
the Subscriber, has eloped from my Bed and Board; and to prevent her from running me in Debt, I hereby caution all Persons from trusting her, as I will not pay one Farthing she may contract after this date.
    JOHN TAYLOR.
The Independent Chronicle and the Universal Advertiser, June 24, 1779; July 1, 1779.

RANAWAY on Sabbath Evening last, from the Parish of Bethany, in the Town of New-Haven, two young Men, about the Age of 18 Years; the one named *Nathan Beers,* an Apprentice to Stephen Sanford. Said Nathan is a tall thick-set Fellow, has short dark Hair commonly clubbed behind, took with him two check'd linen Shirts, one linen Coatee, one striped Vest, two Pair striped Linen Trowsers. The other named *Uri Sperry,* Son of Isaac Sperry, a tall well built Person, with strait brown Hair; had on when he went away, a striped linen Coatee, and Vest and Overhalls of the same Cloth. Whoever will send Word to either of said Subscribers, or return them to either of said Subscribers, shall receive Fifty Dollars Reward, and all Charges.   STEPHEN SANFORD, ISAAC SPERRY.
               New-Haven, June 28, 1779.
The Connecticut Journal, June 30, 1779; July 7, 1779.

WHEREAS Mary the Wife of the Subscriber has eloped from my Bed and Board: I do hereby warn all people from trusting her on my account, as I declare I never will pay one single farthing of any debt that she shall contract from the date hereof.
    JOHN DINGLEY.   Windham, June 15, 1779.
The Connecticut Gazette; And The Universal Intelligencer, July 1, 1779; July 8, 1779.

RAN away from the subscriber, about the first Inst. an apprentice girl named LYDIA PRESTON, about 14 years old, born in this town.—Whoever will return her to the subscriber in New-London, North-Parish, shall have 6d. reward.
    SAMUEL FOX, jun. N. London, North-Parish, June 28, 1779.

The Connecticut Gazette; And The Universal Intelligencer, July 1, 1779; July 8, 1779; July 14, 1779.

WHEREAS David Baldwin, Leicester, hath advertised my Son Benjamin Barton as his apprentice, absenting himself from his service on the 4th day of May last: I say the assertion is false, and I forbid any person or persons taking up said Benjamin on said advertisement, as they would avoid the penalty of the law. TIMOTHY BARTON. Granby, June 27, 1779.
The Massachusetts Spy Or, Thomas's Boston Journal, July 1, 1779; July 15, 1779. See *The Massachusetts Spy Or, Thomas's Boston Journal*, June 10, 1779.

BOSTON, June 24.
At the Superior Court held last week at Ipswich, the famous Isaac Taft (who was lately pillored in this town, for a public cheat) pleaded guilty for two indictments; one for defrauding the government—sentenced to stand in the pillory one hour at Ipswich, with a label attached to his breast, with the words *a public cheat*, wrote or painted; to be whipped 30 stripes upon his naked back at the whipping post, pay cost of prosecution, and stand committed until sentence is performed:—The other for defrauding the town of Danvers; sentenced to be whipped 20 stripes upon his naked back, at the public whipping post, in Salem, and pay costs of Court, and stand committed until the sentence be performed.
The Massachusetts Spy Or, Thomas's Boston Journal, July 1, 1779. See *The Independent Chronicle and the Universal Advertiser*, March 11, 1779, *The Independent Chronicle and the Universal Advertiser*, July 29, 1779, and *The Boston Gazette, And The Country Journal*, November 1, 1779.

R*UN away, from the Subscriber, the night following the* 1*st of July instant, a negro man named Quam, about* 30 *years old,* 5 *feet* 8 *inches high, very black, strait built, speaks quick; had on and carried with him* 1 *great Coat, light blue cape, lin'd with red baize, strait bodied coat and vest pale blue, the back of said vest deep blue,* 1 *pair leather breeches,* 1 *pair long trowsers,* 3 *flannel and* 1 *stript linen shirt,* 2 *pair stockings,* 2 *new castor hats and* 1 *old do. hat,* 1 *scythe and tackling,* 1 *sickle,* 1 *knapsack markt W. W. and about forty or fifty pounds in money. Whoever will take up and secure said negro, or return him to me, shall receive* 50 *dollars reward and all necessary charges*
    paid by   WILLIAM WILLIAMS. Colchester, July 3, 1779.
The Connecticut Courant, And The Weekly Intelligencer, July 6, 1779; July 20, 1779; *The Connecticut Gazette; And The Universal*

Intelligencer, July 8, 1779; July 13, 1778; July 28, 1779. Minor differences between the papers.

Hartford, June 19, 1779.
ESCAPED from the goal last Tuesday afternoon; 3 prisoners of war, viz. Joseph Bradly, a tall lusty man, perhaps near 40 years old, was a serjeant of grenadiers, very poorly cloathed, his outside covering was a very poor almost worn out blue great coat. Another named Thomas Slate, a sailor, also a tall lusty man, about the same age. The other is a Thomas Ward, who was taken up at Waterbury and returned. It is hoped they may be taken up and returned, and when I am informed of it necessary charges shall be paid,
by   E. WILLIAMS, Dep. Com. Pris.
The Connecticut Courant, And The Weekly Intelligencer, July 6, 1779.

BROKE out of the County Goal in New-London, the Night after the 5th Inst. one THOMAS DOUGLASS, 25 Years old, 5 Feet 6 inches high, has short brown Hair, ruddy Complexion; strait and well made; had on a brown Holland Coattee and linen Breeches; committed for Theft and Desertion from the ship WARREN. Whover will return him to the Subscriber, shall have TEN DOLLARS Reward.
NATHAN BALEY, ju. *Goaler.*
NEW-LONDON, JULY 6, 1779.
The Connecticut Gazette; And The Universal Intelligencer, July 8, 1779; July 14, 1779; July 28, 1779.

RUN away from the subscriber, in Rehoboth, a mulatto fellow named CATO, about five feet nine or ten inches high, pretty long favoured. Whoever will return said mulatto to his master, shall have a handsome reward and all necessary charges,
paid by   DANIEL HUNT.
N. B. All masters of vessels and others are forbid harbouring or concealing him at their peril. Providence,   July 14, 1779.
The American Journal And General Advertiser, July 15, 1779; July 22, 1779; July 29, 1779. See *The Providence Gazette; And Country Journal*, July 24, 1779.

Six Pence Reward,
RANAWAY from his Master on the night of the 9th of July Instant a boy about 15 years old, named Benjamin Brown, had on a snuff colour'd coat, red broad cloth Jacket &c. Whoever takes up said boy and conveys him to his master shall have the above reward. And all persons are cautioned against harbouring, concealing or trading with him.
BENJAMIN BROWN.   South Hampton, July 10.

The New-Hampshire Gazette, Or, State Journal, and General Advertiser, July 20, 1779; July 27, 1779; August 3, 1779.

WHEREAS ANNA, Wife of me the Subscriber, hath eloped from my Bed and Board, and refuseth to return to her Duty, and to live with me. These are therefore to forbid all Persons entertaining or trusting her on my Account for I will pay no Debts of her Contracting, after this Date.
                NATHAN BURROWS, 2d.   GROTON, July 21, 1779.
The Connecticut Gazette; And The Universal Intelligencer, July 21, 1779; August 4, 1779.

TWO HUNDRED DOLLARS REWARD.

    BROKE *out of the Gaol in this town,*
On the night of the 16*th instant,* WILLIAM MOSMAN, *of Lancaster, in the County of Worcester, five feet* 10 *inches high, light hair, sandy complection, about* 35 *years of age, had on when he broke Gaol, a white shirt, red coat and waistcoat.* TIMOTHY POWERS, *of Princetown, aged* 37 *years, has short dark hair, smooth face, of middling size, wore a blue jacket without sleeves, and a woolen shirt, long white trowsers, and a foxskin cap. Whoever will take up said* Mosman *and* Powers, *and send them to me, shall receive the above reward, or one hundred dollars, for either of them, with necessary charges.*
    INCREASE BLAKE, Goal-Keeper.   *Worcester, July* 17, 1759.
Thomas's Massachusetts Spy Or, American Oracle Of Liberty, July 22, 1779; July 29, 1779; August 5, 1779; August 12, 1779. See *Thomas's Massachusetts Spy Or, American Oracle Of Liberty*, October 28, 1778, for Mosman.

WHEREAS Phoebe the Wife of the Subscriber, hath misbehaved herself; I therefore forbid any Persons trusting her on my Account, as I will not pay any Debt of her contracting from the Date hereof.
                JOHN COLE.   Warwick, July 24, 1779.
The Providence Gazette And Country Journal, July 24, 1779; July 31, 1779.

RAN away from the Subscriber, a Negroe Man, named CATO, about 50 Years of Age, of a middling Stature, speaks broken English, has his Country's Marks in his Face; had on when he went away an outside Cloth coloured woollen Jacket, a Linen striped under Jacket, Linen Shirt and Stockings, and a Pair of good Shoes. Whoever shall take up said Negroe, and return him to his Master, in Rehoboth, shall have Twenty Dollars Reward, and all reasonable Charges,
           paid by me,   DANIEL HUNT.

N. B. All Masters of Vessels and others are cautioned against harbouring or concealing said Fellow, as they would avoid the Penalty of the Law. Rehoboth, July 25, 1779.
The Providence Gazette; And Country Journal, July 24, 1779; July 31, 1779; August 7, 1779. See *The American Journal and General Advertiser*, July 15, 1779.

FORTY DOLLARS REWARD.

RUN away from the subscriber, a negro man named TITE, who was lately taken from the enemy; he is about 5 feet 6 inches high, looks very surly; has very thick lips, can play on a fiddle, and stole one that he took with him. Whoever will take up said negro and secure his so that the right owner may have him again, shall have the above reward and all necessary charges paid,
by JAMES ELLIOT, of Philadelphia,
or NATHANIEL PATTEN, of Hartford.
N. B. Said Negro can work at Farming very well, and it is likely will try for employ. Hartford, July 24. 1779.
The Connecticut Courant, And The Weekly Intelligencer, July 27, 1779; August 3, 1779; August 10, 1779.

Broke out of the Goal at Salem, on the Night of the 25th Instant, the noted *Isaac Taft*, in the Continental Service, who has been convicted three Times for hireing Men into said Service, and has received his Punishment the last at Salem, and has the Marks of Part of his Punishment streak'd on his Back: He is a thick well made Fellow, light Complection, and short light Hair, 26 Years of Age, 5 Feet 10 Inches high—Also *George Stacnon*, a soldier Col. Jackson's Regiment, dark Complection, black Hair, about 5 Feet 10 Inches high; and two Negro Fellow, Prisoners of War, taken by the Ship Hunter.—Whoever shall take up any, or all of the above named Prisoners, and confine them in any Goal within the United States of America, shall receive ONE HUNDRED DOLLARS Reward for each of them,
by me, MICHAEL FARLEY, Sheriff.

Ipswich, July 26, 1779.
The Independent Chronicle and the Universal Advertiser, July 29, 1779, August 5, 1779; September 2, 1779. See *The Independent Chronicle and the Universal Advertiser*, March 11, 1779, *The Massachusetts Spy Or, Thomas's Boston Journal*, July 1, 1779, and *The Boston Gazette, And The Country Journal*, November 1, 1779, for Taft.

RAN a-way from *Reading*, or absconded last Sunday night three Highland prisoners of war, viz. *John Division*, 22 years of age, five feet ten inches

Coat, a home-made striped Waistcoat, and a new Pair of Deerskin Breeches. He was inticed away by on *Thomas Payden*, a Shoemaker by Trade, who is very apt to change his Name. Said *Payden* stole and carried off with him, a Quantity of Hard-Money, and about 30 Weight of Tobacco: He had on, when he went away, a rifle Frock and Trowsers trimed with blue Fringe. Whoever will secure said Lad, or the Thief, so that the Lad may be returned to his Master again, or the Thief brought to Justice, shall have FIFTY DOLLARS Reward, and all necessary Charges
paid, by me, DANIEL BARBER, of Worthington.
The Independent Chronicle and the Universal Advertiser, July 29, 1779; August 5, 1779.

RUN away from the subscriber on the night after the 22d day of July, a young negro man, called his name ROGERS, about 5 feet 10 inches high, light colour'd hair, slow of speech; had a blue coat and vest, check shirt, stript trowsers, a large pair of diamond silver shoe buckles, and an old fashioned large watch, and a large pack, with a pillow coat knapsack, with a rope tump line, and a great coat. Stole from the subscriber one white shirt, one check do. one pair blue broadcloth breeches, one pair of thread stockings, one pair striped long trowsers. Whoever will take up said fellow and commit him to any goal so that the subscriber may have him, shall have 50 dollars reward and all necessary charges paid,
by SETH GARY. Enfield, July 23. 1779.
The Connecticut Courant, and Hartford Weekly Intelligencer, August 3, 1779; August 10, 1779; August 17, 1779; August 24, 1779.

ESCAPED from Lennex, in the county of Berkshire, on the 22d inst. *Joseph Murrin*, a man who has long had a suspected character, and of late evidenced himself an enimical person to the cause of these State by harbouring and secreting a person who has had a trial, and judged an inimical and dangerous person; said Murrin disposed of his Estate in a private manner before he escaped, by which it appears probable he is going to the enemy. He is supposed to have gone to the State of Connecticut. He is a man of middling stature, about 30 years of age, dark complexion, short curled hair. Whoever will take up said runaway, and convey him to the subscriber in Lennex, will render escencial services to his country, and shall be intitled to one hundred dollars reward, and all necessary charges
paid by CALEB HYDE, Chairman of the
Committee of Lennex. Lennex, July 23, 1779.
The Connecticut Journal, And The New-Haven Post Boy, August 4, 1779.

WHEREAS Hannah, the wife of me the subscriber, hath eloped from my bed and board: These are to forbid all persons from entertaining or trusting her on my account, for I will pay no debts for her after this date.
DANIEL ROGERS.   Colchester, August 10, 1779.
The Norwich Packet and the Weekly Advertiser, August 10, 1779; August 17, 1779; August 24, 1779. See *The Norwich Packet and the Weekly Advertiser*, August 17, 1779.

RUNAWAY from the subscriber on the 9th Inst. a Negro Boy named Frank, about 15 years of age, has sharp teeth, suppos'd to have been filed, with a remarkable scar of a cut on his under lip, had on a dirty woollen shirt, blue breeches, and tow cloth waistcoat; 'tis suppos'd he will try to get to Long Island. Whoever will apprehend and secure said Negro, will be well rewarded and have charges
paid, by   CHRISTOPHER HUGHES.
The Connecticut Journal, And The New-Haven Post Boy, August 11, 1779; August 18, 1779.

ONE HUNDRED DOLLARS REWARD.
AGREEABLE to regimental orders from Col. Jonathan Dimon, dated Stratford, July the 28th, 1779, to me the subscriber, to arrest the body of *Henry Bradford*, a person inimical to the United States, and bring him before the said Colonel for trial: Accordingly I took the body of the said Bradford, and upon his request gave him parole for two hours, but the said Bradford most shamefully forfeited his honour, and has fled from trial. Whoever shall take up said Henry Bradford, and bring him to me the subscriber, or secure him so that he may be brought to trial, shall be intitled to the above reward.
BENJAMIN NICHOLS, Capt.   Stratford, August 3, 1779.
The Connecticut Journal, And The New-Haven Post Boy, August 11, 1779; August 18, 1779; August 25, 1779.

RUN away from the subscriber on the 1st instant, an apprentice boy named Albrow Cleaveland, between 17 and 18 years of age, is well set, of a light complexion, wears his hair; had on when he went away, a dark coloured broad-cloth coat, a striped flannel jacket, a white tow shirt, striped trowsers, and a felt hat; carried with him a white tow shirt and trowsers. Whoever will return said fellow to the subscriber, shall have ten dollars reward and reasonable charges paid,
by NATHANIEL LOVELL. . Scituate, Aug, 8.
N. B. All masters of vessels and others are forbid harbouring or concealing him at their peril.

The American Journal and General Advertiser, August 12, 1779; August 19, 1779; August 26, 1779.

Mr. TRUMBULL,
SIR,
As an unjust aspersion has been thrown upon me by my husband, in an advertisement of your last paper, relative to my having eloped from him; I take this opportunity to desire you to insert the following facts in your next publication, that the judicious and impartial Public may form a judgment whether my leaving my husband is justifiable or not.

EVER since last May I have been in a distressed situation by sickness, my disorder being a consumption; and a great part of my distress lying in my throat, it was not every kind of sustenance I could take; necessary foods and cordials I was obliged to my friends for, as my husband absolutely refused to purchase any thing which was proper for me: Brown bread, pork and milk, was all that was allowed me. I therefore asked him to let me go to my own house, and amongst my friends, in hopes of finding some relief from their care and tenderness, to which he never would give any answer; however, as he did not absolutely deny me, I requested my son-in-law to come for me, which he did, and then my husband told me he was unwilling I should go; I told him in case I recovered, I would return; to which he gave no answer.

As I have alledged nothing by the truth, I hope the candid Public will commiserate the situation of a poor, distressed woman, languishing in the last stage of a consumption, cruelly accused by a pitiless and unjust husband of having eloped from him.—If he denies these facts, they can readily be proved by

HANNAH ROGERS.   Norwich, (Great Plains,) August 17, 1779.
The Norwich Packet and the Weekly Advertiser, August 17, 1779. See *The Norwich Packet and the Weekly Advertiser*, August 10, 1779.

RAN away from the Subscriber, on Wednesday last, a Negro Man Servant, about 18 Years old, named DERRY, about 5 Feet 7 Inches high, well built, has large Scars on both his Shins, speaks broken English. Had on a check Shirt, striped Trowsers and an old Hat, being all the Cloaths he had on or carried off. Whoever will return said Negro to the Subscriber in Windham, shall be well rewarded for their Trouble, and all necessary Charges paid by
JOHN HOWARD.   WINDHAM, Aug. 10, 1779.
The Connecticut Gazette; And The Universal Intelligencer, August 18, 1779; August 25, 1779.

WHEREAS Hannah the wife of me the subscriber, hath behaved herself in an indecent manner, has left my bed and board, and refuses to live with me.

These are therefore to forbid any person keeping or trusting her on my account, for I will not pay any debts of her contracting after this date.
    SILAS CHAMPLAIN,   Stonington, Aug. 2d, 1779.
The Connecticut Gazette; And The Universal Intelligencer, August 18, 1779; August 25, 1779.

       ONE HUNDRED DOLLARS Reward.
Ran-away from the subscriber on Sunday the 15th instant, a NEGRO BOY, named *Dublin*, aged about 15 years, of low stature, thick and well sett, stammers a little in his speech, of the Cormantine nation.—Whoever takes up, and him safely conducted to his master at *Boston*, shall have the above reward, and all necessary expences paid by
    HECTOR McNEIL.   BOSTON, August 18th, 1779.
 All masters of vessels and others, are hereby cautioned against carrying off or concealing said servant.
 The Continental Journal, And Weekly Advertiser, August 18, 1779; August 26, 1779; September 2, 1779.

WHereas LYDIA, the wife of me the subscriber, hath eloped from my bed and board; this is to forbid any person trusting her on my account, as I am determined not to pay any debts of her contracting after the date hereof.
    NATHANIEL DAGGETT. Westmoreland, July 15, 1779.
 The American Journal and General Advertiser, August 19, 1779; August 26, 1779; September 9, 1779.

WHEREAS Hannah Huffman, wife of me the subscriber hath lately eloped from me, and left contrary to me will. I hereby forbid all persons trusting her on my account, as I will not pay any debt contracted by her after this date. SIMON HUFFMAN.   Middletown, August 17, 1779.
 The Connecticut Courant, and Hartford Weekly Intelligencer, August 24, 1779; August 31, 1779.

      Whereas Hannah Davis,
Wife of me Jabez Davis of Barrington, absents herself from me at Times, and I have Reason to think she contracts Debts without my Knowledge, therefore I forbid any Person or Persons crediting her on my Account, as I will not pay any Debts of her contracting from the Date hereof.
    Jabez Davis.   Barrington, August 17, 1779.
 The New-Hampshire Gazette, Or, State Journal, and General Advertiser, August 24, 1779; August 31, 1779.

STOLEN from the Subscriber at New-London, the 18th inst. a BAY HORSE, 13 and half Hands high, a white Strip in the Face, has a small

Burst on the near Side and another on the off Side under his Flank, hind Feet white, trots and paces, with a Saddle without a Housen, and Bridle something soiled. The Thief calls himself by the Name of John Thomson, is about 5 Feet 9 Inches high, light Complection, long Hair, something pitted with the small-pox, has on a light coloured Coat, white Jacket and Breeches, white Stockings, A Pair old Shoes, with round Brass or Steel Buckles, says he belongs at Providence. Whoever will secure said Horse and Thief, so that the Thief may be brought to Justice, and notify me thereof, shall have THREE HUNDRED DOLLARS Reward, or for the Horse only, a handsome Reward,
     paid by SAMUEL CLEVELAND.
The Connecticut Gazette; And The Universal Intelligencer, August 25, 1779; September 1, 1779.

RAN away from the Subscriber, on the 20th Day of June last, a Mulatto Man Servant, called Primus, about 25 Years of Age, a likely well made Fellow, speaks good English; had on, and took with him, when he went away, a Pair of Leather Breeches, almost new, two Pair of Linen Trowsers, two Linen and two Woollen Shirts, three Flannel Waistcoats, two Pair of Hose, one Pair of good Shoes, a new Beaveret Hat, one Irish Linen Shirt, a Suit of green Cloaths, not much worn, and an old Great-Coat; also took with him a considerable Sum of Money. Also ran away the last Evening, a Mustee Apprentice Boy, called Primus Watt, alias Toby, aged about 14 Years; had on when he went away a Linen Shirt, Flannel Waistcoat, a thick homespun Jacket over it, a Pair of Shoes, and a small old Hat, lopped, and pieced round the Brim. If either of them will return to their Master, before taken up, they shall be forgiven their Crimes; but whoever shall take up said Servant, and convey him to his Master at Warwick-Neck, in the County of Kent, shall have Twenty Dollars Reward; and whoever shall take up said Apprentice, and return him to his said Master, shall have Ten Dollars Reward, and all
    reasonable Charges, paid by BENJAMIN GREENE.
N. B. All Masters of Vessels, and others, are cautioned against harbouring or concealing said Servant or Apprentice, as they would avoid the Penalty of the Law, in such Cases provided. Warwick-neck, September 2, 1779.
The Providence Gazette; And Country Journal, September 4, 1779; September 11, 1779; September 18, 1779.

FIFTY DOLLARS REWARD.

RUN away from the subscriber, living in Hartford, in June last, a small LAD named William Johnstone, alias William Sutherland, about 4 feet [*sic*] high, 14 years old, sandy hair, grey eyes.—Whoever will return said

run away to the subscriber or give information where he may be found, shall have the above reward.
                 FREDERICK BULL.   Hartford, Sept. 6. 1779.
The Connecticut Courant, And The Weekly Intelligencer, September 7, 1779; September 14, 1779.

WHEREAS my wife DEBORAH SEDGWICK abuses me with insolent behaviour, [   ] carriage, and hard provoking words, too bad to publish; has sold and imbezzell'd my goods and estate, and persists in so doing. It is therefore necessary from me to forbid all persons trading with or trusting of her, or harbouring her, for I will not pay any debts shall contract after this date.   SAMUEL SEDGWICK.   Canaan, Aug. 12, 1779.
The Connecticut Courant, And The Weekly Intelligencer, September 7, 1779.

WHEREAS my servant boy FREDERICK GIBBS, about sixteen years of age, light complexion, about five feet and seven inches high, absented from my service on the twenty-seventh of August last, and has not returned. Whoever will take up said servant and return him to me shall receive ten dollars reward.
       N. B. All persons are hereby cautioned against concealing or harbouring said servant as they would avoid the penalty of the law.
                BOAZ MOORE.   Princeton, Sept. 1st, 1779.
The Massachusetts Spy Or, Thomas's Boston Journal, September 9, 1779; September 23, 1779; September 30, 1779.

THIS is to forbid all persons trusting or harboring PATIENCE the wife of me the subscriber, for I will pay no debt of her contracting after this date.
                JOSEPH BUEL.   Wethersfield, Sept. 13, 1779.
The Connecticut Courant, and Hartford Weekly Intelligencer, September 14, 1779; September 28, 1779.

ON Tuesday night, the 6th instant, was stolen out of the enclosure of the subscriber, at Harrington, in the county of Litchfield, in Connecticut, a brown MARE, about nine years old, fourteen hands high, a natural pacer, low carriage, and has no other white than a streak or two round one of her hind legs. The thief has been heard of on the road from Hartford to Providence, and from thence over Pawtucket bridge with said Mare. He is a young man, had on a striped jacket and trowsers, and went by the name of WOOD. Whoever will take up and secure said thief and Mare, so that he may be brought to justice, and the Mare recovered, shall have two hundred dollars, and all reasonable charges paid,
                by THOMAS MOODY.   Harrington, September 8, 1779.

The American Journal and General Advertiser, September 16, 1779; September 23, 1779; September 30, 1779.

Whereas *Lydia*, my Wife, has eloped from my Bed: This is, therefore, to forbid any Person trusting her on my Account, as I will not pay any Debt she may contract after the Date hereof.　　DANIEL PARKS.　　*Lincoln, September* 11, 1779.
The Independent Chronicle and the Universal Advertiser, September 16, 1779.

Whereas MARY, the Wife of me the Subscriber, has eloped from my House and her Family, this is to caution any Person trusting said MARY on my Account, for I do hereby declare that I will not pay any Debt, or Debts whatever, by her contracted, after this Date.
　　　　MOSES BAKER.　　　　　　　Braintree, Sept. 2, 1779.
The Independent Chronicle and the Universal Advertiser, September 16, 1779.

RUN away the evening after the 9th instant, two BOYS, about 14 and 15 years of age, check shirts, old frocks, brown trowsers, one of them had light coloured hair, the other dark brown, one of them had on a streaked flannel jackets, [sic] both had old felt hats bound round the brim with white cloth, and had a few leather pocket books for sale. Whoever will take them up and bring them to me, or secure them and send me word, shall have fifty dollars reward for each and necessary charges
　　　　paid, by　ZEBULON WOODRUFF.
N. B. Said boys are brothers, one named Jasper the other Tobias Woodruff.
　　　　　　　　　　　　　　　　　　Farmington, Sept. 20. 1779.
The Connecticut Courant, and Hartford Weekly Intelligencer, September 21, 1779; September 28, 1779; October 5, 1779.

WHEREAS my wife Catharine Case, uses me with insolent behaviour, and undutiful carriage, has sold and embezzled my goods and estate, and persists is so doing. It is therefore necessary for me to forbid all persons trading with, trusting or harboring her, for I will not pay any debt she may contract after this date.
　　　　ELIJAH CASE, jun.　　　Barkhempsted, Sept. 13, 1779.
The Connecticut Courant, and Hartford Weekly Intelligencer, September 21, 1779; September 28, 1779.

For the BENEFIT of the PUBLIC.
NOTICE is hereby given, that a certain ABRAHAM S. REMSAN, of Westerly, State of Rhode-Island, is a public Cheat, and as such I think it my Duty to make him known to the Public, to prevent their being imposed on by him, as I myself and a Number of others have been. I shall mention several Instances of his Fraud;—on the 4th of September Inst. said Remsan, bought a Horse of me in Norwich, for which he gave me an Order for 110 Gallons of Rum of Major Hart of Say-Brook, and John Foster, Esq; of East Haddam, pretending that he had Effects in their Hands, which was entirely false. I afterwards pursued him to South Kingston and got my Horse from him. Not long since he went from Mr. John Denison's, Tavern Keeper in Stonington, after their three Days entertained at his House, without paying his Expences;—at a public House in Rhode-Island he changed his Name;—about ten Days ago he kept at Capt. Douglass's Tavern in New-London, and left the House without paying his Bill;—he also lately left the Houses of Mr. Ephraim Miner, Tavern Keeper in New-London, and Mr. Azariah Lathrop in Norwich, under the like Circumstances, but it is presumed these are but a few Instances of his Fraud. As he may change his Name, which he has heretofore done, it may be proper to describe him, he is about 5 Feet 10 Inches high, well set, about 40 Years of Age, cross Eyed and near sighted, brown Complexion, well dressed, writes a good Hand, and had the Appearance of a Gentleman, talks smooth, and a little on the Dutch.
    SAMUEL DELIVAN. of Crompond, State of New-York.
The Connecticut Gazette; And The Universal Intelligencer, September 22, 1779.

    WHEREAS Catherine the Wife of
Moses Thomas, hath for some years past been quarreling with her husband, desturbing the peace of his family, and destroying his interest, wishing all mannur of bad wishes to him and his interest, and vilifying his character in every manner possible, and striking him with every instrument that comes to hand, and frequently deserting his bed and board, carrying away his wearing clothes and other household goods, and selling and disposing of his interest: I therefore, with the advice of my friends and neighbours, take this method to forbid all persons harbouring her, or any of my goods, or trading with her to my damage, as they may expect trouble: I furthermore declare I will pay no debts of her contracting after the date hereof.
    MOSES THOMAS. Salem, September the 13th, A. D. 1779.
The Connecticut Journal, September 22, 1779; September 29, 1779.
See *The Connecticut Journal,* September 29, 1779.

WHEREAS Sarah my wife has without just cause absented herself from me, and carried with her some of my household furniture, apparel, &c. and fearing she may run me in debt; therefore all persons are hereby notified and cautioned not to pay any debt that she may contract after this day, also all persons are cautioned against harbouring my said Wife or concealing things of mine she has carried away, as she may expect to be prosecuted.
     THOMAS LANCEY.
     Bedford, (State of New-Hampshire) August 28th, 1779.
The Massachusetts Spy Or, Thomas's Boston Journal, September 23, 1779; September 30, 1779; October 14, 1779.

WHEREAS SEBBEL LADD, my wife, hath lately eloped from me contrary to my will, and by the advice of other people has carried away my household goods. And I having a desire she would return to her duty again and live with me as she ought, do therefore forbid all persons harboring, trading with, or trusting her on my account, for I will not pay any debt of her contracting after this date.
    EZEKIEL LADD, jun.   East-Windsor, Sept. 15, 1779.
The Connecticut Courant, and Hartford Weekly Intelligencer, September 28, 1779; October 5, 1779.

WHEREAS Moses Thomas has advertised me his wife as disposing of his interest, and running him in debt, deserting him, &c. I hereby notify the public, that I when was so unfortunate as to marry said Thomas, I had a good interest sufficient to have supported me and my family well—That my moveable estate which belonged to me and my children he has squandered away, even a ring, which I have reckoned much of, he took from me and gave to his daughter on the contrary I have been so careful of his interest, as not to have spent to the valuation of one dollar without his consent; have have endeavoured to do my duty as dutiful wife and tender mother; but have been so evil [   ]ed and cruelly beaten by him that I was obliged to heave him for my own safety; for the truth of which [   ] I appeal to my neighbours. CATHARINE THOMAS.
The Connecticut Journal, September 29, 1779. See *The Connecticut Journal,* September 22, 1779.

    Whereas *Sarah,* the Wife of me the subscriber, has eloped from my bed and board:—I do hereby forbid all persons from trusting her on my account, as I do declare that I will not pay on farthing of her contracting from the date hereof.
    SAMUEL HARTLEY,   Sept. 30.

The Continental Journal, And Weekly Advertiser, September 30, 1779; October 14, 1779; November 12, 1779.

ONE HUNDRED DOLLARS REWARD.
STOLEN from the Subscriber the following Articles, viz. One Hairbine Coat & Waistcoat, one Chints ditto, 3 pair Cotton 1 pair Worsted and 1 pair of Yarn Hose, 1 Ruffled and 3 plain Shirts, 3 Stocks, 1 Stock Buckles, and one pair Thread Gloves.—The Thief who stole them goes by the name of *John Marvell,* he is about 5 feet 8 inches high, very much Pock-broken, and has lost one of his Fore Teeth.

Whoever will secure said Thief and give Notice thereof to Mr. James Boyd, of Boston, shall receive the above Reward, and all necessary Charges paid.   ROBERT BOYD.

The Boston Gazette, And The Country Journal, October 4, 1779; October 11, 1779; October 18, 1779.

RUN away from the subscriber a Negro Man about 40 years of age, about 5 feet 4 inches high, the grizle of his nose eat out; and the top sunk in. Whoever will take up said run away and confine him so that his master can have him again, shall have one hundred dollars reward, and all necessary charges paid, by
    ABRAHAM CASE.   West Simsbury, Sept 29. 1779.

The Connecticut Courant, and Hartford Weekly Intelligencer, October 5, 1779; October 12, 1779; October 19, 1779. See *The Connecticut Gazette; And The Universal Intelligencer*, July 4, 1777.

RANAWAY from the subscriber about the 12th of September last, a Negro Man named *Charles*, about 30 Years old, slender built, speaks broken English; it is supposed he is concealed in this Town by some evil minded Person—Whoever shall take up said Negro and return him to the Subscriber, and discover the Person who has conceal'd him, shall be handsomely rewarded, and have all necessary Charges paid
    HEZEKIAH JOHNSON.   Wallingford, October 5, 1779.

The Connecticut Journal, October 6, 1779; October 13, 1779; October 20, 1779.

TEN DOLLARS Reward:
RUN away on the night of the 21st instant, a servant BOY, 15 years old, about 5 feet high, slim built, brown complexion, short brown hair, named Abel Burton, took with him a red great coat cape lin'd with pink tammy, old butternut colour'd short coat with new sleeves, a durant coatee a blue and white striped vest, a flanning striped jacket red white and blue, a vest of the same and felt hat, one new ditto, cut in the fashion two pair of

butternut colour'd breeches, two pair home made striped trowsers, one pair blue and white, the other black and white, one pair blue stockings, pair of single soal shoes half worn, and trode on one side, brass home made figur'd shoe buckles, and an old home spun striped shirt. Whoever shall take up said boy, and return him to me, shall receive the above reward, and all necessary charges by
    MORDECAI MARKS.   Ripton, *Sept.* 22. 1779.
All masters of vessels are forbid taking him.
 The Connecticut Journal, October 6, 1779; October 13, 1779; October 20, 1779.

   BROKE Goal in this town on Saturday evening last, the following persons, viz. JOSEPH MULLENS, JOHN JOLLY, DANIEL KIRBY, ROBERT CRAIG, and JOSEPH MOTTE, Mariners, who were committed some time since for piracy, &c. Whoever shall apprehend and secure the afore-named pirates, so that justice may have its due course, shall be handsomely rewarded by
   JOSEPH OTIS, Dep. Goaler.   *Boston,* October 6.
 The Continental Journal, And Weekly Advertiser, October 7, 1779; October 14, 1779.

   Whereas *Mable,* Wife of me the subscriber, has absented herself from my bed and board:—These are therefore to caution all persons from trusting her on my account, as I will not pay one farthing of any debt she may contract after the date hereof.
   JOSEPH CHAPHEY.   *October* 3, 1779.
 The Continental Journal, And Weekly Advertiser, October 7, 1779; October 14, 1779; November 12, 1779.

      SIX PENCE REWARD.
RUN-AWAY from the subscriber, on the night of the 10th instant, a Molatto Girl, named *Abigail Gummer,* about 17 years old, large of her age, with a bushy head of hair. Whoever will take up said Girl, and return her to the subscriber, shall have the above reward.
   ELIPHALET CAREW.   Norwich, October 12, 1779.
 The Norwich Packet, October 12, 1779. See *The Norwich Packet,* February 22, 1780.

RAN away last night from head quarters, a likely dark Mulatto Fellow, 18 years old, 5 feet 6 inches high, smooth face, is very artful, and speaks good English; carried with him a crimson coat (military cut) a good hat and furr cap, with a variety of other clothes of value, his design is to go a privateering, and probably will put on a sailor's dress. Whoever take up

said fellow, and secures him so that his master may get him again, shall receive Two Hundred Dollars reward, paid by
JAMES BROWNE, S. G. M. H. W. D.

Providence, October 11. 1779.
The Connecticut Gazette; And The Universal Intelligencer, October 13, 1779; October 27, 1779. See *The American Journal and General Advertiser*, October 14, 1779, and *The Providence Gazette; And Country Journal*, October 16, 1779. Browne was a Surgeon General in the Hospital Department of the Continental Army.

Head Quarters, Providence, Oct. 13, 1779.
DEserted last Saturday night, one William Berry, a mulatto fellow, 20 years of age, five feet eight inches high. Whoever will return him to Dr. JAMES BROWN, at Head-Quarters, shall receive two hundred dollars reward, and all necessary charges.

The American Journal and General Advertiser, October 14, 1779; October 21, 1779; October 28, 1779; November 4, 1779. See *The Connecticut Gazette; And The Universal Intelligencer*, October 13, 1779, and *The Providence Gazette; And Country Journal*, October 16, 1779.

Head-Quarters, Providence, Oct. 11.
RAN away, last Night, a likely dark Mulatto Slave, named William Barry, 18 Years of Age, about 5 Feet 7 Inches high, has a smooth Face, is very artful and speaks good English: Had on, and carried with him, a crimson Coat, with yellow Metal Buttons, a good Hat, Furr Cap, and may other Cloaths of Value. His Design is to get on board a Privateer, and will probably put on a Soldier's Dress. Whoever takes up said Slave, and secures him so that his Master may have him again, shall receive Two Hundred Dollars Reward, paid by
JAMES BROWNE, Surgeon-Gen. Military Hospitals, N. D.

The Providence Gazette; And Country Journal, October 16, 1779; October 23, 1779; October 30, 1779; November 6, 1779; *The Independent Chronicle and the Universal Advertiser*, October 21, 1779; October 28, 1779. See *The Connecticut Gazette; And The Universal Intelligencer*, October 13, 1779; October 20, 1779, and *The American Journal and General Advertiser*, October 14, 1779.

WHEREAS ABIGAL the Wife of me the Subscriber, has elop'd from by Bed and Board: This is therefore to forbid all Persons harbouring or trusting her, as I am determined not to pay any Debts of her contracting from the Date hereof.
JACOB BASFORD. Chester, October 8, 1779.

The New-Hampshire Gazette, Or, State Journal, and General Advertiser, October 26, 1779; November 2, 1779. See *The New-Hampshire Gazette, Or, State Journal, and General Advertiser*, December 7, 1779.

WHEREAS Joseph Green, a bound Servant to me, has left my Service, and I hear has inlisted himself into the Continental Service.—This is to give Notice, that I will not pay any Debts he may contract, while absent from me. Enoch Barker. Greenland, October 25, 1779.

The New-Hampshire Gazette, Or, State Journal, and General Advertiser, October 26, 1779; November 2, 1779.

25 Silver Dollars Reward.

LAST Monday morning was stolen from two Frenchmen, at Mr. Chappel's house in New-London, *Twenty-two Half Johannes* in gold and silver, supposed to be taken by one John Allen, about 6 feet high, about 30 years of age, brown complexion, dark brown hair, black eyes, one ancle thicker than the other and pitted with the small pox, had on a red coat and waistcoat, with yellow anchor buttons, blue velvet breeches, blue ribb'd stockings, new shoes, round brass shoe buckles, silver carv'd knee buckles, and a blue pocket handkerchief with white stripes in it. Whoever will take up said thief with all the money or part, so that the owners may get it, shall receive the above reward, and all necessary charges, paid by
LOUIS TOUSSON. New-London, October 21, 1779.

The Connecticut Gazette; And The Universal Intelligencer, October 27, 1779; November 3, 1779.

Whereas one *Roger Kane*, First-Lieutenant of the ship Batcheldor, who was taken into custody for rioting, &c. made his escape from the subscriber,—he was a very stout man, of a light complexion, blue eyes, and a large Roman nose. Whoever will apprehend said *Kane*, so that he may be brought to justice, shall have *Two Hundred Dollars* reward, and all charges paid,
by DANIEL PARKS, Constable.

N. B. A reward of *One Hundred Dollars* will also be given for one *Scranton*, who was concerned with said *Kane*.

Boston, October 27, 1779.

The Independent Chronicle and the Universal Advertiser, October 28, 1779; November 5, 1779; November 11, 1779.

WHEREAS Perces the wife of me the subscriber, has absented herself from me and family, and refuses to return to her duty, although often requested by myself and others, and I am

apprehensive she may run me in debt. These are therefore to caution all persons against trusting her on my account for I will not discharge any debt she may contract from and after this date.
    DANIEL ADAMS.
                Westborough, (State of Massachusetts-Bay) October 19, 1779.
The Massachusetts Spy Or, Thomas's Boston Journal, October 28, 1779; November 5, 1779; November 11, 1779; November 25, 1779; December 2, 1779. See *The Massachusetts Spy Or, Thomas's Boston Journal,* November 25, 1779, and *The Massachusetts Spy Or, Thomas's Boston Journal,* April 27, 1780.

                Broke out of the County Goal in
Boston, last Thursday Night, the following Persons, viz.—JOHN HERBERT, about 5 Feet 7 Inches high; had on a blue Coat, a red Waistcoat, and striped Cap.—ISAAC TAFT, about 9 Feet [sic] 5 Inches; had on a blue Jacket, white Waistcoat, brown Trowsers; has short brown Hair.—DANIEL Mc'INTOSH, 5 Feet 5 Inches high; had on a Chocolate-coloured out-side Jacket; has light-coloured Hair: confin'd for Theft,.—PATRICK OBRIAN, about 5 Feet 7 Inches high; had on a dark-coloured brown Coat; had black Hair.
    Whoever will take up either of the above Persons, and confine them in any Goal in this State, shall have Forty Dollars Reward,
                paid by   JOSEPH OTIS, jun. Dep Goaler.
                                                                   Boston, Oct. 30, 1779.
The Boston Gazette, And The Country Journal, November 1, 1779; November 8, 1779; November 15, 1779. See *The Massachusetts Spy Or, Thomas's Boston Journal,* July 1, 1779, and *The Independent Chronicle and the Universal Advertiser,* July 29, 1779, for Taft.

RUN AWAY, from Caleb Turner, jun. and Samuel Turner, one PELETIAH TURNER, of Hartford, who lies under a bond to the county-court, for the sum of 200 pounds, he being draughted to go into the Continental service for nine months. This is therefore to forbid all Continental officers, or other officers upon their peril not to take away the said Peletiah into the service; as we have given bond for his appearance at court; and we cannot be released until he is delivered up to court; and stands as a prisoner to Caleb Turner, jun. & Samuel Turner. Whoever will take up said Peletiah Turner, and return him to the subscribers, shall have TWO DOLLARS Reward.
                CALEB TURNER, Jun. SAMUEL TURNER.
                                                                     Hartford, Oct. 1779.
The Connecticut Courant, and Hartford Weekly Intelligencer, November 2, 1779.

RUNAWAY from the subscriber, on the 13th instant, a servant lad named Roswell Smith, about twelve years of age, light coloured hair, eyes, and complection. Whoever will return said lad to me, free from charge, shall have six pence reward for their trouble, by their humble servant,
    EBENEZER MOSELEY. Windham, Sept. 26, 1779.
N. B. All persons are forbid harbouring said lad, under the penalty of the law in such case provided.

The Norwich Packet and the Weekly Advertiser, November 2, 1779; November 9, 1779; November 16, 1779; November 23, 1779; December 7, 1779.

RAN away from the Subscriber, a Negro Fellow named WOODER, about 22 Years of Age, this Country born, about 5 Feet 8 Inches high, thick Lips, something long favored, has a Scar on the Back of one of his Hands that was burnt when he was a Child, when he stoops down the Small of his Back sticks up as though it had been broke, wore away a full Cloath butternut coloured Jacket, striped blue and white under Jacket without Sleves, checkt black and white woolen Shirt, and checkt Trowsers much the same; carried of a checkt linen Shirt, two striped black and white woollen Jackets much worn. Whoever will take up said Fellow, and confine him in Gaol and notify me thereof, or convey him to me, shall have ONE HUNDRED and FIFTY DOLLARS Reward, and all necessary Charges, paid by
    JOSHUA POWERS. Lyme, October 16, 1779.

The Connecticut Gazette; And The Universal Intelligencer, November 3, 1779; November 10, 1779; November 17, 1779; *The Boston Gazette, And The Country Journal*, November 29, 1779; December 6, 1779; December 13, 1779; *The Connecticut Courant, and Hartford Weekly Intelligencer*, December 7, 1779; December 14, 1779; December 21, 1779. Minor differences between the papers.

Stop Thief!

STOLEN out of the Pasture of Joab Stafford, in New-Providence, in the State of Massachusetts-Bay, on the Night of the 22d Inst. a sorrel HORSE, 4 Years old, 14 Hands high, has a large white Streak on his Face, black Hoofs, the lower Part of his Legs white, a natural Pacer. The Thief is named Francis Clafford; had on a Snuff coloured Coat and Breeches, a white Hat, is round-shouldered, and pretty well built, has a flat Nose, light-coloured Eyes, and one crooked Ancle. Whoever will take up said Horse, and secure the Thief in the nearest Gaol, shall have One Hundred Dollars Reward, and all necessary Charges, or Fifty Dollars for the Horse only, paid by
    JOAB STAFFORD, in New-Providence,
    or EDWARD SPALDING, in Providence.
        New-Providence, Oct. 28, 1779.

The Providence Gazette And Country Journal, November 6, 1779; November 13, 1779; November 20, 1779.

Whereas my Wife ANNE, has eloped from my Bed and Board, and has refused to live with me; this is therefore to caution any Person from harbouring or trusting her, as I am determined not to pay one Farthing she may contract after this Day.
          SIMEON TURNER.   *Harvard, Nov.* [ ], 1779.

The Independent Chronicle and the Universal Advertiser, November 11, 1779.

RUN away from the subscriber on the night following the 14th of August last, an apprentice boy named SETH RANNEY, about 5 feet 6 inches high, 18 years of age, wore away a red brown jacket, checkt shirt, brown trowsers, new shoes, felt hat, had a variety of other cloaths with him. Whoever will take up said run-away and return him to the subscriber shall have fifty dollars reward and necessary charges paid, by
         AMOS SAGE.   Middletown, November 9 1779.

The Connecticut Courant, and Hartford Weekly Intelligencer, November 16, 1779; November 23, 1779.

BROKE out of the gaol in New-Haven on the night of the 13th instant, Nov. one Enoch Moultrop, about 35 years old, about 5 feet and an half high, black curled hair, had on a light colour'd great coat, a small hat newly cockt, committed for joining the enemy on Long Island; also one Samuel Butler, about 50 years old, black hair, had on a brown great coat, flopt hat, about five feet high, also one Samuel Pierpont, six feet high, light hair, light colour'd great coat, flopt hat, committed for attempting to join the enemy; also Benjamin Seeley, of Stratford, six feet high, brown hair, flopt hat, short brown jacket, leather breeches, committed for harbouring a deserter. A reward of twenty dollars is offered for the above persons, or five dollars for each of them, if returned to the gaol in New-Haven,
      paid by   STEPHEN MUNSON, Gaoler.

The Connecticut Journal, November 17, 1779; November 24, 1779.

WHEREAS *I the subscriber through my own weakness and imperfection, have inadvertently advertised and cried down, PERCES my Wife in the three preceding weekly papers; these are therefore to give public notice, that I am convinced of my imprudence in so doing, am very sorry for my conduct and for the injury done her, desire her forgiveness, and do now recall the former inconsiderate publication.*
         DANIEL ADAMS.

The Massachusetts Spy Or, Thomas's Boston Journal, November 25, 1779; December 2, 1779; December 16, 1779. See *The Massachusetts Spy Or, Thomas's Boston Journal*, October 28, 1779, and *The Massachusetts Spy Or, Thomas's Boston Journal*, April 27, 1780.

Ran-away from the subscriber last Sabbath-day morning, a Negro Fellow named CATO, about 25 years of age, about 6 feet high—had on when he went away a hair cap, a short blue coat, with blue horn buttons, and lin'd with red baize, a pair of long cloth coloured duffled trowsers—he carried off a black hair knapsack, part if the hair wore off. Whoever shall take up said Negro and bring him to the subscriber, shall have THIRTY DOLLARS reward, and all necessary charges paid by

EDWARD CARNES.   *Boston, November 25. 1779.*

The Continental Journal, And Weekly Advertiser, November 27, 1779; *The Independent Chronicle and the Universal Advertiser*, November 27, 1779. Minor differences between the papers.

LYME, in Connecticut, November 16, 1779.

STOLEN out of Ashfield, on Black Point, a black Mare, about Nine Years old, has some white Feet, a hollow Face, Hind Legs something Crooked, Paces chiefly, high life. The same Night stolen, a good Hunting Saddle, with a light cloth Housing, with a white Facing, a few scratches on the Seat. It is supposed to be a fellow who calls his Name William Winslow, who left his Guard at Black Point about this Time, he has a sandy Complexion, thin Faced, a little odd Cast with his Eyes, about 5 feet 9 inches high, a talkative Fellow, Maccaroni Hat, wears a rusty Claret-colour'd Surtout. Whoever will take up said Fellow, Mare, and Saddle, and will secure him in any Goal, and give Notice, or bring the Thief, Mare and Saddle, to me, shall have One Hundred Dollars Reward, and all necessary Charges paid, or Fifty Dollars for the Horse, and Fifty for the Thief.

By   JOSEPH POWERS.

The Boston-Gazette, And Country Journal, November 29, 1779; December 6, 1779; December 13, 1779. See *The Connecticut Gazette; And The Universal Intelligencer*, June 21, 1782.

WHEREAS LYDIA, the lawful Wife of the Subscriber, has eloped from her Bed and Board, and, as I understand, cohabits with one James Ray—These are to forwarn all Persons from trusting her on my Account, as I hereby declare I will not pay one Farthing of any Debt she may contract on my Account from the Date hereof.—And I also forwarn all Persons, particularly say Ray, from harbouring, concealing or entertaining her, on Penalty of the Law.

             TIMOTHY BRIMER.   Nov. 27, 1779.

The Boston-Gazette, And Country Journal, November 29, 1779; December 6, 1779; December 13, 1779.

             TWENTY DOLLARS REWARD.

Ran-away from the Subscriber on the 28th of November last, a Negro Man named PRINCE, about 27 years of age, 5 feet 2 inches high, had mean cloaths on when he Ran-away. All Masters of Vessels and others, are cautioned against harbouring or concealing said Negro, as they would avoid the Penalty of the Law.

    N. B. It is supposed said Negro is gone to Salem, in order to go a Privateering.

             JOSHUA BOYLSTON.   Brooklyne, Nov. 19.

The Continental Journal, And Weekly Advertiser, December 2, 1779; December 10, 1779.

WHereas Mary, the wife of the subscriber, has left his bed and board, and refuses to live with him: He hereby forbids all persons crediting her on his account, as he is determined not to pay any debts of her contracting from the date hereof.

             ROBERT LETSON.   Coventry, Dec. 2, 1779.

The Providence Gazette; And Country Journal, December 4, 1779; December 11, 1779; December 18, 1779,

             Whereas I the subscriber have posted my Wife ABIGAIL, by taking up with bad Advice of my Friends, wherein I blame her not, whereas she may act and do as before.

             Jacob Basford.   Chester, Nov. 25, 1779.

The New-Hampshire Gazette, Or, State Journal, and General Advertiser, December 7, 1779. See *The New-Hampshire Gazette, Or, State Journal, and General Advertiser*, October 26, 1779.

MY Wife Margaret, having behaved in a disrespectable and refractory Manner and in numerous Instances shamefully treated and abused me, all which I have long born with a degree of Patience beyond a Parallel. To prevent the said Margaret from involving me in Debt, I do forbid all Persons trusting her on my Account, or entertaining of her, for I will pay no Debts of her contracting after this Day.

             THOMAS BLACKLE.   New London, December 7, 1779.

The Connecticut Gazette; And The Universal Intelligencer, December 8, 1779.

FORTY DOLLARS REWARD.

RAN away from the subscriber on the night following the 10th inst. a negro man servant named CESAR, about 25 years old, something of low stature, about midling size, talks good English, can read considerable well, carried away with him, a serge coat and jacket of a claret colour, considerably faded, with flowered brass buttons, a belt velvet jacket of a lightish brown, black breeches, mix'd worsted stockings, two strip'd tow shirts almost new, one old fine shirt, an old bever hat with yellowing lining and tinsey loops, a pair of cow-skin shoes with double soals, and brass buckles. Whoever will return said negro to the subscriber in Plainfield or secure him in any goal in the United States, shall receive the above reward, and necessary charges paid by

JOHN PEIRCE. Plainfield, Dec. 13, 1779.

N. B. All Masters of Vessels and others are hereby forbid harbouring or carrying off said Negro on Penalty of the Law.

The Connecticut Gazette; And The Universal Intelligencer, December 15, 1779; December 22, 1779.

Broke out of the County Goal in Boston, on the evening of the 12th instant, one Capt. Owen Sullivan, about 5 feet 9 inches high, red full face, and black hair; had on a red baize outside Jacket, check'd Shirt, and blanket trowsers. Whoever will apprehend said Sullivan, and return him to said Goal, shall have *one hundred Dollars* reward, and all necessary charges paid. He being assisted in breaking out by two persons unknown; a reward of *Five hundred Dollars* is offered for apprehending and bringing them to justice, by

JOSEPH OTIS, Dep. Goaler. Boston, Dec. 15, 1779.

The Continental Journal, And Weekly Advertiser, December 23, 1779; December 30, 1779.

Whereas *Sarah*, the Wife of me the Subscriber, has absented herself from my Bed and Board: These are therefore to caution all Persons from trusting her upon my Account, as I will not pay one Farthing of any Debt she may contract after the Date hereof.

WILLIAM APPLETON. Ipswich, December 21, 1779.

The Independent Chronicle and the Universal Advertiser, December 23, 1779; December 30, 1779; January 6, 1780.

1780

WHEREAS, Mary, wife to me the Subscriber, left my house on the 9th of Jan. 1779, in a manner unexpected. I forbid all persons trusting or harbouring her from that date, as I shall prosecute them as the law directs.
    ROB. BROWN, jun.   Brimfield.
The Connecticut Courant, And The Weekly Intelligencer, January 4, 1780; January 18, 1780.

BROKE out of the County Goal in New-London, on the Night following the 10th Instant, one RICHARD DUTTON, committed for Debt, he is about 40 Years old, about 5 Feet 8 Inches high, Pock marked, an Irishman, had on an old brown Coat, and old Leather Breeches. Whoever will return him to me the Subscriber, shall have TWELVE DOLLARS Reward.
    NATHAN BALEY, jun. Goaler. New-London, Jan. 11, 1780.
The Connecticut Gazette; And The Universal Intelligencer, January 12, 1780.

BROKE out of the county goal in New-London, on the night after to 24th instant, one JOHN ARMSTRONG, committed for debt, he is about 24 or 25 years old, short and well set, had on a dark coloured surtout, and linen trowsers. Whoever will return him to me the subscriber, shall have Twelve Dollars reward.
    NATHAN BALEY, jun. Goaler. New-London, January 25 1780.
The Connecticut Gazette; And The Universal Intelligencer, January 26, 1780; February 2, 1780; February 9, 1780.

TO THE PUBLIC

WHEREAS I the Subscriber posted my Wife in March, 1777,—I now inform the Public that she is returned home and all Matters of Difficulty between us are happily settled to mutual Satisfaction, and as what I did then was rather sudden, I do now with Pleasure recall it, and restore her to all the Privilege, of a good and beloved Wife.
    JAMES GEER,   Preston, Nov. 19, 1779.
The Connecticut Gazette; And The Universal Intelligencer, February 2, 1780; February 9, 1780; February 23, 1780. See *The Connecticut Gazette; And The Universal Intelligencer*, March 14, 1777. The wife's name was Mary.

ON the night after the 9th instant, Litchfield county goal was broke and the following prisoners made their escape, viz. Thomas Knap, confined for treason, of a middling size short black curled hair, black eyes, quick spoken, a fellow of great address. Also, William Thompson, confined for theft, lately belonged to Col. Sheldon's regiment of Light Dragoons, a small likely looking fellow, about 22 years of age. Also, William Simmons, confined for treason, a young fellow about 22 years of age, thick set, appears to be and ignorant worthless fellow. Also, Eno. Blakesley, confined for desertion from the continental army. The Cloaths of the above cannot be described, as they have lately made some exchanges. Whoever will apprehend and return the above prisoners to said goal again shall have for Knap 50 dollars, and for Thompson and Simmons 20 dollars each as a reward; and for Blakesley the thanks of the public's humble servant,

LYNDE LORD Sheriff.   Litchfield, Feb. 10, 1780.

The Connecticut Courant, And The Weekly Intelligencer, February 15, 1780; February 22, 1780.

Extract of a Letter from Litchfield, Feb. 10.

"You have doubtless heard that the house of Caleb Mallery of Washington was consumed by fire last Thursday night, and five persons, viz. Mr. Mallery, his wife, and three children all burnt in it, which was the whole of the family that was at home that night: and this day one Barnet Davenport, (who was a hired man to said Mallery at the time) was committed to our goal, and confesses he knocked Mr. Mallery and his wife on the head, robbed the house, and then set it on fire, and when said Davenport was taken up was cloathed in Mr. Mallery's cloaths."

The Connecticut Courant, And The Weekly Intelligencer, February 15, 1780. See *The Connecticut Gazette, And The Universal Intelligencer*, February 16, 1780, *The Connecticut Journal*, February 16, 1780, and *The Connecticut Courant, And The Weekly Intelligencer*, May 9, 1780.

Stop a Murderer.

ON the night after the 3d last, was destroyed by Fire, the Dwelling House of Caleb Mallery, of this Town, Caleb Mallery, his Wife, and three small Children were consumed with the House, (the whole Family except one Davenport.) It is supposed that one *Nicholas Davenport*, as he called himself, his true Name is *Barnard Davenport*, a Deserter from the American Army, a stout well built Fellow, about five Feet ten Inches high, light Complexion, hard favoured, light Eyes, about Twenty Years of Age, a Native of New-Milford, plundered the House, murdered the Persons, set Fire to the House, and then run-away by the Light of it. Every Friend to Justice, the Ties of Society, and the Laws of God and Man, is earnestly requested to use every Method and Means to apprehend the aforesaid [Villai]n—Whoever shall apprehend the Perpetrator of this horrid Villainy, will be generously rewarded, and all necessary Charges paid, and receive the Thanks of every Friend of Mankind in General.

Washington, Litchfield County, State of Connecticut, Feb. 8, 1780.
The Connecticut Gazette, And The Universal Intelligencer, February 16, 1780. See *The Connecticut Courant, And The Weekly Intelligencer,* February 15, 1780, *The Connecticut Journal,* February 16, 1780, and *The Connecticut Courant, And The Weekly Intelligencer,* May 9, 1780.

NEW-HAVEN, February 16.

The following are all the particulars we have been able to collect of a most barbarous murder, committed at Washington, in this State. On the night of the third inst. the dwelling house of Mr. Caleb Mallery, a wealthy farmer, of that town, was observed to be on fire, but standing remote from neighbours, it was not discovered until the house was nearly destroyed; and as none of the family were to be found, it was concluded at first, that they had all perished in bed, while asleep; it consisted of Mr. Mallery, his wife, and three grandchildren, and one Barnard Davenport, a youth of about 20, a native of New Milford, who had for some time been in the employ of Mr. Mallery. On searching the rubbish, after the fire was out, the bones of Mr. Mallery, his wife, and the children, were found near the apartment where they lodged, but as the bones of Davenport, who lodged in another part, could not be found, and several other circumstances made it strongly suspected that he had murthered the family, robbed the house, and then set it on fire, to hide his villainy. We hear he has been taken up, and committed to Litchfield gaol, and owns he is guilty of the black crimes of having first inhumanly murthered Mr. Mallery, then Mrs. Mallery, and two of the children, while in bed, and after plundering the house, set it on fire, and that he heard the child, whom he had spared for a more painful death, calling for help, from the flames. The mother of the children being from home, escaped the unhappy fate of the rest of the family.

The Connecticut Journal, February 16, 1780; *The Boston Gazette, And Country Journal,* March 6, 1780. See *The Connecticut Courant, And The Weekly Intelligencer,* February 15, 1780, *The Connecticut Gazette, And The Universal Intelligencer,* February 16, 1780, and *The Connecticut Courant, And The Weekly Intelligencer,* May 9, 1780.

ONE DOLLAR REWARD.

RAN-AWAY from the subscriber on the night of the fourteenth inst. ELISHA WATERMAN, an Apprentice boy, between 18 and 19 years of age.—Whoever will take up said Apprentice and return him to the subscriber, shall have the above reward.

ISAAC GRISWOLD. *Norwich, Feb.* 22 1780.

The Norwich Packet And The Weekly Advertiser, February 22, 1780; March 14, 1780; March 28, 1780.

SIX PENCE REWARD.

RUN-AWAY from the subscriber, on the night of the 12th instant, a MOLATO GIRL, named ABIGAIL GUMMER, about seventeen years old, large of her age, with a bushy head of hair. Whoever will take up said Girl and return her to the subscriber, shall have the above reward.
    ELIPHALET CAREW.   *Norwich, Feb.* 15, 1780.
The Norwich Packet and the Weekly Advertiser, February 22, 1780; March 14, 1780. See *The Norwich Packet*, October 12, 1779.

RAN away from the subscriber, an apprentice Boy named JEREMIAH CANNON, about 15 Years Old, very small of his Age, very much of a talkative. Whoever will return him shall have Six Pence reward.
  Wm. MOOR.   New-London, Feb. 20th, 1780.
N. B. All Masters of Vessels and Others, are forbid harbouring or carrying off said Fellow, at the Peril of the Law.
The Connecticut Gazette; And The Universal Intelligencer, February 23, 1780; March 15, 1780.

WHEREAS Elizabeth Bishop, the Wife of James Bishop, of New Haven, hath for some Time past, behaved herself in a turbulent Manner, and refused to bed and board with her Husband: This is therefore to forewarn and forbid all Persons trusting her, as no Debts contracted by her after this Date shall be paid by me the Subscriber, Conservator to said James Bishop.
    JAMES HUMESTON. New-Haven, February 9, 1780.
The Continental Journal, February 23, 1780; March 8, 1780.

TWO HUNDRED DOLLARS Reward.

Broke out of the common Goal in *Cambridge*, on the night of the 31st of January, 1780, one BENJAMIN HEAVERLIN, dark complexion, about 30 years of age, and about five feet two inches high; had on when he went away a snuff-coloured coat, and light-blue shag velvet waistcoat and breeches, and a blue surtout with a crimson cape. Whoever shall take up said prisoner, and return him to said goal at *Cambridge*, shall receive the above reward
    by ISAAC BRADISH. *Cambridge*, January 31, 1780.
The Continental Journal, And Weekly Advertiser, February 24, 1780.

  Mr. GILL, *Please to insert the following*—
LAST Tuesday month came into my house, a middle siz'd youngish woman, bought three pounds of candles, and gave me a seventy dollar bill,

and I gave her to the best of my knowledge fifty-two dollars change; wore a red calico gown with white sports, a red handkerchief with white sports, a dark check'd apron, a short scarlet cloak trim'd with ermine, dark riding hood outside the hood of the scarlet cloak over her head, a scallopt cushion, a brownish head of hair, a black hat trim'd with gauze, a white silk pocket-book work'd with silver thread, a sharpish nose.—Any person or persons that will give intelligence of that above described woman, so that she may be apprehended, or if any of her accomplices will give information, they shall receive a handsome reward.
     THOMAS LEECH.
The Continental Journal, And Weekly Advertiser, February 24, 1780.

RUN away from the Subscriber, living in South-Kingstown, an Indian Servant Woman, named PATIENCE, about 30 Years of Age, short and thick, has a Scar on one Side of her Face, and is very talkative. Had on, when she went away, a black quilted Petticoat, somewhat worn, a spotted green woollen Cooler, a blue Cloth Bonnet; and took with her a large white Blanket. Said Indian has been known to change her Name. Whoever will take up said Servant, and secure her in any of the Gaols of the United States, so that her Master may have her again, or return her to her Master in South-Kingstown, shall have One Hundred Dollars Reward, and all necessary Charges,
    paid by STEPHEN POTTER.
N. B. All Persons are forbid to harbour said Servant. Feb. 23. 1780.
 The Providence Gazette; And Country Journal, February 26, 1780; March 4, 1780; March 11, 1780.

ABSENTED from the subscriber, 4 months past, a negro woman named DINAH, of a middling stature, very black complexion and about 20 years of age, somewhat pock-broken about her nose, has large lips, a sharp eye and speaks broken English: Any person that will apprehend said servant and give information thereof, shall be handsomely rewarded and all necessary charges paid. All persons are hereby forbid harbouring said servant.
     Wm. TAYLOR.
N. B. She passes herself for a free Negro, and supposed to be in the country.
 The Boston-Gazette, And Country Journal, February 28, 1780; March 6, 1780; March 13, 1780. See *The Boston-Gazette, And Country Journal*, July 17, 1780.

RUN away from the subscriber the 5th instant, a Negro Man named Juos, about 24 years of age, and about five feet six inches high, has a small scar in his forehead, broken in speech, has on a flopt hat, brown jackets and trowsers, check'd woolen shirt, black and white mix'd coloured stockings,

and a pair of thick shoes cap'd. Whoever will take up said Negro, and secure him, so that the owner may have him again, shall be reasonably rewarded by me,
    GILES PIERPOINT.   New-Haven, March 7, 1780.
The Continental Journal, March 8, 1780; March 15, 1780.

RUN away from me the subscriber about the 28th of February last, a Negro Man named LONDON, about 50 years of age, had on when he went away, a strait bodied blue coat and leather breeches, as to his other cloathing I am not certain; he is a middling sized fellow, speaks faint and slow, but tolerable good English, is a crafty subtle sly fellow, and has and can pretend sickness when well. Whoever will apprehend said Negro and bring him to me in Hartford, or secure him in any goal in this or the neighbouring States and send me word so that I may have him again, shall have 50 dollars reward, and all necessary charges paid. I also forewarn all persons from either harboring, secreting or employing said Negro, as they will answer the same at the peril of the law.
    H. LEDLIE.   Hartford, March 13, 1780.
The Connecticut Courant, And The Weekly Intelligencer, March 14, 1780; March 21, 1780.

RAN away from the Subscriber on the Night of the 14th Inst. an Apprentice Boy, named WILLIAM JOHNSON, he stole and carried away with him a Gun. Whoever will take up said Johnson and return him to me, shall have One Hundred Dollars Reward, and for the Gun One Hundred Dollars.
    DANIEL SHAW.   Millington, Feb. 24, 1780.
N. B. All Persons are forbid to harbour or conceal him.
The Connecticut Gazette; And The Universal Intelligencer, March 15, 1780.

RAN away from the Subscriber about the 1st of March, an Apprentice named John Plumbe. Whoever will return him shall receive Six Pence Reward. All Persons are forbid harbouring him.
    DANIEL CAULKINS.   Lyme, March 21, 1780.
The Connecticut Gazette; And The Universal Intelligencer, March 22, 1780; March 29, 1780; April 5, 1780.

KNOW all Men by these Presents, that I David Smith forbid all Persons to trust my Wife Eunice, on my Account, as I will not pay one Farthing of her Debts.   DAVID SMITH.   Gloucester, March 24, 1780.
The Providence Gazette; And Country Journal, March 25, 1780; April 1, 1780; April 8, 1780.

FRIDAY the 17th of this inst.
Went from Exeter, a Person who calls himself by the name of *James Lord*, sometimes *Gordon Burnham*, of which last is known to be his true name. He is of a small stature, a likely man, of about 25 or 30 Years of age.—Had a small Hat bound with Velvet, a brown Coat, light blue Jacket, white Breeches and Stockings, and a dark brown loose Coat—He had hired a Horse of *James Thurston* of Exeter, of a light grey, trots and paces, and said he was bound to Newbury, but it's suspected his Design is not to return the Horse, as it is said he has a wife in Old-York. Whoever will take up said Man and Horse, and return the Horse to *James Thurston*, or the Printers hereof, shall receive FIFTY DOLLARS Reward, and all necessary charges paid.

The Independent Ledger, and the American Advertiser, March 27, 1780; April 17, 1780.

RAN away from the Subscriber on the 22d Instant, a Negro Man Servant named CAESAR, slim built, about 5 Feet 10 Inches high, speaks pretty good English, plays on the Violin, and is much inclined to Liquor; took with him a large Bundle of Cloathes, about one Thousand Dollars and a Violin. Whoever will take up and return said Negro, shall have Two Hundred Dollars Reward, and necessary Charges
   paid by ENOCH LORD. Lyme, March 17, 1780.

The Connecticut Gazette; And The Universal Intelligencer, March 29, 1780; April 5, 1780.

RAN away last Night from the Subscriber, an Apprentice Boy named WIAT HINCKLY, about 16 years old. Whoever will return him to the Subscriber, shall have Eighteen Pence Reward. Masters of Vessels and others are forbid harbouring or carrying off said Apprentice on Penalty of the Law.
    MOSES TYLER. Preston, February 29, 1780.

The Connecticut Gazette; And The Universal Intelligencer, March 29, 1780; April 5, 1780.

WHEREAS Mary Nichols, who is sometimes called Mary Davis, is bound to me by an Indenture of Apprenticeship, and hath absented herself from my Service: I hereby forbid any Person or Persons from harbouring or concealing her, or by any Means keeping her from my Service.
    NATHAN BUDLONG. Warwick, March 30, 1780.

The Providence Gazette; And Country Journal, April 1, 1780; April 8, 1780; April 15, 1780.

RAN away from the Subscriber, a Negro Man named JO, (was lately altered to Dick) about 5 Feet high, 22 Years of Age; he is a stocky strait limb'd Fellow, speaks good English, and is much inclined to Liquor; wore and carried away a blue outside Jacket, stout Cloth, about half wore, lin'd with white Flannel, a strip'd under Jacket, a Pair of new Shoes, a coarse white Shirt and a strip'd ditto, two Pair of long Trowsers, an old Great-Coat mended with different Cloth, and two Pair of good yarn Stockings, mark'd D one pair blue the other mix'd; he was seen at New-London about the 17th Inst. and at Chester in Say Brook about the 18th. Whoever will take up and return said Negro, shall have TWO HUNDRED DOLLARS Reward, and all necessary Charges.
    SAMUEL P. LORD. East-Haddam, March 30, 1780.
The Connecticut Gazette; And The Universal Intelligencer, April 5, 1780.

PROVIDENCE, April 6, 1780.

On Friday night last the house of Mr. Nathaniel Sprague, in Cranston, was broke open and he was robbed of about 300l. L. M. in silver and gold, and some private securities. The next day a warrant for hue and cry and search after suspected persons was issued; in consequence of which Thomas Waterman and Abraham Andrews, both of Cranston, were apprehended on suspicion of being concerned in the above robbery, and examined, but wholly denied having been any way accessary to the offence. But several circumstances appearing strongly against them, the Justices who took their examination ordered them to be confined for trial. On Monday Waterman, on a second examination, made a confession of the whole matter, whereby it appeared, that the persons who committed the burglary and robbery, were Abraham Andrews, Nathan Carpenter, and the said Thomas Waterman, all of Cranston. In the course of their examination it appeared, that on the evening the fact was perpetrated, they all disguised themselves and went to Mr. Sprague's house, when it was agreed that Andrews should guard the door, while Waterman and Carpenter entered the house, the former was to secure any person who might attempt to oppose them, while the latter broke open the chest that contained the money. Mr. Sprague, on hearing a noise in the house, got out of bed, but was immediately knocked down by Waterman. They then effected the robbery. Carpenter was apprehended at Warren early last Tuesday morning, and brought to town the same day. They are all confined to goal in order to take their trial at the next Superior Court which will be holden here the 4th of September next.

The American Journal And General Advertiser, April 6, 1780; *The Providence Gazette; and Country Journal*, April 8, 1780. Minor differences between the papers. See *The Massachusetts Spy Or, Thomas's Boston Journal*, April 20, 1780.

RAN away from the subscriber, on Sunday the 16th of March, a Negro Man named Caesar, about 27 years of age, small stature, very crooked legs, was brought up to the paper making business. Whoever will take up said servant and bring him to his master in Dorchester, shall have One Hundred Dollars reward, and all charges paid. All masters of vessels are hereby cautioned against harbouring or carrying away said servant, as they would avoid the penalty of the Law.
     GEORGE CLARKE.   Dorchester, April 4, 1780.
The Boston-Gazette, And Country Journal, April 10, 1780; April 24, 1780.

            Hartford, 22d March, 1780.
LAST night made his escape from the goal in this place, one BENJAMIN HICKOX, a Tory Prisoner; is a middling sized man, about 45 years old, had on a light coloured surtout, old bever hat, leather breeches and a tailed wig. Whoever will take up said Prisoner and confine him in this or any other goal in this state, shall have one hundred dollars reward and reasonable
     charges, paid by EZ'l. WILLIAMS, Sheriff.
N. B. He has a family at Braintree, in Boston State, and likely he has gone that way.
The Connecticut Courant, And The Weekly Intelligencer, April 11, 1780.

WHEREAS my wife ANN hath, for years passed, conducted herself in such a manner as to give me reason to believe she hath prostituted herself to other lovers, and become a harlot and concubine to another man.—These are therefore to forbid any person entertaining or trusting her on my account, as I will pay no cost nor debt she may contract or be the occasion of for the future.
     JOHN TURNER.   Norwich, April 11, 1780.
The Norwich Packet and the Weekly Advertiser, April 11, 1780; May 4, 1780.

       Whereas ELIZABETH, the
Wife of the Subscriber, has eloped from House: This is to forbid any Person trusting her on my Account, as I will not pay any Debts she may contract after the Date hereof.
     DAVID SHEAL, jun.   Stoughton, April 4, 1780.
The Independent Chronicle and the Universal Advertiser, April 13, 1780.

Whereas LYDIA, Wife of me the Subscriber hath eloped from my Bed and Board, this is to caution all Persons from trusting her on my Account, as I will pay no Debt of her contracting after the Date hereof.
                    GAMALIEL GERELD.   Medford, April 6, 1780.
The Independent Chronicle and the Universal Advertiser, April 13, 1780; April 20, 1780; April 27, 1780.

Stop the RUNAWAY.
Runaway the ninth of the Instant April from his Master William Cotton of Portsmomt, [sic] Tanner, a Negro man about 5 feet 10 Inches high, about 25 Years of Age, a Stout spry Fellow, upon the yellow order. a stripe upon his Cheeks, left Hand little Finger broke off; two S[   ]es from his Nable round to his Nable, had on a yellow colour'd Pea Jacket lin'd with Woolen check, and a blue Jacket, Buck Leather Breeches, a dark brown Cap mill'd,—Whoever will take up said Negro and convey him to his Master shall have Forty five Pounds Reward and necessary Charges
        paid by me.   William Cotton.   Portsmouth,   April 14, 1780.
The New-Hampshire Gazette; Or, State Journal, and General Advertiser, April 15, 1780. See *The Independent Chronicle and the Universal Advertiser*, April 20, 1780, and *The New-Hampshire Gazette; Or, State Journal, and General Advertiser*, September 16, 1780.

PROVIDENCE, April 8.
ON Friday night, last week, a robbery was committed at the house of Mr. Nathaniel Sprague, in Cranston, by three persons in disguise, who broke open the house, and robbed him of about 380 dollars in silver and gold, about 300 l. in paper currency, and sundry notes of hand. Mr. Sprague being awaked by the noise, and enquiring who was there, at the same time attempting to rise from his bed, was knocked down by one of the persons; another guarded the door, while the third passed through the room where Mr. Sprague lodged into another room, and broke open a chest which contained the money. A warrant for Hue and Cry and Search for suspected persons being issued next day, and some Circumstances appearing against Abraham Andrews and Thomas Waterman, they were apprehended and committed to goal. On examination, they denied being any way accessary to the offence; but not giving a satisfactory account of themselves, the Justices who took the examination committed them for trial. Waterman upon a second examination on Monday, confessed the whole, whereby it appeared that in the year 1778 an agreement was between him and Nathan Carpenter, (who is half-brother to Mrs. Sprague) that they should take into Confidence

a third person, and rob houses from whence there was a probability of obtaining money. Many were proposed, but Mr. Sprague's was finally agreed upon. They mentioned their intentions to several persons, who they expected might join them, but all finally failed them, except Andrews. Carpenter was apprehended at Warren early on Tuesday morning, and on his examination also confessed the whole matter; he likewise informed where the money was buried, which has been recovered. They are all confined in goal, to take their trials at the next Superior Court.

The Massachusetts Spy Or, Thomas's Boston Journal, April 20, 1780; *The Connecticut Journal*, April 27, 1780. See *The American Journal And General Advertiser*, April 6, 1780. Minor differences between the papers.

TWO HUNDRED DOLLARS Reward.

STOLEN from the Subscriber out of the Stable of Job Stiles, in Granville, on the 30th Day of March instant, a dark bay or brown MARE, about 14 ½ Hands high, with a small Star in her Forehead; said Mare has a genteel Canter, and is a Racer, and is shod for that Purpose. The Thief is one *Amos Rose*, aged 25 or 26 Years, had on when he took the Mare, a light coloured Coat, green Vest, light coloured Breeches, no Great Coat, and is a small Man. Whoever shall take up said Mare and Thief, so that the Owner may have the Mare, and the Thief brought to Justice, shall have the above Reward, and all necessary Charges paid per me,

SAMUEL STILES. Granville, (Berkshire County, State of Massachusetts-Bay) March 31, 1780.

The Connecticut Journal, April 20, 1780.

ON the night of the 16th instant, the following prisoners broke out, and made their Escape from the gaol in New-Haven, viz Dan Fairchild, of Newtown, in Fairfield county, committed for horse-stealing, aged about 30 years, and more than five feet high, had on a light colour'd great coat, boots, and a hair cap; also Malcom M'Callam, committed for passing counterfeit money, middling size, age not known, a native of Scotland, but late resident at Middletown. Whoever shall take up the above persons, and secure them, so that they be brought to justice, shall receive one hundred dollars for both, or fifty for either of them, paid by

STEPHEN MUNSON, Gaoler. New-Haven, April 19, 1780.

The Connecticut Journal, April 20, 1780; April 27, 1780.

Ran away from William Cotton, of Portsmouth, a Negro Man named GARRACK, about five Feet ten Inches high something of a yellow Colour, his little Finger on the left Hand, squat off half way the Nail, speaks broken and very grum, about 25 Years old, has

two Streeks round his Middle, with Notches cut between, from his Navel to Navel; had on when he went off, a light coloured cloth Jacket, lined with check'd homespun Cloth, his under Jacket blue Cloth, Leather Breeches, striped Trowsers, woolen Shirt, grand about his Hair. Whoever will take up said Negro, and convey him to his Master, or secure him in some Goal, shall have Forty-Five Pounds L. M. for their Trouble, and necessary Charges, paid by   WILLIAM COTTON.
Portsmouth, April 11, 1780.
The Independent Chronicle and the Universal Advertiser, April 20, 1780; April 27, 1780; May 4, 1780. *The New-Hampshire Gazette; Or, State Journal, and General Advertiser*, April 15, 1780, and *The New-Hampshire Gazette; Or, State Journal, and General Advertiser*, September 16, 1780.

RUN AWAY from the subscriber, on the evening of the 23d instant, an apprentice boy, named PAUL SAYRE, a native of Long Island, by trade a goldsmith, about nineteen years of age, about five feet seven or eight inches high, a thick set fellow, thick lips, flat nose, light eyes, somewhat pitted with the small pox, has short, straight, dark hair. Had on and carried with him, a broadcloth blue coat, jacket and breeches, a light brown short coat, with open sleeves, a jacket about the same colour, a blue great coat, a pair of brown broadcloth breeches, a large castor hat, almost new, two pairs of shoes, a pair of open work silver shoe buckles, and sundry other articles of cloathing. Whoever will take up said apprentice, and return him to his master, or confine him so that he shall get him again, shall have One Hundred Dollars Continental Money Reward, and all necessary Charges   paid by   JAMES TILEY.
N. B. It is supposed that he will endeavour to go on Long Island. All Masters of Vessels and others, are forbid carrying him off, or harbouring or concealing him at their Peril.   April 24 1780.
The Connecticut Courant, And The Weekly Intelligencer, April 25, 1780; May 9, 1780, *The Connecticut Journal*, April 27, 1780; May 11, 1780, and *The Connecticut Gazette; and the Universal Intelligencer*, May 5, 1780. Minor differences between the papers. The *Journal* spells the apprentice's name as Sayer.

NOTICE is hereby given to all concern'd, That a certain negro girl, named *Violent*, [sic] alias *Sansy*, is now in custody of the subscriber, who has instituted a petition in her behalf, to the General Assembly, of this State, to be holden at Hartford, on the 2d Thursday of May next, in order to obtain her freedom; when and where all persons claiming said girl, (if any such there are) may, if they please, appear, and make good their claim.—She was born at Wallingford of a negro woman, named *Nancy*, who is now free,

from whence she was, by some means, about 12 years since, sent into the case of *Joshua Chandler, Esq; late of New Haven, politically deceased,* from whence, she was afterwards sent to *Middletown,* and from thence, to *Sunderland,* from thence to *Cambridge,* near *Boston,* from whence she was lately transported, together with several miserable Africans, to Dutchess county, in the State of New-York, by a number of *South Carolina Negro-Drivers,* who being in danger, on account of attempting to smuggle flour, &c. out of *that state,* fled precipitately in the night, leaving the girl above mentioned, with some other articles of their bounty, in the care of one —— *Sheldon,* of *Quaker Hill,* in said Dutchess County, from whence said girl, by the assistance of her master, made her escape. Said girl in now about 13 or 14 years of age.—she has an undoubted right to her freedom, of which, said *Negro Drivers* seem'd sensible, as they travelled with their cargo, in the night season only. Said South Carolina Negro Drivers, said Sheldon, or any one authorised by them, or him, are hereby forbid molesting said girl, during the pending of said petition, either openly, or clandestinely, upon their peril. DANIEL EVERITT. New-Milford,
Litchfield County, State of Connecticut, March 22d, 1780.
The Connecticut Journal, April 27, 1780.

PROVIDENCE, April 8.

On Friday Night, last Week, a Robbery was committed at the house of Mr. Nathaniel Sprague, in Cranston, by three Persons in disguise, who broke open the House, and robbed him of about 380 Dollars in Silver and Gold, about £. 300 in Paper Currency, and sundry Notes of Hand. Mr. Sprague being awaked by the Noise and enquiring who was there, at the same Time attempting to rise from his Bed, was knocked down by one of the Persons; another guarded the Door, while the third passed through the Room where Mr. Sprague lodged into another Room, and broke open a Chest which contained the Money. A warrant for Hue and Cry and Search for suspected Persons being issued next Day, and some Circumstances appearing against Abraham Andrews and Thomas Waterman, they were apprehended and committed to Gaol. On examination, they denied being any Way accessary to the Offence; but not giving a satisfactory account of themselves, the Justices who took the Examination committed them for trial. Waterman upon a second Examination on Monday, confessed the Whole, whereby it appeared that in the Year 1778 an Agreement was between him and Nathan Carpenter, (who is Half-Brother to Mrs. Sprague) that they should take into Confidence a third Person, and rob Houses from where there was a Probability of obtaining Money. Many were proposed, but Mr. Sprague's was finally agreed upon. They mentioned their Intentions to several Persons, who they expected might join them, but all finally failed them, except Andrew Carpenter was apprehended at Warren early on

Tuesday Morning, and one his Examination also confessed the whole Matter; he likewise informed where the Money was buried, which was recovered. They are all confined in Gaol, to take their Trials at the next Superior Court.
The Connecticut Journal, April 27, 1780. See *The Massachusetts Spy Or, Thomas's Boston Journal*, April 20, 1780, and *The American Journal And General Advertiser*, April 6, 1780.

Deserted last Tuesday night, from on board the ship *Protector*, in Nantasket road, the following seamen, *viz. William Bell, John Robinson, John Butler, William Maxwell, William McKinley, Robert Ireland* and *Francis Wood.* Whoever will detect all or either of the above persons, and convey them to the subscriber, or confine them in goal, shall receive One Hundred Dollars for each, and all necessary charges paid by   JOHN F. WILLIAMS, Captain.
N. B. *All masters of vessels and others are hereby cautioned against concealing or carrying off either of the above deserters, as they would avoid the penalty of the law.*   Boston, April 26, 1780.
The Continental Journal, And Weekly Advertiser, April 27, 1780.

To all whom it may concern.
KNOW YE, That *Elizabeth Bemis,* my Wife, left my House in Lexington in my Absence, and refuses to return to it, though I have repeatedly requested her to return home, and promised to receive and treat her kindly, and provide for her according to my Ability:—I therefore forbid all Persons entertaining, trading with, or supplying her with any Thing on my Account, as I will not pay any Debt she has contracted since she left me, or shall contract which she absents herself from me.
SAMUEL BEMIS.   Lexington, April 25, 1780.
The Independent Chronicle and the Universal Advertiser, April 27, 1780; May 4, 1780; May 11, 1780.

Mr. Thomas.
IN October, 1779, I advertised my wife PERCES; previous to which I went to her to solicit her return, and to enquire whether she had ran me in debt; her supposed friends, would not exhibit any account against me, nor discharge me, neither would she return to live with me: In this perplexed situation I thought proper to advertise her, for it seem to me hard to support my wife from home, when I conceived I was not the blameable cause of her going away. Soon after one of her friends came to me offering to be her sponsor until the first of April ensuing, and that time being now expired, and she still persists in her obstinacy in not returning to live with me, but

insists upon my maintaining her where she pleases to live, which appears so unreasonable to me, that I do hereby recall the last piece I put in your paper relative to my wife, which I never should have done, had I not been in hopes she would have returned to live with me again; not that I was the blameable cause of her going away, or meant to clear her of blame in so doing; and I do hereby caution all persons against harbouring my said wife PERCES, as they may expect to answer at the peril of the law; neither will I discharge any debt she may contract from and after this date.
       DANIEL ADAMS.
N. B. All persons that have trusted her before this date, are desired to settle the same immediately with the subscriber.
             Westborough, April 24th, 1780.
The Massachusetts Spy Or, Thomas's Boston Journal, April 27, 1780; May 11, 1780. See *The Massachusetts Spy Or, Thomas's Boston Journal*, October 28, 1779, and *The Massachusetts Spy Or, Thomas's Boston Journal*, November 25, 1779.

       ONE GUINEA REWARD.
RUN AWAY from his Master, on Tuesday last, a Negro Boy, named PRINCE, about fifteen years old, a small likely looking lad, speaks good English, is rather talkative and saucy. He carried with him, an old blue coat with steel buttons; a short, redish, brow coat, with yellow cape, cuffs, and lining; a striped wilton great coat; a leather jockey cap, and an old flop'd hat, with several shirts, &c. Its supposed said boy was lurking about town for several days. He formerly lived at Lyme. Whoever will take up said Negro Boy, and bring him to the Subscriber, at Hartford, shall have the above reward and all charges, paid by
  JOSIAH W. GIBBS.   Hartford, May 1st, 1780.
The Connecticut Courant, And The Weekly Intelligencer, May 2, 1780.

       Ran-away from Capt. Caleb
Sanborn, an apprentice Boy, named SIMON GODFREY, about 17 Years old; had on when he went away, a lightish coloured Coat, brown Jacket, light coloured Breeches, short brown Hair. Whoever will take up said Boy, and bring him to his said Master, shall have Ten Shillings Reward,
    by the Subscriber. CALEB SANBORN.
N. B. This is to forbid all Masters of Vessels from concealing or carrying off said Boy, in suffering the Penalty of the Law.
           Hampton-Falls, April 28, 1780.
The Independent Chronicle and the Universal Advertiser, May 4, 1780; May 11, 1780.

MADE his Escape from the Subscriber, on the Evening of the [10]th Instant, at Capt. Wheeler's Tavern in New-London, one DANIEL DAVIDS, a Dutchman about 30 Years of Age, about 5 Feet 4 Inches high, well set, with black Hair; had on a white Coat and blue Plush Jacket and Breeches. Said Davids was born in Albany but has lately lived in Symsbury, Turkey-Hill Society, Connecticut, and is a great Horse-Jocky; he being, when he made his Escape, under an Arrest for Debt. Whoever will secure said Davids in either of the Goals in the County of New-London, or deliver him to me shall receive One Hundred Pounds Reward.
    STEPHEN MAYNARD,
     (Constable. New-London, April 19, 1780.
The Connecticut Gazette; and the Universal Intelligencer, May 5, 1780.

ALL Persons, are forbid trusting ISABEL DELONG, on my account; as I shall pay none of her contracts, after this date.
    ELIAS DELONG.   Spencertown, April 21, 1780.
The Connecticut Courant, And The Weekly Intelligencer, May 9, 1780.

    HARTFORD, May 9,
At a special superior court, holden at Litchfield, April 25th, Barnett Davenport, was indicted before the grand jury, for the horrid murder of Mr. Caleb Mallery, and his wife, and burning three grand children, with the house. And Nicholas Davenport was indicted as being an accessory. Bills were secured against both of them. Barnett confessed, and plead guilty to the Court. Said Nicholas as tried, April 17th, and the next morning the jury brought him in guilty. Barnett Davenport was sentenced to be hanged on the 8th of May, between the hours of twelve and three, P. M. Nicholas was sentenced to sit on the gallows one hour, with a rope about his neck, to be whipt thirty-nine lashes, and to be imprisoned ten years; to be confined in Litchfield gaol, till Newgate is repaired, and then to be sent there to continue said term.—One Austin, for attempting to join the enemy, was also sentenced to six months imprisonment.
 The Connecticut Courant, And The Weekly Intelligencer, May 9, 1780. See *The Connecticut Courant, And The Weekly Intelligencer*, February 15, 1780, *The Connecticut Gazette, And The Universal Intelligencer*, February 16, 1780, and *The Connecticut Journal*, February 16, 1780, for Davenport. See *The Connecticut Courant, And The Weekly Intelligencer*, June 13, 1780, for Austin. See *The Connecticut Courant, And Weekly Advertiser*, May 22, 1781, for Nicholas Davenport.

RAN away from the subscriber, a negro man named Peter, he is about 4 feet [sic] 2 inches high, of a short smallish stature, plays upon the violin, carried away with him 3 good coats, 3 waistcoats, 2 pair leather breeches, 4 shirts, 4 pair trowsers, one great coat, 2 pair shoes 5 pair stockings and 2 hats. Whoever will take up said negro and secure him, so that the right owner may have him again, shall have One Shilling lawful money,
     paid by JOHN EDDY, of Chatham.
The Connecticut Gazette; And The Universal Intelligencer, May 12, 1780; May 19, 1780; May 26, 1780.

     Whereas Elizabeth, my Wife,
has during my Absence in the Continental Service, misbehaved herself greatly to my Injury. This is to forbid all Persons trusting her on my Account, for I will not pay any Debt of her contracting hereafter.
    Benjamin Dockum.   Epping, May 8, 1780.
The New-Hampshire Gazette; Or, State Journal, and General Advertiser, May 13, 1780; May 20, 1780.

    ONE HUNDRED DOLLARS REWARD.
LAST night escaped from the subscribers with whom they were permitted to work in Hartford, MICHAEL MURREY and JOHN SCOVEL both prisoners of war. Said Murry is a short thick set fellow, about 5 feet 6 inches high, dark complexion, small eyes, short curl'd black hair; had on a dark brown out side jacket, short under vest and overhalls of the same kind, an old bever hat, small brim'd, old check shirt much town, is about 20 years of age, a native of Ireland. Scovel is a short thick set fellow, about 5 feet 6 inches high, light complexion, large white eyes, short strait brown hair; had on an old outside vest much torn, short under vest both lightish brown, a pair of corduroy breeches, old shoes, a pair of mixt blue and white cotton stockings, an old coarse white shirt, small round hat, was born near Horseneck. Whoever will take up and confine said prisoners or send them to the goal in Hartford, shall have 50 dollars for each.
    ELIAKIM FISH. STEPHEN AUSTIN.
              Hartford, May 15, 1780.
The Connecticut Courant, And Hartford Weekly Intelligencer, May 16, 1780; May 30, 1780.

WHEREAS Susannah, the wife of me the Subscriber, hath, for ten or eleven months past, eloped from my bed and board, contrary to my will, and hath embezled my effects. I do hereby forbid all persons harbouring or dealing with her on my account, as I will not pay any debt of her contracting, from this date.
    WILLIAM ORCUTT.   Somers, Feb. 19, 1780.

The Connecticut Courant, And Hartford Weekly Intelligencer, May 16, 1780; May 30, 1780.

RAN away from me the subscriber on the 18th of April last, SALMA KEYES, a servant of mine in his 18th year, of a fresh complexion, black hair, blue eyes, about five feet and an half high, had on when he went away, a wrapper, with a black cape, the coat of a greyish colour, jacket of a dark colour, brown coat and breeches, grey stockings, stripped woolen shirt. Whoever will take said servant and convey him to me, shall have two Dollars reward. And all persons are cautioned against entertaining said servant, as they must answer it in the law.
    ELISHA JACKSON.   Westminster, May 5, 1780.
Thomas's Massachusetts Spy Or, American Oracle of Liberty, May 18, 1780; May 25, 1780; June 1, 1780; June 8, 1780.

WHEREAS on Thursday Evening last, a Person who called himself Jacob Johnson, hired a Mare Saddle and Bridle of the Subscriber, to go to Weston, and said he would return her the next Morning, but has not. Said Johnson had on dark chocolate colored Cloaths, and is a stout Man, with light Hair, about five Feet 9 or 10 Whoever will apprehend said Johnson, Mare, &c. so that the Subscriber may have her again, shall have One Hundred Dollars Reward, or for the Mare, &c. only, Fifty Dollars and all necessary Charges paid by
    BENJA. PIPER.   *Charlestown, May* 25, 1778.
N. B, The Mare is of a Chesnut Colour, about 15 *or* 16 *Hands high, with a Blaze in her Face, and has about half of the near Side of her Mane cut off, both Paces and Trots well.*
  The Boston Gazette, and Country Journal, May 25, 1778; June 8, 1778.

RUN away from his keeper, one William Prindle, a delirious person, about 35 years old, had on when he went away, a black and blue jacket, linen trowsers, no stockings, and has a small bunch in his forehead. In his former deliriam he killed a man, and as some time in Fairfield county gaol. I would earnestly intreat those that may see or hear of said person, and secure him, and give me notice, shall have all reasonable charges paid by me,
    ABIJAH HUBBELL.   Stratford, May 29th, 1780.
The Connecticut Journal, May 25, 1780; June 1, 1780; June 8, 1780; June 15, 1780. See *The Connecticut Journal,* July 11, 1782.

WHEREAS my Wife JANE hath absented herself from my Bed, I do therefore forewarn all Persons from harbouring or trusting her, as I am determined not to pay any Debts of her contracting from the Date hereof.

THOMAS TRACEY. Boston, May 29, 1780.
The Boston Gazette, And Country Journal, May 29, 1780; June 12, 1780.

WHereas Elisabeth, my wife, hath eloped from my bed and board, and contrary to my orders doth run me in debt: I am necessitated to, and hereby do forbid all person trading, dealing with, or trusting her on my account, as I will pay no debts of her contracting after the date hereof.
JAMES DAILEY. New-Milford, May 8th, 1780.
The Connecticut Journal, May 25, 1780; June 1, 1780; June 8, 1780.

WHEREAS my wife BEULAH,
has behaved in the most indecent and uncertain manner—disposed of my property, and cohabited with other men, in my absence. This is therefore to request all persons not to trust her on my account, as I shall hereafter pay no debts of her contracting.
ELEAZER COLLINS. Rutland, May 19, 1780.
Thomas's Massachusetts Spy Or, American Oracle of Liberty, June 1, 1780; June 8, 1780.

WHEREAS Amy, Wife of the Subscriber, has behaved in a very lude and indecent Manner, and by her Ludeness is guilty of a Breach of the marriage Covenant, and there is great Danger of her running me in Debt:—This is therefore to warn all Persons not to trust her on my Account, as I will not pay any Debt of her contracting after the Date hereof.
JOHN DANIELS. Groton, May 26, 1780.
The Connecticut Gazette; And The Universal Intelligencer, June 2, 1780.

WHEREAS my Wife ANNA, hath for some time past been disposed to disturb the peace and harmony of my family to that degree that I have reason to fear that she will run me in debt. These are therefore to forbid all persons trusting her on my account, as I will pay no debt contracted by her after this date.
STEPHEN HOTCHKISS. Farmington, May 30, 1780.
The Connecticut Courant, And The Weekly Intelligencer, June 6, 1780.

WHereas MARY, the wife of me the subscriber, has absented herself from me and family and refuses to return to her duty, although often requested by myself and others; and as I am apprehensive she may run me in debt: These are to caution all persons against trusting her on my account, as I will not discharge any debt she may contract after this date; and whoever harbours the said Mary may expect to be dealt with as the law directs.

JOHN DYAR. Dudley, May 24, 1780.
The American Journal And General Advertiser, June 7, 1780; June 21, 1780.

BOSTON, June 5.
Tuesday last one David Phelps, late of Sherburne, was apprehended in this town and committed to gaol for passing counterfeit Continental 50 dollar bills, of the emission of September, 1778. Upon examination several of the bills, as also some letters wrote at New-York, were found upon him. The work of these bills is well executed, but may easily be detected by the omission of the comma, at the word Philadelphia, on the face of the bills.
Thomas's Massachusetts Spy Or, American Oracle of Liberty, June 8, 1780. See *The Continental Journal, And Weekly Advertiser*, June 29, 1780.

550 *Continental Dollars Reward.*
ON the evening after the 30th of May instant, Litchfield County Gaol was broke open, and the following prisoners made their escape, viz. JOHN WELCH, a deserter from the British, an Irishman; confined for murder, thick set, about 21 years old. NICHOLAS DAVENPORT, about 21 years old, a short thick fellow; sentenced by the Honorable Superior Court, to 10 years imprisonment in New-Gate, CALEB AUSTIN, Jun. of Suffield, about 20 years of age; confined by judgment of Court, for attempting to join the enemy. EBENEZER REED, of Stamford, about 22 years of age, short of stature; confined on suspicion of treason. NATHANIEL HUSTEAD, PHINEAS RUNDLE, JOSEPH BEARD, and CHARLES BUCKSTON, all of Horse-Neck, confined for treason. Hustead, Rundle and Beard, are all young fellows, of a middling size, about 20 years of age. Buckston is about 32 years of age, tall slim built. Also, one WILLIAM THOMSON, Pennsylvania born about 21 years of age, small of stature; confined for debt. Whoever will apprehend and return the above prisoners, to said goal again, shall have as a reward for Welch and Davenport, 100 Dollars each: And for Austin, Reed, Hulstead, Rundle, Beard, Buckston and Thomson, 50 Dollars each, paid by
  LYNDE LORD, Sheriff.   Litchfield, May 31, 1780.
N. B. The Cloathing of the above fellows cannot be described.
The Connecticut Courant, And The Weekly Intelligencer, June 13, 1780; June 20, 1780. See *The Connecticut Courant, And The Weekly Intelligencer*, May 9, 1780, for Austin.

Ranaway from the Subscriber, living at Bellingham, sometime last April, a likely Negro Man, named *CAESAR*, about 22 Years of Age, speaks good English.—This, therefore, is to caution all Commanders of Vessels, and

Recruiting Officers, against inlisting said Negro Man, and any other Persons from harbouring or trading with him, upon Penalty of the Law.
JOHN CORBETT.
The Independent Chronicle and the Universal Advertiser, June 22, 1780; June 29, 1780.

BROKE out of the gaol in New-Haven, on the night of the 17th of June, inst, one John Jackson, 3d. committed for attempting to go to Long-Island, a lad about 16 years of age, thick set, had on a blue jacket, and striped trowsers, he belonged to Fairfield. A reward of 50*l.* will be given for the above lad, if returned to the gaol in New-Haven, or secured in any gaol in this state.   *S. Munson* Gaoler.   (June 29)
The Connecticut Journal, June 29, 1780; July 6, 1780.

BROKE out of the Goal in *Boston,*
on the evening of the 27th instant, DAVID PHELPS of *Sherburne,* about 40 years of age, black hair, about 5 feet 9 inches high; had on a brown homespun great coat, and striped trowsers, was committed, for uttering counterfeit bills.— JACOB YOUNG, of *Broad-Bay,* was confin'd for being inimical to the United States, about 5 feet 5 inches high, round face, had on a short blue jacket, and long trowsers.—ROBERT ALLEN, confin'd for theft, about 5 feet 7 inches high, a thin face, black strait hair wears it loose in his neck, broke out very much with the itch, had on a chocolate colour'd coat, white flannel waistcoat and breeches.— JOHN PAINE, confin'd for theft, about 5 feet 6 inches high, black hair, about 21 years of age, had on a hat with a gold button and loop, light coloured cloathes.— STEPHEN PAINE, confin'd for theft, about 5 feet six inches high, brown hair, about 19 years of age, had on a brown coat faced with blue, light colour'd waistcoat and breeches.— JAMES DENNIS, a molatto, about 5 feet 8 inches high, wore a wig, brown short coat and long trowsers.—Whoever will take up and secure said villains, that they may be brought to justice, shall receive FIVE HUNDRED DOLLARS for PHELPS—THREE HUNDRED DOLLARS for YOUNG—and TWO HUNDRED DOLLARS for each of the four last, and all charges paid by
JOSEPH OTIS, Dep. Goaler.   Boston, June 28, 1780.
The Continental Journal, And Weekly Advertiser, June 29, 1780; July 6, 1780; July 13, 1780. The Paines are not listed in the second and third ads. See *Thomas's Massachusetts Spy Or, American Oracle of Liberty,* June 8, 1780, for Phelps. See *The Boston-Gazette, And The Country Journal,* August 7, 1780, for the Paines.

Drove on the shore of Connecticut River, a few days since at Chatham, a dead body, supposed to be the noted burglarian John Brown, a short thick set man, about 5 feet three inches in height; had on a brown linnen coat, black breeches and boots, his ears cropt. A watch was found on him which he stole last week from one Goodrich of Chatham, and in attempting to make his escape across the river in a canoe, fell overboard and was drowned.

The Connecticut Gazette; And the Universal Intelligencer, June 30, 1780. See *The Connecticut Courant, and Hartford Weekly Intelligencer*, June 19, 1775, *The Connecticut Courant,* From November 6, to November 13, 1770, *The Connecticut Journal, And New-Haven Post-Boy*, November 30, 1770, *The Connecticut Journal, and New-Haven Post-Boy*, January 4, 1771, (2 ads), *The Connecticut Journal, and New-Haven Post-Boy*, January 18, 1771, *The Connecticut Courant,* From April 16, to April 23, 1771 (two ads), *The Connecticut Courant,* From July 23, to July 30, 1771, *The Connecticut Courant,* From January 28, to February 4, 1772, *The Connecticut Courant,* From March 3, to March 10, 1772, *Connecticut Journal*, April 15, 1774, *The Connecticut Courant, and Hartford Weekly Intelligencer*, October 3, 1774, *The Connecticut Gazette; And The Universal Intelligencer*, December 2, 1774, *The Connecticut Courant, and Hartford Weekly Intelligencer*, December 5, 1774 (two ads), and *The Connecticut Courant, and Hartford Weekly Intelligencer*, August 28, 1775.

Broke out of goal in Boston, June 30th, 1780, Richard Pomroy, confin'd for high treason, about 5 feet 7 inches high, round face, very red, pretty thick set, dark hair, had on a round hat with a silver lace, a blue coat, red waistcoat and blue breeches.

John Fellerton, confin'd for high treason, about 5 feet 6 inches high, had on short brown clothes, long trowsers, pretty thick set, wore his own hair: Whoever will apprehend said runaways and secure them so that they may be brought to Justice, shall have FIVE HUNDRED DOLLARS reward for each, and charges
         paid by   JOSEPH OTIS, dep. goaler.

The Boston-Gazette, And Country Journal, July 3, 1780; July 10, 1780; July 17, 1780, and *The Independent Chronicle and the Universal Advertiser*, July 6, 1780; July 13, 1780.

Whereas Molly, my wife, has eloped from me, has run me in debt, and disposed of my effects; and as I have been informed, has in my absence co-habited with another man, and still refuses to co-habit with me: Therefore this is to forbid any person trusting her for any thing on my account, for that I will not henceforth pay any debt she shall contract, or has lately contracted on me account.

Eleazer Ferguson.   Exeter, July 7, 1780.
The New-Hampshire Gazette; Or, State Journal, and General Advertiser, July 8, 1780.

WHEREAS Phoebe, the Wife of the Subscriber, has, without Cause, left his Bed and Board, and refuses to live with him: He hereby forbids all Persons to credit her on his Account, as he is determined not to pay any Debts of her contracting from the Date hereof.
   AMOS BLISS.   Rehoboth, June 29, 1780.
The Providence Gazette; And Country Journal, July 8, 1780; July 15, 1780.

FIVE HUNDRED DOLLARS REWARD.

RUN-away from the subscriber, on Wednesday the 5th instant, a likely Negro Man, named BILL, about 25 years of age, 5 feet 6 or inches high, plays well on the flute and fife; had on a short green coat with a red cape, took with him a fine blue broadcloth coat, with red cuffs and cape, and sundry other cloaths: It is supposed he will attempt to get to New York, or within the enemy's lines. Whoever will secure said servant, and return him to the subscriber shall receive the above reward, and all necessary charges.
   JEREMIAH PLATT.   Hartford, July 10. 1780.
The Connecticut Courant, And The Weekly Intelligencer, July 11, 1780; July 18, 1780; July 25, 1780. See *The Connecticut Journal*, January 22, 1777.

Whereas *Sarah* the wife of me the subscriber has eloped from my bed and board: These are therefore to caution all persons whatsoever from trusting her on my account, for I will not pay one farthing of any debt she may contract after the date hereof.
   DAVID PARKER.   Boston, July 12, 1780.
The Continental Journal, And Weekly Advertiser, July 13, 1780; July 20, 1780.

RAN AWAY from the subscriber, on the 17th inst. a Negro Man named WARREN, about 22 years of age, a remarkably stout well-made fellow, near 5 feet 8 inches high, and has an exceeding black and greasy look.—Had on, when he went away, a cloth-coloured coat faced with red, a white cloth waistcoat and breeches, a white holland shirt, tow stockings, new shoes, and a beaver hat.—Whoever will take up said Negro, and secure him, so that his Master may have him again, shall receive ONE HUNDRED and TWENTY CONTINENTAL DOLLARS Reward, and all necessary charges paid, by
   JOHN BARBER.   *North-Kingston, June* 30, 1780.

N. B. As he went off in company with another Negro fellow, who has been used to privateering, it is imagined they will endeavour to get on board some vessel for that purpose.—All masters of vessels and others are therefore forbid carrying him off.
The Newport Mercury, July 15, 1780.

Four Hundred Dollars Reward.
RAN away from the Subscriber, a Negro Man, named Anthony, a likely well-made Fellow, near 6 Feet high, about 23 Years of Age, and has a Scar in his Forehead: Had on a white Blanket Coat, a blue Jacket, and Ozenbrigs Overalls. Whoever will secure the above Negro, and give Notice to his Master, in Providence, so that he may have him again, shall have the above Reward, and all necessary Charges, paid by
    SILAS TALBOT.   Providence, July 14, 1780.
The Providence Gazette; And Country Journal, July 15, 1780; July 22, 1780; July 29, 1780.

ABSCONDING NEGRO.
ABSENTED from the subscriber, about eight months past, a negro woman named DINAH, of a midling stature, very black complexion and about 30 years of age, somewhat pock-broken about her nose, has large lips, a sharp eye and speaks broken English: Any person that will apprehend said servant and give information thereof, shall be handsomely rewarded and all necessary charges paid. All persons are hereby forbid harbouring said
    servant. Wm. TAYLOR.
N. B. She passes herself for a free Negro, and supposed to be in the country; and if she returns to her duty her offences shall be forgiven.
The Boston-Gazette, And Country Journal, July 17, 1780; July 24, 1780; August 7, 1780. See *The Boston-Gazette, And Country Journal*, February 28, 1780.

SIX HUNDRED REWARD.
RUN away from Elisha Hall, Constable, on the 2d instant, JOHN STRORG, under and arrest for passing counterfeit eighty dollars bills, continental currency of the emission of January 1779; is a thick set fellow, has short black hair, about 5 feet 9 inches high. Whoever will take up said prisoner and return him to me, or secure him in any goal and give me intelligence so that I can have him again, shall have the above reward and necessary charges paid, by
    ELISHA HALE Constable. Glastonbury, July 10, 1780.
The Connecticut Courant, And The Weekly Intelligencer, July 18, 1780; July 25, 1780; August 8, 1780. The second and third ads show the runaway's name as STRONG.

ONE THOUSAND DOLLARS REWARD.

STOLEN from Waterbury, the night after the 7th instant, a dark bay HORSE, about 9 years old, about 15 hands high, a blaze in his face, black mane and tail, some white on his hind feet, trots and paces, carried his head something high, shod all round. The thief is a fellow of middling stature, looks to be about 30 years of age, dark complexion, short black hair, a small round hat, with a narrow yellow lace round the crown, blue coat, streaked waistcoat, white shirt and stock, leather breeches, blue yarn stockings. The above fellow crossed Hartford Ferry about sun-rise the 8th instant, passed through Enfield below noon, and there called his name Smith, passed through Wilbraham just before night; it is supposed he is gone to the north. The above reward for the thief and horse, for the horse only five hundred dollars and all necessary charges paid, by
   DAVID SHAW.   East-Windsor, July 11, 1780.
The Connecticut Courant, And The Weekly Intelligencer, July 18, 1780; July 25, 1780; August 1, 1780.

WHEREAS HANNAH the wife of me the subscriber, has eloped from my bed and board, and otherwise behaved herself in a scandalous manner: These are therefore to caution all persons whatsoever from trusting her on my account, for I will not pay one farthing of any debt she may contract from the date hereof.
   SAMUEL T. COFFIN.   Newport, July 22, 1780.
The Newport Mercury, July 22, 1780; July 29, 1780; August 12, 1780.

RAN away from the Subscriber, on Apprentice Lad, named Abimelech Arnold, between 17 and 18 Years of Age, about 5 Feet 8 Inches high, has dark Hair, of a dark Complexion, and is left-handed. Had on, when he went away, a Rateen Coat, and striped Trowsers, and carried with him other Cloaths. Whoever will secure him, and inform me thereof, shall have Twenty Dollars Reward. All Masters of Vessels, and others, are forbid harbouring or employing said Apprentice.
   CALEB BARTLETT.   Gloucester, July 20, 1780.
The Providence Gazette; And Country Journal, July 22, 1780; July 29, 1780; August 12, 1780; August 19, 1780.

RUN away from the subscriber, on the 18th of July, a negro man named Alexander, 36 years old, about six feet six inches [*sic*] high, speaks good English, in a high and polite stile. Had on when he went away, a light coloured sleeve jacket, striped shirt, and two trowsers, carried with him a blue great coat, with a black velvet collar, trim'd with basket buttons. It is supposed he will attempt to get to Long Island. Whoever will take up and return said negro, shall be entitled to one hundred dollars reward, and all necessary charges paid by

        ELIAS DUNNING, Woodbury.   July 25.

The Connecticut Journal, July 27, 1780; August 3, 1780; August 10, 1780.

RUNAWAY NEGROES!

ON the 26 Inst. two Negroes were taken up in the Sound near the West End of Fisher's-Island in a Canoe, and supposed to have absconded from their Master or Masters, and intending for Long-Island; one of then says his Name is Prince, and the other Gilliam. Prince is about 45 Years old, large and well set, had on a grey Jacket, Towcloth Shirt and white Hat; says he belongs to John Williams, Esq. of Stonington. Gilliam is 19 Years old, small and very black and likely; had on a blue Camblet Coat and brown Cloth Overalls, says he came from Swansey; but he's said was lately inlisted in the Continental Army; they are both committed to Goal. The Owner may have them, paying Charges, by applying to

        JAMES HOLT,   in New-London.

The Connecticut Gazette; And The Universal Intelligencer, July 28, 1780.

RUN away from the subscriber on the 18th of June last, a Servant Boy, about 15 years of age, named Gideon Owen, of a light complection and light hair, a guilty fox eye; had on when he went away, a light brown coat and vest, linen trowsers and a straw hat. I do hereby forbid all persons harbouring or crediting him on my account.—Whoever will take up said Boy and return him to me the subscriber at Canaan, shall have five dollars reward and no charges paid.

        DANIEL BEEBE.   June 22, 1780.

The Connecticut Courant, and Hartford Weekly Intelligencer, August 1, 1780; August 8, 1780.

        Broke out of Goal last Thursday

Morning, James Ryder Mowet, about 5 feet 9 inches high, had on a short green coat, trimmed with narrow gold lace, striped trowsers, light complexion.— David Mowet, about 5 feet 6 inches high, had a brown coat, round hat, very red face.— Samuel Chapman, had a green short coat, trimmed with narrow gold lace, a fur cap, wore boots, short curl'd hair, about 5 feet 10 inches high, very full fac'd, prisoners of war.— William Sampson, about 5 feet 7 inches high, had a round hat, a blue crape coat, thin fac'd, long black hair.— John Paine, about 5 feet 6 inches high, had a uniform coat, brown hair.— Stephen Paine, about 5 feet 7 inches high, had light colour'd cloaths, long grown hair, a small hat, with a gold button and

loup. Whoever will take up any of the above persons and secure them, so that they may be brought to justice, shall have Five Hundred Dollars reward for each, by
     JOSEPH OTIS, Dept. Goaler.   Boston, Aug. 5, 1780.
The Boston-Gazette, And The Country Journal, August 7, 1780; August 14, 1780; *The Independent Chronicle and the Universal Advertiser*, August 10, 1780; August 17; August 24, 1780. Minor differences between the papers. See *The Continental Journal, And Weekly Advertiser*, June 29, 1780, for the Paines.

RUN away from the subscriber the 26th of July last, a Negro Man named BILL, about 29 years of age, 5 feet 10 inches high, a well set fellow, talks good English, has been brought up to farming; had on when he went away a linen coat and vest, and carried with him a sacking bag full of cloaths, markt A P H; had a brown surtout coat, a brown coat and vest, a pair of deer-skin breeches, and a number of other cloathing; and stole a likely red roan Mare, 14 hands high, with a white streak in her forehead, a natural pacer, no shoes one, no brand; also an old breasted Saddle without housing or crooper. Whoever will take up said thief, and mare and return them to the subscriber at Simsbury, or secure them so that they may be had and send word, shall have three hundred dollars reward, or two hundred for either, and charges paid, by
     AHIJAH PETTIBONE.   August 4, 1780.
The Connecticut Courant, And The Weekly Intelligencer, August 8, 1780; August 15, 1780. See *The Connecticut Gazette; And The Universal Intelligencer*, September 8, 1780.

     One Hundred Dollars Reward.
STOLEN out of the House of the Subscriber, in Richmont, on the eighth instant, two pair of Leather Breeches, one pair of white Cotton Stockings, one pair white Woollen one pair of pale blue Worsted, a striped linen Vest, a check'd linen Shirt, a check'd silk Handkerchief, a linen half Handkerchief, mostly blue, also about 50 or 60 Continental dollars, some small pieces of Silver: Supposed to be taken by one James Shepard who came over with Burgoyne, an Englishman, had on a dark brown Coat, a new pair of two trowsers, a tow vest threaded, an old pair shoes, tied with strings, a felt hat, with small brims, with a white hair [o]. Whoever will take up said thief, so that he may be brought to condign punishment shall be intitled to the above reward, and necessary charges, paid by
     CALVIN TILDEN.   Richmont, August 10, 1780.
The Connecticut Courant, And The Weekly Intelligencer, August 15, 1780; August 22, 1780.

Three Hundred Dollars Reward.
RUN AWAY from the Subscriber in Westfield, on Sunday Night the 13th Instant, a Negro Man named JIM, about 27 Years old; he formerly belonged to Mr. Isaac Jones, and afterwards to Mr. Douglass of New Haven, who call'd him by the Name of HARRY; he is about 5 Feet 10 Inches high, well proportioned, pretty black, has an Impediment in his Speech; 'tis thought he will endeavour to get to Long Island; 'tis uncertain what Clothes he will wear; carried with him a loose Coat of a butternut Colour with a little Mixture of White and a red plush Cape, a dark brown broadcloth Coat and Vest, a short blue broadcloth Coat, a brown linen Ditto, a striped damascus Vest, a homespun butternut coloured Ditto, a good Pair of Buckskin Breeches, a Pair of blue broadcloth Ditto, a Pair of white linen Ditto, several Pair of Stockings, a good pair Shoes, Silver Shoe and Knee Buckles, a good Felt Hat and straw Ditto. Whoever will take up said Negro, and return him to the Subscriber at Westfield, or Mr. John Atwater at Cheshire, or secure him in some Goal and give Notice so that the Subscriber may have him, shall receive three Hundred Dollars Reward, and necessary Charges paid.
          JOHN ATWATER.   Westfield, 14th August, 1780.
The Connecticut Journal, August 17, 1780; August 24, 1780; August 31, 1780. See *The Connecticut Courant, And The Weekly Intelligencer,* August 22, 1780.

Two Hundred Dollars Reward.
Ran-away from the Subscriber,
living in *Berkly* in the County of *Bristol,* a Negro Boy named *Titus,* about 15 Years old, had on when he went away, a white Shirt, a pair of striped Trowsers pretty much worn, and a round painted Hatt.—Whoever will take up said Negro, and secure him in any Goal in this State, or bring him to me, shall receive the above Reward, and all necessary Charges.
          JAMES NICHOLLS.
The Independent Chronicle and the Universal Advertiser, August 21, 1780; August 28, 1780; September 4, 1780 *The Independent Ledger, and the American Advertiser,* August 21, 1780; August 28, 1780; September 4, 1780; September 11, 1780

Three Hundred Dollars Reward.
RUN-away on sunday night the 13th instant, a Negro Man named JIM, 27 years old; he formerly belonged to Mr. Isaac Jones, and afterwards to Mr. Douglass of New-Haven, who called him by the name of Harry; is about 5 feet 10 inches high, well proportioned, has an impediment in his speech, 'tis uncertain what cloaths he will wear; carried with him a loose coat of a butternut colour with a little mixture of white, and a red plush cape, a dark

brown broadcloth coat and vest, a short blue broadcloth coat, a striped damascus vest, a home-made butternut coloured ditto, a good pair of buckskin breeches, a pair of blue broadcloth do. a pair of linnen do. a white holland shirt, a homespun checked do. a brown linen coat, a pair of brown tow cloth trowsers, a felt and a straw hat, several pair of stockings, a good pair of shoes, silver shoe and knee buckles. Whoever will take up said Negro and return him to the subscriber at Westfield, or Mr. John Atwater at Cheshire, or secure him and give notice so that the subscriber may have him, shall receive the above reward and necessary charges paid.
    JOHN ATWATER.   Westfield, August 14, 1780.
The Connecticut Courant, And The Weekly Intelligencer, August 22, 1780; August 29, 1780; September 5, 1780. See *The Connecticut Journal,* August 17, 1780.

TAKE NOTICE, That on Saturday last, a Lad about 11 years of age, named John Alley, went away from his Habitation. He had on a blue Jacket, white long Trowsers, striped Shirt, light Hair, and without a Hat. Whoever will give information of him to the Printers hereof, shall be well rewarded for their Trouble.
The Boston Gazette, And Country Journal, August 28, 1780.

RUN-AWAY from the Subscriber, a certain THOMAS KELVIN, Prisoner of War to the United States: had on when he went away, a Tow Cloth Coat, Vest and Breeches, a brass Button to his Hat: about five Feet six Inches High, dark curl'd Hair. Whoever will up and return said Prisoner to EZEKIEL WILLIAMS, Esq. Commissary of Prisoners, shall have all reasonable Charges paid,
    by Wm. JEPSON.   Hartford, August 26, 1780.
The Connecticut Courant, And The Weekly Intelligencer, August 29, 1780; September 5, 1780.

Broke out of the Goal in this
Town, on the Night of the 3d Instant, the following British Officers, Prisoners of War, viz.—Capt. *Thomas Sandford,* Lieut. *Hugh Davis,* and Lieut. *John Miller.* Said *Sandford* had on a Red Coat, trimmed with Silver, and Nankeen Waistcoat and Overalls, about 5 Feet 9 Inches high, brown Hair; *Davis* and *Miller* had on short green Coats trimmed with narrow Gold Lance, and Nankeen Waistcoat and Overalls, about 5 Feet 9 Inches high, brown Hair.—Whoever will apprehend any of the above Persons, and secure them so that they may be brought to Justice, shall have 400 Dollars reward for each, by
    EPHRAIM JONES, Dep. Goaler. *Concord, September* 4, 1780.

The Continental Journal And Weekly Advertiser, September 7, 1780; September 14, 1780; *The Independent Chronicle and the Universal Advertiser,* September 7, 1780; September 14, 1780; September 21, 1780. See *The Connecticut Journal,* September 14, 1780, and *Thomas's Massachusetts Spy Or, American Oracle of Liberty,* September 14, 1780.

RAN away from the Subscriber the 26th of July last, a negro Man named BELL, about twenty nine Years old, a well set lusty Fellow, talks good English, has been bro't up to farming Business, had on when he went away a linnen Coat and vest, carried with him a sacking Bag full of Cloaths, had a brown Surtout, a brown Coat, a Pair of deer-skin Breeches, and a Number of other Cloathing, the Bag was marked A. P. He stole a likely redish brown MARE, about six Years old, fourteen Hands high, natural paces, has a white Streak in her Forehead, rode and old breasted Saddle, without any housing or Crooper, she had no shoes on, nor any Brand. Whoever will take up said Thief and Mare and bring them to me at Simsbury, or secure them so that they may be had and send Word, shall have THREE HUNDRED DOLLARS REWARD, or two Hundred for either, and all necessary Charges paid by
    ABIJAH PETTIBONE.   Simsbury, Aug. 6, 1780.
The Connecticut Gazette; And The Universal Intelligencer, September 8, 1780; September 15, 1780; September 22, 1780. See *The Connecticut Courant, And The Weekly Intelligencer,* August 8, 1780.

Twenty Silver Dollars Reward.
STOLEN out of the pasture of Israel Gardner, of Swanzey, on the night of the 4th inst. a pair of oxen. The theft was committed by one John Arnold, who took them to Rhode-Island, and sold them to Robert Lawton; he there called himself William Smith. He is about five feet ten inches high, well set, has long black hair, much pitted with the small-pox, born, in Morristown, New-Jersey; had on a striped linen coat, jacket and breeches, and white ribbed thread stockings. Whoever will take up said thief, and deliver him to either of us the subscribers, so that he may be brought to justice, shall have the above reward, and all necessary charges, paid by
    ISRAEL GARDNER, of Swanzey.
    ROBERT LAWTON, of Portsmouth.   September 8, 1780.
The Newport Mercury, September 8, 1780; September 25, 1780. See *The Providence Gazette; And Country Journal,* September 9, 1780.

Ranaway from the subscriber
in Berwick, on Saturday the second Instant, a Negro Man named Boston, about 34 years old, about five Feet eight inches high; a thick set Fellow;

speaks good English. Whoever will apprehend said Negro, and convey him to his said Master of commit him to any Goal, and give Information to the subscriber, shall receive One Hundred Dollars Reward, and all necessary Charges paid.
     Noah Ricker.   Berwick, Sept. 8, 1780.
The New-Hampshire Gazette; Or, State Journal, and General Advertiser, September 9, 1780; September 16, 1780; October 7, 1780; October 14, 1780; October 21, 1780. See *The New-Hampshire Gazette, and Historical Chronicle*, August 12, 1774.

Twenty Silver Dollars Reward.

S*Tolen out of the Pasture of Israel Gardner, of Swanzey, on the Night of the 4th Inst. a pair of oxen. The theft was committed by one John Arnold, who took them to Rhode-Island, and sold them to Robert Lawton; he there called himself William Smith; he is about 5 Feet 10 Inches high, well set, has long black Hair, much pitted with the Small-Pox, born, in Morristown, New-Jersey; had on a striped Linen Coat, Jacket and Breeches, and white ribbed Thread Stockings. Whoever will take up said Thief, and deliver him to the Subscriber, or to said Lawton, at Portsmouth, Rhode-Island, so that he may be brought to Justice, shall have the above Reward, and necessary Charges.*
    ISRAEL GARDNER.   *Portsmouth, Sept.* 8, 1780.
The Providence Gazette; And The Country Journal, September 9, 1780; September 16, 1780; September 30, 1780; October 4, 1780. See *The Newport Mercury,* September 8, 1780.

A Woman who call'd herself

by the Name of Mrs. Griffin, belonging to Boston, living in Pudding-Lane, hired of me the Subscriber a Horse and Chaise to go to Worcester; a black Mare, Hog Main, with White on her hind Feet, about Nine Years Old, 14 Hands high, Trots all; the Chaise of a Chocolate Colour, with a Canvas Top, Roll up all Round. Said Horse and Chaise was hired from me the 5th Day of August: Whoever will inform me of said Horse and Chaise, and said Woman that carryed off said Horse and Chaise, and bring them to me shall receive *One Thousand Dollars* Reward, with all necessary Charges; or *Five Hundred Dollars* for the Horse and Chaise without the Woman.
    Per me, RICHARD TRUMBALL, of Charlestown.
The Boston-Gazette, And The Country Journal, September 11, 1780; September 18, 1780; September 25, 1780.

THREE HUNDRED DOLLARS Reward.

ON Friday might, the first instant, a negro man, named Reuben, escaped from the subscriber, innholder in East Haven; he is about 23 years old, very

black, five feet and an half high, thick-set, is simple, affects to be very complaisant, and talks but little; had on a redish homespun surtout, with a red cape, pretty much worn, a striped linen shirt, brown homespun jacket, striped over-halls, and a felt. [sic] As the subscriber had a white wood canoe, (with a crack in her stern, and a wooden bolt to secure it) taken off at the same time, it is supposed the negro went off in her, intending to reach Long Island, but has not been heard of since. Whoever shall take up the negro and canoe, and return them to the owner, shall receive the above reward, or 200 dollars for the negro, and 100 for the canoe, and all necessary charges paid by me,
                  SAMUEL HEMINWAY.   New Haven, Sept. 14, 1780.
The Connecticut Journal, September 14, 1780; September 21, 1780; September 28, 1780.

Last Monday night broke goal at Concord, where they were confined for violating their paroles, the imperious Capt. Sanford, and Lieuts. Miller and Davis, of the infamous, renegado, Tarlton's cavelry, [sic] in the service of the tyrant of Britain.
The Connecticut Journal, September 14, 1780. See *The Continental Journal And Weekly Advertiser,* September 7, 1780, and *Thomas's Massachusetts Spy Or, American Oracle of Liberty,* September 14, 1780.

Last Monday night broke gaol at Concord, where they were confined for violating their paroles, the imperious Capt. Sanford, and Lieuts. Miller and Davis, of the infamous, brutal, renegado Tarlton's cavalry, in the service of the tyrant of Britain, now at Charlestown, South Carolina, where he has lately evidenced the most inhuman acts of cruelty that were ever heard of, viz. in the massacre of the gallant, amiable Col. Buford and 170 of his corps at Lynche's creek in that State, and which Mr. Clinton congratulated his banditti upon.
Thomas's Massachusetts Spy Or, American Oracle of Liberty, September 14, 1780. See *The Continental Journal And Weekly Advertiser,* September 7, 1780, and *The Connecticut Journal,* September 14, 1780

RANAWAY from his Master WILLIAM COTTON, of Portsmouth, about five Week ago [sic] a NEGRO MAN named Garrack, 25 Years of Age, a stout Fellow, of a yellowish Colour, five Feet ten Inches high, speaks very grum and broken, has scars on his Forehead; part of the Nail of his little Finger on the left Hand squashed off. Had on light Cloth colour'd Breeches, striped Linnen Shirt. Whoever apprehends said Negro, and conveys him to

his said Master, shall have Thirty Pounds Reward, and necessary Charges paid by me
     WILLIAM COTTON. PORTSMOUTH, Sept. 15. 1780.
The New-Hampshire Gazette; Or, State Journal, and General Advertiser, September 16, 1780. See *The New-Hampshire Gazette; Or, State Journal, and General Advertiser*, April 15, 1780, and *The Independent Chronicle and the Universal Advertiser*, April 20, 1780.

FIVE HUNDRED DOLLARS REWARD.

A PERSON who calls his name NATHAN STODER formerly of Groton, having produced forged certificates and orders to the Committee of Pay Table, has hereby obtained from the Treasurer the balances due from the State to William Dansey, and Jonathan Munger, for service in the Continental Army in four notes for each; Those in favor of Dansey are from 5201 to No. 5204; those in favor of Munger are from No. 5197 to 5200, inclusive. The said Stoder is 5 feet 7 or 8 inches high, well set, short dark brown hair, about twenty four or twenty five years old.

 Whoever will apprehend and secure him in Hartford Goal, shall be entitled to the above reward, and all necessary charges paid.
Pay Table Office, ELEAZER WALES,
      FENN WADSWORTH, Committee.
      SAMUEL LYMAN.   September 16th, 1780.
N. B. All persons are cautioned against purchasing the above Notes.

The Connecticut Courant, And The Weekly Intelligencer, September 19, 1780; September 26, 1780; *The Connecticut Journal*, September 28, 1780; October 5, 1780; October 12, 1780. Minor differences between the papers. See *The Connecticut Gazette; And The Universal Intelligencer*, September 22, 1780.

FIVE HUNDRED DOLLARS REWARD.

A PERSON who calls his Name Nathan Stoddard, having produced Certificates and Orders on the Committee of Pay-Table, and thereby obtained the Treasurer's Notes for the Balance due to William Dansey and Jonathan Munger for Service, which Orders and Certificates are supposed to be forged. Whoever will apprehend and secure the said Stoddard in Hartford Goal, shall be entitled to the above Reward, and all necessary Charges. He is about 5 Feet 7 Inches high, has short dark Hair, and is about 25 Years of Age. FENN WADSWORTH,
      ELEAZER WALES, Committee.
      SAMUEL LYMAN.
          Pay-Table Office, September 15. 1780.

The Connecticut Gazette; And The Universal Intelligencer, September 22, 1780; September 29, 1780; October 6, 1780. See *The Connecticut Courant, And The Weekly Intelligencer*, September 19, 1780.

ON the 9th instant, two men, by the names of John Allen and Robert Pulveytaft, hired a horse and mare of us the subscribers to go to Providence, and as they have not yet returned, it is imagined they have run away. The said Allen is upwards of six feet high, had a quantity of cloathing with him, which makes it uncertain as to his dress, and talks the French language very fluently. The dress of Pulveytaft not known. The Mare was a sorrel, with a bald face, white legs, thin of flesh, and had a saddle on her somewhat worn, with a black dressed sheepskin on it for a covering, and a pair of sealskin saddle bags. The Horse was a black, about eight or nine years old, fourteen hands high, branded G. R. on the near fore shoulder, has a white streak on his near fore foot just above his hoof, a full round forehead, and trots and paces freely; had on a bridle, and saddle, the back part of the skirts of which was torn. They likewise carried off another horse, and were seen passing through Little-Rest the same day, in company with two other men, all armed. Whoever will apprehend the said Allen and Pulveytaft, so that they may be brought to justice, and the subscribers recover their Horses, &c. shall receive Five Silver Dollars Reward for each Horse, if found in this State, and Ten Dollars for each, if out of the State, with all necessary charges, paid by
TIMOTHY WATERHOUSE, WILLIAM ANTHONY.
Newport, September, 18, 1780.
The Newport Mercury, September 25, 1780.

WHEREAS my wife ANNA CRYRENA hath had unlawful concern with another man, while I have been absent from her about ten months in the army, by which means she is now pregnant.—I therefore hereby forbid all persons harbouring or trusting her on my account, for I will not pay any debts she shall contract after the date hereof, as I intend to take lawful measures to get rid of her as soon as may be.
REMEMBRANCE FILEY.
Winchester, September 11, 1779. [*sic*]
The Connecticut Courant, And The Weekly Intelligencer, September 26, 1780; October 10, 1780.

BOSTON, September 25.
Last Thursday *Ebenezer Burbank* of Sudbury, who was convicted at the Superior Court, lately held here, for passing counterfeit 50 dollar bills, sit on the gallows one hour with a rope about his neck, agreeable to his sentence. Same day *Thomas Gibbs*, convicted of passing counterfeit 50

dollar bills, received 35 stripes, as also *John Atkinson,* 28, *John Pattin,* 10, *Mary M'Lean* 16, *Mary Higgins* 30, and *Amy Pattin,* 30, at the whipping post, convicted of stealing.
The Norwich Packet and the Weekly Advertiser, October 3, 1780.

BROKE out of the County Goal, the Night after the 21st, one JAMES CHAMPLIN, about 5 Feet high, about 26 Years of Age, had on a white Hatt, red Coattee, and Trowsers. Whoever will take him up and return him to the subscriber shall have THIRTY DOLLARS Reward,
paid by   NATHAN BAYLEY, jun. Goaler.
New-London, 24th Sept. 1780.
The Connecticut Gazette; And The Universal Intelligencer, October 6, 1780; October 17, 1780.

NEW-LONDON, Oct. 10.
At the Superior Court held here last Week, one Asa Chadwick, of Windsor, was convicted of passing a counterfeit 80 Dollar Bill, Continental Currency, and sentenced to three Months Imprisonment in New Gate Goal, and to forfeit his Estate.
The Connecticut Gazette; And The Universal Intelligencer, October 10, 1780.

New-Salem, September 19, 1780.
RAN away from my house in my absence
a woman, aged near 40 years—said woman about 3 weeks before this date, came to my house to seek labour, I consented to take her upon tryal—she was pretendedly from Boston, said she was a widow, and called herself by the name of Allen—the evening before she went away, she discovered a very unhappy and abusive temper to my family—she went off in the morning very early—stole and took with her a Worsted Gown with an Apron, a Linnen Shirt and a Quilted Coat—she may be known by a scald in her left hand which has scarred and crippled her fingers, also by a lying tongue, for since she left my house she had spread many false and prejudicial reports which ought to be suppressed—all persons are cautioned against taking her into their families as their names and estates will be endangered thereby.

N. B. Since she left my house it is supposed that she came from the Barracks at Rutland and returned thither. If any person will apprehend said thief, recover the things stolen, and bring her to justice, they shall be entitled to the respects of the subscriber, and to a reasonable reward.
JOEL FOSTER.
Thomas's Massachusetts Spy Or, American Oracle of Liberty, October 12, 1780; October 19, 1780; October 26, 1780.

WHEREAS Abigal wife to the subscriber, has behaved in a very unbecoming manner, and there is danger of her running me into debt. This is to warn all persons not to harbor or trust her on my account after this date, on peril of the law.   ANDREW SPALDING. Nov. 4. 1780.
The Connecticut Courant, And The Weekly Intelligencer, November 14, 1780. See *The Connecticut Courant, And The Weekly Intelligencer*, April 10, 1781.

WHEREAS ANNA, the wife of me the Subscriber, regardless on the solemn obligation of the marriage covenant, did in the month of August last, elope from my bed and board, and hath ever since absented herself, and hath falsely reported that she receives such abuses from me that she could not dwell with me: by all which false reports she is endevouring to scandilize and blacken my character, and destroy my interest. As to the pretended abuses, I leave to be judged by the candor of those acquainted with my family, I know of no grounds for such reports, but ever acted the part of a kind husband to her, and did in April last give her a large sum of money, to expend for her comfort and support: and at the time she left my house there was nothing on my past that in the least could justify her conduct therein: but as she is subject to fits, I have reason to think, that while she is under the opperation she is desirous to seek other company, which fits are hereditary to the family from which she originated. I do therefore forbid all persons harbouring or trusting the said Anna on my account, as I will not pay any debt of her contracting after the date hereof.
       JOHN THOMSON.   Palmer, October 25, 1780.
The Connecticut Courant, And The Weekly Intelligencer, November 14, 1780.

One Thousand Dollars Reward.
STOLEN from the Subscriber, a very likely Black HORSE; 15 hands high, 6 years old, branded on his near buttock with the letters B. B. trots and canters well: The thief, calls his name John Clark, had on a light blue coat, red vest, striped overhalls, is about 25 years of age, pock-broken; was seen in Colchester the 15th of September last. Whoever will take up said horse and thief, shall have the above reward, or five hundred for the horse only, paid by
Wm. GOODRICH.   Stockbridge, October 5, 1780.
The Connecticut Courant, and Hartford Weekly Intelligencer, October 17, 1780; October 24, 1780.

Two Hundred Dollars Reward.
RUN-AWAY from the Subscriber, the 2d of Sept. last, a yellowish likely Negro Boy, named TOM, about 15 years old; had on when he went away, a dark brown vest; has a scar on his right arm, near the shoulder. Whoever will return said negro to me, shall receive the above reward, and necessary charges.   JOHN PHELPS.   Westfield, October 3, 1780.
The Connecticut Courant, and Hartford Weekly Intelligencer, October 17, 1780; October 24, 1780.

MADE their escape from the goal in this place the following prisoners, viz. Easton Trowbridge, Miner Miles, Henry Gibbs, assigned for New-gate; also John Frost, or Bush, for passing counterfeit money, assigned for New Gate: It is supposed they will make for the sea shore, it is desired the friends of the country will look out for them, Whoever will secure the above prisoners so that the goaler can get them into his custody, shall be handsomely rewarded and all reasonable charges paid, by
EZEKIEL WILLIAMS, Sheriff.   Hartford, October 26, 1780.
The Connecticut Courant, And The Weekly Intelligencer, October 31, 1780. See *The Connecticut Gazette; And The Universal Intelligencer*, November 14, 1780.

WHEREAS NOMY, Wife of the Subscriber, has behaved in a very indecent Manner, and there is great Danger of running me in Debt: This is therefore to warn all Persons not to trust her on my account, as I will not pay any Debt of her contracting, after the Date hereof.
NED FREEMAN.   Groton, October 16, 1780.
The Connecticut Gazette; And The Universal Intelligencer, October 31, 1780.

RAN away from the Subscriber, on the 2d Instant, an Apprentice Boy, named Joram Hopkins, about 15 Years of Age, of a light Complexion; had on a Kersey Jacket and Trowsers, and new thick Shoes. All Masters of Vessels and others are forbid to harbour or carry him off. Whoever will return said Apprentice to his Master, shall have One Shilling Reward.
JOHN WELLS.   Gloucester, Nov. 6, 1780.
The Providence Gazette; And Country Journal, November 8, 1780; November 15, 1780; November 22, 1780; November 29, 1780.

Medford, Nov. 8. 1780.
On the Evening of Saturday, 23d Ult. was taken from the House of the underwritten, by a certain Edmund Purk, a small deep bay Horse, black Mane and Tail, with a black Stripe down his Rump, well built, trots chiefly, rising 9 Years—Also a Saddle and Bridle,

the Saddle without Sadle Cloth, the Bridle a black one with a Snaffle Bit.—The said absconded Purk has on a small round Hat, a blue Coat, with a Gold Sprig work'd Button, rib'd Velvet Jacket and Breeches of a brownish Colour, white Cotton Stockings, square plated Buckles. I now offer a Reward of *One Thousand Dollars* to any Person who will apprehend the Fellow, or one moiety for either.
BEN. SHAW.

As the above Fellow was low in Cash, 'tis presumed he sold the Horse in Boston, or its Circumj[ecen]ies.

The Independent Chronicle and the Universal Advertiser, November 9, 1780; November 16, 1780.

Three Hundred Dollars Reward.

RUN-AWAY from the subscriber, living in New-Britain, on the 6th inst. an Apprentice Lad, named SILAS SEARE, a native of Long Island, about 19 years of age, very thick set, 5 feet 8 inches high; had on, or carried with him, a reddish brown coat and vest, 1 pair of light coloured cloth breeches, 1 do. leather, a new large brim'd hat, silver shoe and knee buckles, a brown surtout, with a velvet cape, and sundry other articles too tedious to mention. Whoever will take up said runaway and return him to the subscriber, shall receive the above reward.

ELIJAH HINSDALE. New-Britain, Nov. 10. 1780.

The Connecticut Courant, and Hartford Weekly Intelligencer, November 14, 1780; November 21, 1780.

RANAWAY from the subscriber about three weeks since, a NEGRO MAN named DICK; about five feet high, speaks good English and Low-Dutch; had on a frock, and an old brown coat, an old felt hat, with a leather strap round the crown, a pair of tow-cloth trowsers, a new pair of double-solaed shoes.—'Tis supposed he is now lurking about Westfield or Northampton.—Whoever will return said Negro to his master, shall receive FIVE HUNDRED DOLLARS reward, paid by

ABEL TILLOTSON. Granville, Nov. 6. 1780.

The Connecticut Courant, and Hartford Weekly Intelligencer, November 14, 1780.

NEW-LONDON, Nov. 14.

Last Saturday night, was taken out of the harbour of New-Haven, Capt. Brown's pettiaugre and Capt. Gourly's boat, laden with lumber, and carried over to Long-Island, by one Miles and Trowbridge, who broke out of Hartford Goal.

The Connecticut Gazette; And The Universal Intelligencer, November 14, 1780; *The Providence Gazette; And Country Journal*, November

29, 1780. See *The Connecticut Courant, And The Weekly Intelligencer*, October 31, 1780.

FRIDAY Evening the 17th Instant, made his Escape from the Custody of his Keepers at Cambridge, in the County of Middlesex, one THOMAS SACKVILLE TUFTON, of Groton, indicted the same Day for passing Counterfeit Money, knowing it to be such. Said Tufton is a small, genteel, well-dressed Man:—Had on when he made his Escape, a Suit of light colour'd Cloaths, a blue Hussar Cloak with a red Lining.—Whoever will apprehend and secure the said Tufton in any of the Public Goals in this Commonwealth, shall receive TWENTY DOLLARS Reward in Money of the new Emission, and all necessary Charges paid by

LOAMMI BALDWIN, Sheriff of the County of Middlesex.

Cambridge, Nov. 18, 1780.

The Boston-Gazette, And Country Journal, November 20, 1780; November 27, 1780; December 4, 1780.

Two Hundred SILVER DOLLARS *Reward.*
State of Rhode-Island, &c.

BROKE GAOL, this Evening, *GEORGE HOWELL*, confined on Suspicion of being a SPY from the Enemy: He is a slim tall Man, about 22 Years of Age, of genteel, easy Address, and bred as a Physician, which Character he may assume to effect his Escape, though lately he has dealt largely in dry Goods, as a Merchant. The Dress he went off in cannot be described, as he escaped in the Dark, and had Friends capable of lending him every possible Assistance to get off.

Whoever will apprehend said *George Howell*, and secure him in any of the Gaols of this or either of the United States, shall have *Two Hundred Silver Dollars Reward*, and Charges, paid by

JOHN BEVERLY, Sheriff.   *Providence, Nov.* 19, 1780.

The Providence Gazette; And Country Journal, November 22, 1780; November 29, 1780; December 6, 1780.

WHEREAS Abigail the wife of the subscriber, has left my bed and board without any just occasion. These are to desire all persons not to trust her on my account, as I will pay no debts of her contracting after this date.

JEREMIAH BEEBE.   Norwich, Nov. 28.

The Norwich Packet and the Weekly Advertiser, November 28, 1780; December 12, 1780.

One Joe Reward.

Ran away from the Subscriber, a Negro Man, about 5 and a half Feet high, Coal black, Bermuda born, goes by the Name of WILL STILES or WILL

POST. Whoever will take up said Negro, and consign him in any Goal, and give Notice to the Printer hereof, shall receive one Joe Reward and all Charges.   JOHN LITHLOURN.   Nov. 30.
The Independent Chronicle and the Universal Advertiser, November 30, 1780; December 7, 1780.

SATURDAY Night escaped from the Goal in this Place, *Isaac Doolittle*, of Cheshire, committed for passing counterfeit Money, about 23 Years old, middling Size; had on a regimental red Coat. Whoever will return him to said Goal, shall be paid Twenty Dollars Reward for their Trouble.
STEPHEN MUNSON, Goaler. New Haven, Nov. 30, 1780.
The Connecticut Journal, December 6, 1780; December 21, 1780.

Whereas *Susan*, my Wife, hath eloped from me, and every Means hath been used, both by my own invitations as well as the Persuasions of sundry Friends, to reclaim her, but to no purpose: I therefore forbid all Persons from trusting her on my Account, as I will pay no Debts she may contract from the Date hereof.
N. B. I forbid Simon Mellon, Nathaniel Pike, jun. and Jonathan Pike from harbouring said Susan.
JOSEPH HANCOCK.   Hopkinton, Oct. 30, 1780.
The Independent Chronicle and the Universal Advertiser, December 7, 1780; December 21, 1780.

Whereas SARAH, who should have been the wife of me the subscriber, hath acted ridiculous to the marriage covenant, right reason and common sense:—This is therefore to forewarn all persons from trading, bargaining or contracting any thing with her, as they shall answer it at the peril of law.
SIMEON PALMER, Charlton.
Thomas's Massachusetts Spy Or, American Oracle of Liberty, December 14, 1780; December 21, 1780. See *Thomas's Massachusetts Spy Or, American Oracle of Liberty*, December 21, 1780.

Sixteen Hundred Dollars Reward.
BROKE out of the Gaol in this town, in the night of the 15th instant, one George Bailey, an old countryman, 5 feet 8 inches high, about 25 years of age, light complexion, long reddish hair pin'd on the top of his head; had on a light coloured serge coat, brown rib'd velvet jacket and breeches, and a felt hat with a large brim.

Also made his escape at the same time, John Ryley, (alias King) an Irishman, a sailor, 5 feet 8 inches high, 25 years of age, darkish complection, a sprightly fellow; had on a striped flannel jacket, a striped linen shirt, a pair of brown woollen drawers, and an old round beaver hat; likewise took with him a green rug.

Whoever will apprehend and return said villains to the subscriber, or give information so that he may secure them again, shall receive the above reward; or one thousand dollars for Bailey alone, or six hundred for Ryley, and all reasonable charges.

MOSES CLEVELAND, Gaoler.   Norwich, Dec. 5.

The Norwich Packet and the Weekly Advertiser, December 19, 1780; December 26, 1780; January 2, 1781.

TWENTY ROUND DOLLARS REWARD,
and all reasonable Charges.

Ran away from *James Mitchell*, of Weathersfield, in the State of Connecticut, two Servants; one a Molatto Boy, about 15 Years old, named PRINCE, very large of his Age; had on, when he went from home, white Yarn Stockings with small Seams, Leather Breeches, a light Waist and Coatee Coat, and light Great-Coat, grey Wool Hat, striped Woolen Shirt, and Copper Buckles—The other a middling Size, well set, named ROBIN, rather black, with a light brown Great-Coat, and very old Breeches, when new a Logwood-colour, a Blemish in one Eye, so that he keeps it always shut.—Any Person take takes up said Negroes, and secures them, so that I may have them again, shall be entitled to the above Reward, or *Ten Dollars* for either.—All Masters of Vessels are cautioned against harbouring or carrying off said Negroes.   Boston, Dec. 10, 1780.

The Independent Chronicle and the Universal Advertiser, December 21, 1780; December 28, 1780; January 4, 1781. See *The Providence Gazette; And Country Journal*, December 27, 1780, and *The Connecticut Courant, And Weekly Advertiser,* January 2, 1781.

Charlton, December 18, 1780.
WHEREAS SIMEON PALMER,
man delirious, has of late forbid any person trading with SARAH his wife, as he will not pay any debt she may contract, which will operate very much to the inconvenience of said Sarah as he the said Simeon has since took a journey and left her, and no person to take any care of her, which we are confident he would not have done had he been in the free exercise of his reason.   CALEB AMMIDOWN, ISAIAH BLOOD,
JOHN BLOOD, CALEB RIDER, RICHARD DRESSER.

Thomas's Massachusetts Spy Or, American Oracle of Liberty, December 21, 1780; December 28, 1780. See *Thomas's Massachusetts Spy Or, American Oracle of Liberty*, December 14, 1780.

Hartford, December 18, 1780.
LAST night the county goal was broke open, and the following prisoners made their escape, viz. ENOCH JOHNSON, JAMES WILSON, FRANCIS NOBLE, and DANIEL FAIRCHILD, Traitors. DARLING SEALECK, NATHAN SEALECK, HEREKIAH SCRIBNER, ARCHIBALD HIGENS, Prisoners of War. Whoever will take up said prisoners, and secure them, so that the subscriber can get them into his custody again, have HANDSOME REWARD and reasonable charges.
WILLIAM BARNARD, Goaler.
The Connecticut Courant, And The Weekly Intelligencer, December 26, 1780.

RAN away from the subscriber, a Negro Woman named Esther, 36 years old, carried with her a Negro girl about 3 years old.—Whoever will return said slaves to the subscriber shall be handsomely rewarded, and all necessary charges paid, by
JOHN CARTEY.   Colchester, December 12, 1780.
N. B. All Persons are forbid harbouring said slaves on penalty of the law.
The Connecticut Gazette; And The Universal Intelligencer, December 26, 1780; January 2, 1781; January 9, 1781.

Twenty hard Dollars Reward.
RAN away from James Mitchell, of Weathersfield, in the State of Connecticut, two Servants; one a Mulatto BOY, about 15 Years of Age, very large of his Age; had on, when he went from Home, white Yarn Stockings, Leather Breeches, a light Vest and Coat, a light Great-Coat, a grey Wool Hat, and a striped woollen Shirt:—The other a middle-sized well-set NEGRO; had on a light brown Great Coat, and very old Breeches; has a Blemish in one Eye, which he keeps always shut. Any Person take takes up said Servants, and secures them, so that they may be had again, shall be entitled to the above Reward, or TEN DOLLARS for either, and all reasonable Charges. *JAMES MITCHELL.*
N. B. All Masters of Vessels are cautioned against harbouring or carrying off said Servants.
The Providence Gazette; And Country Journal, December 27, 1780; January 3, 1781; January 10, 1781. See *The Independent Chronicle and the Universal Advertiser*, December 21, 1780, and *The Connecticut Courant, And Weekly Advertiser*, January 2, 1781.

Five Thousand Dollars Reward.
BROKE Gaol this morning, and made his escape from my custody, John Williams, jun. of Shrewsbury,

Innholder, very dark complexion, about five feet six inches high, confined for passing counterfeit money, and supposed to be guilty of High Treason. Whoever will take up said Williams, and bring him to me, or confine him in any Gaol in the United States, so that I may have him again, shall have the abovementioned reward, and all necessary charges paid by
INCREASE BLAKE, Gaoler. *Worcester, December* 25th, 1780.
N. B. A young Woman, of my family went off with said Williams, and took with her several silk gowns: she is supposed to be still with him.
Thomas's Massachusetts Spy Or, American Oracle of Liberty, December 28, 1780; January 4, 1781; January 11, 1781; January 18, 1781.

1781

1500 *Continental* Dollars Reward.
Made his escape from the Subscriber, last Night, one *Moses Pond*, of Medway, who was under a conveyance to Goal, suspected of being concerned in knowingly uttering and passing Counterfeit Bills. He is of a stall Stature, light Complection, and loud spoken. Whoever will take up said Pond, and deliver him to me, or secure him in any Goal, so that he may be bro't to justice, shall receive the above Reward.
Moses Mann, Constable of Medway.
Medway, Dec. 26, 1780.
The Independent Ledger, and the American Advertiser, January 1, 1781; January 8, 1781; January 15, 1781; January 22, 1781; February 5, 1781. See *The Providence Gazette; And Country Journal,* March 3, 1781.

RUN AWAY from JAMES MITCHELL, of Weathersfield, in Connecticut, a negro man, called ROBBIN, about thirty years of age, a middle sized, well set fellow. Wore away a light coloured coat and vest, the coat without buttons or buttonholes; had with him a brown great coat, the cape ripped open. He has a blemish in his left eye and keeps it shut, a scar in his forehead. Whoever will take up said negro, and return him to the subscriber, or secure him and send word where he may be found, shall have TEN SPANISH MILLED DOLLARS as a reward, and all reasonable charges paid, by   JAMES MITCHELL.
All masters of vessels are forbid harbouring or carrying off said negro.
The Connecticut Courant, And Weekly Advertiser, January 2, 1781; January 9, 1781; January 16, 1781. See *The Independent Chronicle and the Universal Advertiser*, December 21, 1780 and *The Providence Gazette; And Country Journal*, December 27, 1780.

STOPPED about the last of December from a strolling Fellow who calls his Name Robinson, a fine LAWN APRON, rough dried almost new, on Suspicion it was stole. The right Owner may have it, by applying to Capt. Douglass's Tavern in New-London, and paying Charges.
The Connecticut Gazette; And The Universal Intelligencer, January 9, 1781.

One Thousand Dollars Reward.
ABsconded from his Master, last Saturday Evening, a Negro Man, named JERICHO, a likely well made Fellow: He had on when he went away, a green outside Jacket, lined with red Baize, and a Pair of red Baize Trowsers. Whoever will apprehend the said Servant, and convey him to Mr. JOHN JENKINS, shall be entitled to the above Reward.
N. B. All Masters of Vessels and others, are hereby cautioned not to conceal or carry off the said Servant, as they would avoid the Penalty of the Law.   Providence. January 9, 1781.
The American Journal And General Advertiser, January 13, 1781; January 20, 1781; January 27, 1781.

Whereas *Violet*, my Wife, neglects her Duty in my Family, going abroad and idling her Time, to my great Damage; so that, to keep from Ruin, I am obliged to remove to a Place where she may have less Company to tempt her abroad; and whereas she hath refused to go with me, and so in my Absence may run me in Debt, to my utter Ruin: I therefore forbid any Person or Persons crediting her to my Account, as I am determined not to pay any Debt she may contract from the Date hereof.
                    CATO GARDNER.   Boston, January 17, 1781.
The Continental Journal, And Weekly Advertiser, January 25, 1781.

RUNAWAY from the Subscriber, on the night of the 9th instant, an Apprentice Boy, named LEMUEL COOL; 14 years of age, about 5 feet high, light complexion, dark brown hair: had on when he went away, a light brown coat, blue vest and overhalls, and mix'd colour'd stockings. Whoever will return said boy to the subscriber, shall have SIX PENCE reward, paid by
                    NATHANIEL EDGERTON.   Salisbury, January 28, 1781.
The Connecticut Courant And Weekly Advertiser, January 30, 1781; February 13, 1781.

WHEREAS, Susannah Hurlbut of Farmington. (a single woman) resided at my house, a few days, the last Summer, during which time I lost a pair of linen Sheets (the said Susannah being a stranger, and I not acquainted with her character) I had suspicions, in my own mind, that she, the said Susannah, has taken them; and did inadvertently say, that I thought and believed she had taken the sheets from my house. I am now fully satisfied that my suspicions were ill founded; and in order to restore the said Susannah's character, I do hereby voluntarily declare, that after the most strict scrutiny, I could find no evidence or traces of evidence to warrant such suspicions against the said Susannah, and do acquit her of the same, and recommend her to the good esteem and charity of all and every person whatsoever, and that I am free and willing that the said Susannah publish this writing to whom she please.
As witness my hand, in Farmington,
this 20th day of Jan. 1781. JAMES JUDD.
The Connecticut Courant And Weekly Advertiser, January 30, 1781.

RUN away from the subscriber the 14th inst. a negro fellow named Isaac, about 25 years of age, has a down cast look, large eyes, very thick lips, and a large scar under his throat, had on a brown homespun jacket and trowsers and striped woollen shirt, took away two coats, one blue broad cloth coat, one brown homespun ditto, went off in company with a free negro wench named Bet, belonging somewhere near Providence. Whoever shall apprehend said fellow, and confine him so that his master may be apprized thereof, shall be handsomely rewarded, and all necessary charges
paid by TITUS HURLBUT. New-London, January 21st. 1781.
The Connecticut Gazette; And The Universal Intelligencer, January 30, 1781; February 9, 1781.

COLCHESTER, January 18th, 1781.
WHEREAS Abigail, Wife of the Subscriber, has in numberless Instances, behaved in the most indecent and scandalous Manner, and on the 18th inst. absconded with another Man, and carried with her a Number of Household Articles and my two Children. These are therefore to forbid all and every Person trusting or entertaining her or harbouring my said Children on Penalty of the Law: And I hereby declare that I will not pay any Debt of her contracting after the Date hereof.
BENJAMIN HOPKINS.
The Connecticut Gazette; And The Universal Intelligencer, January 30, 1781; February 9, 1781.

SIX PENCE REWARD,
CONTINENTAL CURRENCY.

RUN-AWAY from the subscriber, on the twenty-first instant, an Apprentice Lad, named William Mc Carty, about sixteen years of age, had on a brown coat, and breeches of the same, mixt yarn stockings, and a new felt hat.—Whoever will apprehend said Apprentice, and return him to his master, shall be entitled to the above reward—but no charges.
     WILLIAM MORGAN.   Norwich, January 30.
The Norwich Packet; And Weekly The Advertiser, January 30, 1781;February 6, 1781; February 13, 1781; February 20, 1781.

WHEREAS a transient person being taken at Ripton, for passing counterfeit money, made in imitation of the true bills of credit of this State of Connecticut, of Forty Shillings, dated the 1st day of June, 1780, and taken before authority for examination, and upwards of twenty pounds of counterfeit money found with him; and in the evening of the 29th instant January, in a crowd of persons made his escape; he called himself by the name Joseph Higgins, but his name is Joseph Pine Cable, and is said to belong to the State of New-York; is about 5 ½ feet high, 19 years old, fresh complection, short hair, with a false tail; had on when he went away, a small round hat, a light brown great coat, white metal buttons, a brown coat, a red jacket, black breeches, white stockings, and a pair of boots. Whoever will take up said man, and him convey to me the subscriber, or secure him in any gaol in this State, so that I may have him again, shall receive Five Hard Dollars Reward, and all charges
  paid by NATHANIEL BLACKMAN, Constable of Stratford.
                Ripton, January 30. 1781.
The Connecticut Journal, February 2, 1781; February 8, 1781; February 15, 1781; February 22, 1781.

WHEREAS MARY, the Wife of the Subscriber, hath left his Bed and Board, and refuses to live with him: He hereby cautions all Persons against crediting her on his Account, as he will not pay any Debts of her contracting, from the Date hereof.
    CHARLES KING.   *Providence, Feb. 3, 1781.*
The Providence Gazette; And Country Journal, February 3, 1781; February 10, 1781.

WE the Subscribers being appointed by the Town-Council of Westerly, in the State of Rhode-Island, Guardians to Capt. Joshua Thompson, of said Westerly, who is reputed by said Town-Council delirious, distracted, or *non compos-mentis*, notify the Public, that all Debts, Bargains or Contracts, made by said Capt. Joshua Thompson, after the Publication of this Notification, will be considered by us as null, void, and of no Effect.

JAMES BABCOCK,
ABRAHAM PERKINS, Guardians.   *Westerly, Feb.* 2, 1781.
The Providence Gazette; And Country Journal, February 3, 1781.

Whereas *Joshua Winslow* hired of the Subscriber last Friday evening, to go to Cambridge, and to return the next morning, a dark sorrel MARE, in good flesh, 7 years old, 14 ½ hands high, with a small white stripe in her forehead, hind feet white, main cut but grown out again and inclines to the near side, switch tail, low carriage, forward, and carried a good tail, trots and paces, with a saddle and briddle, white wollen saddle cloth, and the pads made of wollen; and as said *Winslow* is not returned, it is presumed he intended to carry off said Mare, this is to give notice to any person that will bring the said *Winslow* and Mare, saddle and briddle, to the subscriber, shall receive 200 Pounds old
currency, by THOMAS ROBBINS.   Charlestown, February 8, 1781.
N. B. Said *Winslow* is 32 years of age, 5 feet 9 inches high, light complexion, wore a green coat with overalls.
The Continental Journal, And Weekly Advertiser, February 8, 1781; February 15, 1781; *The Independent Chronicle and the Universal Advertiser*, February 8, 1781; February 15, 1781; February 22, 1781.

ON the 7th Instant, at Night, escaped from the Goal in New-Haven, William Burton, and Samuel Graham, committed for being concerned with the Enemy; Burton is short and thick set; Graham is lusty. Also David Sturge, of Reading, in Fairfield County, committed for passing counterfeit Money, he was handsomely dress'd. They are all young Men, about 23 years old. Whoever returns them to said Goal, shall receive Five Pounds Reward, paid by
STEPHEN MUNSON, Goaler.   New-Haven, February 15, 1781.
The Connecticut Journal, February 15, 1781; February 22, 1781.

WENT away from Braintree, in the Month of December last, one *Judas Ned*, about 5 Feet 4 Inches high, with white Hair and a Bull Neck and Head, and a large Wall Eye, destitute of Truth or Honor; had on when he went away, an old red Coat: But as much as People that pass the Road are not so likely to be threatened to be sent to Hell are heretofore, others not to be deceived by his Lies, Women not so likely to be insulted in their own Houses, Days of Fasting and Prayer more regarded. Rioting and Cock-fighting more likely to cease on the Lord's-Day, and the Land is more likely to enjoy the Sabbath than for two Years past, and as there is nothing in his Character that recommends him to the Place again, there will be no Reward given for bringing him back.

N. B. All Persons that are about purchasing Lands of said *Ned*, are desired to search the Records, as they would avoid being cheated as others has heretofore, by purchasing mortgaged Lands of said *Ned.*
The Independent Chronicle and the Universal Advertiser, February 15, 1781.

LET to one GEORGE CALDER, of Boston, to go to Princetown, a large black HORSE, about six years of age, 15 hands high, with switch tail, and a very short dock, and thin mane, very good carriage, with continental mark, trots, paces and canters, with hunting saddle and bridle: The said Calder is about 30 years old, 5 feet 6 inches high, light complexion, grey eyes, brown hair, a Sail-maker by trade, he went off the 17th January. Whoever will take up said Calder and horse, and return them to me, shall have 1000 dollars, old emission, reward; or 100 pounds for said Calder, dead or alive.
    RICHARD TRUMBALL.   Charlestown, Feb. 17.
The Boston-Gazette, And Country Journal, February 19, 1781; February 26, 1781; March 5, 1781.

RUNAWAY from his Master, in Suffield, on the 3d inst. a Negro Man, named BOSTON, about 27 years old, thick set, and well built, of a copper colour: Had on when he went away, a lightish brown broadcloth coat (which has been turn'd) a dark brown broadcloth vest, light coloured camblet breeches, white yarn Stockings, and a white Holland ruffled shirt. Said negro is about 5 feet 6 inches high, speaks good English, and plays poorly on a fiddle. Whoever will return said negro to me, shall have 500 dollars reward, and charges: or, if secured in any of the States gaols, and notice given me, 100 dollars, and all charges paid, by
    SHEM BURBANK.   Suffield, February 6, 1781.
The Connecticut Courant, And Weekly Advertiser, February 20, 1781; February 27, 1781; March 6, 1781. See *The Independent Chronicle and the Universal Advertiser*, March 22, 1781.

RAN away from his master on the 17th ult. an apprentice boy named Cephas Todd, in the 13th year of his age, middling size, of a middling light complection. Whoever will take him up, and return him to his master, shall have Five Shillings reward;—and all masters of vessels and others are forbid carrying off or entertaining said apprentice on penalty of the law.
    GEORGE CONE.   East-Haddam, February 1, 1781.
The Connecticut Gazette; And The Universal Intelligencer, March 2, 1781; March 9, 1781; March 16, 1781.

TAKEN from Canterbury, the 23d inst. a likely iron grey Horse, about 14 hands high, a star in his forehead and a white spot on his heel, by one Samuel

Smith alias Sherman, of Rhode-Island, who was entrusted with said horse, saddle and bridle, and a note against a gentleman in Windham for 28 hard dollars, which note he got satisfied, and run away with the horse, saddle and bridle, money, &c. he is a light coloured man, with a light coloured great coat, leather breeches and handsome boots; he also carried off a note against Jonathan Hebard, of Windham, which is discharged, therefore the public are hereby notified, that they may not be imposed upon, it is supposed he will expose said note for sale. Whoever will take up and secure said thief, so that he may be brought to justice, shall be handsomely rewarded, and for the horse, saddle and bridle Ten Silver Dollars, and necessary charges, paid by
    DANIEL MOREY, of Boston, in Massachusetts.
Windham, Feb. 24, 1781.
The Connecticut Gazette; And The Universal Intelligencer, March 2, 1781; March 16, 1781.

New London, 28th February, 1781.
WHEREAS my wife Nabby, has eloped from my bed and board, and refuses to live with me: I do therefore forbid any person from trusting her on my account, as I will pay no debts of her contracting after this date.
    RICHARD ATWELL.
The Connecticut Gazette; And The Universal Intelligencer, March 2, 1781; March 9, 1781; March 23, 1781.

Four Thousand Dollars Reward.
MADE his Escape from the Subscriber, in the Night preceding the 26th of December last, one MOSES POND, who was apprehended for passing Counterfeit Sixty Dollar Bills: He is of a tall Stature, of a light Complexion, and speaks loud.—Whoever will take up and secure said Pond, shall have the above Reward, paid by
    RALPH MANN, Const.   Medway, March 1, 1781.
The Providence Gazette; And Country Journal, March 3, 1781; March 10, 1781; March 17, 1781. See *The Independent Ledger, and the American Advertiser,* January 1, 1781.

Whereas *Benjamin Hooker,* Apprentice
to me the subscriber, has absented himself from my service several months past, without my consent; this is therefore to forbid all persons harbouring or trusting him on my account, as I will not pay any debts he may contract.
    PATRICK WATSON.   Palmer, February 3, 1781.
The Continental Journal, And Weekly Advertiser, March 8, 1781.

RAN away from the subscriber, a negro fellow named JACK, about five feet two inches high, about thirty-three years old; had on when he went away, a

mixt coloured pair of breeches, full'd cloth jerking and great coat, of a mill colour; he is a very likely black, and most commonly has a fiddle with him. Whoever will take up said fellow and bring him to me, shall have THREE SILVER DOLLARS Reward, and all necessary charges paid, by
   SAMUEL HASSARD. South-Kingston, Feb 28, 1781.
The Connecticut Gazette; And The Universal Intelligencer, March 9, 1781; March 16, 1781; March 23, 1781; March 30, 1781. See *The Connecticut Gazette; And The Universal Intelligencer*, September 15, 1775.

        M. Wm. SCARFE.
IF M. Wm. Scarfe, alias Day, originally of the Town of Cambridge, in England, who left London in the Month of March 1775, and took shipping as it is supposed, at Deal, in the County of Kent, and was in company with one M. Sanders, supposed to be a Clergyman, is in any Part of North America, he is desired to apply personally, or send his direction, To Messirs. BRECK & GREEN, Merchants in Boston—where he will learn of something which concerns him very much. Any Person knowing of the said M. Scarfe, whether he be dead of alive, or that they have or do new Correspondence with him, or with the above M. Sanders, they will oblige very much the Advertiser by favouring him with a Line for A. B. at the above Messirs. Breck and Green's Store.
 N. B. M. Scarf is a short thick Man, of a dark Complexion, and about 64 or 65 Years of Age.
 The Boston Gazette, And The Country Journal, March 12, 1781; March 19, 1781.

R*UN away from the subscriber of Stratford, a NEGRO Man, named JACK, a short thick set fellow much pock broken, with a small spot bald on the crown of his head, had on when he went away, a Kersey great coat and a strait bodied coat of the same. Whoever will take up said Negro and return him to me, shall be generously rewarded by*
   EBENEZER EURD. Stratford, Feb. 28, 1781.
 The Connecticut Journal, March 15, 1781; March 22, 1781; March 29, 1781.

RUN AWAY from the subscriber, on the 12th instant, an apprentice boy, named DAVID BAXTER, 19 years of age, about five feet eight inches high, light complexion, short hair, had on when he went away, a light brown coat and vest, dark brown breeches, white yarn seamed stockings. Whoever will return said boy to the subscriber, shall have six pence reward, paid by
   JOSEPH BEWELL. Glastonbury, February 12, 1781.

The Connecticut Courant, And Weekly Advertiser, March 20, 1781; March 27, 1781.

       Ranaway from his Master in Suffield, on the evening of the 3d Instant, a Negro Man, named BOSTON, about 27 Years old, had on when he went away, a light brown broadcloth Coat which had been turned, a dark brown broad cloth Vest, a pair of light-brown camblet breeches, white yarn Stockings, and a white Holland ruffled Shirt. Said Negro is about 5 Feet 6 Inches high, speaks good English, plays poorly on a Violin, of a Copper Colour, whoever will take up said Negro and return him to me, shall have 500 Dollars Reward, and all necessary charges paid, otherwise secure him in any Goals and give me Notice thereof, shall have 150 Dollars and Charges paid by me,
    SHEM BURBANK.   Suffield, February 6, 1781.

The Independent Chronicle and the Universal Advertiser, March 22, 1781. See *The Connecticut Courant, And Weekly Advertiser*, February 20, 1781.

THIS is to forbid all Persons harbouring or trusting LYDIA, wife to the Subscriber: she having behaved in a very unbecoming manner.
    BENJAMIN HOSKIN.   Torrington, February 16, 1781.

The Connecticut Courant And Weekly Intelligencer, March 27, 1781; April 3, 1781. See *The Connecticut Courant And Weekly Intelligencer*, August 14, 1781.

RAN AWAY from the Subscriber this Morning, a Negro Man named Christopher, but called KIT, 25 years old, about 6 feet high, full faced, smooth Black, pretty thick Lips, carried away one pair white Yarn seamed Stockings, and wore away a mixed grey black and white outside Jacket and striped under Jacket and Shirt, striped woolen Trowsers, black yarn Stockings, turn'd Pumps, brass Shoe Buckles; plays on a Violin. Whoever will take up said Negro and return him to the Subscriber or secure him in any Goal in the United States so that the Subscriber shall have him again shall have Twenty Silver Dollars Reward, and all necessary Charges
    paid by AMASA RANSOM.
N. B. All Persons are forbid to harbour, conceal or carry off said Negro on Penalty of the Law.

The Connecticut Journal, March 29, 1781; April 5, 1781; April 12, 1781, *The Norwich Packet and the Weekly Advertiser*, April 26, 1781; May 4, 1781; May 10, 1781; May 17, 1781. Minor differences between the papers.

TAKEN from the subscriber last evening, a brown Dutch MARE, with a white strip in her face, natural trotter, about fourteen hands high, 11 or 12 years old, had on a hunting Saddle with a yellowish cloth, and a grey homespun great Coat, with horn buttons, was taken by one Augustus Burgoyne, who has been by the names of Thomson and Smith, he is about 31 years of age, light complexion, bald on the top of his head, cat hammed, had on his legs two large scars, about six feet high; had on when he went away, a black coat, vest and breeches, has been keeping school in this place some time. Whoever will take up said mare and said Burgoyne, and deliver them to me shall have five hundred dollars reward, and all reasonable charges paid, by me
    SAMUEL BILLING. Bennington, March 13, 1781.
The Connecticut Courant, And Weekly Advertiser, April 3, 1781; April 10, 1781; April 17, 1781.

RAN away from his Master, on Saturday the 24th ult. a Negro LAD, 17 Years of Age; he is a strait, well-built Fellow. Said Negro had on a grey outside Coat, with plain Pewter Buttons, a grey Jacket, striped woollen Trowsers, and a striped Flannel Shirt.—Whoever will take up said Negro, and return him to the Subscriber, in Attleborough, shall have Two Hundred Dollars Reward, and necessary Charges, paid by
    EBENEZER DRAPER. Attleborough, April 2, 1781.
The Providence Gazette; And Country Journal, April 7, 1781; April 14, 1781; April 21, 1781.

WHEREAS the subscriber some time since Advertised his wife, and forbid all persons trusting her on his account. This is therefore to inform the public that their former disagreement was occasioned by some ill advisers, which is now fully compromised. I do therefore revoke said advertisement, and desire all persons to treat her in the same manner as tho' she had not been advertised.
    ANDREW SPALDING. Hartford, April 9, 1781.
The Connecticut Courant, And Weekly Intelligencer, April 10, 1781.
See *The Connecticut Courant, And Weekly Intelligencer,* November 14, 1780.

        Middletown, Nov. 9th, 1780. [*sic*]
WHEREAS MARGARET (who should be) my wife, has for a long time absented and dealt fraudulent and deceitfully with me, and refuses to return to her duty, though often requested, for which reason I forbid all persons crediting or dealing with her in my name for I will pay none of her debts, or answer any of her contracts or obligations, as I am satisfied of her intentions to ruin me, in combination and advice of some evil persons.
    SAMUEL WILLIS.

N. B. If any person has demands on me for any transactions or debts of hers, they are requested to exhibit them forthwith, or I will not be accountable for them. S. W.
The Connecticut Gazette; And The Universal Intelligencer, April 20, 1781.

SPRINGFIELD, April 10, 1781.
Three Hundred Dollars Reward.
JOHN COLLINS, whose Name, Crimes and Punishment, is published by Order of General WASHINGTON, sentenced by a General Court Martial—Having broke Goal at Springfield last Evening, being about 28 Years old, slim built, about 5 Feet 10 Inches high, very light Complection, Femenine Voice, dress'd in good brown Cloth Clothes, French Lapell'd, &c. —Whoever will take up said COLLINS, that he may be had again, shall have the above Reward, and all necessary Charges paid,
by me, JOHN MORGAN, Goaler.
The Boston-Gazette, And Country Journal, April 23, 1781; April 30, 1781; *The Independent Chronicle and the Universal Advertiser*, May 4, 1781; May 10, 1781; *The Independent Ledger, and the American Advertiser*, May 7, 1781; May 14, 1781; May 21, 1781; May 28, 1781. Minor differences between the papers. See *The Independent Ledger, and the American Advertiser*, May 7, 1781.

WHEREAS my wife Sarah, has been and is endeavouring to waste and ruin my estate as much as in her power, by running me in debt and in conveying it away. These are to forbid all persons trusting her on my account, as I will not pay any debt of her contracting,
NATHAN TIBBALS.   Washington, April 17, 1780. [*sic*]
The Connecticut Courant, And Weekly Intelligencer, April 24, 1781; May 1, 1781.

STOLEN out of the stable of the subscriber, on the night of the 19th instant, two Horse kind, one a HORSE of a brown colour, about six years old, one white hind foot, trots and canters.—The other a red Rone MARE, about 14 hands high, about 10 years old, with a burst upon her near flank, paces and canters. Supposed to be taken by two men, one a short thick very pock broken fellow, with a green baize sailor's jacket, mix brown tar'd over alls, with a hair or wool cap, the other a tall slim fellow, with a brown coat, blue jacket, white breeches. Whoever will take up said Theives and Horses, shall have FIVE HUNDRED DOLLARS REWARD, and all necessary charges paid by the subscriber.
DAVID BISSEL.   *East Windsor, April* 20, 1781.
N. B. For either of the Horses, shall have ONE HUNDRED DOLLARS.

The Norwich Packet and the Weekly Advertiser, April 26, 1781.

Stop Runaway Negro.

RAN away from the Subscriber in *Portsmouth*, on Saturday Evening the 28th Instant, a NEGRO *MAN* named CESAR, about 32 Years old, about five Feet five Inches high, and of a tawny Colour; a thick set Fellow, speaks good English, Had on when he went away, a grey homespun Coat, striped Wollen Shirt, old grey Breeches, and grey Stockings. Whoever will apprehend said Negro, and convey him to the subscriber, or commit him to any Goal, and give Information thereof to him, shall receive two hundred Dollars Reward, and all necessary Charges

          paid by me   SAMUEL LANGDON.

N. B. All *Masters* of Vessels and others are forbid entertaining or carrying off said Negro, as they would avoid the Penalty of the Law.

Portsmouth, April 30, 1781.

The New-Hampshire Gazette, OR, State Journal and General Advertiser, April 30, 1781; May 14, 1781. See *The New-Hampshire Gazette, And Historical Chronicle*, May 11, 1779; May 18, 1779 and *The Exeter Journal, or The New-Hampshire Gazette and Tuesday's General Advertiser*, May 18, 1779.

WHEREAS my Father, Jonathan Allen, of Greenland, is adjudged Non-compes mentis, and I the Subscriber being appointed by the Honorable Phillips White, Esq; Judge of the Probate of Wills, &c. Guardian to my said Father, do hereby forbid all Persons trading with or trusting him, as I will pay no Debts that he may contract.

          Jonathan Allen, Junr.   Greenland, April 21, 1781.

The New-Hampshire Gazette, OR, State Journal and General Advertiser, April 30, 1781.

Dutches County, Southeast Precinct, April 17, 1781.

LAST week was taken up in this place one John Pain, about 19 years of age, born (he says) at Charlestown, near Boston.—In the course of enquiry, it appears, that the said Pain, together with his two brothers, viz. Joseph and Stephen, has been at Crumpond and the neighbourhood adjacent thereto, for about nine months last past: That they have served as soldiers in the Continental army for several years: That during their residence hereabout, they have appeared not of affluent, but indigent circumstances. That about the first of March last, the said John, his brother Stephen, and one or two others, whose names were unknown, set out for a tour Eastward. The said Pains apparel very indifferent, having only one change of shirts and stockings: That in about three weeks the two Pains returned through this place, with considerable quantities of gold and silver, of which they expended at every state very largely.—The said John when taken, had about 140 Spanish milled dollars (generally ting'd with a sort of yellow rust) about 20 crown pieces, 1 half johannes, and one guinea; a scarlet superfine broadcloth coat, lined with white, and gold gilt buttons; a light brown corduroy jacket and breeches broad strip'd, with silver buttons of an oval figure on each; silver watch, makers named J. Aiden, London; one string of gold beads; a silver broach, embellished with red and white stone; a pair of silver shoe buckles, new mode, very large; a large new beave hat.—The said Pain says, That he carried from Crumpond with him, when he went Eastward, about 100 dollars, and that he received at a town called Pelham (above Hartford) 40 dollars, of a gentlemen with whom he had labor'd some years ago, whose name he could not recollect, but that he lived about a mile and a half from one Mr. King's of that town; the cloth for his coat, jacket and breeches he bought at Hartford, where the former was made up, and the latter at Farmington, on the whole, his own story, taken together, does not by any means account for the sudden change of his circumstances, to the advantage of his character; his money and other things mentioned, are detained, while he, at his own request, is liberated, to the end that he may collect circumstances, for the removal of suspicions had against him.

The Connecticut Courant And Weekly Intelligencer, May 1, 1781.

FIVE HUNDRED DOLLARS REWARD.

WENT away from the subscriber
on the 25th of April inst. a Negro BOY named NERO, about 21 years old, a well set likely fellow, speaks good English, and has much of a musical voice, he carried with him two felt hats, one with a gold lace for a band, a new stripped woolen shirt, one red baize waistcoat, a brown home-made coat, cuffed and lappeled with red, a pair of new moose-skin breeches, with Mathewman's buttons, one pair blue broad-cloth breeches, one pair white ribbed, one pair black, and one pair grey yarn stockings, one pair doubled soled and one pair single soled shoes, a pair of brass square shoe-buckles a pair of silver knee buckles, with brass chapes and tongues, and an old violin. Whoever will give intelligence of him that he may be recovered, or convey him to me, shall receive the above reward and all necessary charges paid by
THOMAS LEGATE, of Leonminster.

All persons are cautioned against harbouring or carrying off said Negro as they would avoid the penalty of the law.

Thomas's Massachusetts Spy Or, American Oracle of Liberty, May 4, 1781; May 10, 1781; May 17, 1781; May 24, 1781; *The Independent Chronicle and the Universal Advertiser*, May 31, 1781; June 7, 1781; *The Continental Journal, And Weekly Advertiser*, June 14, 1781. Minor differences between the papers. The *Chronicle* is dated May 1, 1781 at the bottom of the ad.

HEAD-QUARTERS New-Windsor Friday March 23d 1781
At a General Court Martial, held by Order of his EXCELLENCY at Springfield, the 1st inst.
Colonel SHEPARD President.

Mr. John Collins Deputy-Commissary of Military Stores, was tried on the following charges viz.

1st For defrauding the Public of a Quantity of Salt Petre, and employing a Person to receive the same as his Property, but to conceal his Name, as he was a public Officer, and to sell the Salt-Petre for cash or Cash-Articles and he would satisfy him for his trouble.

2dly. For breaking from his arrest, and deserting from his Quarters contrary to Orders given him, and carrying off one of the Public's best Saddles compleat, and endeavouring to make his Escape from justice by every possible Method in his Power; and using his utmost Efforts to get a Birth on board some Vessel to go to Sea.

3dly. For feloniously robbing E. Cheevers D. C. G. of Military Stores of some public papers and carrying off with him, to serve his own Purpose.

The Court after serious and mature Deliberation on the Case of Mr John Collins are unanimous in Opinion, that he is guilty of the two first Charges exhibited against him, being Breaches of the 1st Article of the 6th and 12th sections of the Articles of War; but that he is not amenable to the Act of Congress of the 22d of August, it not being published at the Time the Crime was committed; and do adjudge him to forfeit all his Pay due to him from the United States; make Restitution to the United States for all the Damages they may have suffered on this Occasion.

That he be rendered ever incapable of holding any Office under the United States; that he serve on board a Continental Ship of War during the present Contest, without permission to put his Foot on Shore; and that his Name, Crimes and Punishment be published in public Prints.

The Commander in Chief confirms the Sentence of the Court and orders it carried into Execution.

Transcript of General Orders.
EDWARD HAND, Adjt. Gen.
A true Copy. Attest. SETH BANISTER, Captain
per Order Col. Shepard.
SPRINGFIELD, April 10, 1781.
Three Hundred Dollars Reward.

JOHN COLLINS, whose Name, Crimes and Punishment, is published by Order of General WASHINGTON, sentenced by a General Court Martial—Having broke Goal at Springfield last Evening, being about 28 Years old, slim built, about 5 Feet 10 Inches high, very light Complection, Femenine Voice, dress'd in good brown Cloth Clothes, French Lapell'd, &c.

—Whoever will take up said COLLINS, that he may be had again, shall have the above Reward, and all necessary Charges paid,
   by me, JOHN MORGAN, Goaler.
The Independent Ledger, and the American Advertiser, May 7, 1781; May 14, 1781; May 21, 1781; May 28, 1781. See *The Boston-Gazette, And Country Journal,* April 23, 1781.

      Whereas GRACE, the wife of
the Subscriber embezzles my Estate, and refuses to Live with me: This is to give notice to all Persons not to Credit her on my Account, for I hereby declare I will not pay one Farthing of any Debt she may contract from the Date hereof, as witness my Hand.
    THOMAS CARE.   Sudbury, May 4, 1781.
The Boston Gazette, And The Country Journal, May 14, 1781.

      Whereas MARY, the Wife of
me the Subscriber embezzles my Estate, and refuses to live with me.—This is therefore to give Notice to all Persons, not to credit her on my Account, for I do hereby declare I will not pay one Farthing of any Debt she may contract from the Date hereof. Witness by Hand.
    PAUL JEBBLING.   Boston, May 14, 1781.
The Boston Gazette, And The Country Journal, May 14, 1781.

     TWENTY SILVER DOLLARS REWARD.
STOLEN on the 10th inst. a Chesnut or sorrel coloured MARE, five years old, trots and paces well, fourteen hands high, with a white stripe on her face, small white spots behind her ears, and a white spot on one of her buttocks; a saddle with a red plush housing, and a red fringe, together with a new bridle; supposed to be stolen by a transient person, between 20 and 24 years of age, light complexion, about five feet seven inches high; had on a light mix coloured blue coat, jacket and breeches, and a pair of boots, and a fur cap, he went by the name of Hagar, alias Willington. Whoever will take up and secure said Mare and thief, or convey them to me, shall be intitled to the above reward, and for the Mare or Thief only, TEN SILVER DOLLARS, for each, and all necessary charges paid by
    REUBEN SPAULDING.   *Pomfret,* May 11, 1781.
Thomas's Massachusetts Spy Or, American Oracle of Liberty, May 17, 1781; May 24, 1781. See *The Connecticut Gazette; And The Universal Intelligencer,* May 25, 1781.

     WHEREAS ESTHER, the Wife
of me the Subscriber, hath eloped from my Bed and Board, and hath behaved herself in a very unbecoming Manner: I do therefore forbid any Person or

Persons to trust her on my Account, or maintain her son CONVERSE WILLIAMS on my Account (he having been born at Otter-Creek, in the Town of Clarendon, where my Estate now lieth) as I will not pay any Debts of her contracting, or for maintaining her said Son, from the Date hereof.
JOSEPH WILLIAMS.
Clarendon, on Otter-Creek, Dec. 1, 1780. [*sic*]
The Providence Gazette; and Country Journal, May 19, 1781; May 26, 1781. See *The Providence Gazette; and Country Journal,* June 2, 1781.

STOP VILLIANS!

THE prison of Newgate was broke up last night, one of the guard killed, and a number more wounded, and the following prisoners escaped (and carried with them the arms and ammunition belonging to the guards, viz. Chadwell Parsons, Luke Morris, William Young, and Stephen Prentice, committed for making and passing counterfeit money; Nicholas Davenport for being accessary in murder and house burning; Pelatiah Turner, for horse stealing, attempting to join the enemy, &c. David Worster, Samuel Doolittle and Henry Worster, for illicit trade and joining the enemy, Benjamin Prescott, for illicit trade; Peter Shackett, Jo. Heacock, Ebenezer Hathaway, Thomas Smith and William Wharton, for joining the enemy; Elihu Hennels, James Derby, Heth Baldwin, Samuel Hoit, Ephraim Palmer and James Bush, by sentence of a court-martial, and it's supposed, they will attempt to join the enemy: All persons are, therefore warned to take care of their vessels and boats, and by order of his Excellency the Governor, all officers, civil and military, are authorized and directed to call to their assistance, such of the military as they shall judge necessary, and enter and search such places as they shall have reason to suppose any of said prisoners are concealed in, and apprehend and return them to the said prison; and all persons are directed to give all the aid and assistance in their power, and secure and return the said Prisoners to the said prison, for which they shall be generously rewarded and all necessary charges paid.
ROGER NEWBURY, Brigadier-General.
Windsor, May 19, 1761. [*sic*]
N. B. More effectually to prevent said prisoners getting off, all Persons are notified and desired to take up and secure all travellers they have reason to suspect to be said prisoners, and carry them before some lawful authority to be examined.
The Connecticut Courant, And Weekly Advertiser, May 22, 1781; May 29, 1781. See *The Connecticut Courant, And The Weekly Intelligencer,* May 9, 1780, for Davenport. See *The Connecticut Courant And Weekly Intelligencer,* March 26, 1782, for Hoit.

Last night broke out of the County goal, in York, in the county of York, *Samuel Kelley, George Burbage, Richard Cooms,* and *John Martin,* Prisoners, taken on board a schooner in the British service, and carried into Biddeford, in said county. Now if any person will apprehend the abovenamed persons, and commit them to any goal in these States, shall receive a handsome reward, and all necessary charges paid.

JOHNSON MOULTON, Sheriff. York, May, 17, 1781.
The Independent Chronicle and the Universal Advertiser, May 24, 1781; May 31, 1781.

Ran away from the Subscriber, on the 17th instant, one DANIEL HAYDEN; about 14 Years old. All Persons are cautioned against harbouring, concealing, or carrying off the said Lad, as they would avoid the Penalty of the Law.

THOMAS GREEN. Boston, May 25.
The Independent Chronicle and the Universal Advertiser, May 24, 1781; May 31, 1781.

STOLEN last night from the subscriber, a chestnut coloured MARE, 5 years old, has a white strip in her face, trots and paces, 14 ½ hands high; and a saddle with a red housen and red fringe, and a bridle; supposed to be stolen by a transient person, about 24 years of age, light complexion, about 5 feet 7 inches high, had on a light mixed coloured blue coat, jacket and breeches, boots, and a fur cap. Whoever will take up and secure said mare and thief, shall have Twenty Silver Dollars reward, or for the mare Ten Dollars, and all necessary charges, paid by

REUBEN SPAULDING. Pomfret, 11th May, 1781.
The Connecticut Gazette; And The Universal Intelligencer, May 25, 1781; June 8, 1781. See *Thomas's Massachusetts Spy Or, American Oracle of Liberty,* May 17, 1781.

WHereas SARAH, the Wife of me the Subscriber, hath eloped from my Bed and Board, and hath behaved in a very unbecoming Manner: I do therefore forbid any Person or Persons to trust her on my Account, as I will not pay any Debts of her contracting from the Date hereof.

WILLIAM TUCKER. Attleborough, May 25, 1781.
The Providence Gazette; And Country Journal, May 26, 1781; June 2, 1781; June 9, 1781.

BROKE from the county gaol in Newport on the 9th of May, 1781, SAMUEL GARDNER, of Exeter, and RUFUS CASE, of West-Greenwich, confined on

suspicion of burning a barn and several stacks of hay within this State.—Whoever will secure and return them to the county gaol in Newport, shall be handsomely rewarded and all necessary charges paid by
WILLIAM DAVIS, Sheriff of said County.
The Newport Mercury, June 2, 1781; June 9, 1781.

To the PUBLIC.

IN a late Providence Paper I observed a false and scandalous Advertisement, signed Joseph Williams, of Clarendon, on Otter Creek, setting forth that Esther his Wife had eloped from him Bed and Board, and behaved herself in a very unbecoming Manner. In Justice to said Esther Williams, I must inform the Public, that in April, 1778, I received a Letter from said Joseph Williams, then living on Otter Creek, requesting me to remove my Sister Esther Williams and her Children to Rhode-Island, he not being able to support them. I accordingly went to Otter Creek, and brought down my said Sister, and four Children, at my own Expence, and have supported and taken Care of her and two of her Children ever since; the other two Children my Father, Samuel Smith, of Johnston, maintains. The Behaviour of said Joseph was such, that his Neighbours requested me never to suffer my Sister, Esther his Wife, to return to him. The base Aspersions thrown on her by the said Advertisement cannot affect her, as her Character as a virtuous Woman is established where she is known.
SAMUEL SMITH.   East-Greenwich, June 1, 1781.
The Providence Gazette; and Country Journal, June 2, 1781; June 9, 1781; June 23, 1781. See *The Providence Gazette; and Country Journal*, May 19, 1781.

TEN-SILVER DOLLARS REWARD.

RODE away on the 29th of May, a chestnut coloured Horse, thick set, a star in the forehead, off hind foot white, paces chiefly; had on a bridle with a strap just below the eyes, a strap for a throat latch; an old saddle with leather house, a patch set on the fore part of the saddle, a pair of saddle-bags—Said Horse was rode away by one Jeremiah Hutchinson, darkish complexion, had on when he went away, a blue sagathee coat, white waistcoat and breeches, a feather and a black ribbon in his hat is about 30 years old, about 5 feet 7 inches high, was inlisted by Mr. Barber of Torrington for three years. Whoever will take up said man and horse and secure them shall have the above reward, and necessary charges, or five dollars for the horse only, by
NOAH STONE.   Litchfield, June 2, 7781. [*sic*]
The Connecticut Courant, and Hartford Weekly Intelligencer, June 5, 1781; June 12, 1781; July 3, 1781.

JOSEPH WAY made his Escape from New-Haven Goal the last of May; he is of a middling Size, dark long hair braded and club'd, and is very lame; had on a brown Coat and brown Vest. Whoever will return said Way to the Goal in New-Haven, or any Goal in this State, so that he may be brought to Justice, shall receive a Reward of Five Pounds.
The Connecticut Journal, June 7, 1781; June 14, 1781; June 21, 1781.

Whereas my Wife *Lucy,* has eloped from my Bed and Board, and refuses to live with me: I do therefore forbid all Persons from trusting or trading with her on my own or Children' account, as I will not suffer any of my Estate to be sold by her, nor pay any Debts of her contracting after this Date.
                 BENAJAH TRACY.   Preston, June 2, 1781.
The Connecticut Gazette; And The Universal Intelligencer, June 8, 1781; June 15, 1781; June 22, 1781.

Ten Silver Dollars Reward.
RAn-away from the Ship
Marquis la Fayette, a Negro Man, named JACK, belonging to Messirs Wells Cooper and Co. of Virginia; he is a low built, well set Fellow, was born in the North of England, speaks after their Manner, his Face is marked with a Number of Scars. Whoever will take up said Negro, and deliver him to the Captain on board said Ship, or to Mr. JOHN BROWN in Providence, shall receive the above Reward, and all necessary Charges.
                                                    Providence, June 9, 1781.
The American Journal And General Advertiser, June 9, 1781; June 13, 1781; June 30, 1781.

WALK'D away from his Master, early on Friday Morning, a Negro Man, named *TOM,* about 50 Years of Age, but has an older Look; is much Pock-broken, has the Mark of an old Scald on one of his Wrists, was well cloathed, is about 5 Feet high, a civil well-behaved Fellow, very ingenious at Painting and Drawing, and has the necessary Pencils and Paints with him; is supposed to have been seduced away, and as he has frequently expressed a Desire of going privateering, he may be gone towards Newbury-Port, Salem, Boston or Rhode-Island.—Any person who will stop said Negro, and keep him till his Master can be informed where to send for him, shall be gratefully rewarded, and have all Charges paid, by
                 JOHN WENDELL.   Portsmouth (N. Hampshire) May 28.
The Providence Gazette; And Country Journal, June 9, 1781; June 16, 1781.

RAN AWAY from the Subscriber, on the 16 of May last, an apprentice boy, nam'd DAVID HARRIS; about 15 years of age, 5 feet 6 inches high, pock mark'd: He carried with when he went off, two coats, on a blue broadcloth, faced with white—two vests—one pair of fulled cloth breeches—two check shirts, and one white ditto—4 pair stockings; one pair open work'd silver shoe buckles—Also, one suit of linen cloths. Whoever will return said boy to the subscriber, shall have Five Shillings State Money.
    ELIPHAS SPENCER.   Salisbury, June 7, 1781.
The Connecticut Courant And Weekly Intelligencer, June 12, 1781; June 19, 1781; June 26, 1781.

WHEREAS Sarah, my wife, hath eloped from my bed and board, I therefore forbid all persons to credit her on my account, as I will not pay any debts that she may contract after this date.
    JOHN BROWN.   Farmington, May 20, 1781.
The Connecticut Courant And Weekly Intelligencer, June 12, 1781; June 19, 1781.

STOP VILLAIN!
TEN POUNDS REWARD, STATE MONEY.
MADE his escape from the gaol in Norwich, on the evening of the 11th inst. one SAMUEL CHARD, alias CULVER, who was committed for passing counterfeit State money, of July emission, 1780: He is about 5 feet 10 inches high, about 25 years of age, darkish complexion, long brown hair; had on a pair red and white striped overhauls, pair old stockings, a stamped under jacket, and white shirt; no hat, coat, or shoes; he is a carpenter by trade, and supposed to have come from Long-Island.—Whoever will apprehend said villain, and deliver him to the subscriber, in Norwich, or secure him in any gaol in this State, shall have the above reward, and all necessary charges.
    MOSES CLEVELAND, Gaoler.   Norwich, June 14.
The Norwich Packet and the Weekly Advertiser, June 14, 1781; June 21, 1781; June 28, 1781.

    WHEREAS Cesar, my negro man,
has absented himself from me, and is employed by several persons, without my consent: This is to caution all persons from harbouring or employing said negro, or trusting him on my account, from the date hereof. Those who entertain him, may expect to be dealt with according to law.
    JAMES WILDER.   *Lancaster, May,* 7th, 1781.

Thomas's Massachusetts Spy Or, The Worcester Gazette, June 14, 1781; June 21, 1781; June 28, 1781; July 5, 1781.

WHERAS Martha Ballou, my Wife,
has eloped from my Bed and Board: These are therefore to notify all Persons not to trust her with any Thing on my Account, as I will not pay one Farthing of any Debt that she shall contract after the Date hereof.
    DANIEL BALLOU.   Gloucester, June 16, 1781.
The American Journal And General Advertiser, June 20, 1781; June 23, 1781; June 27, 1781; June 30, 1781; July 4, 1781; July 7, 1781; July 11, 1781.

Whereas NANCY my Wife,
(and Daughter to Mrs. Haden of this Town) whom I Married in March, 1780, and in June following I went in the Service of my Country for during the War, leaving my Wife orders &c. to draw upon my interest for her subsistence, but she my said Wife, lost to every sense of conjugal virtue, and by the advice of her aforesaid Mother, Mrs. Haden, and of her Sister, Mrs. Cassidy, in seven months after my before mentioned departure to the army, married again to Mr. John Newning, who is now gone a cruize in the armed ship Essex: And as my said wife has drawn much upon my interest in my absence, even since here last marriage, and has secreted herself from me: This is to caution all persons from trusting her on my account, as I will not pay any debt shall may contract after the date hereof. The Agents of the Essex will please to take notice of the above, as I intend to recover, if possible from her present or last Husband, the amount of my interest which she has drawn since her last marriage. Mrs. Haden and Mrs. Cassidy live opposite Dr. Cooper's Meeting-House.
    HUGH Mc KOWN, Serj't 6th Massa'tts Regt.
              Boston, June 19, 1781.
The Continental Journal, And Weekly Advertiser, June 21, 1781.

At the last Superior Court, held at East-Greenwich, for the County of Kent, Thomas Case, Thomas Reynolds, Samuel Gardner and William Hopkins, were convicted of burning a Barn belonging to Othniel Gorton, Esq; and a Stack of Hay belonging to Rufus Spencer, Esq; and were each sentenced to stand in the Pillory at the Town of East-Greenwich for the Space of one Hour, to pay a Fine into the General-Treasury One Hundred Pounds Lawful Money, or in Default thereof each to be whipped at a Cart's Tail thirty-nine Lashes, to pay Costs of Prosecution and Conviction, and to

recognize with Sureties for their good Behaviour during the War.—This Sentence was by Order of Court to be executed Yesterday.
> *The Providence Gazette; And Country Journal*, June 22, 1781. See *The Newport Mercury*, June 2, 1781. See *The Providence Gazette; And Country Journal*, June 22, 1781.

WHereas DORCAS, the Wife of the Subscriber, has left his Bed and Board, and behaved otherwise in a shameful Manner: I hereby caution all Persons against trusting her on my Account, as I will not pay any Debts or her contracting from the Date hereof.
SILAS BATES.   Exeter, June 22, 1781.
> *The Providence Gazette And Country Journal*, June 23, 1781; July 7, 1781; July 21, 1781.

Essex ff.   June 23, 1781.
In the night preceeding this Day, the noted *John Long*, broke out of Salem goal—he is about 35 years of age, 5 feet 8 inches high, and well proportioned, of a ruddy complexion, long black hair, lost four of his upper teeth.

Whoever will take up said *Long* and secure him in any of the jails of this or the United States, shall have a reward of sixty hard dollars, and all necessary charges paid by me.
MICHAEL FARLEY, Sheriff.
> *The Independent Chronicle and the Universal Advertiser*, June 28, 1781.

RAN away from the subscriber, a Negro Man Slave, named NERO; he is a well grown, stout built fellow, about 6 feet high, he is a good singer and dancer, and is ingenious and active, has large feet, his little finger on his left hand something crooked, and one of his upper teeth is a little on the blueish order, different from the rest, he is pitted in the face with the small-pox, and is about 25 years of age; when he went away he carried with him a pair kersey tow trowsers, a pair strip'd ditto, a pair blue short breeches, four under jackets, two of them striped, one brown linen, the other brown broad cloth, one white shirt, two check'd ditto, a beaver hat, a red and yellow silk handkerchief, four pair stockings, one pair shoes, a pair silver shoe buckles, and a pair stone silver sleeve buttons: Whoever will take up said negro and return him to the subscriber, shall be handsomely rewarded and all necessary charges paid, by
JAMES STODDARD.   Groton, June 21, 1781.

N. B. All masters of vessels are forbid carrying away or harbouring said Negro.
The Connecticut Gazette; And The Universal Intelligencer, June 29, 1781; July 6, 1781; July 13, 1781. See *The Connecticut Gazette; And The Universal Intelligencer*, August 10, 1781.

STOLEN from the subscriber, the night after the 25th of June last, a light brown STONE HORSE, nine or ten years old, about 14 hands high, trots and canters, lame in his fore feet, newly shod before; supposed to be taken by one JOHN SELAH, a Continental soldier, about five feet four inches high, dark complexion, twenty-four years old. Whoever will take up said horse and thief, and deliver them to the subscriber, shall have FIVE DOLLARS, hard money, reward, and all necessary charges paid, or Three Dollars or either the horse or thief.
    OLIVER BELDING,   Lenox, July 2, 1781.
The Connecticut Courant, And Weekly Intelligencer, July 10, 1781; July 17, 1781; July 31, 1781.

    THIRTY hard dollars REWARD.
RUN away from Nathaniel Durkee, jun. and Capt. Nathan Bomford of New-Milford, 2 NEGRO Men on Tuesday night. One named BUD, about 21 years old about 5 feet 6 inches high, wore a brown coat home made, and small cut castor hat, two holland shirts, one pair leather breeches, and sundry other articles.—The other named PETER, about 18 years of age, six feet high, very stocky, had with him a brown homemade coat, a new felt, leather breeches, one or two pair of trowsers, two check'd shirts, and sundry other articles—Also a NEGRO woman named NABBY, about 21 years of age, very short and stocky, has a suite of brown, and suit of white linen with her, Said NEGROES are supposed to be in the woods, or concealed by some person nigh the sea shore, with an intent to get to Long-Island. Any person that will take up the said NEGROES, shall have the above reward, or for either of them ten dollars, and necessary expences, by committing them to goal or sending word to
    NATHANIEL DURKEE, jun. New Milford, June 30th, 1781.
The Connecticut Journal, July 12, 1781; July 19, 1781; July 26, 1781.

WHEREAS *Eunice* my Wife has behaved in such a Manner, as Necessity and Duty constrain me to forbid all Persons trusting the said *Eunice* on my Account, for I positively declare that I will not pay any Debts of her contracting to any Person whomsoever.

ISAIAH EDES. Groton, July 16, 1781.
The Independent Chronicle and the Universal Advertiser, July 19, 1781; The Boston Gazette, And The Country Journal, July 30, 1781.

TWENTY hard dollars REWARD.
RUN away from the subscribers, two NEGRO Servants, in the night after the 8th instant, named *Hampton* and *Gad*, one about 30 years old, about 5 feet 7 inches high: the other about 22 years old, and is near 6 feet high, and walks bent forward, and between them when they went away, two tow-cloth shirts, and one check'd linen shirt, each had on a pair of tow cloth trowsers, and a striped linen jacket with sleeves, as also, a light colour'd great coat, it is supposed that they will endeavour to get to Long-Island by way of Horse-Neck, as Gad has serv'd in the State Corps upon that stature, is heavy eyed, has a great appearance of honesty. Whoever takes up said run-aways, and return them to the subscribers, shall receive the above reward, and necessary charges paid by, JOSEPH JOHNSON,
SIMON BRISTOL. New-Haven, July 17, 1781.
The Connecticut Journal, July 19, 1781; July 26, 1781.

State of New-Hampshire, *Exeter, June* 25, 1781.
CHARITY WELCH, *Wife of* Benjamin Welch, *late of Portsmouth, in the County of Rockingham, and State aforesaid, Marriner, having petitioned the General Court, setting forth, that about fourteen Years ago, she was married to the said* Benjamin, *who about seven Years last past left her destitute of any Support, went to Sea, entered on Board a British Man of War, and has continued with the Enemy ever Since. She is informed, and expects to prove, that the said* Benjamin *is married again in England, and has a Child there: wherefore she prayed, that the Bond of Matrimony between the said* Benjamin *and her may be dissolved.*

Upon which Petition, the General Court Ordered, that the Petitioner by heard thereon before them on the second Tuesday of their next Session; and that in the mean time she cause the Substance of the Petition and Order of Court thereon, to be published three weeks successively in the New Hampshire Gazette, that any person may then appear, and shew cause (if any they have) why the prayer thereof should not be granted.
Attest. Joseph Pearson, *D. Sec:*
The New-Hampshire Gazette State Journal, and General Advertiser, July 23, 1781; July 30, 1781; August 6, 1781.

The Subscriber, last Saturday, let a sorrel white face Horse, about 14 hands high, trots and paces, and an English Saddle, to a Frenchman, by the name of PETER MARTIN, about 5 feet 5 inches high, had on a green coat, turn'd up with white, silver button

and loop in his hat, talks broken English. The Horse and Saddle was let to be returned in 4 hours but has not since been returned.—Whoever will take up said MARTIN, Horse and Saddle, and give intelligence to the subscriber, shall receive FIFTEEN HARD DOLLARS, or TEN DOLLARS for Horse and Saddle, by
                SYRANUS COLLINS.   Roxbury, July 18, 1781.
The Connecticut Journal, August 2, 1781.

PROVIDENCE, August 4.

On Monday Morning three Men and two Women, were apprehended here, on Suspicion of having been concerned in breaking open and robbing the House of Capt. Lewis Thomas, on the Night of the 19th ult. The Persons apprehended are, Francis Johnson and his Wife, who have resided here but a short Time. John Clarke and his Wife, transient Persons, and Cornelius Smith, alias Staggs. Most of the Articles stolen from Capt. Thomas, with some others stolen from Capt. Larshar, were found in Johnston's House, where the other Persons taken into Custody resided.—They were all committed to Goal, in order to take their Trials at the Superior Court in Sept. next.
    The Providence Gazette; And Country Journal, August 4, 1781.

WHEREAS Abigail, the wife of me the subscriber, has refused to bed and board with me, I therefore forbid all person or persons to harbour or trust her on my account, as I declare I will not pay any debt or her contracting, after this day.   PHINEAS CARE.   Salisbury, July 20.
    The Independent Chronicle and the Universal Advertiser, August 2, 1781.

Newbury-Port, July 16, 1781.

                STOLEN out of a pasture in New-
bury, on the 12th inst. two MARES, one a Bay with a long main and tail; the other a light chesnut with a white streak down her face, trots all, about thirteen or fourteen hands high; supposed to be stolen by one *Welch* or *Brown*, riding upon a large grey stone horse and a red horse. Whoever will take up said thiefs, or thief, so as the owners may have their horses again, shall have TWENTY hard DOLLARS from each, and all necessary charges
                paid by   JOHN LITTLE, ANTHONY DAVENPORT.
N. B. Said *Welch* is much scared [*sic*] under his throat, wears a Calico coat, Green velvet breeches, boots and shoes. *Brown* wore a light Broad cloth coat

and jacket, and brown plush breeches, they said they belonged to Hartford, in Connecticut.
Thomas's Massachusetts Spy Or, American Oracle of Liberty, August 9, 1781.

DESERTED from the subscriber, on the 4th inst. one SIMON BAXTER, a Lieut. of the Convention troops, about 5 feet 10 inches high, thick set, short greyish hair, had on a faded claret coat, white jacket, tow-cloth over-alls, pair of boots, rode a light sorrel horse. Whoever will take up said Baxter, and send him to Worcester goal, or the Barracks in Rutland, shall have TEN DOLLARS reward by me   SAMUEL RUGGLES, Serjeant of
the Guards at Rutland.
Worcester, August 5, 1781.
Thomas's Massachusetts Spy: Or, American Oracle of Liberty, August 9, 1781; August 23, 1781; August 30, 1781.

RAN away from the subscriber on the 23d inst. an apprentice boy named Asa Larabee, about 15 years old, small and weakly, dark complection, dark eyes, strait dark hair, had on a striped jacket, tow-cloth trowsers, and a hat bound with white. Whoever will return said boy to the subscriber, shall have One Shilling Reward.
　　　　　AMOS CULVER.　　　　　　Groton, July 31, 1781.
The Connecticut Gazette; And The Universal Intelligencer, August 10, 1781; August 17, 1781. See *The Connecticut Gazette; And The Universal Intelligencer*, September 7, 1781.

Ten hard DOLLARS reward.
RAN away from the subscriber, a Negro Man Slave, named NERO; sometimes calls himself CAESAR QUOMMINO; he is a well grown stout built fellow, about 6 feet high, is a good singer and dancer, and is ingenious and active, has large feet, his little finger on his left hand something crooked, and one of his upper teeth is a little on the blueish order, different from the rest, he is pitted in the face with the small-pox, and is about 25 years of age; when he went away he carried with him a pair kersey tow trowsers, a pair strip'd ditto, a pair blue short breeches, four under jackets, two of them striped, one brown linen, the other brown broad cloth, one white shirt, two check'd ditto, a beaver hat, a red and yellow silk handkerchief, four pair stockings, one pair shoes, a pair silver shoe buckles, and a pair stone silver sleeve buttons: Whoever will take up said negro and return him to the

subscriber, shall be handsomely rewarded and all necessary charges paid, by
JAMES STODDARD.   Groton, June 21, 1781.
N. B. All masters of vessels are forbid carrying away or harbouring said Negro.

The Connecticut Gazette; And The Universal Intelligencer, August 10, 1781; August 17, 1781; August 24, 1781. See *The Connecticut Gazette; And The Universal Intelligencer*, June 29, 1781.

WHEREAS the subscriber some time since advertised his Wife, and forbid all persons trusting her, I do now hereby revoke and make void the same.
BENJAMIN HOSKIN.   Torrington, July 21, 1781.

The Connecticut Courant And Weekly Intelligencer, August 14, 1781. See *The Connecticut Courant And Weekly Intelligencer*, March 27, 1781.

STOP THIEF.

Stolen from the pasture of *Michael Dalton*, of Londonderry, on the night of the 10th instant, a Chesnut HORSE, about 14 hands high, 5 years old; his ears are thin, small and neat; his neck thin and elegant; his hind feet white, and a large scar on the near one; supposed to be stolen by one *Phelps* and *Anthony*; said *Anthony* was missing, and *Phelps* made his escape, and left a chesnut Mare about 14 hands high, which fell into the said *Dalton's* hands, and is supposed to be stolen from some other person.—Whoever takes up said Horse and the thief, and return them to said *Dalton*, shall have FIVE GUINEAS reward and all charges paid, or TWO GUINEAS and charges for the Horse only.
MICHAEL DALTON.   Londonderry, July 19, 1781.

The Continental Journal, And Weekly Advertiser, August 16, 1781; August 23, 1781.

My wife, *Anne Mason*, hath eloped from me, and hath left my bed and board: I forbid all persons trusting her on my account, as I will not pay any debt of her contracting.
SAMUEL MASON.   Stonington, August 4th, 1781.

The Connecticut Gazette; And The Universal Intelligencer, August 17, 1781; August 24, 1781.

Two Guineas Reward.

RAN away from the Subscriber last Night, a likely Negro Man, named Prince, about 20 Years of Age, 5 Feet 9 or 10 Inches high, speaks good

English:—Had on when he went away, a Beaver Hat, Chocolate colour'd Coat and Waistcoat, Pair of blue and white striped Trowsers, a Pair Silver square Buckles in his Shoes. Carried away with him, a white Coat, blue and white striped Holland Waistcoat, Pair of black Knit and a Pair of Leather Breeches, one white and two striped Cotton and Linnen Shirts, and a Number of other Articles, also a Firelock. Whoever will take up said Negro and return or secure him until they can give Information to his Master, shall receive the above Reward and all necessary Charges.

    EBEN. BREED.   Charlestown, Aug. 15.

N. B. All Masters of Vessels are forbid carrying off said Negro, as they would avoid the Penalty of the Law.

The Boston Gazette, And The Country Journal, August 20, 1781; August 27, 1781; September 3, 1781.

WHEREAS *LOWIS* my wife, has deserted my bed and board: I hereby caution all persons whatsoever against harbouring or concealing my said wife, or trusting her on my account, for I hereby declare that I will not pay one farthing of any debt she may contract, from the date hereof.

    JAMES HOLDIN.   Westford, Aug. 16, 1781.

The Boston Gazette, And The Country Journal, August 20, 1781; August 27, 1781; September 3, 1781.

             Worcester, August 10, 1781.

BROKE gaol last Saturday evening, and made their escape from my custody, THOMAS COOK, and ISAAC MOORE, both belonging to Sudbury, and confined for theft. Whoever will apprehend said Cook or Moore, and bring or send them to me shall receive FOUR DOLLARS reward for each of them, and all necessary charges paid by

    INCREASE BLAKE, Gaoler.

Thomas's Massachusetts Spy Or, The Worcester Gazette, August 23, 1781.

MADE his escape, the 16th of August instant, from the custody of the subscriber, the infamous JOSEPH KILBORN, sometimes calls himself Doct. Kilborn; he was put in custody by virtue of a mittimus signed by William Noyes, Esq. directing him to be committed to Norwich goal, being bound over to November court, for illicit trade with the enemy, he was taken in the act, crossing Long Island sound; had on when he escaped, a light brown coat, very narrow back'd, long trowsers, felt hat, &c. he is supposed to be that villain that stole a quantity of flour from Capt. James Ransom of Colchester, some time past. Whoever will take up said Kilborn, and return him to the subscriber in Lyme, shall have Twenty Silver Dollars reward, paid on sight, by ELIJAH BINGHAM, Constable.

Lyme, 20th August, 1781.
The Connecticut Gazette; And The Universal Intelligencer, August 24, 1781, August 31, 1781; September 7, 1781. See *The Norwich Packet and the Connecticut, Massachusetts, New-Hampshire, and Rhode-Island Weekly Advertiser*, October 18, 1781.

WHEREAS SARAH, the wife of the subscriber, has behaved in a very unbecoming manner, this is to forbid all persons from harbouring or trusting her on my account, as I will pay not debts of her contracting from the date hereof.   JESSE HALL.

Granville, Berkshire county, Massachusetts, Sept. 4, 1781.
The Connecticut Courant, And Weekly Intelligencer, September 4, 1781; September 11, 1781; September 18, 1781. See *The Connecticut Courant, And Weekly Intelligencer*, October 9, 1781.

Lunenburgh, (State of Vermont, August 23, 1781.
WHEREAS SARAH my Wife has without
just cause, left my bed and board, and absented herself from my family, and now resides at Westminster, (State of Massachusetts): I therefore caution all persons from trusting her on my account, as I am determined not to pay any debts of her contracting from the date hereof.
Cursed are they that part man and wife—Amen—*praise ye the Lord!*
As the Lord liveth before whom I stand, he will judge between my wife and me, and between her mother and me, and between any who will disturb me or my children, and discomfort us.
        JACOB EMERSON.
Thomas's Massachusetts Spy Or, The Worcester Gazette, September 6, 1781; September 20, 1781; September 27, 1781.

ESCAPED from the county gaol in New-London on Friday night last, one Asa Larabe, about 15 years old, a meagre looking lad, has dark eyes, and strait dark hair: had on a striped linen jacket, tow cloth trowsers, old flop'd hat, no stockings or shoes. Whoever will return him to the subscriber shall have One Dollars reward.
        JOHN POTTER, Gaoler.   New-London, Sept. 4, 1781.
The Connecticut Gazette; And The Universal Intelligencer, September 7, 1781. See *The Connecticut Gazette; And The Universal Intelligencer*, August 10, 1781.

STolen out of the Pasture of the Subscriber, on the Night of the 25th ult. a sorrel MARE, about 15 Hands high, 8 Years old, a natural Pacer, with a white Strip in her Face, newly shod. Also stolen, out of the House of the Subscriber, the last Evening, a Pinchbeck WATCH, double cased, gilt with Gold, runs on Diamonds, with a Steel Chain, and two Keys. The Person who undoubtedly took the Watch called himself John Craige; he is tall and slender, has black Eyes and black Hair, supposed to be about 22 Years of Age, two of his upper fore Teeth gone; had on a small old Beaver Hat, bound with Ferret, partly worn off, an old yellow Bandanoe Handkerchief round his Neck, a blue Sailor's Jacket, lined with white Baize, a spotted Waistcoat, long striped Trowsers, with a Pair of black Breeches under the Trowsers. Whoever will secure either or both of the Thieves, [*sic*] in any of the Gaols in this State, or deliver him or them to me, with the Mare and Watch, shall have Thirty Silver Dollars Reward, and for the Mare or Watch only, a reasonable Reward, and necessary Charges paid by,

   ANDREW CRAIGE.   Coventry, September 3, 1781.

The Providence Gazette And Country Journal, September 8, 1781; September 15, 1781; September 22, 1781. See *The Norwich Packet and the Weekly Advertiser*, September 20, 1781.

RUN-away from the subscriber on the 31st of May last, an apprentice Boy named David Washbourn, about 16 years of age, about 4 feet [*sic*] 10 inches high; he wore when he went off a dark gray fulled cloth Coat, a darkish colour'd linen Vest, a check Linen Shirt, a pair of Linen Trowsers, a pair of white woolen Stockings and a Straw Hat. Whoever will return said boy to the subscriber, shall have Five Shillings State Money Reward, paid by

   JOSEPH WHITCOMB.   East-Windsor, July 28, 1781.

The Connecticut Courant, And Weekly Intelligencer, September 11, 1781; September 18, 1781.

THIRTY DOLLARS REWARD.

STOLEN from the subscriber, the 2d inst. a Pinch-Back WATCH, gilt with gold, had a double case, runs upon two diamonds, steel chain, a large yellow seal, two keys for a portmanteau; it was stolen by one James French, of New-London, who says his name is John Craige—He is a slim built fellow, has lost one of his fore teeth; had on a blue jacket, with white lining, and striped linen trowsers. Whoever will take up and secure said Thief in any gaol in the United States, or bring him to the subscriber, shall have the above reward, and all reasonable charges.

   ANDREW CRAIGE.   Coventry, Sept. 6.

The Norwich Packet and the Weekly Advertiser, September 20, 1781; October 11, 1781; October 18, 1781. See *The Providence Gazette And Country Journal*, September 8, 1781.

RAN-away from the Subscriber, an indented Lad, named James Taylor, about 14 Years old, had on when he went away, cloth colour'd Cloathes, and white Stockings. Whoever will take up the abovesaid Servant and secure him that his Master may have him again, shall have Three Dollars Reward and all necessary Charges paid. All Masters of Vessels and others are forbid harbouring and carrying said Servant off, as they would avoid the Penalty of the Law.   JOSEPH LEE.   Concord, Sept. 22.
The Boston Gazette, And Country Journal, September 24, 1781; October 8, 1781.

MADE his Escape on the Night of the 18th Instant, from the Goal in New-Haven, one Joseph Dickerman, a tall slim Man, with short black Hair, lame in one Leg. Whoever shall take up said Dickerman, & return him to this or Hartford Goal, shall be reasonably rewarded by
STEPHEN MUNSON, Goaler. New-Haven, Sept. 25, 1781.
The Connecticut Journal, September 27, 1781; October 4, 1781.

RUN-away from his master, an Apprentice boy named Abraham Witaker, tall slim stature, about 17 years of age. Whoever will take up said apprentice and return him to he said master, shall be entitled to Six Pence reward, paid, by HARPER HOWARD WOOD.   Somers, Sept. 24, 1781.
The Connecticut Courant, And Weekly Intelligencer, October 2, 1781; October 9, 1781; October 16, 1781.

RAN away, about the 22d of last Month, a Molatto Boy, named JOE, about 10 Years old, thick set; had on when he went away a dark Waistcoat and Trowsers. Whoever will take up said Boy, and bring him to the Printers hereof, shall be handsomely rewarded for their Trouble.
N. B. All Masters of Vessels are hereby forbid carrying off said Lad, if they will avoid the Penalty of the Law.
The Boston-Gazette, And Country Journal, October 7, 1782; October 14, 1782; October 21, 1782. See *The Boston-Gazette, And Country Journal*, December 23, 1782.

WHEREAS I the subscriber lately advertised my wife Sarah, in the Hartford News Paper, as misbehaving and forbidding all persons to trust her on my account, or to entertain her, a writing from under my hand hath since been obtained by force and threats, recommending her as of good behaviour and in full credit, I do notwithstanding the said writing obtained as foresaid, further forbid all persons trusting her on my account, or keeping her in their houses, as I am willing to provide for her in my own house if she will come home to her duty.

           JESSE HALL.   Farmington, October 4, 1781.

The Connecticut Courant, And Weekly Intelligencer, October 9, 1781; October 30, 1781. See *The Connecticut Courant, And Weekly Intelligencer*, September 4, 1781.

           I Have a Son by Name of JOSIAH FOOT, aged 24 Years, who has always been under a Degree of Infirmity of Mind, and is wont to wander from Town to Town, which has put me to much Trouble and Expence: This is therefore to request of such People as have Opportunity to see or be conversant with him, to treat him with Humanity and Tenderness, but not to harbour or detain him in their Service, (as has been too often the Case) but to dismiss him that he may come home, thus they will oblige their very humble Servant,

           GEORGE FOOT.   New-Town, October 10, 1781.

The Connecticut Journal, October 11, 1781; October 18, 1781; October 25, 1781.

                                                  Worcester, October 3, 1781.

           Yesterday made his escape from the Subscriber, a Negro Man named Prince, about 20 Years of Age, 5 Feet 8 or 9 Inches high, a pale Black, large flat Nose, speaks moderate and good English, had on when escaped, a round black Wool Hatt, a light blue Coat, green jacket, checked Woolen Shirt, a pair of long tow Trowsers, bare footed and bare leged. He was apprehended by Authority for Stealing several ruffled Shirts, some Cloth, Shoes, Leather, and a Variety of other Articles, from Gentlemen in Salisbury in Connecticut, and supposed to have stolen a considerable sum of Money. Whoever will apprehend said Negro Man, with the Goods, and return him to Salisbury, or secure him and Goods that he may be brought to Justice and the Owners receive their Property, shall have Forty hard Dollars Reward and all necessary Charges paid, and for the Negro Man, Three Guineas Reward, and all necessary Charges

           paid by   STEPHEN KEYS.

N. B. All Masters of Vessels are requested to secure the above mentioned Negro, on his offering to come on board.

The Independent Chronicle and the Universal Advertiser, October 11, 1781; October 18, 1781; October 25, 1781.

                            WORCESTER, October 11.

           The supreme judicial court, which lately sat at Springfield, County of Hampshire, adjourned without day [sic] after passing sentence of death on

Michael Lobidal for the murder of James MacMullen. William Thelly was convicted of the crime of Manslaughter in carelessly administering such a quantity of rum to an infant under the age of six years as to occasions its death, for which he was burned in the hand. Thomas Gibbs, and old offender, for uttering counterfeit new emission eight dollar bills, to be whipped thirty stripes, and to suffer six months imprisonment; and for having a large quantity of counterfeit money in his custody, with an intent to utter the same, to stand one hour in the pillory in the several towns of Springfield, Northampton and Hadley.

Thomas's Massachusetts Spy Or, The Worcester Gazette, October 11, 1781.

ON the night of the 4th instant the house of the subscriber was broke open while he was in it by Amos Hull, Fred. Way, and Betty Way, Mulattoes, and robbed of the following articles, viz. One white and one striped Linen Shirt, one waistcoat, one pair of white silk Breeches, one Dollar and some small silver. The ruffians also attempted to murder the subscriber. Whoever will apprehend the above persons and give information, shall receive Ten Pounds reward, or in that proportion for each.

      JOSEPH MUNN.   Farmington, October 8.

The Connecticut Courant, And Weekly Intelligencer, October 16, 1781; October 23, 1781.

     Whereas *Jemima*, Wife of the Subscriber,
has eloped from me without Cause. These therefore are to forbid any Person from harbouring or trusting her on my Account, for I declare I will not pay any Debt she may contract.

     BENJAMIN FORSTER, Jun. Reading, October 4, 1781.

The Independent Chronicle and the Universal Advertiser, October 18, 1781.

FORTY DOLLARS REWARD.

MADE their escape from Norwich goal, on the night of the 15th instant, JOSEPH KILBORN and ROBERT RANSOM: Kilborn is about 27 years old, near 6 feet high, dark complexion, long dark brown hair, a large boned fellow; had on a blue coat, snuff coloured breeches, white stockings, and a felt hat. Ransom is about 18 years of age, 5 feet 6 inches high, light complexion, long light coloured hair, turned back on the top of his head; had on a black coat and waist-coat, white cloth breeches, and a pair of boots.—Whoever will apprehend said villains, and secure them in any gaol in the United States, or return them to the subscriber, shall receive the above reward, or Twenty Dollars for either of them.

    MOSES CLEVELAND, Gaoler.   Norwich, October 18.

The Norwich Packet and the Weekly Advertiser, October 18, 1781; October 25, 1781; November 1, 1781. See *The Connecticut Gazette; And The Universal Intelligencer*, August 24, 1781, for Kilborn.

WHEREAS Mary my wife hath eloped from my bed and board, and hath carried away considerable of my substance, this is therefore to forbid all persons trusting her on my account, for I will not pay any debt of her contracting after this date.
          ELISHA TUCKER.   Coventry, October 23, 1781.
The Connecticut Courant And Weekly Intelligencer, October 23, 1781; October 30, 1781; November 6, 1781.

RUN-away from his master, on the 16th of September, a servant boy named Allen Bill, about 17 or 18 years of age, small of stature, of a brindled complexion, and very full of his own importance; had on when he went away an old Castor Hat, an old speckled Flannel Jacket, striped tow and linen Shirt, white tow cloth long trowsers, pale blue stockings, old Shoes newly mended. Whoever will take up said run-away and return him to his master, shall have Six Pence reward and no charges paid by
          REUBEN STILES.   Coventry, October 16, 1781.
The Connecticut Courant And Weekly Intelligencer, October 30, 1781; November 6, 1781.

RUN away from the Subscriber on Monday 8th inst. a Negro Man, named Cuff, about 24 Years of Age, about 5 Feet, 9 or 10 inches high—Whoever will apprehend said Negro, and return him to his Master, shall have one Continental Dollar, old Emission Reward, and no charges paid; all Persons are hereby cautioned and forbid harbouring or concealing him if they would avoid the penalty of the Law.
          J. CUZZINS, of Holliston.
The Independent Chronicle and the Universal Advertiser, November 1, 1781; November 8, 1781.

          Millington, (East-Haddam) Nov. 1, 1781.
RAN away from the subscriber last night, a negro man named TOM, about 40 years old, tall, well-built, very black, speaks good English, marked with three straight strokes on the temple; had on striped woollen breeches, his jacket ragged, checked woollen shirt, and plain silver shoe buckles. Whoever will return said servant to the subscriber, shall have TEN HARD DOLLARS reward.   GREEN HUNGERFORD.
The Connecticut Gazette; And The Universal Intelligencer, November 2, 1781; November 9, 1781; November 16, 1781. See *The Connecticut Courant, And Weekly Intelligencer*, November 20, 1781.

WHEREAS Sarah the wife of me the subscriber has behaved herself in a very indecent, unbecoming and disobedient manner, by raising and spreading slanderous reports, which is ruinous to a good name, and has now forsaken my bed and board, I have reason to fear she will involve me in debt. These are therefore to forbid all persons whatsoever from trusting her on my account, as I am determined not to pay any debt of her contracting after this date.
               SAMUEL STEEL.   Tolland, October 25, 1781.
The Connecticut Courant And Weekly Intelligencer, November 6, 1781; November 13, 1781. *The Connecticut Courant And Weekly Intelligencer*, April 9, 1782.

STOLEN from the dwelling house of the subscriber, in East Windsor, on the evening of the first instant, a new beaver hat, of the best kind, with black lining, round looping, and the front of the crown lined with green hat case. The supposed thief is a slim built young fellow, about five feet ten inches high, fair skin, dark hair, had on a light brown coat, redish coloured silk handkerchief, striped or checked trowsers, and a small round black hat, said he belonged to Union.
    Whoever will detect the thief so that he may be brought to justice and the hat recovered, shall receive ten dollars in silver, paid by
               ELI MOORE.   East Windsor, Nov. 8, 1781.
N. B. Six Dollars will be given for the hat only.
The Connecticut Courant, And Weekly Advertiser, November 20, 1781; November 27, 1781.

RUN AWAY from the subscriber, the night of the third inst. a Negro Man named TOM, 40 years old, tall, well built, very black, speaks good English, marked with three strait streaks on one or both temples, had on and carried with him two checked and one white shirt. A grey surtout, a cut velvet snuff coloured jacket, and an otter coloured ditto, and one old ragged ditto, blue yarn stockings and old shoes. Whoever will return said servant to his master shall have ten hard Dollars reward.
             GREEN HUNGERFORD.   East-Haddam, Nov. 4, 1781.
The Connecticut Courant, And Weekly Intelligencer, November 20, 1781; November 27, 1781. See *The Connecticut Gazette; And The Universal Intelligencer*, November 2, 1781.

STOLEN from the subscriber in the night of the 13th inst. by a British deserter, who calls his name Henry Brown, about 5 feet 7 or 8 inches high, says he was born in Germany, but speaks good English, had on a pale blue short jacket, light coloured cloth breeches, white woolen stockings, checked

woolen shirt, and stole from the subscriber, a red duffil great coat, a light coloured surtout, a pair of green plush breeches, a holland shirt, two pair of worsted stockings of a greyish colour, a pair of channel pumps, a pair of boots, a pair of silver buckles, a napkin marked E. I. and a considerable sum in hard cash, and sundry articles too tedious to mention. Whoever takes up said thief shall be handsomely rewarded and charges paid by me
JONATHAN HEBARD, of Windham.
Danbury, November 13th, 1781.
The Connecticut Courant, and Weekly Intelligencer, November 20, 1781; November 27, 1781.

RUN AWAY, my apprentice JOHN NEFF, a tall young man of about 17 years of age, masculine, hearty, raw country boy, of a good disposition, light coloured short hair; had on when he went away light colour'd cloaths.—As he has always behaved well, and appeared contented and happy, I suppose he has been enticed away by some designing person—Therefore, if the young man will return soon I will forgive him; but if he refuses it is desired he may be taken up or secured, and notice given to me.—All reasonable charges shall be duly paid, besides a handsome reward.
THOMAS DENNY.   Wethersfield, Nov. 8, 1781.
The Connecticut Courant, And Weekly Advertiser, November 20, 1781; November 27, 1781; December 11, 1781.

MADE his Escape from the Guard at Mill-stone Point, in the Night after the 20th Instant, a young Man who called his Name JOHN COLEMAN, and said he belonged to Hatfield; he was taken with a Number of Horses going to Long-Island; had on when he absconded a blue Coat and Jacket, and Boots, was about 5 ¼ Feet high, light Complexion: Whoever will take up said Fellow and deliver him to into the Custody of the Guard at Fort Trumbull, shall have Four Dollars Reward, and reasonable Charges
    paid by   JERE. HARDING, Serjeant of the Guard.
New-London, Nov. 22, 1781.
The Connecticut Gazette; And The Universal Intelligencer, December 7, 1781.

PORTSMOUTH, December 8.
We hear from Charlestown, in the county of Cheshire, in this State, on the East side of Connecticut River, that Col. Enoch Hale of Rindge, the High Sheriff of said county, having received orders to proceed to that town, and there to liberate two prisoners who were confined in the county gaol by the usurped authority of Vermont, having demanded the keys, and being denied, he attempted to break open the prison doors, but was knocked down by two

men and much wounded: And application being made to one Giles, a new made Justice in Vermont, (who has been in commission under New-Hampshire all the war 'till lately) very readily made and a warrant, and committed the High sheriff close prisoner, where he remained at the last account.
The Salem Gazette, December 14, 1781.

AFTER committing sundry burglaries and thefts ran away from his master last night, a negro man named FELIX, about twenty years old, near six feet high, speaks good English, tells lies with art and confidence, was born in Dedham, in Massachusetts State, one of his ancles a little bigger than the other, but cannot be easily discovered without pulling off his stocking, he is very well proportioned. Whoever will take up said negro and convey him to me, shall have TEN DOLLARS reward, and all necessary charges paid.
        HENRY CHAMPION.   Colchester, December 23, 1781.
N. B. Said negro when taken must be handcuff'd with iron or depend he will effect an escape. H. C.
The Connecticut Gazette; And The Universal Intelligencer, December 28, 1781; January 4, 1782; January 18, 1782.

        RUN-AWAY from his Master,
in Roxbury, on Wednesday last, a black SERVANT MAN, called NED, about 5 Feet 7 or 8 Inches high, speaks bad English, and one of his Legs is much longer than the other: Had on a black Broad-Cloth superfine Coat and Waistcoat.
    Whoever will secure or bring back the said Negro to the Subscriber, shall be handsomely rewarded.—All Persons are requested not to harbour him, as he has stolen some valuable Articles from
        HENRY MITCHELL.   BOSTON, 28th December, 1781.
The Boston Evening-Post and the General Advertiser, December 29, 1781.

1782

FIVE DOLLARS REWARD.
RAN away from the subscriber, on Tuesday the 8th instant, a negro man named JACK, about six foot high, slim built, talks very broken; had on when he went away, a dark brown jacket, oznabrigs trowsers, check'd shirt, new shoes, and a large black hat. Whoever will take up said negro, and return him to me the subscriber, shall have the above reward, and all necessary charges paid, by
        GILES MUMFORD.   New-London, Jan. 10, 1782.

The Connecticut Gazette; And The Universal Intelligencer, January 11, 1782; January 18, 1782; January 25, 1782.

DESERTED yesterday from the ship St. John, lying in this harbour, a sailor, named THOMAS BROOKS, he is near six feet high, about 27 years of age, had on a red jacket, a pair of lead coloured duffil trowsers, and a red cap. Whoever will apprehend said fellow, and confine him in any of the gaols of the United States, and giving notice to Capt. WILLIAM CREED, in Providence, shall be handsomely rewarded, and all necessary charges paid.
          OLIVER BOWEN.   Newport, January 12, 1782.
The Newport Mercury, January 12, 1782; January 19, 1782.

WHEREAS on Wednesday the 9th Instant, a Person about 32 Years of Age, who called himself by the Name of Doctor HENRY THOMAS NEATES, who had on an Olive-coloured Coat, blue Surtout, a white Hat, black Silk Stockings, about 5 Feet 5 Inches high, light Complexion, Pock mark'd, hired of the Subscriber, a Bay Horse, with a small Star in his Forehead, about 14 Hands high, a natural Trotter, about 8 Years old, with a very good Bridle and Saddle, the Saddle had Silver Oval Buttons, with a Cypher W C the Saddle Cloth red and white striped; the iron on the hind post of the Saddle-Tree broke.

The above Person is suspected of having stole 3 Shirts, a red India Handkerchief, 1 white ditto, with a red Border, 2 Cambrick Stocks, a white Cotton Waistcoat and Breeches 1 Pair Breeches, 1 Pair Shoes and 1 Pair Knee Buckles plated with Gold, polished in the Middle, on of then is broke on one Side, the Flukes of the Knee Buckles made of Steel.

Whoever will apprehend the above Neates, and return him to the Subscriber, with the above Horse and Goods, or confine him in any Goal on this Continent, so that the above Horse and Goods may be recovered, shall have FIFTY DOLLARS Reward, or Ten Dollars for the Horse, &c. and the same Sum for the Goods, or Twenty Dollars for the Man himself, paid by
          JOHN BALLARD, or JULES NEUVILLE.
                                      BOSTON, Jan. 12, 1782.
N. B. All Masters of Vessels and others are hereby cautioned against carrying off said Neates, as they would avoid the Penalty of the Law.
The Boston Gazette, And Country Journal, January 14, 1782; January 23, 1782.

WHEREAS MARY, the Wife of the Subscriber, hath eloped from my Bed and Board: I do hereby forbid all Persons trusting her on my Account, as I am determined not to pay any Debt of her contracting from the Date hereof.
          JOHN KING,   Coventry, January 18, 1782.

The Providence Gazette And Country Journal, January 19, 1782; January 26, 1782; February 2, 1782.

RAN AWAY on the 15th of September last, my Negro man LANKTON, about thirty-two years of age, talks but indifferently, handsomely pitted with the small-pox, has his two fore teeth remarkable sharp, being filed in his youth to a point, his wool, the fore part, grey by sickness, walks very upright.—Whoever will take up said Negro, and return him to the subscriber, shall have TEN DOLLARS reward, and all necessary charges paid, by
    JOHN BELDEN.   Weathersfield, January 26, 1782.
The Connecticut Courant and Weekly Intelligencer, January 29, 1782; February 5, 1782; February 12, 1782.

      Ten Dollars Reward.
RAN away from the subscriber, and indented NEGRO BOY, about 12 years old, a likely smart boy, had on a green waistcoat and Overalls, a jockey-cap, and white surtout.—Whoever will apprehend said Boy, and return him to his Master shall receive the above reward and all necessary charges paid.
 All Masters of Vessels and others are cautioned against harbouring or concealing said indented servant, as they would avoid the penalty.
    D. D. ROGERS.   Boston, January 29, 1782.
The Continental Journal, And Weekly Advertiser, January 31, 1782; February 7, 1782.

HANNAH WHITTEMORE, of New-Ipswich, in the county of Hillsborough, and State of New Hampshire, wife of Peletiah Whittemore, late of said New-Ipswich, having petitioned the General Court of said State, representing that she had been married to the said Peletiah about nineteen years and that he without any just cause on her part, had within eighteen months last past at a place called Peck-Kiln, in the State of New-York, married another woman, and now actually lives and cohabits with woman at said Peck-Kiln, and had utterly forsaken her the petitioner: For which reason, she pray that a divorce from the said Peletiah, *a vinculo matrimonii* might be granted her.—On which petition, the General Court ordered that the petitioner be heard before said court, on the second Tuesday of their next session; when any person may appear and shew cause why the prayer should not be granted.
    Attest. E. THOMPSON, Sec'y.   January 11, 1782.
The New-Hampshire Gazette, And General Advertiser, February 2, 1782; February 9, 1782.

ELOPED from my bed and board HANNAH wife of me the subscriber, and refuses to return to live with me again, these are therefore, to warn all persons

against trusting her on my account, as I will not pay any debts of her contracting.
    JOHN EPHRAIM, jun.   *Natick, February 9th, 1782.*
Thomas's Massachusetts Spy Or, The Worcester Gazette, February 14, 1782; February 21, 1782.

Yesterday se'nnight two men from New-Plymouth, in the state of New-Hampshire, were taken up in Newbury-Port, for uttering and passing counterfeit dollars. Upon examination, upwards of fifty were found upon them, only one of which was good. The name of one of these culprits is Paul Hovey, son to a Baptist preacher, who said he received it from one Brown of New-Plymouth. There were strong reasons for supposed them guilty, and they were committed to goal for trial.—These dollars are easily discovered from the true ones, being made of pewter only, dated 1770, and the work badly executed. Tis probable more of them may be offered in other towns, as it is supposed several others in Cohoss are equally concerned.
 Thomas's Massachusetts Spy Or, The Worcester Gazette, February 14, 1782.

WHEREAS my wife HULDA has given me reason to suspect that she will run me in debt, I therefore hereby forbid all persons trusting with her or trusting her any thing on my account; for I declare I will not pay any debt of her contracting after the date hereof.
    THOMAS ROBBLEE. Lanesborough, February 1, 1782.
 The Connecticut Courant And Weekly Intelligencer, February 19, 1782; February 26, 1782.

WHEREAS Ruth, the Wife of me the Subscriber, hath eloped from my Bed and Board, and during my Absence at Sea hath behaved herself in a very unbecoming Manner: I hereby caution all Persons against trusting her on my Account, as I shall not pay any Debts of her contracting from the Date hereof.
    EZEKIEL HARRIS. *Cumberland, March 1, 1782.*
 The Providence Gazette And Country Journal, March 2, 1782; March 9, 1782; March 16, 1782.

STOLEN from the subscriber on or about the 1st of February last, a large Sorrel MARE, with a star in her forehead, natural trotter, about 14 hands and half high, well built, about 6 years old. The person who is suspected to take her, likewise received a quantity of Cloaths belonging to my son and has carried them away with him; the cloathing consists of the following articles, viz. One red Hairb[in]e Coat, a pair of Velveroy Breeches, a pair of Shoes, a pair of plated Shoe Buckles, two pair of white woolen Stockings, two Stocks, one light coloured homespun Great Coat, two white linen Shirts; likewise 5

yards Corduroy, and 3 and half yards white Shalloon, and a Bridle which was on said Mare. Whoever will take up said thief and the articles stolen, and secure the thief in any of the goals in the United States and give the subscriber notice, shall have Ten Dollars reward and all necessary charges paid, by   REUBEN HURLBUT.
N. B. The person suspected to be the thief, is a tall stout built fellow, about 26 years old, wears long dark hair, black eyes, his name is Timothy Holcomb, and originally belonged to Simsbury.   Simsbury, March 1, 1782.
The Connecticut Courant And Weekly Intelligencer, March 5, 1782; March 12, 1782. See below. See *The Connecticut Courant And Weekly Intelligencer*, March 26, 1782.

WHEREAS the above advertisement, published by REUBEN HURLBUT, of Simsbury, purports, that he has had a HORSE stolen, and a quantity of his son's cloaths carried off by the thief, bidding a reward to have him taken up and the horse and cloathing secured, and charges one Timothy Holcomb of said Simsbury with the theft: We therefore, would represent to the candid public the truth of the affair, which is this, that his son Reuben Hurlbut, jun. being arrested for stealing some articles from Mr. Burr, of Hartford, made his escape from the officer, taking his father's mare, described in said advertisement against Holcomb, and runs away, meets with Holcomb white he was absent, and puts his father's said mare into Holcomb's hands. Holcomb returns home and informs, that he had exchanged horses with young Hurlbut, and gave a watch and some money for odds, and likewise that he had bought some cloathing of him: Immediately on this young Hurlbut comes home, with a horse and watch, which he said he had of Holcomb, and had let Holcomb have his horse and some cloaths. Therefore, if the horse described in said advertisement was stolen, he who run from the arrest for theft must be the thief: Therefore, we trust, the candid public will treat the advertisement, signed Reuben Hurlbut, with that contempt which such scandalous publications ought to meet with from all honest people.
    CALEB HOLCOMB,   STEPHEN GRIFFIN, 2d.
    JESSE HOLCOMB.   Simsbury, March 4, 1782.
The Connecticut Courant And Weekly Intelligencer, March 5, 1782; March 12, 1782. See above. *The Connecticut Courant And Weekly Intelligencer*, March 26, 1782.

TAKEN away from the subscriber, a BAY HORSE about 14 hands high, white on the end of his nose, a star on his forehead, and one white hind foot. The person who took him is an Irishman of a middling size, light complexion and red hair, had on a grey great coat. Whoever shall take up the man and horse, and secure them so that the subscriber recovers his horse and the man

brought to justice, shall receive Six Dollars reward, or three dollars for the horse, and all necessary charges paid by
ZEBULON PLATT.   Redding, March 1, 1782.
The Connecticut Journal, March 7, 1782; March 21, 1782.

BOSTON, March 16.

At the Honorable Supreme Judicial Court held at Boston, in the county of Suffolk, on Saturday the 5th of March inst. the following persons received sentence for crimes by them committed, viz. Ebenezer Griffin, William Hannon, and John Carrol, indicted for robbery, the two former acquitted and Carrol acquitted of the robbery but convicted of theft, sentenced to pay David Child (the person injured) 34 l. 10s. being, with the goods restored, three times the value of the goods stolen, to be whipped 20 stripes upon his naked back, at the public whipping-post, pay costs of prosecution, and stand committed till the sentence is performed. William Sayles convicted of a fraud, sentenced to be whipped 20 stripes, &c. to recognize in 100 l. with sufficient surety for his good behavior for two years, pay costs, &c. Oliver Ware, and William Sayles, convicted upon another indictment for fraud, sentenced to stand one hour in the pillory, (which sentence was executed last Thursday) pay costs, &c. and David Tuman, sentenced to be whipped 20 stripes, to pay costs, &c.—Oliver Ware who pleaded guilty to another indictment for fraud, sentenced to be whipped 20 stripes, recognize in 50 l. with sufficient surety for his good behavior for two years, pay costs, &c.—Jesse Fowler who pleaded guilty to an indictment for theft, sentenced to pay Joseph Crosby (the person injured) 14 l. 4s. 6s. being treble damages, and to pay a fine to the Commonwealth of 5 l. pay costs, &c. David Tuman who pleaded guilty to an indictment for fraud, sentenced to suffer 3 months imprisonment, pay costs, &c.—Williams Sayles convicted for uttering and passing counterfeit money, knowing it to be such, sentenced to pay Jonathan Scott (the person injured) 36 l. being treble the value of the bills uttered, to pay a fine to the Commonwealth of 50 l. to suffer three months imprisonment pay costs &c. William Sayles convicted upon another indictment for the same crime, sentenced to pay Joseph Steel (the person injured) 43 l. 4s. to pay a fine to the Commonwealth of 50 l. the suffer 3 months imprisonment, to pay costs, &c.

The Boston Evening-Post and the General Advertiser, March 16, 1782.

Whereas Bridget, the Wife of
the Subscriber, has Eloped from me, this is to forbid all Persons from trusting her on my Account, as I will not pay any Debt contracted by her.
James Kelsey.   Nottingham, March 4. 1782.
The New-Hampshire Gazette, And General Advertiser, March 16, 1782; March 23, 1782.

Hartford, March 22, 1782.

LAST night made their escape from the Goal in this place, Samuel Hoit, about 23 years old, wore his own hair, light coloured Jacket, red brown Overhalls, middling sized fellow belonged to Delancy's corps, one of the number that broke out of Newgate in May last. Also, Elijah Smith, confined for theft, small fellow, about 32 years old. Whoever will take up and confine said fellows, or either of them, in any goal in the United States, shall have reasonable charges paid and the thanks of the public.
     EZ'L. WILLIAMS, Sheriff.
 The Connecticut Courant And Weekly Intelligencer, March 26, 1782; April 2, 1782. See *The Connecticut Courant, And Weekly Advertiser*, May 22, 1781, for Hoit.

WHEREAS my wife MARTHA hath eloped from my house, while I was in the army, serving my country, and hath been guilty of adultery, and behaved herself in such a manner as I have reason to think she will run me in debt. These are therefore to forbid all persons trusting her on my account, as I will not pay any debt of her contracting from this date.
    SETH ARNOLD.   Farmington, March 21, 1782.
 The Connecticut Courant, And Weekly Intelligencer, March 26, 1782; April 9, 1782.

      Twenty Dollars Reward.
THE public have undoubtedly observed in the Connecticut Courant and advertisement, published by me the subscriber; advertising one large Sorrel Mare, about six years old, fourteen hands and half high, with a star in her forehead, natural trotter, belonging to me, as also a number of articles of cloathing, belonging to my Son Reuben Hurlbut, jun. consisting of the following articles, viz. five yards of Corduroy, 3 yards and half of white Holland, 2 white Shirts, one red Hairbine Coat, one pair of white Velveroy Breeches, one pair of Shoes, one pair of plated Buckles, 2 pair of white Stockings, 2 Stocks, one light coloured Great Coat, one Bridle on said Mare, as being stolen; in which I informed the public that I suspected the thief to be one Timothy Holcomb, of Simsbury, being a stout well built fellow, about 26 years old, with long dark hair, and black eyes, and therein I proffered a reward of Ten Dollars, for the thief and articles: the thief being secured in any goal in the United States, and notice given to me: In consequence of which, I was under written by a brother and some near kinsmen of said Timothy, who would endeavour to impose upon the public that my Son Reuben Hurlbut, jun. and said Timothy, being abroad together, exchanged Horses for valuable considerations: I would therefore assure the public, that on a strict enquiry into the matter which the pretended exchange was made, find in fact that one the contrary there never was any exchange made, so that of course all

assertions of a bargain being this made is false.—And further, that upon the return of said horse home, which they pretend said Timothy let my son have in a way of exchange, Caleb Holcomb, one of the subscribers to said underwriting, having a demand against said Timothy, immediately seized, as being the estate of said Timothy.—Therefore it is obvious, that said underwriting was designed, only to prevent my said advertisement taking effect; and as to what the underwriters say they had from my mouth, concerning any exchange of said horses, I affirm I never gave such an account; and as to the theft that they would scandalously cast on my said Son, respecting Mr. Burr's goods, another person undertook to settle as being the thief himself, and settled by the assistance of said Caleb Holcomb, one of said underwriters, before my Mare and Son's cloathing were stolen, but from a consciousness of the honesty of my intention, which was and is to obtain a compensation for the wrongs I have suffered, as well as that such felony may be punished; I would therefore repeat my said advertisement, that whoever will take up the thief and said articles, (stolen on or about the fourth day of February last) and secure the thief in any common goal of the United States, and give me notice, shall have the above reward of Twenty Dollars and all necessary charges, if only the thief Ten Dollars, by me

REUBEN HURLBUT. Simsbury, March 22, 1782.

We the subscribers under-written, having had acquaintance with the above named Reuben Hurlbut, for a number of years past, do esteem him to be a man of truth and fidelity, and is reputed an honest judicious man, he is now Captain over a company of militia in this town, and has behaved as a great friend to the cause of his country—would beg that the public would assist him in the recovery of his goods, &c.

Simsbury, March 22, 1782.

JONATHAN PETTIBONE, ELISHA CORNISH,
DUDLEY PETTIBONE, JOSEPH TULLER,
DAVID PHELPS, ABEL PETTIBONE,
DANIEL HUMPHREY, NOAH PHELPS,
JOE CASE, JONATHAN HUMPHRY.

The Connecticut Courant And Weekly Intelligencer, March 26, 1782; April 2, 1782. See *The Connecticut Courant And Weekly Intelligencer*, March 5, 1782, two ads.

5 Dollars Reward.

Ran away from the subscriber, a servant man, named Francis Muray, a native of France, 4 feet [*sic*] 7 inches high, his face much scar'd, the left eye blind, had on when he went away a stone-grey outside jacket and breeches, and red waistcoat; he took with him a watch, silver face and case, and leather string in lieu of a chain. Whoever will secure said servant so that he and the watch may be recovered, shall receive the above reward.

NORMAN CLARK. Newton, March 27.
The Independent Chronicle and the Universal Advertiser, March 28, 1782; April 4, 1782; April 11, 1782; April 18, 1782.

WHEREAS Elizabeth, the Wife of me the Subscriber, hath eloped from my Bed and Board: I hereby give Notice, that I will not pay any Debts of her contracting from the Date hereof.
JOHN COLE. Warren, March 29, 1782.
The Providence Gazette And Country Journal, March 30, 1782; April 6, 1782; April 20, 1782; April 27, 1782.

Left his master's service in Boston, on Thursday the 7th of March inst. a servant Boy, named Walter Jackson, 12 years of age, and about 4 feet 8 or 9 inches high—had on when he went away a black broad cloth coat, much worn, a light-grey cloth waistcoat, leather breeches, and white ribb'd yarn stockings. As the parents of said boy are very anxious to know what has become of him, if any person can give any intelligence of where he is, by leaving word with the printer hereof, they will much oblige a distress'd mother, and shall also be rewarded for their kindness.
The Independent Chronicle and the Universal Advertiser, April 4, 1782; April 18, 1782.

RAN AWAY from the Subscriber in Groton, on Tuesday last, a Negro Man named FLETUS, his Nose pitted, but not with the Small Pox, one of his fore Teeth broke and split; had on a short brown Jacket something old, buckskin Breeches, mix'd yarn Stockings, an old felt Hat fopp'd. Whoever will return him to the Subscriber, shall have TEN DOLLARS Reward, and all necessary Charges.
All Masters of Vessels and Others are hereby forbid to conceal or carry off said Negro on Penalty of the Law.
THOMAS GARDINER, jun. Stonington, April 3d. 1782.
The Connecticut Gazette; And The Universal Advertiser, April 5, 1782; April 12, 1782; April 19, 1782.

I JOSEPH SLATE, do hereby warn any persons of trusting my wife SOVIA, on my account, as she has eloped from my bed and board.
JOSEPH SLATE. New-London, March 27, 1782.
The Connecticut Gazette; And The Universal Advertiser, April 5, 1782; April 12, 1782; April 19, 1782.

RAN away from the Subscriber, on the Evening of the 28th of March, a Negro Boy, named Warwick, about 5 Feet 6 Inches high, about 18 Years of Age, has the Guinea Marks on his Forehead, Cheeks and Chin, and Holes through the Sides of his Nose: had on when he went away, a Pair of thick Mooseskin Breeches, white Stockings, woollen Shirt, black and white mixed Coat, white woollen Jacket, Cloth coloured Great-Coat, and an old Beaver Hat, newly dressed; carried with him a striped Linen Coat, a Pair of white Stockings, a Pair of blue and white mixed Ditto, one fine Home-made Shirt, and a white Linen Jacket and Breeches. Whoever will take up said Negro, and deliver him to the Subscriber, or secure him so that he may be had again, shall have Ten Dollars Reward, and all necessary Charges, paid by
EBENEZER CRAFT.
N.B. All Persons are forbid to harbour or carry off said Boy, as they will answer the contrary at the Peril of the Law.   Sturbridge, April 2, 1782.

The Providence Gazette And Country Journal, April 6, 1782; April 13, 1782; April 20, 1782; April 27, 1782; May 4, 1782.

THE Public, and my friends in particular, are hereby informed, that the late advertisement in the Connecticut Courant, under the signature of Samuel Steel, is without any just foundation. He has wantonly sported with truth, in the many epithets he has bestowed on an unhappy wife.

That I married Samuel Steel is my misfortune; that I have as his wife behaved indecent or unbecoming I deny, and whether my connexion with him, or behaviour towards him, or reports of him, have hurt his good name, let his best friends judge.

He left my bed two month before I left his board; I never run him in debt nor even threatened it. What he took from me I hope he will return; what he took from me, that is my innocence, let him settle that with God and his own conscience; and if for the future he will not hurt his own character, I promise him I will not do it for him.

Marriage, O sacred ordinance of Heaven,
The last best seal of love to mortals given,
In public prints must now thy frowns and smiles
'Twixt man and wife, ride post for scores of miles.
            SARAH STEEL.   Pittsfield, February 16th, 1782.
The Connecticut Courant And Weekly Intelligencer, April 9, 1782; April 23, 1782. See *The Connecticut Courant And Weekly Intelligencer*, November 6, 1781

MADE their Escape from the Gaol in this Town, in the Night of the 5th instant, one Joel Jennings, of Fairfield, committed for attempting to break open a House in Milford; he is a tall slim Man, had on a light coloured Great-Coat.—Also John Anthony, of Wallingford, committed for Debt, is a small Man, poorly dressed, but a great Talker. Whoever shall return to above Persons to this Gaol, shall receive a generous Reward, and the Thanks of
111STEPHEN MUNSON, Gaoler.   New-Haven, April 9, 1782.
   The Connecticut Journal, April 11, 1782; April 18, 1782; April 24, 1782.

THE Subscriber, on the 2d of this instant, lent to a Stranger, who called himself Jones, a red roan MARE, about 14 Hands high, trots and paces, her hind Feet appear as if she had Ring-Bones; she is about 8 Years old or upwards; had on a hunting Saddle, with a Deerskin Seat, and a single-rein'd curb Bridle.—He hired said Mare to go to Taunton, to stay one Night; but as he has not since been heard of, the Subscriber supposes he is gone off with said Mare. Said Jones appears to be a Foreigner, is short, of a light Complexion, has blue Eyes and light Hair; wears a green Coat, and a light coloured Surtout, walks rather wide, and appears to be somewhat lame. Whoever will apprehend said Jones, and secure the Mare, so that the Owner may have her again, shall have Fifteen Dollars Reward for both, or Ten for the Mare, and Five for the Man, and all necessary Charges, paid by
            SIMEON THAYER.   *Providence, April* 12, 1782.
   The Providence Gazette And Country Journal, April 13, 1782; April 20, 1782.

WHEREAS I Samuel Hale, of Granby, in the County of Hampshire, and State of Massachusetts Bay, Cooper, do hereby notify all Persons, that my Wife, Elizabeth Hale, has for some Time past, forsook and acquitted my Bed and Board, for which Reason I hereby forbid all Persons trusting said Elizabeth, on any Terms, as I will not pay any Debt of her contracting.
            SAMUEL HALE.   Granby, April 5th, 1782.
   The Boston Gazette, And Country Journal, April 15, 1782; April 29, 1782.

RUN AWAY on the evening of the 15th instant, my hired man JOHN ROWLAND LENOX, who before this lived with me some time as my hostler, served me faithful and well untill this time, is a good looking fellow, about five feet ten inches high, talks broad and open English, stammers a little, dark coloured hair, his foretop carelessly turned back, handsomely pitted with the small pox, fair complexion, about 25 years of age, is a deserter from the British army; well cloathed, in white plain home made cloth waistcoat, vest and overalls; stole a likely black Horse, fourteen hands and

an half high, white star in his forehead, marked with a Dutch brand TB, about twelve years old, has lost one eye, marked on his hoof if not worn out IWebb. He stole the following things besides said horse, viz. One exceeding genteel pair of plated jointed Stirrup Irons, one pair plated spurs, one genteel plated curb bridle, two pair steel common stirrups, half a dozen fine razors, some of them in a shagreen pock-book, with scissors, &c. two watch coats, one a light brown lined with green baize, the other a new dark brown Bath-Coating, a number of stockings, silk and linen handkerchiefs, five linen shirts, and a number of other articles of wearing apparel, most of them marked with the initials of some of my family's name's. Whoever will take up the said thief, and secure him, shall have eight Dollars reward, and eight Dollars for the things, and all necessary charges paid, by their humble servant,
   JOSEPH WEBB.   Wethersfield, April 16, 1782.
The Connecticut Courant, and The Universal Weekly Intelligencer, April 19, 1782; April 30, 1782; May 7, 1782. See *The Connecticut Gazette; And The Universal Advertiser,* April 19, 1782.

RUN away on the evening of the 15th instant, my hired man JOHN ROWLAND LENOX, who before this lived with me some time, a good looking fellow, of about 32 years of age, talks broad and open, dark coloured hair, his foretop turned back, handsomely pitted with the small-pox, fair complexion, about 5 feet 11 inches high, dressed in white plain cloth, home made, white overhalls; stole dark brown great coat, a number of stockings, a number of pocket handkerchiefs, some linen shirts, a genteel pair of plated swiveled stirrups irons, a plated bridle bit, a genteel pair of plated spurs; also a number of raisors in a black leather case like a pocket-book, and a number of other articles;—also a black horse, with one eye. Said horse is 14 ½ hands high, about 12 years old, a good trotter. The fellow also stole and carried off a gun; by which it is supposed he will turn up said horse and endeavour to pass with a gun and knapsack as a soldier; he is a deserter from the British army, and likely gone towards Rope-ferry. Whoever will secure the thief and things, shall be handsomely rewarded by their humble servant,
   JOSEPH WEBB.   Wethersfield, April 16, 1782.
The Connecticut Gazette; And The Universal Advertiser, April 19, 1782; April 26, 1782; May 3, 1782. See *The Connecticut Courant, And Weekly Intelligencer,* April 19, 1782.

     WHEREAS *MIRIAM* the wife of me the subscriber, has behaved in such a disorderly manner towards me in various instances, as to forfeit my protection, affection, and her marriage vows, I therefore forbid any person trusting her on my account, as I will not discharge any debt of her contracting from the date hereof.
   DAVID NEWTON.   *Rutland, April* 26, 1782.

Thomas's Massachusetts Spy Or, The Worcester Gazette, April 26, 1782; May 9, 1782.

STOLEN from the Subscriber in the Night of the 30th of April last, a grey Great-Coat, a pair new Boots, pair leather Breeches, a new Silk Cloak, 2 pair Stockings, 6 pair Sheets, 6 do. Pillow-Cases, a Chintz Gown, a new Hat, and a number of small Articles. The Person who stole the above-mentioned Articles is a Servant of the Subscriber's/ called his Name Richard Greenelch, an Old Countryman, about 20 Years old, short stocky Fellow, has a down look, and weak Eyes. Whoever will apprehend the above Thief, so that the Owner may recover his Property again, shall have Six Dollars Reward.
     EDWARD LARKIN.   New-Haven, May 1, 1782.
The Connecticut Journal, May 2, 1782.

RAN away from the Subscriber, in North-Kingstown, in the State of Rhode-Island, the 27th inst. a likely young coloured Mulatto Servant, named ROBIN, about 19 Years of Age, and near 5 Feet 10 Inches high, walks a little bending forward, has a Scar on one of his Feet, and a small one on his Forehead; had on when he went away, a black and white Kersey Jacket, white Kersey Breeches, white Flannel Shirt, a Pair of black and white Yarn Stockings, and took with him another pair of white Yarn ditto, had on old Shoes, and an old Felt Hat with small Brims.—Whoever will take up said Fellow, and bring him to his Master, or secure him in Gaol, so that his Master gets him again, shall receive TEN SILVER DOLLARS, and reasonable Charges paid, by
     EZEKIEL GARDNER. North-Kingstown, April 30, 1782.
The Newport Mercury, May 4, 1782; May 11, 1782.

RAN away, from the subscriber, on the 27th of April last, a Negro man named PERO, about 5 feet 7 inches high, middling well set, was bred in the country, and speaks good English, is a quiet peaceable fellow, looks somewhat sleepy with his eyes, had on when he went away, a white flannel shirt, a pair of light grey broad-cloth breeches, with dark gray waistband thereto, a dark grey full-cloth jacket, a striped flannel jacket, grey yarn stockings, old shoes, one cap'd at the toe, a grey kersey full cloth great coat, and a felt hat, it is supposed he went off with a couple of Mulatto fellows, or at least they looked like such: Whoever will take up said fellow and return him to me, or secure him so that I might get him again, shall have EIGHT DOLLARS reward, and reasonable charges paid, by
     JOSEPH RAYNOLDS.   Exeter, May 2, 1782.
The Newport Mercury, May 4, 1782; May 11, 1782; May 18, 1782.

RAN away from the Subscriber, in the Evening of the 28th ult. a NEGRO FELLOW, named BRISTOL, about 19 Years of Age, about 5 Feet 9 Inches high, rather clumsily made, slow of Speech, walks upright, not over-witted; had on, when he went away, a blue Coat, a Pair of old striped Flannel Trowsers, patched with Cloth of a different Colour, and an old check'd Shirt; carried with him two white Shirts, a white Jacket, white Breeches, and old white Worsted Stockings. Whoever will take up said Fellow, and secure him so that his Master may have him again, shall have Eight Dollars Reward, and all necessary Charges, paid by
          JOSIAH FINNEY.   *Bristol, May* 3, 1782.
N. B. All Masters of Vessels are forbid to carry him off at their Peril.
The Providence Gazette And Country Journal, May 4, 1782; May 11, 1782; May 18, 1782; May 25, 1782; June 1, 1782; June 8, 1782.

WHereas SARAH, the Wife of BENJAMIN DEXTER, hath eloped from him, and in her Carriage towards him, both as to Bed and Board, and acting contrary to his loving and lawful Requests respecting his Interest, hath conducted herself in a very indecent and unbecoming Manner: He hereby forbids any Person trusting her on his Account, as he will pay no Debts of her contracting.
          BENJAMIN DEXTER.   *East-Greenwich, May* 3, 1782.
The Providence Gazette And Country Journal, May 4, 1782; May 11, 1782; May 18, 1782; May 25, 1782.

Fifty Dollars Reward.
STOLEN from the harbour of *Nantucket*, on the morning of the 29th of April last, a SCHOONER BOAT, burthen about 15 tons, her quarters was painted a bluish colour, bottom red, stern not coloured, she had two gangways on her quarter deck, one aft to stand and steer, the other with a companion way over it, her mainsail very old, foresail good and made of tow cloth. The persons that carried away said Boat, called their names George Burrage and Peter Little John. Burrage is a very small sized man, and Little John of a middling size.—As the above persons came from the Eastward it is supposed they have gone that way. Whoever will apprehend and secure said men so that they may be brought to justice, and the owner have his Boat again, shall have the above reward paid by
          HUSSEY & SNOW.   *Boston,* May 7, 1782.
The Continental Journal, And Weekly Advertiser, May 9, 1782; May 30, 1782.

WHEREAS Susanna my wife, has eloped from my bed and board, without any provocation. This is to forbid any persons harbouring, or trusting her on

my account, as I solemnly declare I will not pay one farthing, contracted on my account from this day forward.
     JOHN BEACH.   April 30, 1782.
 The Connecticut Courant, And Weekly Intelligencer, May 14, 1782; May 21, 1782; May 28, 1782. See *The Massachusetts Gazette Or The Springfield and Northampton Weekly Advertiser*, May 21, 1782.

WHEREAS Massy, my wife, has eloped from my bed and board, and still refuses to live with me; this is to cautions all persons from trusting her on my account, as I will pay no debts of her contracting, after the date hereof.
    MOSES VARNEY.   Rochelle. April 27, 1782.
 The New-Hampshire Gazette, And General Advertiser, May 18, 1782.

WHEREAS on Friday last, one William Lameson, aged 28 Years, 5 Feet 7 Inches high, light Complexion, grey Eyes, and brown Hair, Labourer, enlisted for the Term of three Years for the Town of Salem, having on Callico Clothes, hired of the Subscriber a Horse and Chaise to go the Watertown, but has not yet returned—The Horse was or a Sorrel Colour with a white Face, Trots and Paces; the Chaise painted Yellow, with a white Lining. Whoever will bring the Man, Horse and Chaise to the Subscriber, shall have TWENTY DOLLARS Reward, or the Horse and Chaise only Ten Dollars, and all reasonable Charges paid.
    JOHN NEWELL.   Boston, May 20, 1782.
 The Boston Gazette, and Country Journal, May 20, 1782.

WHEREAS JOHN BEACH, my husband, has advertised me as eloped from his bed and board, this is to certify the public, that we parted by previous agreement, and mutual consent before witnesses, and that on my leaving him, he consented to deliver me my goods. Said John Beach never took the care in providing for his family, that is the indispensable duty of every man, and allowed his son to behave toward me in a scandalous, indecent manner, which, together with his own ill homour, [sic] rendered my life very unhappy: For these causes I left him, and hope the candid world will pity rather than condemn an unfortunate woman,
     SUSANNA BEACH.
N. B. This is to forbid all women from harbouring, concealing, or having connection with said John Beach, as I will not be answerable for the consequences. S. B.   *Springfield, May* 21, 1782.
 The Massachusetts Gazette Or The Springfield and Northampton Weekly Advertiser, May 21, 1782; June 4, 1782. See *The Connecticut Courant, And Weekly Intelligencer*, May 14, 1782.

WHEREAS PATIENCE, the Wife of the Subscriber, hath eloped from my Bed and Board: I hereby forbid all Persons trusting her on my Account, As I will not pay any Debts of her contracting from the Date hereof.
    BENJAMIN BROWN.   Rehoboth, May 25, 1782.
The Providence Gazette And Country Journal, May 25, 1782; June 1, 1782; June 22, 1781.

WHEREAS LUCY, my Wife, hath eloped from my Bed and Board, and refuses support from me.—These are therefore, to caution all persons from harbouring or trusting her on my account, as I will not pay any debt of her contracting from the date hereof.
    ASA PARMELE.   Richmond, May 24, 1782.
The Connecticut Courant, And Weekly Intelligencer, May 28, 1782; June 4, 1782.

WHEREAS my wife MARTHA, hath conducted herself in such a scandalous manner, that I purpose not to cohabit with her—This is therefore to forbid any person or persons trusting her on my account, as I will not pay any debt of her contracting after the date hereof.
    SETH HUNT. Shaftsbury, (State of Vermont)
                   April 2d, 1782.
The Connecticut Courant, And Weekly Intelligencer, May 28, 1782; June 4, 1782.

STOP THIEF.

RUN away from the subscriber, one EDWARD BRISTOL, says he was born in the city of Bristol; he is a small man, about 5 feet 4 or 5 inches high, thin face, something round shoulder'd; he is very talkative, speaks through his nose, and takes snuff; had on when he went away, an old coat which has been turn'd, the original colour was claret, but much faded, with white figur'd buttons, an old purple cloth waistcoat with silver wash'd buttons in imitation of basket work, coarse white shirt, a round felt hat new, a pair of shoes almost new, plain brass shoe and knee buckles; stole about twelve dollars in cash. Whoever will secure said fellow in any goal in this State, and give me information, or return him to me, shall have EIGHT DOLLARS reward, and all reasonable charges paid, by
    HENRY TRUMAN.   New-London, 27th May, 1782.
The Connecticut Gazette; And The Universal Intelligencer, May 31, 1782; June 7, 1782; June 14, 1782.

WHEREAS GERUSHA, the Wife of the Subscriber, hath eloped, and refuses to live with me.—This is to forbid all Persons trusting her on my Account, As I will pay no Debts of her contracting after this date.

CALEB WOLCOTT. Wethersfield, May 27, 1782.
The Connecticut Courant, And Weekly Intelligencer, June 4, 1782; June 18, 1782; June 25, 1782.

SPRINGFIELD, June 4.

On Friday last a certain person appearing in a public house in this town, offering to serve in the continental army for the term of three years, was inlisted by the name of Samuel Smith, and on the same day was presented to the officer of this post for mustering. After many enquiries and a very *minute* examination, this adventurer (altho artfully dressed in mans apparrel) was discovered to be of the female sex; and soon conducted to goal. This discovery prevented the payment of 80 dollars bounty, which she was to have received for her promised services, after having been duly mustered. Since her confinement her accounts of herself have been many and various, at one time she asserts this to be the first scrape the devil ever led her into; at another that she has been a soldier and in actual service for three months, undiscovered. It is known however that her real name is Anne Smith originally from Ashford in Connecticut, and lately from Ashfield in this State. It appears also that our heroine began this rout with stealing a horse at Ashfield, that she swoped him for another at Northampton, sold the last to a tavern-keeper about five miles from this for a dram, a dinner, and an old coat. She acted the man so perfectly well through the whole she might probably have passed, had not the want of a beard, and the redundance of some other matters led to a detection.

The Massachusetts Gazette Or The Springfield and Northampton Weekly Advertiser, June 4, 1782; *The Independent Ledger, and the American Advertiser,* June 10, 1782, *The Salem Gazette,* June 13, 1782, and *The Connecticut Gazette; And The Universal Intelligencer,* June 14, 1782, *The Pennsylvania Packet or the General Advertiser,* June 25, 1782, and *Thomas's Massachusetts Spy Or, The Worcester Gazette,* June 27, 1782. Minor differences between the papers.

Ran away from the Subscriber,
a NEGRO BOY, about 12 Years old; he is a very likely, cunning, arch, little Fellow; had on when he went away, a Leather Jockey-Cap, green Waistcoat, redish Breeches, and check Shirt.—Whoever will take up said Runaway, and convey him to his Master, or confine him in any of the Goals of the United States, shall receive TEN DOLLARS reward, and all necessary Charges paid.
DANIEL DENNISON ROGERS.
The Independent Chronicle and the Universal Advertiser, June 13, 1782; June 20, 1782; June 27, 1782; July 4, 1782.

RUN away from the subscriber on the evening of the 8th inst. an apprentice negro boy, named CAESAR, about 17 years of age, about 5 feet high, thick set; had on when he went away, a double-breasted grey jacket, all wool cloth, a white belted under jacket without sleeves, all wool cloth, brown tow-cloth long trowsers, striped linen shirt, and an old felt hat; had on no stockings or shoes. If any Person will take up said negro boy and return him to me, so that I may have him again, shall receive TEN DOLLARS reward, and all necessary charges paid, by
        ISAAC AVERY.   Groton, June 10, 1782.
The Connecticut Gazette; And The Universal Intelligencer, June 14, 1782; June 21, 1782; June 28, 1782.

RUN away from the subscriber living in Green's-Farm Parish, Fairfield, a NEGRO WENCH, named TAMOR, the 10th inst. about 19 years of age, having a child with her about 15 months old, and pregnant with another, night her time. Whoever will take up and secure said Negro so that the owner may have her again, shall be generously rewarded and all necessary charges paid, by   JOSEPH HIDE.   Green's-Farms, June 12, 1782.
The Connecticut Journal, June 20, 1782; June 27, 1782; July 4, 1782.

20 Dollars Reward.

ON Thursday Night last, four armed Ruffians came on board my Sloop, lying in the Mill-Creek, and by Force entered the Cabin, with a dark lanthorn, made diligent Search, but finding nothing they could convey away, soon departed. One who was particularly active, had a long Nose, straw Hat, and a Pair of short sailor Trowsers; but from the Appearance of his under Cloths, and some other Circumstances, I have reason to suppose it to be a Person in disguise, who thinks he supports the Character of a Gentleman in this Town. Whoever will give Information to convict one or more of said Gentlemen, shall receive the above Reward, and the sincere Thanks of one who wished to detect Knaves, under the Mark of Gentlemen.
        W. TUCK.   Boston, June 15, 1782.
The Independent Chronicle and the Universal Advertiser, June 20, 1782; July 4, 1782.

Forty Dollars Reward.

Windham, 4th June, 1782.
LAST Evening the SHOP of the Subscriber was broke open, and the following Articles stole, viz. 10 Dozen Silk Barcelona Handkerchiefs—1 Piece black Mode—1 Piece blue Do.— 1 Piece Dove coloured Persian.—1 Piece yellow Batavia Silk—20 whole and part Pieces Ribbans—1 Piece Irish Linen—3 or 4 whole and part Pieces Cambrick—17 Dozen Gold spangled coat and vest Buttons, and a Number

of other Articles—a Quantity of Cash in Coppers, small Silver, and Connecticut Bills. Whoever will take up and secure the Thief or Thieves, recover the Goods and return them to me, shall receive the above Reward, and Charges paid by me; and for either Thief or Goods only, Twenty Dollars.
EBENEZER BACKUS.
N. B. The above Goods are supposed to have been stolen by one WILLIAM WINSLOW, a transient Person, about five feet nine Inches high, slim Built, short curl'd Hair, of a sandy Complexion, a great Talker, speaks fast, and much in his own Praise; has a bad Sore on his right Ancle; his Clothing is a redish brown Coat, and Great-coat, brown strip'd Flannel Trowsers, a small cut macaroni Hat, a check'd Silk Handkerchief, and often enquires for a Place to keep School.
The Connecticut Gazette; And The Universal Intelligencer, June 21, 1782; June 28, 1782; July 5, 1782. See *The Providence Gazette And Country Journal*, June 22, 1782.

FORTY DOLLARS REWARD.
LAST Night the Shop of the Subscriber was BROKE OPEN, and the following Articles stolen therefrom, viz. 10 Doz. Barcelona Handkerchiefs, 1 Piece of black Mode, 1 Piece of blue Ditto, 1 Piece of yellow Batavia Silk, 1 Piece of Dove coloured Persian, 20 whole and part Pieces of Ribbons, 1 Piece of Irish Linen, 3 or 4 whole and part Pieces of Cambrick, 3 or 4 Doz. Jack and Penknives, and a Number of other Articles; also a Quantity of Cash, in Coppers, small Silver, and Connecticut Bills. Whoever will take up and secure the Thief or Thieves, so that he or they may be brought to Justice, and the Goods recovered, shall receive the above Reward, and have all necessary Charges paid.   EBENEZER BACKUS.
N. B. The above Goods are supposed to have been stolen by one William Winslow, a transient Person, about 5 Feet 9 Inches high, slim built, has short curl'd Hair, is of a sandy Complexion, a great Talker, and speaks much in his own Praise; he has a bad Sore on his right Ancle. Said Winslow had on a brown Coat and Greatcoat, a Pair of striped Flannel Trowsers, a small cut Hat, and a Silk Handkerchief; he often enquires for a Place to keep School.
Windham (Connecticut) June 4, 1782.
The Providence Gazette And Country Journal, June 22, 1782; June 29, 1782. See *The Connecticut Gazette; And The Universal Intelligencer*, June 21, 1782. See *The Boston-Gazette, And Country Journal*, November 29, 1779.

SPRINGFIELD, June 18.
On Wednesday last, between the hours of 4 and 6 o'clock, P. M. a number of men, from the north-west part of this county, to the amount of about 150, armed with swords, guns, and bayonets, made their appearance in

this town, marched to the common gaol, and demanded the keys thereof, which being denied them, they proceeded with axes and levers, broke open said gaol, and released therefrom Samuel Ely, one M'Knoll, a debtor, and a runaway negro; and then marched off in the same manner they came with the said Ely. The principal part of the male inhabitants of the parish in which said gaol stands were gone to the funeral of the late reverend and pious Mr. Stephen Williams, of the parish of Long Meadow; those that remained in said parish collected under arms and pursued and overtook the said party, and received from them three persons as hostages for the return of the said Samuel Ely, who had been condemned by the Supreme judicial Court of this county to suffer six months imprisonment, pay a heavy fine, &c. for his seditions and disorderly behaviour.

The Providence Gazette; And Country Journal, June 22, 1782. See *Thomas's Massachusetts Spy Or, American Oracle of Liberty*, September 26, 1782.

RAN away from the subscriber on the 25th instant, an apprentice boy about 18 years old, named RUFUS MILLER, dark swarthy complexion, black eyes and hair, slim built, tall of his age; had on when he went away, a check linen shirt, striped linen trowsers, old shoes, a waistcoat without sleeves, and an old felt hat. Whoever will return said boy or secure him and give notice so that he may again be obtained by the subscriber living in Lyme, shall be handsomely rewarded, and all necessary charges paid. All masters of vessels and others are hereby forbidden to carry off or harbour said apprentice boy, as they will answer it at the peril of the law.

    JOHN GRIFFING.   Lyme, 26th June, 1781.

The Connecticut Gazette; And The Universal Intelligencer, June 28, 1782; July 5, 1782; July 12, 1782.

Newport, June 27, 1782.

WHEREAS POLLY, the Wife of me the Subscriber, has contracted a Number of Debts in my Absence: This is therefore the caution any Person or Persons against trusting her on my Account, as I am fully determined not to pay any Debts of her contracting.

    GODFREY MALBONE, jun.

The Newport Mercury, June 29, 1782; July 6, 1782; July 13, 1782.

RAN from the Subscriber, in Westerly, on the night of the 17th Instant, one WILLIAM WYATT, a white Man, born at Bristol, in England, 23 Years of Age, 5 Feet 8 Inches high, fresh coloured, has short dark brown Hair; he deserted from the British Fleet in Gardner's Bay, in the Month of October, 1780: Had on, when he went away, a short Felt Hat, bound with black Velvet,

a short blue Sailor's Jacket, lined with white Flannel, long striped Breeches, and Neats Leather Shoes. He stole two Silver Watches, one very large, with a Silver Face, Steel Chain, and Stone Seal set in Pinchbeck; the other small, with a China Face, Steel Chain, and Stone Seal set in Silver—both Seals having the Figure of a Man's Head; he also stole a Number of Shirts, long Breeches, Stockings, and two Pair of new Calf-Skin Shoes. Whoever will take up said Thief, and confine him in any Gaol in the United States, or deliver him to the Subscriber, shall have Ten Dollars Reward, and all necessary Charges, paid by
    JOSEPH NOYES.   Westerly, June 27, 1782.
 The Providence Gazette and Country Journal, June 29, 1782; July 6, 1782.

        To the PUBLIC.
WE the subscriber having by evil counsel undertaken a wicked scheme, and in its tendency ruinous to the cause of America, as well as our own characters; impressed with a deep sense of the wickedness of our purposes, and hoping that a humble confession will in some degree atone therefor, do in this public manner declare, that we were persuaded by one FOSTWICK, of Bolton, in the county of Worcester, to list for three years service in the continental army by fictitious names, and did give false accounts of ourselves with design to deceive the continental muster-masters, and were to share the promised bounty of 60 l. each with FOSTWICK, then assume our real names, and return to our respective homes to enjoy the fruits of our wickedness; but, by the scrutinous examination at mustering we were detected in our designs, have most sincerely repented of them, and hoping the candid world (in consideration of our future good behaviour) will throw the veil of charity over the folly of unguarded youth, do humbly ask the pardon of the public, the muster master and all good men for our intended imposition. We also have willingly and cheerfully paid twenty dollars each as smart money to be appropriated to public use in advertising deserters, detecting deceivers, &c. at the discretion of the Muster-Masters.
  Witness our hands,
  GERSHOM BROWN, jun. ELIAS SWAN.
             Springfield, June 27 1782.
 N. B. The above-mentioned villain, FOSTWICK, after seducing Brown and Swan, to join in his nefarious schemes, on the detection of the villainy, took the first opportunity to make his escape, leaving the others in the trouble he himself created, and clandestinely conveyed a hat belonging to Swan and a pair of silver shoe buckles the property of Swan.
 It is hoped every friend to justice will use his endeavors to bring to condign punishment so attrocious an offender.

The Massachusetts Gazette Or The Springfield and Northampton Weekly Advertiser, July 2, 1782; July 9, 1782; *The Boston Gazette, And The Country Journal,* July 22, 1782. The Boston Gazette adds: *The above Fostwick, was in this town last week, and very narrowly escaped being apprehended. People are cautioned to be on their guard, lest they should be taken by him.* Boston, July 22.

MADE their escape from the goal in this town, on the night of the 28th ult. George Monro, of Branford, pitted with the small-pox, middling size, and John Daton, about five feet high, wore his hair, had on a blue coat, both resident of Branford; committed for corresponding with the enemy; also John Johnson, and John Burns, transient, suspicious persons. Whoever shall return them, or either of them to the above goal, shall be well rewarded.
            STEPHEN MUNSON, Goaler.   New-Haven, July 4, 1782.
The Connecticut Journal, July 4, 1782; July 11, 1782. See *The Connecticut Journal,* November 27, 1782, for Monro.

ON Saturday the 29th instant, was robbed on the high-way between Guilford and Branford, about one mile and an half or two miles on the side Guilford, by five armed men, the subscriber, Marsh Ely, of Lyme, of ten guineas, three dollars, and a crown; one of the robbers had on a frock and trowsers, has a large scar from his right eye, down the side of his nose, almost to his mouth, another a thick-set man with curled hair, and of a dark complexion; had on a red jacket & green baize overalls; another of a light complexion, long hair, middle size, has on a green coat, a particular description cannot be given of the other two. Whoever shall take up either of the perpetrators of the above facts, so that they may be brought to justice, shall receive one hundred dollars reward, or two hundred for the whole gang and all necessary charges from
            MARSH ELY.   New-Haven, July 1, 1782.
The Connecticut Journal, July 4, 1782.

ONE GUINEA REWARD.

TO any person who will apprehend a certain black fellow of the name of SQUASH, who came from Rhode-Island, he belonged to a vessel called the Supple Jack, burnt at Sandy Hook, the said fellow stole to the value of Forty Pounds from Humphrey Wadey of Sandy Hook, consisting chiefly of womens cloaths, viz. a Green Silk Gown, 1 Brown Silk do. 1 Brocaded Silk, 1 Chrystal Buckle set in Silver, and several other articles, also Seven or Eight Pounds in cash. Enquire of the Printer.
The Royal Gazette, July 6, 1782.

Absented himself from the house of the subscriber, of Stratford, at a place called Blanket-Meadow, a certain William Prindle, about 37 years of age 5

feet 6 inches high: He has for a number of years been disordered in his mind, and in a fit of insanity, destroyed the life of a person. Said Prindle was, by authority, committed to my care, all persons are forbid to harbour, or employ him. Whoever shall return him to me, shall be paid all necessary charges.
     ELIJAH HUBBELL.   May 29th, 1782.
The Connecticut Journal, July 11, 1782; July 18, 1782; July 25, 1782. See *The Connecticut Journal,* May 25, 1780.

ALL persons are cautioned against harbouring or concealing a NEGRO GIRL named VILOT, about 15 years of age, of a small size, she having left her mistress, as they must expect to be dealt with according to her, by
    ELIZABETH SERVICE.   Portsmouth, July 13.
The New-Hampshire Gazette, And General Advertiser, July 13, 1782. See *The New-Hampshire Gazette, And General Advertiser*, May 24, 1783.

WHEREAS Rachel, the Wife of the Subscriber, hath eloped from my Bed and Board, and behaved herself in a very unbecoming Manner: I do hereby forbid all Persons trusting her on my Account, as I will not pay any Debts of her contracting from the Date hereof.
    JOSIAH HUMPHRY, jun.   Barrington, July 5, 1782.
The Providence Gazette; And Country Journal, July 6, 1782; July 13, 1782; July 20, 1782.

FIVE DOLLARS REWARD,
RAN AWAY from the subscriber, living in Sharon, about the 20th of June last, a NEGRO MAN, named DARBY, about five feet six inches high, 25 years of age, speaks broken; had on when he went away, a tow cloth shirt and trowsers only; he formerly belonged to Canterbury, and is supposed to have gone that way; and as he had an inclination to enter into the service, it is likely he will attempt to inlist.—Whoever will take up said Negro and secure him in any goal in the United States, so that the owner may have him again, shall be entitled to the above reward, and necessary charges paid, by
    LEMUEL BRUSH. Sharon (State of Connecticut)
                   July 16, 1782.
The Connecticut Courant And Weekly Intelligencer, July 16, 1782; July 23, 1782; July 30, 1782.

RAN AWAY from the Subscriber, on Sunday night, the 21st ult. a NEGRO MAN, named DICK, stout built, a scar on the right side of his neck, another on his ancle bone; carried off with him a Grey Coat, a red Under Jacket, a Linen Do. an old Woollen Shirt, a pair of Woollen Trowsers, a pair of Cotton Do. two pair of Ticken Breeches, a pair of Shoes and brass Shoe Buckles,

three pair of Stockings, and an old Caster Hat.—Whoever will take up said Negro, and return him to the subscriber, shall be handsomely rewarded, and all necessary charges paid by
GIDEON LEETE, 2d.
N. B. All masters of vessels or others, are forbid harbouring or carrying off said Negro, on penalty of the Law.
Chester, in Say-Brook, July 27, 1782.
The Connecticut Gazette; And The Universal Intelligencer, July 26, 1782; August 2, 1782; August 9, 1782. See *The Connecticut Courant, and Hartford Weekly Intelligencer*, August 6, 1782.

DEserted from the Ship TARTAR, the following Persons, *Joseph Smith, Silas Morse,* and *Luther Turner*, belonging to Dedham; *Francis Appleton*, belonging to Boston; *Jenkins White*, and *Edward Jones*. Whoever will apprehend said Deserters, and deliver them on board the Ship Tartar, or to the Jail in Boston, shall receive SEVEN DOLLARS Reward for each of them, and all necessary Charges paid by me.
    JOHN CATHCART.   Boston July 27, 1782.
The Boston-Gazette, And Country Journal, July 29, 1782; August 5, 1782; August 12, 1782.

R AN away from me the subscriber, on the first Inst, an apprentice boy, named Samuel Fisk, about 15 years old; about middling for stature; had on when he went away, a cloth coloured homespun jacket without sleves, a pair of tow cloth long trowsers, a large brim'd felt hatt. Whoever will take up said Runaway, and convey him to me again, shall receive three pence lawful money, as a reward for their pains.
    JOHN WEBSTER, junr.   *Salisbury, July* 13, 1782.
The New-Hampshire Gazette, And Historical Chronicle, August 3, 1782; August 10, 1782; August 17, 1782.

RAN AWAY from the Subscriber, on Sunday night, the 21st ult. a NEGRO MAN, named DICK, stout built, a scar on the right side of his neck, another on his ancle bone; carried off with him a Grey Coat, a red Under Jacket, a Linen Do. an old Woollen Shirt, a pair of Woollen Trowsers, a pair of Cotton Do. two pair of Ticken Breeches, a pair of Shoes and brass Shoe Buckles, three pair of Stockings, and an old Caster Hat.—Whoever will take up said Negro, and return him to the subscriber, shall be handsomely rewarded, and all necessary charges paid by
GIDEON LEET, 2d.
N. B. All masters of vessels or others, are forbid harbouring or carrying off said Negro, on penalty of the Law.
Saybrook, July 27, 1782.

The Connecticut Courant, and Hartford Weekly Intelligencer, August 6, 1782; August 13, 1782; August 20, 1782; *The Boston Gazette, And Country Journal*, August 12, 1782. See *The Connecticut Gazette; And The Universal Intelligencer*, August 2, 1782.

JOHN CHAPIN of Springfield have in the last News-paper forbid all persons harbouring or trusting his wife on his account, alledging only in general her late conduct as a reason therefor, without mentioning any particular instances of ill conduct: It is therefore become necessary for the parent of the unhappy women to inform the public, that the said woman is in a disordered state of mind (which is strongly suspected to be owing to the unkindness and ill usage of her husband) whereby she is rendered incapable of performing domestic business, and she now resides in her father's house with two small children, not only with the knowledge but at the particular request of her said husband.
    JOSEPH ELY.   West-Springfield, August 3, 1782.

The Massachusetts Gazette Or The General Advertiser, August 6, 1782; August 13, 1782; *The Massachusetts Gazette Or The Springfield and Northampton Weekly Advertiser*, August 6, 1782; August 13, 1782. See *The Massachusetts Gazette Or the General Advertiser*, August 6, 1782.

WHEREAS MARGARET the wife of me the subscriber, hath by her late conduct rendered it necessary for me to forbid all persons harboring or trusting her on my account. I hereby declare I will not pay any debt of her contracting after this date.
    JOHN CHAPIN.   Springfield, July 29, 1782.

The Massachusetts Gazette Or the General Advertiser, August 6, 1782; August 13, 1782; *The Massachusetts Gazette Or The Springfield and Northampton Weekly Advertiser*, August 6, 1782, August 13, 1782. See *The Massachusetts Gazette Or The General Advertiser*, August 6, 1782.

WHEREAS *Remember*, the wife of me the subscriber, has eloped from my board and bed, and has proved false thereto; this is to forbid all persons from trusting her on my account. And I hereby give notice that I will not pay any debts she may contract.
    his
   Philip X *Messervy.*
    Mark.   *Marblehead, July* 31, 1782.
The Salem Gazette, August 6, 1782.

RAN away from the subscriber on Monday morning the 26th instant an undutiful son, he returned when the family were all out, on Friday afternoon, broke into the hose and stole one linen and one woollen shirt, a pair of woollen stockings, and a pair of silver sleeve buttons. He is about 4 feet 6 or

7 inches high, light coloured short hair, and blue eyes. Whoever will take up said boy and return him to me, shall have a handsome reward and all necessary charges paid.
     JOHN SAVAGE.   Blanford, July 27, 1782.
The Massachusetts Gazette Or the General Advertiser, August 13, 1782; *The Massachusetts Gazette Or The Springfield and Northampton Weekly Advertiser*, August 13, 1782.

       Whereas my Wife *Betiah*,
has gone from my Bed and Board, and has declared that the Marriage Covenant is a Covenant with Death, and an Agreement with Hell, and has renounced all Marriage relations: I do hereby forwarn all Persons harbouring or having any Dealings with her, as I will not discharge any Debt she may Contract, or pay any thing on her Account from the Date hereof.
     OLIVER PRESCOTT.   *Westford,* August 5, 1782.
The Independent Chronicle and the Universal Advertiser, August 15, 1782; August 22, 1782; August 29, 1782.

      Whereas *Hannah*, the Wife
of me the Subscriber, has refused: bed and board with me; These are therefore to forbid all Persons trusting her, as I am determined not to pay any Debt of her contracting after this Date.
     DANIEL CARY.   *Braintree*, August 9, 1782.
The Independent Chronicle and the Universal Advertiser, August 15, 1782; August 22, 1782; August 29, 1782.

WHEREAS Eunice, wife of me that subscriber, in my absence for two years, has not behaved and conducted as she ought to have done; this is therefore to forbid any person or persons crediting her on my account, as I will not pay any debts she may contract after the dat [*sic*] hereof.
     WILLIAM WHIPPLE.   Portsmouth, August 17, 1782.
The New-Hampshire Gazette, And General Advertiser, August 17, 1782; August 24, 1782.

THIRTY DOLLARS REWARD
DESERTED the service of the subscriber on the 7th instant, one John Allibe, a Refugee from Long-Island, of about 28 or 30 years old, and of a midling stature, dark complexion, dark eyes and black hair, combed back and tied with a string behind; had on a flopt Hat, a white Linnen Coat, Vest and Overhalls, a Shoe maker by Trade, but often tells of a large fortune his Father has upon the Island, it is presumed said Allibe has gone into the Country. Whoever will take him up and confine him in Hartford Goal, or being him to

me at Haddam, or give me such information that I may be able to secure him, shall be entitled to the above Reward, and all necessary charges paid, by
    JOHN WILCOX.   Haddam August 14th, 1782.
The Connecticut Courant And Weekly Intelligencer, August 20, 1782; September 3, 1782.

WHEREAS *Peggy Holmes*, wife of me the subscriber, has left my house, without any just cause, and threatens to run me in debt; this is therefore to forbid any person or persons entertaining or crediting her on my account, as I will not pay any debts of her contracting; notwithstanding, if she returns and behaves as she ought to do, I will receive her, and provide for her.
    BENJAMIN HOLMES, jun. *Portsmouth, August* 24.
The New-Hampshire Gazette, And General Advertiser, August 24, 1782; August 31, 1782; September 7, 1782. See *The New-Hampshire Gazette, And General Advertiser*, August 31, 1782.

WHEREAS Grace, *my Wife, has eloped from my Bed and Board, and refuseth to return; I now publickly caution all Persons against trusting her on my account, for I publickly declare that I will not pay one Farthing that she may contract from and after the date hereof.*
    SIMON BEARD.   Pelham, August 13, 1782.
The New-Hampshire Gazette, And General Advertiser, August 24, 1782.

W*Hereas my wife ELZABETH hath behaved in such a debauch'd manner, and threatened to run me in debt. I do hereby forbid all persons trading with her, or trusting her on my account, for I will pay no debts of her contracting. Also, I forbid all persons entertaining or harbouring her, except such places as I provide or her support, viz. Seth Mitchel's, of Roxbury. Dated at Woodbury, this* 26*th of August,* 1782.
    CORNELIUS BROWNSON.
The Connecticut Journal, August 29, 1782; September 5, 1782, September 12, 1782.

DESERTED from Service on Monday Evening the 29th ult. an indented Molatto Girl, named SARAH SEHETER, about 19 years of age, and about 5 feet high; she stole and carried off with her sundry things of value, and is supposed to be gone to Providence or Concord, at both of which places she has formerly resided:—Whoever will apprehend and bring said Girl to the Printer here of, shall receive FOUR DOLLARS Reward.
              Boston, August 28, 1782.

The Continental Journal, And Weekly Advertiser, August 29, 1782; September 5, 1782; September 12, 1782; *The Independent Chronicle and the Universal Advertiser*, October 3, 1782; October 10, 1782. The *Chronicle* does not have the date and location noted.

THIS may certify that Benjamin Holmes, husband of me the subscriber, has without any just provocation posted me, as I can make appear to the public by my neighbours; and then in the same advertisement asserts that if I will return to him, and behave as I ought to, he will again receive me; but I assert that I am afraid to, as he has behaved so very ill to me, and threatened what he would do to me and his two children which he had by me before I left him: if the public had laid before them the treatment he has shown to me, since he first married me, they wou'd not think it acting the part of a prudent woman to return to him; here I would not wish to expose his character more than I possibly can help, as I always bore him the regard of a loving wife.

PEGGY HOLMES.   Portsmouth August 29th.

The New-Hampshire Gazette, And Historical Chronicle, August 31, 1782; September 7, 1782. See *The New-Hampshire Gazette, And Historical Chronicle*, August 24, 1782.

TEN DOLLARS REWARD.

MADE their escape from the Subscriber, on the Night following the 22d Day of Inst. August, from Danbury, in Fairfield County, one Josiah Wright, and one Andrew Bostwick, both having been taken up at Norwalk on the Night of the 13th Inst. and seized with a Quantity of British Goods, Wares & Merchandize; likewise was from in the Custody of said Wright seventy counterfeit French Guineas, the whole imported from Long-Island, or some other Place under the controul of the Enemy. Said Wright and Bostwick had both been sentenced by the Civil Authority in said Norwalk, & sent foreward for Trial before the Honorable Superior Court then sitting at Danbury aforesaid. Said Wright is about 5 feet 9 Inches high, very long black Hair, black Eyes and Eye Brows middling well set, belongs to Pittsfield, in the State of Massachusetts. Said Bostwick has light Eyes, short brown Hair, pitted with the Small Pox, about 5 Feet 10 Inches high, has liv'd and kept a public House at Waterbury, in this State. Whoever will take up said Wright and Bostwick, and deliver them to me the Subscriber, shall have the above Reward, and all reasonable Charges paid, or five Dollars for either of them.

URIAH RAYMOND. *Constable of Norwalk,*

Norwalk, August 24. 1782.

The Connecticut Journal, September 5, 1782; September 12, 1782; September 19, 1782.

WHEREAS *HANNAH* the wife of me the subscriber, has absented herself from my bed and board, this is therefore to forbid all persons trusting her on my account, as I am determined not to pay any debt o her contracting after the date hereof.
    MANASSEH KNIGHT. *Lancaster, August* 21*st,* 1782.
Thomas's Massachusetts Spy Or, The Worcester Gazette, September 5, 1782; September 12, 1782; September 19, 1782.

RUN away from the Subscriber on the night of 6th inst. a Negro SERVANT, about 5 feet high, of a yellow complexion, very crooked legs, about 28 years old, calls himself HENRY BROWNING, had on when he went away, a gray loose Coat, black Jacket, white Waistcoat, check'd Shirt, a pair of old Overalls and Shoes, no Stockings, an old felt Hat. Whoever takes up said Negro and will return him to the Subscriber, in Hartford, or secure him and give information where he is, shall receive Ten Dollars reward and all necessary charges paid, by
    LEVI ROBBINS. Hartford, September 9, 1782.
The Connecticut Courant And Weekly Intelligencer, September 10, 1782; September 17, 1782; September 24, 1782. See *The Massachusetts Gazette Or the General Advertiser*, September 10, 1782.

RAN *away from the subscriber on the night of the 6th inst. a negro man called Henry Browning, 28 years of age, 5 feet 4 inches high, yellow complexion, crooked legs, had on when he went away, an old felt hat, a grey great coat, blue outside jacket, white waistcoat, checked linen shirt, old linen over-alls, old shoes and no stockings. Whoever will return said Negro to ELISHA BABCOCK, in Springfield, or the subscriber in Hartford, shall receive TEN DOLLARS Reward, and necessary charges paid.*
    LEVI ROBBINS. *Hartford, September* 9, 1782.
The Massachusetts Gazette Or the General Advertiser, September 10, 1782; September 17, 1782; September, 1782; *The Massachusetts Gazette Or The Springfield and Northampton Weekly Advertiser*, September 10, 1782; September 17, 1782; September 24, 1782. See *The Connecticut Courant And Weekly Intelligencer*, September 10, 1782.

At the Supreme Judicial Court, held in this town the week before last, Francis Quinn was convicted of the crime of theft, and sentenced to be whipped 20 striped, and to pay a fee of fifteen hundred pounds or to be sold for twenty years. Paul Dustin, at the same Court, was convicted of passing counterfeit money, and sentenced to be set in the pillory for one hour, and to pay a fine of forty-three pounds.

And on Thursday last, the above Francis Quinn was accordingly whipped 20 stripes, at the public post; and the said Paul Dustin was set in the pillory one hour; after which they were both remanded to prison.
The Salem Gazette, September 12, 1782.

RANAWAY,
From the Subscriber,

A SHORT well set Negro Man, named TOM, about 26 Years of Age, 5 Feet 7 Inches high, marked with the Small-Pox; had on, when he went away, a striped Tow Shirt, brown Tow Jacket, full'd Cloth Breeches, white Worsted Stockings, his Shoes mended, one round and one square Brass Buckle, and old Felt hat bound with white; the small Toe of each Foot has been frozen off; took with him two Tow Shirts, and some other Apparel. Whoever will take up said Runaway, and return him, or give Notice to the Subscriber, so that he may have him again, shall receive a Reward of TWENTY SILVER DOLLARS, and all necessary Charges, paid by
   JOHN COOKE.   Tiverton, Sept. 13, 1782.
The Providence Gazette; And Country Journal, September 14, 1782; September 21, 1782; September 28, 1782.

RAN AWAY from the subscribers, on the 15th Instant, a NEGRO MAN, named James Lewis, 24 Years of Age, of a middling Stature, a Shoemaker by Trade, and is handy at Farming Work; had on, when he went away, a light coloured Bearskin Coat without Lining, a woollen Jacket, Tow Trowsers, and an Ozenbrigs Shirt, Shoes partly worn, Steel Buckles plated with Silver, and a Felt Hat partly worn. Whoever will apprehend said Servant, and secure him so that the Subscribers may have hi, again, shall receive Five Dollars Reward.
   ABRAHAM BELKNAP,   AMOS HORTON.
                Johnston, August 21, 1782.
The Providence Gazette; And Country Journal, September 14, 1782; September 21, 1782; September 28, 1782; October 5, 1782.

One Hundred Pounds Reward.

Escaped last Night, from the House of the Subscriber, a Prisoner named WILLIAM PRENTISS, about 27 Years of Age, 5 Feet 6 Inches high, of a light Complexion, has very white and sound Teeth, light coloured Eyes, and light brown Hair; he is a Native of Boston; had on a Cloth coloured Coat, a black Silk Jacket, Nankeen Breeches, blue and white Silk Stockings, a black Beaver Hat, Silver Shoe-Buckles, partly plated with Gold, and a ruffled Shirt. Whoever shall apprehend the above described Person, and secure him in the Gaol in Providence, shall be entitled to the above Reward.
   BENONI PEARCE, D. Sheriff.   Providence, September 7, 1782.

The Providence Gazette; And Country Journal, September 14, 1782; September 21, 1782; September 28, 1782. See *The Providence Gazette And Country Journal*, February 8, 1783.

RUN-away on Monday night the 9th instant, a Negro man named POMP, about 30 years of age, a short thick fellow, lame in his right foot, occasioned by a cut with an ax; carried with him a blue broad cloth coat with a red cape, a green broad cloth coat and vest, one pair of old leather breeches, and one pair of striped ticking ditto, one white dimoty vest, and one white holland short, two check woolen ditto, and one coating loose coat the fore parts lined with red baize. Whoever will take up said Negro, and return him to the subscriber in Hartford, shall have Five Dollars reward, and necessary expences.   DANIEL GOODWIN.

N. B. He went away in company with a young Squaw, and supposed to be gone to New-York or lurking about New-Haven.
September 16, 1782.

The Connecticut Courant And Weekly Intelligencer, September 17, 1782; September 24, 1782; October 1, 1782.

Ran away from the Subscriber, a Negro Man, and indented Servant; he is a tall slim fellow, pleasant looking, and of a good Black, speaks bad English, is a native of Senegal, and answers to the Name of *Pier Sanno*: had on, old blue Breeches and Stockings, strip'd Shirt, and a short Osnaburgh Coat. Whoever may apprehend said Negro and confine him or return him to the Subscriber, or to *Joseph Henderson* Esq; of Boston, shall receive a handsome Reward.

THOs. THOMPSON. *Portsmouth, New Hampshire, Sept.* 8, 1782.

The Boston Gazette, And The Country Journal, September 23, 1782; September 30, 1782; October 7, 1782.

WHEREAS HANNAH my wife hath several times left me contrary to my will, and hath been received back again, and now she hath by the assistance of her father Rowel, and other relations, taken a fat Cow out of my care and hath killed and disposed of her without my knowledge. This is therefore to warn all persons not to trust her on my account, as I will not pay any debt contracted by her from this date.
        NOADIAH BURR, jun.

Farmington, September 21, 1782.

The Connecticut Courant And Weekly Intelligencer, September 24, 1782; October 1, 1782; October 15, 1782. See *The Connecticut Courant And Weekly Intelligencer*, October 15, 1782, and *The Connecticut Courant And Weekly Intelligencer*, October 29, 1782.

WORCESTER, September 26.

On Monday evening last, Col. Porter, High-Sheriff of the county of Hampshire, arrived in this town, having in his custody that noted disturber of the publick tranquility, Samuel Ely; and the next morning the Colonel sat off with his prisoner for Boston. It is remarkable, and an undoubted fact, that only fourteen days past, Ely fled from the county of Hampshire, thinking he could not with safety lie longer concealed from publick justice, and removed into the State of Vermont; the next day after his arrival there his seditious disposition led him to commit some high crime and misdemeanour, for which he was apprehended and committed to goal in Westminster in Vermont, and a few days after had his trial; upon full evidence he was convicted, and was sentenced to be banished from that State; and if consequence of which he was brought under guard to the line of this Commonwealth, and by the vigilance of the officers of the county of Hampshire was soon discovered and secured.

Thomas's Massachusetts Spy Or, American Oracle of Liberty, September 26, 1782; *The Connecticut Journal*, October 3, 1782; *The Connecticut Gazette; And The Universal Intelligencer*, October 4, 1782. Minor differences between the papers. See *The Providence Gazette; And Country Journal*, June 22, 1782, and *The Connecticut Gazette; And The Universal Intelligencer*, November 21, 1783.

MY Wife *Elizabeth* having eloped from me, and taken up her Residence with another Man, I am under the Necessity of forbidding, and I do hereby forbid, all Persons entertaining or trusting her on my Account, as I will pay no Debts of her contracting from the Date hereof. I also forbid all Agents delivering her any Property due to me from any Prizes which I am be concerned in taking.

    ISAAC OAKMAN.   *Salem, September* 24, 1782.
The Salem Gazette, September 26, 1782; October 17, 1782.

STOP THIEVES!

THE subscriber was violently assaulted, in his own house on the night of the 28th inst. and robbed of the following articles. viz

 A Silver Watch. 1 Pair of Buckskin breeches, 1 Beaver Hatt. 2 Holland Shirts. 1 Checked Do. 1 Cotton do. 1 Blue Coat. 1 Snuff Coloured do. 1 Striped Silk Vest. 1 Cloth Coloured, do. 1 pair red Stone Buttons, 1 pair white do. 1 Jack Knife, 1 Stone Broach. 1 Silk Apron. 1 Pair of Shoes. 2 Pair of Silver Shoe Buckles. 1 Pair Thread Hose. 1 white Holland Handkerchief. 2 checked do. 1 Fire Lock, a Powder Horn & a Pound of Powder. 1 Pair of Knee Buckles. 1 Stock Buckle, and three Shillings in Cash.

This attrocious robbery was committed by two persons, nearly of the following description, viz. One of them about 5 feet 10 inches high, full faced, dark cut hair, had on a large hatt, and a light-blue worsted coat, (but took with him a snuff-coloured coat, lining of the same colour0 a brown velvet jacket and dark coloured breeches; the other about 5 feet 7 inches high, dark bushy hair, round faced and had on a scarlet coat and a white jacket, but took with him a light coloured jacket which was some worn, and had a small spot of grease on the bottom side, the fore parts lined with snuff coloured shalloon, and the pockets having worn through lining, also a vest, the fore parts of which is striped silk the back parts white linen, supposed to have on a pair of buckskin breeches lately washed and some of the seams ripped—Any person who will apprehend said Robbers and confine them in Goal shall have a handsome reward and all necessary charges paid by
     LAMMON GRAY.   Pelham, September 29th, 1782.
The Massachusetts Gazette Or the General Advertiser, October 1, 1782; *The Massachusetts Gazette Or The Springfield and Northampton Weekly Advertiser*, October 1, 1782.

RUNAWAY from the subscriber in Voluntown, the 20th of September, a mustee negro boy, named PRINCE, slim built, a slave, about 17 years of age, upon the whitish order, bare footed; had on when he went away, a brown tow cloth shirt, and frock and trowsers the same, a jacket without sleeves, pale blue, an old beaver hat most worn out; carried away with him, a striped tow and linen shirt, short drab breeches. Whoever will that up said slave and return him to me in said Voluntown, or secure him so that I can have him again, shall have FOUR DOLLARS reward, and all necessary charges, by
     me JAMES CAMPBELL.
N. B. All masters of vessels, and all others are forbid carrying away or harbouring said slave on penalty of the law. J. C.
The Connecticut Gazette; And The Universal Intelligencer, October 4, 1782; October 11, 1782; October 18, 1782.

WHEREAS *Submit*, the wife of me the subscriber, hath eloped from my bed and board, and refuseth to dwell with me, and therefore I take this method to warn all persons not to credit her on my account, for I will not pay any debt she shall contract from the date hereof.
     JAMES NEWCOMB.   Lebanon, 23 September, 1782.
The Connecticut Gazette; And The Universal Intelligencer, October 4, 1782; October 11, 1782; October 18, 1782.

WHEREAS *Elizabeth*, wife of me the subscriber, has eloped from my bed and board, and refuses to live with me—and has, and still may run me in debt:

This is therefore to forwarn all persons trusting her on my account, as I will not pay any debt she may contract from the date hereof.
    JOSEPH BURNHAM.   Dover, October 1, 1782.
 The New-Hampshire Gazette, And General Advertiser, October 5, 1782; October 12, 1782; October 19, 1782; October 26, 1782; November 3, 1782.

TWENTY DOLLARS REWARD.

BROKE *out of the Goal in Exeter, on the Night following the twenty second Day of September ultimo,* Henry Tufts *and* John Smith Sanborn, *the former about thirty Years of Age, five Feet ten Inches high, of a light Complection, wears his own Hair, is under conviction of Theft; the latter about forty two Years of Age, six Feet high, of a light Complection, wears his own Hair, was committed on suspicion of Theft: Whoever shall take up, and return them to the said Goal, shall receive the above Reward, or ten Dollars for either of them.* JOHN PARKER, *Sheriff.*
 The New-Hampshire Gazette, And General Advertiser, October 5, 1782; October 12, 1782; October 19, 1782.

RAN-AWAY NEGRO.

Ran-away from his Master, Jonathan Warner *of Portsmouth, New-Hampshire, on Sunday night, September 8, 1782, Negro Man named Prince; had on when he went away, and carried with him, one pair of buff-coloured leather Breeches, with linnen and check'd Shirts, two Coats and Waistcoats, one made of white fustian, the other light cloth, with a light great Coat, with sundry other articles: He is a strait limb'd fellow, about five feet ten inches high, and speaks bad English; has lost two lower fore teeth, and was a house Negro:—Whoever shall take up said Negro, and return him to his Master, shall receive as a reward Twenty Spanish Milled Dollars by*
    JONATHAN WARNER.
N. B. All Masters of Vessels and others, are forbid carrying him off, as they would avoid the penalty of the law. Portsmouth, September 9, 1782.
 The Continental Journal, And Weekly Advertiser, October 10, 1782; October 17, 1782; October 24, 1782; *The New-Hampshire Gazette, And General Advertiser*, October 19, 1782; October 26, 1782; November 3, 1782. Minor differences between the papers.

WHEREAS the Widow ELIZABETH BROAD of Holden, hath for some time past made it her business to ramble up and down the country, and to disturb the people, and hath fomented vexatious lawsuits, and thereby hath already spent a considerable part of what was left her for her support.

We the subscribers do therefore caution all people against harbouring or trusting her, for the future, as the estate is in our hands, and we will not pay one farthing on her account.

JOSIAH BROAD, AARON BROAD, Executors.

September 3d, 1782.

Thomas's Massachusetts Spy Or, The Worcester Gazette, October 10, 1782; October 17, 1782.

WHEREAS I see in the weekly Intelligencer, an advertisement signed by Noadiah Burr, jun. advertising me as his wife, of several times leaving him, contrary to his will, and having been received back again, and now by the assistance of my father Rowel and other relations, killed and disposed of a fat Cow, without his knowledge. Least the world should be led into a mistake, respecting my conduct in regard to my husband, I publish the following facts as truth, though I were to die this moment.

I was married to the said Noadiah Burr, jun. and went to live with him in his fathers family, which was very numerous and in a small house—Soon after I came to live with my husband, his father set up some laws, one of which was, I could not cook, nor eat with my husband, which I took very hard, as he being the closest connection of life, and if this comfort was lost, my hopes of living was at an end. I repeatedly solicited him to procure a house at a distance, that we might enjoy the sweet comforts of a marriage state, but his father refused any such thing, that I must live in his family or else leave my husband—I tried every method to please the family, but to no effect, I must leave my husband or be drove into the chamber and there shut up, till they see cause to let me out, or drove into the chimney corner, and there surrounded by a ruffin crew of girls, and wait their motion for my relief; if I hung on my dish-kettle, it was often took off by the family, and I was not allowed to put it on again—I was kick'd about like a dog, and threatened to be beat, and even my life was as last indangered by the family, proposing to fix a dose which should put an end to it—I then went to my father Rowel's house, who sent me back, but I could not live there long before I see I must be starved to death, or bear the greatest insults from the family, which human nature could not indure; I then being with child, determined to leave my husband, untill after my sickness, and again went to my father Rowels who being poor yet received me—I applied to my husband for my bed and wearing cloths, but his father would not let him deliver them to me; through my sickness I suffered much, and after my recovery I again desired my bed and cloaths, which I took when I went to live with him, but they were refused, and I now have no change of cloaths nor no bed for my two children to lie on, but a blanket sewed up and filled with hay, thus I have lived for several months—I desired the deacons of the parish and others to talk with my husband and the family, that we might have a hearing of our difficulty openly, but it was refused; my life is threatened if I return to my husband, unless at the risque of my life I dirst not, all possible pains I have taken for a reconciliation, but to no effect, they would not give me the least support for myself nor children, thus I have lived till now; they dried up my cow and fatted her, the approaching winter coming on, I was advised to take my cow and kill her, which I have done to save my life and childrens. I should now be glad to live with my husband if we could have a separate house, and believe we might live together peaceably, if his fathers family would let us alone, but so long as they govern him, we cannot—I have received the greatest insults from them that human nature can put up with, and I am not going to excuse myself, when I have been thus abused I have done that which a cool temper would not admit of.—It has been an old saying, tread on a worm and he will turn; here I have stated facts which cannot be denied, and could state many more—As to his advertising Thomas Shepard as being a butcher, I leave it to the public to judge which is the most expert, either one to butcher a cow, or for old Noadiah Burr to butcher a whole family, and an innocent character.

    HANNAH BURR.   Farmington, September 26, 1782.
The Connecticut Courant And Weekly Intelligencer, October 15, 1782.
See *The Connecticut Courant And Weekly Intelligencer*, September 24, 1782, and *The Connecticut Courant And Weekly Intelligencer*, October 29, 1782.

       Broke Goal last week
at Salem, one Joel Smith, about 39 years of age, dark complexion, and one Thomas Gibbs, of a light ditto, and about the same age. Whoever will apprehend and commit to goal either of said prisoners, shall receive Ten Dollars Reward.
    BRIMSLEY STEVENS.   Oct. 10.
The Independent Chronicle and the Universal Advertiser, October 17, 1782; October 31, 1782.

RAN AWAY from the Subscriber, on the 10th Instant, a NEGRO MAN, named PERO, about 20 Years of Age, 5 Feet 4 Inches high, speaks good English; had on, when he went away, a Felt Hat, grey Jacket, Leather Breeches, old Stockings, good Shoes and Buckles.—Whoever will take up said Negro, and return him to the Subscriber, or to Black's Tavern in Rehoboth, shall receive Three Dollars Reward, and necessary Charges, paid
       by OBADIAH REED.
N. B. All Masters of Vessels are forbid to carry him off.
            Rehoboth, October 18, 1782.
 The Providence Gazette; And Country Journal, October 19, 1782; October 26, 1782; November 2, 1782; November 9, 1782. The last two

ads spell the advertiser's last name as Read. See *The Providence Gazette; And Country Journal*, December 27, 1777.

ON the night of the 8th instant, run away from the subscribers, four Negro men, one named GRIG and one JACK, Grig about 51 years of age and Jack about 19, about 5 feet one or two inches high, Grig has a scar on his left cheek and neck occasioned by the kings evil, carried with him one old mixt coloured great coat, one butnut [*sic*] broadcloth do. one scarlet jacket, one white do. one pair of leather breeches, one pair white jane do. one ruffled and one plain Holland shirt, two check do. two woollen do. one pair of check trowsers, one pair of French cut silver shoe Buckles and knee do. two old blue surtouts twiled coating, one Barcelona handkerchief, three pair of stockings, and one fife. Jack carried with him, one blue coat, one white do. homespun, one pair of linen breeches, one pair of striped trowsers, one Holland shirt, one white homespun do. one pair of white yarn stockings, one pair of blue do. one pair of boots. Likewise, one Negro man named FRANK, about the same height, about 24 years of age, had on when he went away, a blue lappel'd coat faced with white, one pair of white woollen breeches and light coloured jackt. Also, one old Negro named PETER, carried with him carried with him, one blue coat, one green do. one brown do. one red great coat and a number of clothes unknown. Whoever will take up said Negroes, and return them to their masters, shall have Ten Dollars Reward for each, except the old Negro, and shall have a reasonable reward for him, and all necessary charges paid for him and the whole.
     ELIAS DUNNING, EBENEZER GURNSEY,
     GIDEON MARTIN, SOLOMON MARSH.
                  Bethlehem, October 9. 1782.
The Connecticut Courant And Weekly Intelligencer, October 22, 1782; October 29, 1782; November 5, 1782.

WHEREAS MARY, my wife, hath eloped from my bed and board, this is to forbid any person trusting her on my account, as I will not pay any debt that she shall contract, after this date.
     LUKE DAY, Senior. West Springfield, October 18, 1782.
The Massachusetts Gazette Or the General Advertiser, October 22, 1782; November 5, 1782. Marcy in second ad. *The Massachusetts Gazette Or The Springfield and Northampton Weekly Advertiser*, October 22, 1782; October 29, 1782; November 5, 1782. Her name appears as Marcy in the last two ads.

WHEREAS *Lydia*, wife of me the subscriber, has wantonly violated the marriage contract in my absence while in captivity; and being now return'd, find her indecent and unchaste conduct so daringly conspicuous, as to render it inconsistent with the principles of a man of character (who once tho't

himself happily settled under the banners of Hymen) further to nourish and cherish her:—I therefore, hereby forbid any person trusting her on my account, as I will not pay any debt contracted by her from this date.
    JOHN REVERE.   Portsmouth, Oct. 19, 1782.
The New-Hampshire Gazette, And General Advertiser, October 26, 1782; November 3, 1782.

WHEREAS I the Subscriber, published in the Hartford weekly paper, sundry abuses I received from my father in law, Mr. Noahdiah Burr, and his family, some of which I acknowledge are false, especially that with regard to the laws set up in his family, for which I acknowledge my fault, and ask the forgiveness of Mr. Burr and his family, my husband and the public.
    HANNAH BURR.   Farmington, October 24, 1782.
The Connecticut Courant And Weekly Intelligencer, October 29, 1782.
See *The Connecticut Courant And Weekly Intelligencer*, September 24, 1782, and *The Connecticut Courant And Weekly Intelligencer*, October 15, 1782.

WHEREAS MARY the wife of me the subscriber, has for some time past behaved in a very unbecoming manner, and I am apprehensive she will do all in her power to injure me. This is therefore to warn all persons from trusting her on my account, as I mean to break off all connections with her and pay no debt contracted by her after this date.
    MATTHEW READ.   Tolland, October 19, 1782.
The Connecticut Courant And Weekly Intelligencer, October 29, 1782.

RAN away from the subscriber in Hartford, the 9th of August last, a negro lad, named Peter, eighteen years old, about 5 feet 5 inches high, very black, speaks good English, wore away a blue coat with white metal buttons, a striped jacket and tow cloth trowsers: and took with him one white linen shirt, two tow cloth and two woollen do. Whoever will take up said Negro, and send word where he may be found, or return him to his master, shall have Eight Dollars reward, and all necessary charges paid by
    JOSHUA HEMPSTED.   Hartford, October 28, 1782.
The Massachusetts Or The Springfield And Northampton Weekly Advertiser, October 29, 1782; November 5, 1782; *The Massachusetts Gazette Or the General Advertiser*, November 5, 1782. See *The Connecticut Courant And Weekly Intelligencer*, November 5, 1782.

Ran from the Subscriber, of Freetown, on the 10th of July last, a female negro Servant, named Selah, of about 50 Years of Age, a little cross-eyed. Whoever will take up said Servant, and return her, or secure her, so that her Master

may have her again, shall have two Dollars Reward, and all necessary Charges paid, by
        PHILIP HATHWAY.
The Independent Chronicle and the Universal Advertiser, October 31, 1782; November 7, 1782; November 14, 1782.

WHEREAS *SARAH*, the wife of me the subscriber, has behaved herself in a very indecent manner towards me; this is therefore to forbid any person trusting her one farthing on my account, as I will not pay any debt of her contracting, from the date hereof.
        STEPHEN BLANCHARD.   *Sturbridge, October 16th, 1782.*
Thomas's Massachusetts Spy Or, The Worcester Gazette, October 31, 1782; November 7, 1782; November 21, 1782.

R*AN away from the Subscriber on the* 25th *Instant, an Apprentice Boy, named DAVID BEEBE, about 13 Years of Age; a likely looking Lad; had on when he went away, a coarse brown Shirt, and Trowsers of the same, a reddish outside Jacket, blue yarn Stockings, felt Hat, and part of a black silk Handkerchief round his Neck. Whoever will return said Boy to the Subscriber in Norwich, shall receive six Pence Reward.*
        JOHN RICHARDS.   *Norwich, October 30, 1782.*
The Connecticut Gazette; And The Universal Intelligencer, November 1, 1782; November 8, 1782; November 15, 1782.

R*AN* away on Monday Night the 28th Instant, a negro Man named DERRY, about 27 Years of Age, six Feet and about 2 Inches high, pretty slim, looks a little cross eyed, his feet very extraordinary large and long, carried with him one caster hat, two checked woolen shirts, one old checked holland do. one white homespun do. one streaked linen do. two pair of old brown linnen trowsers, one pair of striped linen do, one darkish brown woollen vest and one dark do. one short outside dark woolen jacket with white lining, one darkish woolen coat with white lining without pocket lids, one mixed coloured, surtout, one pair of brown woolen breeches, one striped cotton vest, one pair of pale blue stockings, one pair of white cotton ditto, one pair of mixed blue and white ditto, one back silk stampt handkerchief, one checked linen do. marked D, and one fiddle, and play some but not well. And another negro man named DAN, about 5 feet 8 inches high, pale complexion, about 22 years of age, took with him two checked woolen shirts, a calfskin under jacket, a knapsack, brown under jacket, and one pair blue seamed woolen stockings. Whoever will take up said Negroes and return them to the subscribers in Chatham, shall have a generous reward and necessary expences.
        JOSEPH BLAGUE. JONATHAN BUSH.

N. B. They have a mind to go to sea, and it is supposed they have run away for that purpose. This is therefore to forbid all masters of vessels and others harbouring them on the penalty of the law.
October 29th, 1782.
The Connecticut Gazette; And The Universal Intelligencer, November 1, 1782; November 8, 1782; November 15, 1782; November 26, 1782, *The Boston Evening-Post and the General Advertiser*, November 16, 1782; November 23, 1782; November 30, 1782, *The Providence Gazette; And Country Journal*, November 16, 1782; November 23, 1782; November 30, 1782, and *The Connecticut Courant And Weekly Intelligencer*, November 19, 1782. Minor differences between the papers.

RUN away from the Subscriber, living in East-Windsor, Hartford county, a Prisoner, named JOHN STILES, jun. of midling stature, light complexion, pitted with the small pox, about 28 years of age, had on a pale blue or mix'd coloured Body Coat, sky coloured Velvet Vest and Breeches. Whoever shall take up and return said prisoner, or secure him in any goal, so that he may be had, shall receive Ten Dollars reward and all necessary charges
paid, by   JOHN CROSS.
N. B. Said Stiles was taken by attachment, for twenty pounds, due on a note, by writ, dated 26th October instant.
East-Windsor, October 28, 1782.
The Connecticut Courant And Weekly Intelligencer, November 5, 1782; November 12, 1782.

INTICED away by some evil minded person, the 9th of August, a Negro Lad, between 16 and 18 years of age, named PETER, had on a striped linen Coat, and Jacket, plain tow cloth Shirt and Trowsers, an old blue broadcloth Coat, with polished Buttons stamped with a pine-tree, an old felt Hat, an old pair of Shoes with no Buckles, took with him a check'd wollen Shirt, almost new, also a Fiddle and Flute.—Whoever will secure said lad, and give notice to the subscriber, so that he may have him again, shall be handsomely rewarded.
JOSHUA HEMPSTED.   Hartford, October 29, 1782.
The Connecticut Courant And Weekly Intelligencer, November 5, 1782; November 12, 1782. See *The Massachusetts Or The Springfield And Northampton Weekly Advertiser*, October 29, 1782.

STOLEN *out of the House of me, the Subscriber, on Friday the* 8*th Day of November Instant, by* Francis Cowvin, *a Man about* 5 *Feet* 4 *Inches high, dark Complection, much pock-broken, had on a short brown Waistcoat and long Trowsers, he was a Native of France, three Bundles containing* 25 *Shirts,* 7 *Stocks,* 4 *red India Handkerchiefs, five white ditto,* 6 *Pair of ribb'd* brown and white Silk Hose, a Pair of Brown Thread ditto, and one white Waistcoat, all of which were mark'd B C. Also nine Shirts, five Pair plain white Silk Hose, six Linnen Handkerchiefs, red bordered; and one white Waistcoat mark'd R. Whoever shall take up said Thief and bring him to the Subscriber, shall receive SIX DOLLARS Reward and reasonable Charges paid.   WILLIAM GRIDLEY.

Roxbury, Nov. 11, 1782.
The Boston Gazette, And The Country Journal, November 11, 1782; November 18, 1782.

WHEREAS my wife MARY, has eloped from my bed and board, and behaved herself unbecoming the character of a wife. I forbid all persons trusting her on my account, as I will not pay any debt of her contracting from the date hereof.
    WILLIAM WEST.   Litchfield, Sept. 10, 1782.
The Connecticut Courant And Weekly Intelligencer, November 12, 1782; November 19, 1782.

IN the night after the 6th instant, the Prison of New-Gate was burnt, and JAMES GLASS, WILLIAM CRAWFORD, FRANCIS PELHAM and ELISHA PELHAM, who were there confined, made their escape. Any person or persons who will take and secure them or either of them, in any of the goals in this State, shall be reasonably rewarded, and all necessary charges paid.
    ROGER NEWBURY, ASAHEL HOLCOMB,
    JOSEPH FORWARD, MATHEW GRISWOLD.
        Overseers of Newgate Prison.   November 8.
The Connecticut Courant And Weekly Intelligencer, November 12, 1782.

Whereas *Elizabeth*, Wife
of me the Subscriber, has eloped from my Bed and Board, and utterly denies my coming *near her*; this is therefore to forbid any Person trusting her on my Account, as I will not pay any Debt which she shall contract after the Date hereof.
    AARON RUMRILL.   Roxbury, Sept. 13, 1782.
The Independent Chronicle and the Universal Advertiser, November 14, 1782; November 21, 1782; December 5, 1782. See *The Boston Gazette, And The Country Journal*, November 18, 1782.

RANAWAY from the subscriber in New-London, on the 10th instant, a negro man servant named LAMBO, supposed to be between 50 and 60 years old, was lately the property of Mr. Richard Durfee; he is of midling size: had

on a blue jacket and black breeches. Whoever will return him to me, shall have a handsome reward.
JOHN SHEPARD. New-London, November 13, 1782.
The Connecticut Gazette; And The Universal Intelligencer, November 15, 1782; November 22, 1782; November 29, 1782.

Whereas Elizabeth, Wife of me the Subscriber, has eloped from my Bed and Board, and forbids my having any Intercourse with her. This is to forbid any Person trusting her on my Account, for I will not pay any Debt which she shall contract after the Date hereof.
AARON RUMRILL. *Roxbury, Sept.* 13, 1782.
The Boston Gazette, And The Country Journal, November 18, 1782; December 2, 1782. See *The Independent Chronicle and the Universal Advertiser*, November 14, 1782.

WHEREAS my wife RUTH HINE, hath at sundry times run me in debt of considerable sums, without my knowledge or consent, which debts I have been obliged to pay, and hath also sold many things out of the house which belong to me, contrary to my will and orders, and is wasting my estate all that is in her power.—These are therefore to forbid any person or persons, to trade or deal with the said Ruth, either in purchasing of her, or selling any thing to her, as I shall pay no debts of her contracting nor allows any of her contracts.
DAN. HINE. Woodbury, October 14. 1782.
The Connecticut Courant And Weekly Intelligencer, November 19, 1782.

RAN AWAY from his master, Monsieur D'Hiseures, yesterday night, a Negro-Man, named Jaseinte, 5 feet 6 inches high, well set; had on a dark color'd jacket, a grey waist-coat, cloth color'd breeches, red cap, and black hat, was 23 years of age.—Whoever takes up said negro, and conveys him to his master in Portsmouth, shall have FOUR DOLLARS reward, and all necessary charges paid, by Mons. D'HISEURES,
(Capt. Commandant reg. of Venois,
(on board the Auguste.
Portsmouth, Nov. 22, 1782.
The New-Hampshire Gazette, And General Advertiser, November 23, 1782; November 30, 1782; December 7, 1782.

RAN away from the Subscriber, in the Night of the Fifteenth Instant, a Wench, Half Indian and Half Negro, named PHOEBE, Twenty-six Years of Age, large and strong, much pitted with the Small-Pox, has a remarkable piercing Eyes, some Scars round her Neck and back, and is very talkative. Took with her one Calico Gown, one striped Linen Ditto, on Drugget Ditto,

a black Cloak, &c. Whoever will bring said Wench to the Subscriber, shall have Two Guineas Reward; or whoever will give information so that she may be had, shall be handsomely paid for their Trouble.
    JAMES DAGGET.   *Rehoboth, November* 22, 1782.
The Providence Gazette; And Country Journal, November 23, 1782; November 30, 1782.

RUN-away from Isaac Smith of Dutchess County, State of New-York, on the 8th day of May last, a Negro Man named PETER, about 20 years old, about 5 feet 10 inches high, black but not of the blackest sort, thick lips, he was at Deerfield about the first of June last, and proposed going down Connecticut to look for work. Run-away at the same time a Negro man belonging to Lewis Graham, a middle-size fellow, about 30 years old, some marked with the small pox, very talkative, he was lately in the State of Vermont and very narrowly escaped being taken, and now supposed to be gone to look for the above-mentioned Negro, his name is HARRY. Ten Dollars reward and all reasonable charges shall be paid for either of them, by
    ISAAC SMITH, and LEWIS GRAHAM.
            Dutchess County, November 15, 1782.
The Connecticut Courant And Weekly Intelligencer, November 26, 1782; December 3, 1782; December 10, 1782.

BENJAMIN HOWD, *and GEORGE MONRO, both of Branford, in the County of New-Haven, this night having made their Escape from the Sheriff when he was committing them to Goal, by Order of the County Court, on Complaint of the Grand Jury, for going to Long Island, &c. Any Person that shall take up the said Howd and Munro, or either of them, and them bring to me the Subscriber at said Gaol, that he or they may be secured, shall have Ten Dollars Reward for their Trouble for either of said Persons.*
    STEPHEN A. MUNSON, Gaoler.
          Dated at New-Haven, November 15, 1782.
The Connecticut Journal, November 27, 1782; December 12, 1782.
See *The Connecticut Journal,* July 4, 1782, for Monro/Munro.

ON the 7th of September last, one Bartlet, hired a horse, saddle and bridle, of the subscriber, to go as far as Dover, but has not returned it, which creates a suspicion that he is gone off with the same. Said Bartlet is about 6 feet high, wears his own hair, and has on a wrapper with a red velvet cape, and a blue jacket. The horse is of a bay colour, with a white spot in his forehead, about 8 years old, a natural trotter, and 14 hands high. The saddle had a buff seat, and the housen was made out of a flower'd carpet.—Any friend to an injured person, that will give information of the man and horse, or of the horse alone, so that one or both may be come at, shall be handsomely rewarded for their trouble, by   JAMES HASLETT.

The New-Hampshire Gazette, And General Advertiser, November 30, 1782; December 7, 1782; December 14, 1782.

RUN away the second inst. from the subscriber, a negro man, named ZACK, about 19 years old, upwards of 5 feet high, has a blemish in one of his eyes, speaks quick; had on and carried away a whitish colour'd coat, one striped red and white jacket, one white do. one pair white stockings, one pair mix'd do. Whoever will take up said negro and return him to the subscriber, or secure him in any goal in this State, so that I may have him again, shall receive TEN DOLLARS reward, and all necessary charges paid, by
         JABEZ SWAN.   East-Haddam, December 3, 1782.
N. B. All masters of vessels are forbid harbouring or carrying off said negro. J. S.

The Connecticut Gazette; And The Universal Intelligencer, December 6, 1782; December 13, 1782; December 20, 1782. See *The Connecticut Courant And Weekly Intelligencer*, December 17, 1782, for Zack/Jack.

         Mr. Printer,   Boston, Dec. 3d.
WHEREAS James Gardette my lawful husband, has seen fit to leave me, and go off with a *harlot*, and, to support her in some degree of elegance, has in a clandestine manner, in the night, and at a time when I was absent, plundered the house of all the valuable furniture, and left me destitute of almost every necessary of life, with an illegitimate child of his, to maintain, and has had the confidence to declare, (contrary to truth) that I was not his wife, but whore, and written thus to my neighbours, requesting them not to call me by his name, and directed them to forbid me calling myself by his name.—Now, to support my own character against such unjust treatment from a husband, and to bring my said husband to a sense of the injury he has done me and to prevent him from deluding other simple women, it is my request that you would publish this, in *you next* paper, you will oblige your humble servant
         RACHEL GARDETTE.
         Her ℣ mark.
P. S. It is reported that he is now at New-London with a strumpet, by the name of Elizabeth Brown, niece to Capt. John Brown, of Boston, who he has the impudence to call his wife.

The Independent Chronicle and the Universal Advertiser, December 5, 1782; December 12, 1782; December 19, 1782; January 9, 1783; January 30, 1783; *The Connecticut Gazette; And The Universal Intelligencer*, December 6, 1782; December 13, 1782; December 20, 1782. The December 19 edition of the *Chronicle* has the following addition to the above ad:

Plimouth, Dec. 10, 1782.

THIS certifies whom it may concern that on February 12th, 1778, *Jaques Gardine* (alias *James Gardette*) and *Rachel Finley*, both then resident in *Plimoth*, were by the subscriber, then legally joined together in wedlock, as per records will appear, a certificate being first produced of their having been published according to law.

Attest. CHANDLER ROBINS,
Pastor of the 1st church in Plimouth.

WHEREAS Sarah, the wife of me the subscriber, refuses to live with me, these are therefore to forbid all persons trusting her, as I am determined not to pay any debt of her contracting after this; I likewise forbid Daniel Green, or any other persons keeping or harbouring my wife and child, as I am determined not to pay any debt that shall arise thereby.

ISAAC SMITH.   Amherst, Nov. 27, 1782.

The Independent Chronicle and the Universal Advertiser, December 5, 1782; December 12, 1782.

TAKEN up last week, a negro boy named TOM, about 14 years old, says he run away from one Mr. Thomas Edson, of Tower-Hill, State of Rhode-Island. He is now in the care of the subscriber.

DARIUS PECK.   Norwich, 4th Dec. 1782.

The Connecticut Gazette; And The Universal Intelligencer, December 6, 1782; December 13, 1782; December 20, 1782.

RUN away from his Master, at Colonel John Marston's last Evening, a NEGRO MAN, named PRINCE, about 22 Years of age, well set; had on a white Coat, faced with white.—Whoever will apprehend and return him to Comte de SPAUT, Captaine au Regt. Royal a Ponts, at the Bunch of Grapes, shall be generously rewarded.   Dec. 7.

The Boston Evening-Post and the General Advertiser, December 7, 1782; December 14, 1782.

WHEREAS my son, Stephen Jewett, has absented himself from my house and service—this is therefore to caution all persons not to trust him on my account, as I will not pay any debt he shall contract from this date.

As witness *ƒ* my hand,
Jonathan Jewett.   Stratham, Dec. 4.

The New-Hampshire Gazette, And The General Advertiser, December 7, 1782; December 14, 1782; December 21, 1782.

WHEREAS Hannah Dixon, the wife of me the subscriber, has eloped from my bed, and board, with two of my children, and hath put me to cost, in

paying for their boarding. This is therefore to forbid all persons harbouring them, or trusting her on my account; as I will not pay any debt of her contracting, after the date hereof.
    MOSES DIXON.   Westmorland, Nov. 12.
The New-Hampshire Gazette, And The General Advertiser, December 7, 1782; December 14, 1782.

RAN away, about four Months since from the Subscriber, living in Freetown, in the State of Massachusetts, a Negro Woman, named HAGER, about 32 Years of Age, of a middling Stature, very black, has a large flat Nose; she has been absent so long it is uncertain what Clothes she may have on. Whoever will take up said Negro Woman, and return her to me, or confine or in any of the Gaols of the United States, shall have TEN DOLLARS reward, and all necessary Charges paid, by
    JOHN HATHAWAY.
The Newport Mercury, December 7, 1782; December 14, 1782; December 21, 1782.

WHEREAS Tabitha, the Wife of the Subscriber, has eloped from my Bed and Board, and behaved in a very unbecoming Manner; therefore all Persons are cautioned against crediting her on my Account, or having any Dealings with her in my Name, as I will not pay any Debts of her contracting, after the Date hereof.
    JOHN PARKER.   *Scituate, December* 6, 1782.
The Providence Gazette And Country Journal, December 7, 1782; December 14, 1782; December 21, 1782.

Let by the Subscriber, to

one *Dr. Thadeus Jewett* (so called) on Wednesday last, to ride from Newton to Boston, a white roan MARE, with Saddle and Bridle, the Property of the Subscriber, and neither the Mare or Man have since been heard of, whereby it is supposed that the said *Thadeus* has withdrawn himself out of this Commonwealth.—Whoever will take up the said Mare, and give Information to the Subscriber, so that he may obtain his Property again, shall receive Six Dollars reward by
    NOAH HALE, jun.   Newton, December 9, 1782.
The Independent Chronicle and the Universal Advertiser, December 12, 1782; December 19, 1782; December 26, 1782.

RAN away from the Subscriber, on the 28th of November last, a LAD about 15 Years old, of a mustee Complexion; had with him a Great Coat of Sheep's grey, thick Cap, blue Breeches, thick Shoes and homespun Stockings. Whoever will take up said Lad and convey him to me, or secure him in any

of the States Goals, shall have TEN DOLLARS Reward, and all reasonable Charges, paid by
    JOHN WATSON, jun. South-Kingstown, Dec. 3, 1782.
The Newport Mercury, December 14, 1782; December 21, 1782; December 28, 1782; January 4, 1783; January 11, 1783.

RAN away from the Subscriber, in the Evening of the 8th Instant, a Negro Wench named LUCY, about 21 Years of Age; took with her one Calico Gown, one striped Linen Ditto, one green Calimanco Quilt, one blue Worsted Skirt, one dark Petticoat, one striped Kersey Ditto, one red Broadcloth Cloak, one blue Silk Hat, one white Linen Apron, one checked Ditto, one blue woollen Ditto, &c. Whoever will bring said Wench to the Subscriber shall have Ten Dollars Reward, and all necessary Charges; or a reasonable Reward will be paid to any Person who will give Information where she is.
    JOHN RICE. Coventry, December 12, 1782.
The Providence Gazette And Country Journal, December 14, 1782.

RAN AWAY, the 2d instant, from the subscriber, a NEGRO MAN, named JACK, about 19 years old, upwards of 5 feet 4 inches high, has a blemish in one of his eyes, speaks quick; had on and carried away a whiteish coloured Coat, one striped red and white Jacket, one white do. one pair white Stockings, one pair mixed do.—Whoever will take up said Negro, and return him to the subscriber, or secure him in any goal in this State, shall receive FIFTEEN DOLLARS reward, and all necessary charges paid, by
    JABEZ SWAN. East-Haddam, December 12, 1782.
The Connecticut Courant And Weekly Intelligencer, December 17, 1782; December 24, 1782; December 31, 1782. See *The Connecticut Gazette; And The Universal Intelligencer*, December 6, 1782.

    Ran away from his Master,
one *Peter Savanet*, about 25 Years of Age, 5 Feet 3 Inches high, down look, talks not a word of English, Servant to Mr. LABATUT, Officer of the French Navy; carried with him, Money and other Effects, which he stole from his Master.—Whoever will take up said Servant, and convey him to the Officer of Mr. LE CHEVALIER DE L'GUILLE, Major of the French Fleet, at Peck's Wharf, Boston, shall receive 10 Dollars Reward.
The Independent Chronicle, and the Universal Advertiser, December 19, 1782; December 26, 1782.

RAN away from the subscriber a boy named GEORGE GRANT, about thirteen years of age. Whoever will take up said boy and return him to the subscriber, shall have SIX SHILLINGS reward, and all persons are cautioned against harbouring or trusting said boy as they would avoid the penalties of the law.

     JOSEPH CARTER,   *Lancaster, December* 16, 1782.
Thomas's Massachusetts Spy Or, American Oracle of Liberty, December 19, 1782; December 26, 1782; January 2, 1783; January 9, 1783; January 16, 1783.

          Ten Dollars Reward.
SOMETIME in October last, a French officer put into the hands of Benjamin Bagnall, late of this place, watch-maker, a small, flat, single case silver watch, (maker's name Lausquanet, Brest;) the watch being missing, the said Bagnall, a few hours before his death, solemnly deposed, that on the 18th day of November, one Le Verry, a second Lieutenant of one of the French ships in this harbour, took the said watch from him, in lieu of an ordinary silver watch, left with him to repair; it has since been proved that no such officer or persons belongeth to said ships; but that one John Sears, a Frechman, [*sic*] and noted trader in watches, assumed the above named and character, and that a watch exactly of the above description, was seen in this possession, and from many other concurring circumstances, there is not one doubt but that the said Sears had said watch, and disposed of it. Any person that can give intelligence of said watch, so that it may be obtained, shall receive the
      above reward. HALL JACKSON.
The New-Hampshire Gazette, And General Advertiser, December 21, 1782; December 28, 1782. See *The New-Hampshire Gazette, And General Advertiser,* September 6, 1783.

RAN away from the subscriber, a molatto boy named JOE, about ten years of age, had on, when he went away, a blue jacket and strip'd trowsers. Whoever will take up said boy, and convey him to the subscriber, shall be handsomly rewarded, and all necessary charges paid.—All masters of vessels and others are hereby cautioned against harbouring or concealing said boy, as they would avoid the penalty of the law.
     JOHN CATHCART.   Boston, Dec. 21.
The Boston-Gazette, And Country Journal, December 23, 1782; December 30, 1782; January 6, 1783. See *The Boston-Gazette, And Country Journal,* October 7, 1782.

Run away from the Subscriber, on the night after the 15th inst. a Servant Boy, named ROBERT SMITH, about 18 years of age, about 5 feet 4 inches high, dark hair and eyes, had on and carried with him a light coloured great Coat, two brown homespun body Coats, two Vests do. two pair Breeches do. one pair speckled calicoe Breeches, one Vest do. two check'd Shirts, one white do. two pair blue yarn Stockings, one pair white do. one furr Cal, and one caster Hat.—Also, a Negro Man named DICK, about 5 feet high, thick set, talks broken, one of his toes on each foot grows above the rest, have on and took with him, two brown homespun Coats, two Vests do. two pair Breeches do. one velvet Vest, one old great Coat, two check'd woolen shirts, one pair blue yarn stockings, one pair white do. one old hat. Whoever will take up and return to me in Hartford, or secure in any goal in this state, said Boy and Negro, and give me notice, shall be entitled to a reward of Ten Dollars and all reasonable charges paid, or Five Dollars each.

          ISAAC SHELDON.   Hartford, Dec. 21.

The Connecticut Courant And Weekly Intelligencer, December 24, 1782; December 31, 1782; January 7, 1782.

WHEREAS *Ruter,* Wife to me the Subscriber, refuses to labour or do any Thing to support herself, and is running me in Debt, more than I am able to pay: This is therefore to forbid all Persons trusting her on my Account, as I will not pay any Debt that she may contract after the Date hereof.

                his
      BOSTON ╂ PAUL,
              mark.   Boston, Dec. 26, 1782.

The Independent Chronicle and the Universal Advertiser, December 26, 1782.

RAN away from the subscriber, on the 10th inst. an apprentice boy named DANIEL ROGERS, about eighteen years of age, midling stature, and stocky built; took wit him sundry articles of cloathing not exactly known. Whoever will return said apprentice shall have six pence reward.

          SILVANUS HIGGINS.   Lyme, 11th Dec. 1782.

The Connecticut Gazette; And The Universal Intelligencer, December 27, 1782; January 3, 1783; January 10, 1783.

RUN away from the subscriber the night following the 11th inst. an apprentice boy named JAMES DART, a thick set fellow, of a light complection, 18 years old; had on and carried away with him a light coloured coat, one brown outside jacket, one blue broadcloth vest, one Damascus do. one pair black broadcloth breeches, one pair nankeen do. one white holland shirt, one check'd do. and one coverlid; it is supposed he intends to go to sea. Whoever will take up said boy and secure him in any goal, or return him to me, shall be well rewarded for their trouble and all necessary charges paid,

            by   JOHN NUTTER.

N. B. All masters of vessels and others are forbid carrying off or harbouring said boy, if they would avoid the penalty of the law.

                                        Norwich, 25th Dec. 1782.

The Connecticut Gazette; And The Universal Intelligencer, December 27, 1782; January 3, 1783.

RAN-away from the subscriber, on Sunday the third day of November, a servant boy, named James Hutchinson, about seventeen years of age. Whoever will take up said Runaway, and convey him to me the subscriber, shall have one dollar reward, and no charges paid, by
            DANIEL GOULD.   Lyndborough, December 27th, 1782.
The New-Hampshire Gazette, And General Advertiser, December 28, 1782; January 11, 1783.

WHEREAS Mary the wife of me the subscriber has for some time past behaved herself in a very unbecoming manner, in threatening the life of me and my child, and I am apprehensive that she will do all in her power to injure me. This is therefore to warn all persons from trusting her on my account, as I will pay no debt of her contracting after this date.
        MARTIN WILLCOX.   New-Hartford, December 23, 1782.
The Connecticut Courant And Weekly Intelligencer, December 31, 1782. See *The Connecticut Courant And Weekly Intelligencer*, January 14, 1783.

1783

Twenty Dollars Reward.
RAN AWAY from the subscriber, on the 1st instant, a NEGRO MAN, named PRINCE, about 6 feet high, well built, speaks good English, about 23 years old; took with him a short light brown Coat, the buttons marked U. S. A. a grey Great-Coat, an old dark brown Vest and Breeches, one pair of Leather Breeches, one pair of black and blue Stockings, one pair white linen do. a striped linen Coat and Vest, an old beaver Hat, six yards and an half of cloth, mens ware, of a fresh colour, marked T. I. Whoever will take up said Negro, and return him to the subscriber, shall be entitled to the above reward.
        TIMOTHY IVES.   January 4, 1783.
The Connecticut Courant And Weekly Intelligencer, January 7, 1783; January 14, 1783; January 21, 1783.

STOLEN from, the subscriber, on the evening of the 23d of December last, about thirty three pounds, hard money, consisting of two French guineas, about 20 crowns, and the rest in dollars.—The thief is an old countryman, about 28 years of age—5 feet 10 inches high—and passes by the named of David Carncross—he has a bashful look, and is not over talkative—he wore away a blue turn'd coat—no buttons on it. Took with him also a snuff coloured coat and jacket with large yellow buttons—a light coloured serge coat—a light colour'd great coat of plain cloth—two white shirts—one striped collton do. and a number of other articles.—Also, about thirty pounds in soldier's notes, payable in June 1783 and 1784.

Whoever will take up said thief, secure him and return the money and articles to me the subscriber, shall have fifty dollars reward, or twenty five, for securing the thief only.
JUDAH STRONG.   Bolton (Connecticut) Jan. 3. 1783.

The Massachusetts Gazette Or the General Advertiser, January 7, 1783; January 14, 1783; January 28, 1783; *The Massachusetts Or The Springfield And Northampton Weekly Advertiser*, January 7, 1783; January 14, 1783; January 21, 1783.

STOP THIEF!

STOLEN out of the house of the subscriber, on the night of the 2d instant, by a person who calls herself Lydia Newman, who says she belongs to Kennebeck, but suppose she belongs to Groton, she is about five feet eight or ten inches high, light complexion, light blue eyes light hair, no upper teeth, two or three under teeth—had on when she went away, a black sattin hatt with a red sattinet lining, black mode cloak without lining, a narrow striped blue and white cotton and linnen gown, or other colour'd linnen gown, a black short, a blanket under petticoat, and very large feet. Any person that will take up said person, so that she may be brought to justice, and the things returned, shall be handsomely rewarded, and all charges paid, by
THOMAS JENNER CARNES.

The Independent Chronicle and the Universal Advertiser, January 9, 1783.

ONE HUNDRED DOLLARS REWARD.

WHEREAS on the night of the 7th instant, a number of villains did forcibly enter the house of *Cato Devereux*, (a black man) of this town, and by force of arms that from the said house a Negro Woman, named *Violet King*:—Whosoever will take up said Villains, and bring them to justice, and secure said Negro Woman, shall be entitled to the above reward from the Selectmen of Salem.   *Salem, January* 9, 1783.

The Salem Gazette, January 9, 1783; January 16, 1783; January 23, 1783.

OBSERVING yesterdays paper, to my great surprize I found myself advertised by him who ought to have been my friend and husband; who forbids all persons trusting me on his account, which I can safely say they never did nor ever will, until he behaves better than he does at present—but he tells me what he is afraid of, &c. But one story is good till another is told; the truth of the matter is this: It was my misfortune to marry Martin Wilcocks, better than two years ago; for some time after we married he provided a place for us to live, and we lived comfortably together for a few months, although he was considerable in debt, yet I was willing to do every thing in my power to help him out; and for that reason I sold every thing I could possibly spare, and even rob'd myself of cloathing to pay his debts, in hopes to live always happy together.—But it was not long before he enlisted to go in the state service for the town, and took a considerable sum of money for bounty, which he was very careful not to let me have one farthing of. After spending considerable part of the money, he deserted and went into Massachusetts state, and has left me for this 18 months without providing bread, meat or cloathing, or any shelter to put my head in, with an infant child to take care of, and nothing to care of it with; without a friend, relation or acquaintance: As I was a stranger in these parts, I have endured hunger and cold and every thing that is possible for me to undergo, short of death, without any body to pity me or take my part. Finally he has rob'd me of my child, the only comfort of my life, after I have taken so much pains with it, and undergone every thing to support it; considering the matter, it appeared to me so cruel, that I talked unbecomingly and sinfully; for which I ask forgiveness of God and all christian people; and leave it to the world to judge betwixt us, as I was always willing to live with him and behave to him as well as I knew how.

          MARY WILCOCKS.   New-Hartford, January 1st, 1783.

The Connecticut Courant And Weekly Intelligencer, January 14, 1783.

See *The Connecticut Courant And Weekly Intelligencer*, December 31, 1782.

        Broke out of Boston goal on the
night of the 14th instant, four prisoners, confin'd for piracy and theft, viz—

    Jonathan Hewes, about 5 feet 8 inches high, lame in one leg, had on a white out side jacket, long oznabrig trowsers, and a small felt hat.— *John Neal*, slim built, about 5 feet 10 inches high, of a light complexion, short hair, had on a blue jacket and breeches.—*James Webb*, a boy, about 16 years of age, had on a red duffel jacket, long trowsers, a small felt hat, pitted much with the small pox.—*Andrew Fingell*, a Dutchman, about 6 feet high, dark complexion, long hair cued, had on a deep colour'd blue suit of cloths and a large beaver hat.

    Whoever will apprehend the whole or either of them, shall be intitled to receive FIVE DOLLARS for each of them so returned, from the subscriber,

          JOS. HENDERSON, Sheriff.   Boston, January 15, 1783.

The Continental Journal, And Weekly Advertiser, January 16, 1783; January 23, 1783; January 30, 1783; *The Boston Evening-Post and the General Advertiser*, January 25, 1783; February 1, 1783; February 8, 1783; February 15, 1783; February 22, 1783. Minor differences between the papers. The *Post* shows the sheriff's first name as Joseph.

RAN away from the subscriber the 2d inst. one AZEL BENTLEY, an apprentice, about 19 years old, five feet four inches high, darkish complexion; had with him several suits of cloathes, likewise a short gun. Whoever will return said Bently to the subscriber, shall have six-pence reward by
    NAOMI TRACY.   Norwich, January, 1783.
The Connecticut Gazette; And The Universal Intelligencer, January 24, 1783; January 31, 1783; February 7, 1783.

      TWENTY DOLLARS Reward.
RAN-away from the Subscriber of Middletown, about the First of January inst. a lusty stout Negro Man, named CAMBRIDGE, about 26 Years old, about 5 Feet 9 or 10 Inches high, goes a little limping, one of his ancles being considerably larger than the other, plays pretty well on a Fiddle: Had on when he went away, a Felt Hat, a whitened Tow-Cloth Shirt and Linen Stock, a brown homespun closebodied Coat, an old light coloured Great-Coat, a new, white, short woollen homespun Jacket with a Belt to it; a Pair of full cloth homespun gray Breeches, black and white Yarn Stockings. He had inlisted on board a Privateer at Newport, but Inquiry being made for him, he left her, and 'tis supposed he is gone to Providence or Boston to look for a Voyage to Sea for which he has a great Inclination:—Whoever will apprehend said Negro and confine him in the nearest Jail to the Place where he shall be taken, and give Notice thereof to the Subscriber, shall receive Ten Dollars Reward, if taken on Rhode-Island, or Twenty Dollars if taken any where else, and all necessary Charges paid by
    BENJAMIN GARDNER.
All Masters of Vessels and others are hereby forbid harbouring or carrying off said Negro.   Middletown, Rhode-Island, January 16, 1783.
The Newport Mercury, January 25, 1783; February 1, 1783; *The Boston Gazette, And Country Journal,* February 3, 1783; February 10, 1783; February 17, 1783. Minor differences between the papers.

RAN AWAY from the Subscriber on the night after the 30th Day of Sept. last, a MOLATTO PRENTICE MAN, about five feet high, well sett, had about two Years and a half to serve when he ran away, and was bound to me by the Authority of the Town. His Name was called JACK: He has lately been in the Continental Service near a Year; there he called his name JOHN JOHNSON; he is well cloathed, had a large brown great Coat; he is now in Boston, as I have lately heard. Whoever takes up said Fellow and returns him back to the Subscriber, shall have Two Dollars Reward, paid by
    ELIZUR TALLCOTT.   Glastenbury, Jan. 14.
The Connecticut Courant, And Hartford Weekly Intelligencer, January 28, 1783; February 4, 1783.

Stonington, January 29, 1783.

WHEREAS *ANNA*, my wife, has left my house sundrys time before this date, against my mind and will, and has been brought home again by her nigh relations and friends, under a pretence that she was seized with a delirium, and has now willfully left my bed and board again, without any just cause: these are therefore to forbid all persons trusting her on my account, as I will not pay one penny of any debt whatever she shall contract.
AMOS CHESBROUGH.
The Connecticut Gazette; And The Universal Intelligencer, January 31, 1783; February 7, 1783.

RUN-AWAY from the Subscriber, on the night of the 20th inst. a Negro Boy Named JUBA, 18 years of age, 5 feet 8 inches high, had on when he ran away, a white Jacket with sleeves, a brown corduroy Vest, a pair of buckskin Breeches, a pair of Boots, a white holland Shirt, and an old beaver Hat. Also took with him a small horsemans Portmanteau containing the following articles viz. a superfine scarlet broadcloth Coat, faced with blue and trimed with prussion binding and white buttons, a pair of blue cloath Breeches, a white cloath Vest, a striped silk and linnen do. one holland Shirt ruffled, 3 white Stocks, a black leather do, with a false collar, a short blue Jacket with sleeves, a pair of Shoes, Shoe-Brush and Black-Ball. Whoever will take up said Negro and deliver him to me, or to John Whiting, Esq; of Windham, shall receive a generous reward and all necessary charges paid by their humble servant.
FRED. J. WHITING, A. 2d. R. L. D. Newtown, January 27, 1783.
The Connecticut Courant, And Hartford Weekly Intelligencer, February 4, 1783; February 11, 1783.

Two Hundred Pounds Reward.

ESCAPED last Night, from the Gaol in the County of Providence, two Prisoners, viz. WILLIAM PRENTISS, about 27 Years of Age, 5 Feet 6 Inches high, of a light Complexion, has very white and sound Teeth, light coloured Eyes, and light brown Hair; he is a Native of Boston. CHRISTOPHER OSGOOD, of Brattleboro, in the State of Vermont (so called) about 38 Years of Age, 5 Feet 10 Inches high, of a sandy Complexion, has light coloured Eyes, light brown Hair, is round-shoulder'd, and walks stooping he is very long-bodied for a Person of his Height, has a down Look, and has on each Eye-Lid a Number of blue Spots, occasioned by the blowing of Gun-Powder. It is impossible to describe the wearing Apparel of the above named Prisoners, as they have many Friends to help them to an Exchange of Dress. Whoever shall apprehend the above described Persons, and secure them in the Gaol of the County of Providence, shall receive the above Reward, or for either of them One Hundred Pounds Reward.

JOHN BEVERLY, Sheriff of the County of Providence.
Providence, Feb. 4, 1783.
The Providence Gazette And Country Journal, February 8, 1783; February 15, 1783; February 22, 1783. See *The Providence Gazette; And Country Journal*, September 14, 1782, for Prentiss.

SIX DOLLARS REWARD.

RAN away from the Subscriber, in the Evening of the 12th Instant, a Negro Man, named Cash, about 21 Years of Age, speaks good English, small of his Age, carried no Cloathing with him except what he had on, which was a checked woollen Shirt, a grey home-made Coat of fulled Cloth, Jacket and Overalls of home-made woollen unfulled Cloth, grey woollen Stockings, and a Felt Hat. Whoever will take up and return said Fellow to the Subscriber, shall receive the above Reward, and necessary Charges,
paid by   ISAAC MORGAN.
N. B. All Masters of Vessels and others are forbid carrying off said Fellow, as they would avoid the Penalty of the Law, in that Case made and provided.
Plainfield, Feb. 20, 1783.
The Providence Gazette And Country Journal, February 22, 1783; March 1, 1783; March 22, 1783; *The Connecticut Gazette; And The Universal Intelligencer*, March 7, 1783; March 14, 1783; March 21, 1783. Minor differences between the papers.

A notorious Villain,

BROKE into the shop of the subscriber, on the night of the 20th of February instant, and took away, sundry sides of upper leather; likewise a number of calf skins, and a kit of Shoe Makers tools, a light great coat, partly worn, the cape lined with black baize, which it is supposed he wore away.—Had on vest and overalls of a redish gray, trimmed with redish horn buttons, the vest double breasted, calls his name Phillip Morrel, a Shoe Maker by trade, he is about five feet ten inches high, well sett, has short black hair, and is very much pitted with the small pox, and very talkative.—Whoever will take up said Thief, and return him to the subscriber, or secure him in any goal, and give information thereof, so that the villain may be brought to justice, shall be entitled to five dollars reward, and all reasonable charges paid by me
SETH AUSTIN.

Suffield, Feb. 21, 1783.
The Massachusetts Gazette Or The General Advertiser, February 25, 1783; March 4, 1783. See *The Connecticut Courant, And Weekly Intelligencer*, March 4, 1783, and *The Connecticut Courant, And Weekly Intelligencer*, May 13, 1783.

Whereas Eleanor, my wife has injured me greatly by running me in debt, and selling my effects under their full value, by which I am a great suffered, these are to forbid any person dealing with or trusting her on my account, as I will not pay any debt of her contracting after this date.
     WILLIAM JONES. Great Barrington, January 23, 1783.
The Massachusetts Gazette Or The General Advertiser, February 25, 1783; March 4, 1783.

STOP THIEF!

BROKE into the Shop of the Subscriber, on the night of the 20th of February last, and took away sundry Hides of Neat's Leather, black'd for upper-leather; likewise sundry Calf-Skins, and a Kitt of Shoemaker's Tools, also a light Great Coat, partly worn, the cape lined with black baize, which the thief wore away; he had vest and overalls trimmed with redish horn buttons, the vest double-breasted, calls his name Phillip Morrell, and is a good shoemaker; he is about 5 feet 10 inches high, has short black hair, pitted with the small pox, very much addicted to talking.—Whoever will take up said thief, and return him to the subscriber, or secure him in any goal, so that the villain may be brought to justice, shall be intitled to Five Dollars reward, and all necessary charges paid.
    SETH AUSTIN.   Suffield, Feb. 21, 1783.
The Connecticut Courant, And Weekly Intelligencer, March 4, 1783; March 11, 1783. See *The Massachusetts Gazette Or The General Advertiser*, February 25, 1783, and *The Connecticut Courant, And Weekly Intelligencer*, May 13, 1783.

                 Boston, March 4th, 1783.
     TWENTY DOLLARS REWARD.
STOLEN out of the House of the Subscriber, on the Night of the 14th Inst. a neat English FUSEE, clean and bright, three Feet and a Half Barrel, a little Bell-Muzzle, carried 23 Balls to a Pound; it was in a Case. The Person who is suspected, calls himself Frederick Abel, a Dutchman, about 6 Feet high, has lost some of his fore Teeth; had on a brownish great Coat and Breeches, short dark green Coat, and blue Jacket, lined with white. Whoever will secure the Thief, so that he may be brought to Justice, shall be entitled to the above Reward, and eight Dollars for the Gun only, and all necessary Charges paid.
    THOMAS RICHARDS.   Dedham, Feb. 18, 1783.
The Independent Chronicle and the Universal Advertiser, March 6, 1783.

WHEREAS *Hannah*, my wife, has eloped from me; this is to forbid any and every person to trust her on my account—for I will not pay any debt which

she has or shall contract, since I posted her on that account, some time past.—Witness my hand, at Salem, this 5th day of March, A. D. 1783.
          ROGER PEELE.
The Salem Gazette, March 6, 1783; March 13, 1783; March 20, 1783. See *The Salem Gazette*, March 13, 1783.

WHEREAS *Pelige* my wife, has eloped from my house, and hath carried with her, the greatest part of my household furniture, and her child, which makes me suspicious that she is going to run me in debt: These are therefore to forbid all persons from harbouring or trusting her on my account, as I am determined to pay no debt of her contracting after this date.
          SIMON WEATHERBEE.   Westfield, March 7, 1783.
The Massachusetts Or The Springfield And Northampton Weekly Advertiser, March 11, 1783; March 18, 1783; March 25, 1783.

WHEREAS *Roger Peele*, of Salem, has posted me, as eloping from him, and has forewarned all persons crediting me on his account:—This is to assure the public, that I have never run him in debt twenty shillings old tenor, the whole 20 years that he has forsook me; and that the reason I left his house, and retired to one of my daughters, for two years past, is because I conceived my life to be immediately in danger while I lived with him: the reasons for which suspicion are too well known to many.
          HANNAH PEELE.   *Salem, March* 11, 1783.
The Salem Gazette, March 13, 1783; March 20, 1783. See *The Salem Gazette*, March 6, 1783.

          Hallowell, June 20, 1782. [*sic*]
          Whereas *Betty*, the Wife of me
the Subscriber, has eloped from me, forsaken my Bed and Board, and gone away with one JOSEPH NORTH, Esq; (alias Jo Bunker, so called) This is to warn all Persons not to trust her on my Account, for I declare that I will not pay one Debt that she shall contract after the above Date.
          JEREMIAH HILL, Esq:
The Boston Gazette, And Country Journal, March 24, 1783.

          TEN DOLLARS REWARD.
MADE his escape from me the Subscriber, the night after the 10th inst. one WILLIAM WALICE, of East-Windsor, who was legally taken by a special writ. Whoever will take up said Wallice, and return him to me or secure him in any goal in the United States, shall be intitled to the above reward, and all necessary charges paid, by
          HEZEKIAH BISSEL.   East-Windsor, March 22, 1783.

The Connecticut Courant And Weekly Intelligencer, March 25, 1783; April 1, 1783.

RAN away from the subscriber on the 30th of January last, a Negro man servant, named Fortune, the property of Mr. James Wheelock, in the 26th years of his age, about five feet and eight or nine inches high, lame in his right knee and leg, which are crooked and bent inward. Had on when he went away, a coat of knapped cloth, without lining, light brown on the outside, and a light yellow on the inner side, lappels and cuffs with the yellow side on the of the cloth outward, blue plain vest, with pewter flowered buttons, dearskin breeches, felt hat, almost new. Whoever will take up said negro, and convey him to the subscriber, or to Mr. Jabez Bingham, at South Hadley, in the State of Massachusetts, or give notice to either where he may be had, shall be handsomely rewarded, and if conveyed as aforesaid, have necessary charges paid by JABEZ BINGHAM, or
BEZA WOODWARD, (Attorney to said Wheelock.
Dresden, New Hampshire, Feb. 22.
The Massachusetts Or The Springfield And Northampton Weekly Advertiser, March 25, 1783; April 8, 1783. *The Massachusetts Gazette Or the General Advertiser*, April 1, 1783; April 8, 1783; April 15, 1783.

RAN away some time ago from the subscriber, a negro servant man, named PHILBY, between fifty and sixty years of age, about five feet four inches in stature, pretends to be much of a doctor, speaks good English. Whoever will take up the said negro, and return him to his said master, shall have SIX PENCE reward, and no charges paid; and all persons are forbid harbouring or concealing said negro on penalty of the law.
JAMES HAUGHTON.
New-London, North-Parish, March 26, 1783.
The Connecticut Gazette; And The Universal Intelligencer, March 28, 1783; April 4, 1783; April 11, 1783.

IN TOWN-COUNCIL,
Portsmouth, March 10, 1783.
WHEREAS CHRISTOPHER and NATHANIEL LAWTON, have conducted themselves in a Manner very inconsistently with their interest, and from a Number of Complaints and Circumstances it appears, that they will be likely to squander away their Estates and become a Town Charge; whereupon the Council taking the Matter into Consideration, do adjudge the said Christopher and Nathaniel Lawton non compos mentis, and incapable to transact any Business for themselves, and forbidding any Person or Persons from the Date hereof to trade, deal, or transact any Business with them, as it will be null and void.

Signed by Order of Council,
JOHN THURSTON, Council Clerk.
The Newport Mercury, March 29, 1783.

WHEREAS Sarah my Wife has without any just Cause eloped from my Bed and Board; these are to forewarn all Persons from harbouring or trusting her on my Account, as I shall pay no Debt of her contracting after this Date.
JOHN LONG.   *Litchfield, Feb. 10th.*
The Connecticut Courant And Weekly Intelligencer, April 1, 1783; April 8, 1783.

Take Notice.
WHEREAS the subscriber made a promissory note, dated March 24, 1783, for £.78, payable to John Brown or order, in one month from the date, and on interest thereafter, which note was given in part pay for a forged government note, sold to the subscriber by one *Joseph Coit*, alias *Joseph Gardner*, who, it is supposed, is concerned with many others in passing, forging and altering government securities:—This is to notify all persons thereof, that they may not purchase the said promissory note, as the subscriber is resolved not to pay it. He requests all friends to justice to assist in bringing those concerned in the above villanies to condign punishment.
  STEPHEN DUTCH.   *Ipswich, April 2, 1783.*
The Salem Gazette, April 3, 1783.

STOLEN from the subscriber out of the possession of Mr. Jonathan Morgan, one yoke of OXEN, and the yoke and irons with it, on the night of the 29th of March past; the oxen are about nine years old, and are of a blackish colour, near alike, smallish horns, with white stars in the forehead of each of them, part of their tails white; one has his hind feet white part of the way to the gambill, some white on the back part of this rump, and I think the next ox is somewhat speckled on the hips, and of a bluish cast. Whoever will take up said thief and oxen, and them convey to me in New London, shall receive Ten Dollars reward, and all reasonable charges. It is supposed that one Samuel Avery of Lyme, carried off said oxen, as he was lurking thereabout and has carried them up in the Bay state, supposed to Wilbraham or near thereabout.
  JOSHUA HEMPSTED, Collector.
The Connecticut Gazette; And The Universal Intelligencer, April 4, 1783.

DOCTOR PARKER of Coventry, Connecticut, having purchased of Col. Williams of Pittsfield the indentures of DANIEL BRITTON, a lad of about 11 or 12 years old, 4 feet 5 inches high, had on a grey homespun Coat and

Vest, brown cloth Breeches, a chek'd flannel Shirt, white woolen Stockings, high top'd Shoes, of a homely countenance, having a very large mouth and lips and a full light eye, light coloured hair, he was heard of at Feeding Hills, and has since missed his road, he had two dogs with him, which he wishes secured. Whoever will apprehend said boy, and deliver him to said Dr. Parker, or inform Col. Williams, or Mr. Leonard Chester of Wethersfield, shall be handsomely rewarded, by
     CAIDE PARKER.   Coventry, March 28, 1783.
The Connecticut Courant And Weekly Intelligencer, April 8, 1783; April 22, 1783.

     Whereas I have been credibly informed,
by different persons, that Thankful, my wife, hath, since I have been in the service, most shamefully abused me, by cohabiting with other men, and the most undoubtable proofs of her guilt, having appeared against her. This is therefore to forbid all persons trusting her on my account, as I am determined not to pay any debt of her contracting after the date hereof.
    GEORGE SMITH.   Springfield, April 7, 1783.
The Massachusetts Gazette Or the General Advertiser, April 8, 1783; April 15, 1783; April 22, 1783; *The Massachusetts Or The Springfield And Northampton Weekly Advertiser,* April 8, 1783; April 15, 1783.

     TEN DOLLARS REWARD.
STOLEN from the house of Capt. Ebenezer Fisk, of Southampton, on Sunday evening the 6th of April instant, a SILVER WATCH, No. 102, maker's name Thomas Robinson, of London; also a pair of square SILVER SHOE BUCKLES, with wide rims, curiously wrought, and a pair of MEN's PUMPS. They were stolen by a person who said his name was Henry Booth, or Monk; he is of a middling stature, well proportioned, of a sprightly behaviour, lightish complexion, round smooth face, lightish eyes, says he is an Englishman (though he appears to have something of the Irish brogue) and that he deserted from the British army about eight months since, has shortish brown hair, cut short on the top of his head, and the fore-top turn'd back, about twenty-three years old; had on a short brown coat, white vest and breeches, blue stockings, and a pair of boots.
  Whoever will take up the thief, and above articles, and secure them to the subscriber, shall have ten hard dollars reward, and all necessary charges paid; or if only the thief, or watch and buckles, shall be generously rewarded by me
    EBENEZER FISK,   Southington, April 7, 1783.
N. B. The thief says that he work'd with Joseph Pease, of Suffield, two months the beginning of last winter, and at General Wadsworth's, in Durham, the two last months.

The Connecticut Journal, April 10, 1783; April 17, 1783; April 24, 1783.

                        I the subscriber, forbid all
Persons trusting or entertaining a negro Man, named MOSES, now living in Bridgwater, on my Account, for I will not pay any Debt of his contracting after the Date hereof.
                      CHRISTOPHER DYER.   Abington, March 22, 1783.
   The Independent Chronicle and the Universal Advertiser, April 10, 1783.

WHEREAS *Elizabeth Shiels,* Wife of me the subscriber, has eloped from my bed and board, taking my Effects with her; this, therefore, forbids any person trusting her, on my account.
                        EDWARD SHIELS.
   The Independent Chronicle and the Universal Advertiser, April 10, 1783.

THE Subscribers take this Method to inform the Publick, that whereas we have three Notes of Hand, to one JOSEPH MILLER, viz. one Note of *twenty Dollars,* upon demand, one other Note of *sixty-two Dollars and an half,* payable in one Years from Date of said Note; also, one other Note of *sixty-two Dollars and an half,* payable in two Years from the Date of said Note; all bearing date 17th June 1782; which Notes were given to said MILLER, in Consideration that he should serve in the continental Army, three Years; and whereas said MILLER has deserted from said Army. and not fullfiled the Condition, on his Part, this is therefore to caution all Persons against purchasing said Notes, which were put into the Hands of one DANIEL JOHNSON, of SOUTH-BOROUGH, as a Trustee for said MILLER, as we are determined not to pay one Farthing of said Notes.
                  BENJAMIN SAWIN,   JONAS MORSE.
                                                Marlborough, March 15, 1783.
   Thomas's Massachusetts Spy Or, American Oracle of Liberty, April 10, 1783; April 17, 1783; April 24, 1783. See *The Independent Chronicle and the Universal Advertiser,* April 24, 1783.

RAN away from the subscriber the night following the first day of April, an apprentice boy named JONATHAN WEEKS WINTER, about 19 and 20 years of age, and of midling stature. Whoever will take up said boy, and return him to his said master, shall have Four Pence reward, and no charges paid; and all persons are forbid harbouring or concealing said boy on penalty of the law.
                      ABNER BACON.   Canterbury, April 4, 1783.

The Connecticut Gazette; And The Universal Intelligencer, April 11, 1783; April 18, 1783; April 25, 1783.

WHEREAS Mariaba my wife has behaved herself in an indecent manner; this is therefore to forbid all persons crediting her on my account, as I am determined not to pay any debts she may contract after the date hereof.
Uriah Hunskum, Madbury, April 12, 1783.
The New-Hampshire Gazette, And General Advertiser, April 12, 1783.

Forty Dollars Reward.
RAN away from the Subscriber, on the Night of the 7th of April inst. a NEGRO MAN, named Richard, about 5 Feet 10 Inches high, 25 Years of Age, is very much pitted with the Small-Pox; he had on a blue Jacket, dark London brown Breeches, is a Native of Virginia, and speaks good English—has followed the Sea for a Number of Years. He has a Wife in New-York, and is supposed to be gone that Way.—Whoever will apprehend the said Negro, and return him to the Subscriber, shall receive the above Reward, and all necessary Charges.
ALFRED ARNOLD. *Providence, April* 11, 1783.
The Providence Gazette And Country Journal, April 12, 1783; April 19, 1783; April 26, 1783.

Ranaway from the Subscriber,
in the night of the 24th ult. Stephen Hutchinson, an indented servant, 17 years old, near five feet high, light coloured eyes and dark hair, he carried away with him one suite of light coloured cloaths, a good felt hat, a brown waistcoat, and an old red under ditto. two pair of blue stockings, one of which was seemed, and two pair of shoes one check woolen shirt, and one linen ditto, and other articles.

All persons are hereby forbid harbouring, entertaining or securing the said Stephen, or conveying him away by water or otherwise.—Whoever will take him up and bring him to me, shall have three shillings reward, and necessary charges paid.
JOHN AYERS. April 1st, 1783.
The Massachusetts Gazette Or the General Advertiser, April 15, 1783; April 22, 1783; *The Massachusetts Or The Springfield And Northampton Weekly Advertiser,* April 15, 1783; April 22, 1783.

MADE his escape from the goal in New-Haven, on the night of the fifth of April instant, DENNIES HART, a native of Long-Island, about 25 years of age: Had on a blue great-coat, wore his hair: Committed for going over the Long-Island.—Whoever will return said Hart to said goal, or will give information of the person or persons who furnished him with the tools to

made his escape, shall receive THREE DOLLARS for either of them, if delivered to the subscriber,
    STEPHEN MUNSON, Goaler. New-Haven, April 17.
 The Connecticut Journal, April 17, 1783; April 24, 1783.

RAN away from the subscriber, on the 26th ult. an apprentice boy named NATHANIEL WAY, aged 18 years. All persons are forbid to entertain, or carry off said apprentice; and whoever will return him to me shall have one dollars reward.
    PETER ROGERS. New-London, April 8. 1783.
 The Connecticut Gazette; And The Universal Intelligencer, April 18, 1783; April 25, 1783; May 2, 1783.

RAN away from the subscriber on the 5th day of March last, a negro woman servant, about 20 years of age, named CLOE: short and thick set; has a scar on her nose and another on her ear; a tooth which grows out of the roof of her mouth; has been whipped for theft, and carried the marks on her back. Had on when she went away, a short all-wool brown wrapper, and a petticoat of the same; a blue and white handkerchief, a pair white yarn stockings, black cloak, pair men's shoes, and white tow shift: speaks good English. Whoever will take up said negro; and return her to the subscriber, shall have Six Dollars reward, and all necessary charges paid, by
    MORTIMORE STODDER. Groton, April 15, 1783.
N. B. All persons are forbid to entertain or conceal her on penalty of the law.
 The Connecticut Gazette; And The Universal Intelligencer, April 18, 1783; April 25, 1783; May 2, 1783. See *The Connecticut Gazette; And The Universal Intelligencer*, September 29, 1775, and *The Connecticut Gazette; And The Universal Intelligencer*, February 2, 1776.

RAN away from Capt. Timothy Pearce, of Newport, on the 10th instant, an Apprentice Boy, named WILSON MAY, 14 Years of Age, has short black Hair, is very fleshy and likely, and had on a London brown Jacket and Overhauls. This is to forwarn all Masters of Vessels, or other Persons, from harbouring or carrying off said Apprentice, as they must answer for it, if found out. Newport, April 18, 1783.
 The Newport Mercury, April 19, 1783.

WHEREAS *Anne Gardner*, the Wife of the Subscriber, has gone away, and does keep away, though I have desired her to come Home oftentimes and she wont.—I forbid all Persons trusting her on my Account from this Day.
    DAVID GARDNER. *Boston, April* 21.
 The Boston Gazette, And Country Journal, April 21, 1783; April 28, 1783; May 5, 1783.

STOP THIEF.

RAN-AWAY from me the Subscriber, on the 9th of April inst. ROGER ALGOR, about six feet high, round shoulders, long black hair, about 28 years of age, has taken way one pair of silver Shoe Buckles, one check'd linen Shirt, one pair of linen Overhalls, one bag and looms cords. Whoever will take up said villain and return him to me the Subscriber, shall have a handsome reward and all necessary charges paid by
    JOEL BACON.   Middletown, April 4, 1783.
 The Connecticut Courant And Weekly Intelligencer, April 22, 1783; May 6, 1783; May 13, 1783.

WHEREAS Rachel my wife, hath several times left me contrary to my will and hath been received back again, and now she hath again eloped my bed and board, without any provocation. This is to forbid any persons harboring or trusting her on my account, as I solemnly declare I will not pay one farthing, contracted by me on my account, from this day forward.
    JONATHAN BECKWITH.   April 3, 1783.
 The Connecticut Courant And Weekly Intelligencer, April 22, 1783; May 6, 1783.

LEFT in the custody of the Subscriber, by John Lewis, the 2d of April inst. about 50 yards of white woolen cloth fulled—who by examination made his escape, said cloth is supposed to be stolen from some fulling mill in Rhode-Island State. The said John Lewis is about twenty years of age, dark complection, short hair, dark brown coat and vest, a mixed coloured loose coat, and old felt hat, rode away a small bay horse, trots and paces, an old saddle. Whoever will take up said thief and secure him, shall be handsomely rewarded and charges paid by
    ELIJAH HASKEL.
N. B. The owner may have the cloth, by proving his property and paying charges.   Tolland, April 21, 1783.
 The Connecticut Courant And Weekly Intelligencer, April 22, 1783; April 29, 1783; May 6, 1783.

WHEREAS *Lydia*, Daughter of the Subscriber, has lately absconded from me, and greatly run me in Debt:—This is to warn all Persons against trusting her on my Account, as I will not pay any Debt she may contract.
    EBENEZER WARREN.
        Bridgwater, North-Parish, April 23, 1783.
 The Independent Chronicle and the Universal Advertiser, April 24, 1783; May 1, 1783; May 8, 1783.

Marlborough, March 14, 1783.

Whereas the Subscribers did for certain Considerations to be performed by Joseph Miller, sign three Notes of Hand, payable to him or his Order, viz. one Note of Hand for 20 Dollars, payable on Demand, one Note for 62½ Dollars, payable in one Year from the Date, and one other Note for 62½ Dollars, payable in two Years from the Date; all said Notes, bearing date June 17, 1782—And whereas the said Joseph never did perform any Part of the Service which he engaged to do, but has absconded and left the Notes in the Hands of one Daniel Johnson, of Southborough, who may possible convey them away, by which means those not informed of the Circumstances may be defrauded.—This is therefore to notify the Public, that the Subscribers are determined not to pay one Farthing of said Notes.

BENJAMIN SAWEN. JONAS MORSE.

The Independent Chronicle and the Universal Advertiser, April 24, 1783; May 1, 1783. See *Thomas's Massachusetts Spy Or, American Oracle of Liberty*, April 10, 1783.

ON the night after the 10th inst. the subscriber's house was broke open, and the following articles stolen, viz. about £. 18 in silver, crowns and dollars, a silver watch, a claret colour'd great coat, with a red cape, a pale blue coat, black sagathee jacket and breeches, and a check flannel shirt. The thief is supposed to be one David Hessex, about 21 or 22 years old, about 5 feet 6 inches high, of a light complexion, and short hair; had on a short sailor jacket, cloth colour, and striped woolen under-jacket and trowsers. Whoever will take up said thief, and secure him so that the above articles may be recovered, shall have Ten Dollars reward, and for the thief only, Five Dollars, and necessary charges paid, by

JOHN PARISH. (innholder in Windham.

Windham, April 19, 1783.

The Connecticut Gazette; And The Universal Intelligencer, April 25, 1783; May 2, 1783; May 9, 1783.

Whereas MABEL, my wife, has eloped from my bed and board, without any just cause or provacation: this is therefore to forbid all persons from harbouring or trusting her, as they will answer it at their peril, for I will not pay any debts of her contracting after this date; and furthermore, I make a free offer to my said wife Mabel, if she will immediately return to her duty, I will receive her with open arms of friendship.

ELIJAH CHAPPEL, jun.   Lebanon, April 22d, 1783.

The Connecticut Gazette; And The Universal Intelligencer, April 25, 1783; May 2, 1783; May 9, 1783.

STOLEN from the Subscriber, on the evening of the 15th inst. two MARES, a Saddle and a pair of sleigh Leading Lines, one of the Mares of a sorrel colour, with a white spot in her forehead, about 9 years old, natural pacer; the other of an iron grey colour, with one wall eye, a white spot in her forehead, about the same age, natural pacer.—The thief supposed to be a certain Chatwell Persons, who has been convicted before the Hon. Superior Court in this State, for passing counterfeit money—Whoever will take up said Mares and thief, shall have Twenty Dollars reward, and for the Mares only, ten dollars and all necessary charges paid, by
    JONATHAN BIDWELL. Wintonbury, April 29, 1783.
The Connecticut Courant And Weekly Intelligencer, April 29, 1783; May 13, 1783; May 20, 1783.

John Mansfield and William Huggins were last week convicted of Burglary, before the Honourable Judges of the Supreme Judicial Court, began and holden at Worcester last Tuesday se'nnight.
The Continental Journal, And Weekly Advertiser, May 1, 1783. See *Thomas's Massachusetts Spy Or, American Oracle of Liberty*, June 19, 1783.

      Twenty DOLLARS Reward.
RANAWAY from the subscriber on the 26th inst. a negro man servant named SCIP, aged about 23 years, midling stature, well set and very likely, born in the country, can read tolerably well: had on a pair of blue broadcloth breeches, red wastecoat, jacket with buttons covered with blue cloth, pair pale blue seamed stockings, two striped flannel shirts, white wastecoat, green broadcloth coat, brown linen breeches, small beaver hat and a felt ditto. Whoever will take up and return said servant to me in New-London, North Parish, shall have Twenty Dollars reward.
    WILLIAM PRINCE. New-London, April 29, 1783.
The Connecticut Gazette; And The Universal Intelligencer, May 2, 1783; May 9, 1783; May 16, 1783. See *The Connecticut Courant And Weekly Intelligencer*, June 3, 1783.

WHERAS SUSANNAH WILLCOX, Wife of me the Subscriber, has left my Bed and Board, without any just Cause or Provocation, and has already run me considerably in Debt. Therefore all Persons are forbid to trust her in future or to harbour or entertain her, in expectation of Reward from me, for I hereby declare I will pay none of her Debts from the Date hereof.
    ARNOLD WILLCOX. Stonington, April 29, 1783.
The Connecticut Gazette; And The Universal Intelligencer, May 2, 1783; May 16, 1783.

TEN DOLLARS REWARD.

RAN away from the Subscriber, on the 25th ult. a NEGRO MAN, named SIMON, about 5 Feet 4 Inches high, has a Scar on his upper Lip; carried away with him a brown Great-Coat, a blue close-bodied Ditto, a buff Waistcoat, and a Pair of black Velvet Breeches. Whoever will apprehend said Negro, and give Notice thereof, shall receive the above Reward, and all Charges.
SETH JENKINS.
N. B. All Masters of Vessels and others are cautioned against carrying off or concealing said Negro.   Providence, May 2, 1783.
The Providence Gazette And Country Journal, May 3, 1783; May 10, 1783; May 17, 1783; May 24, 1783.

WHEREAS my wife FREELOVE, has eloped from my bed and board, contrary to my will, I do therefore forbid all persons harbouring or trusting her on my account, as I will not pay any debt or her contracting after this date.
EBENEZER PIERCE.   East-Windsor, April 28. 1783.
The Connecticut Courant And Weekly Intelligencer, May 6, 1783; May 20, 1783.

Whereas the wife of me the subscriber, hath absconded from my bed and board, and it is likely she may run me in debt; this is therefore to forbid all persons trusting her, or supporting her, on my account, as I will not pay any debt which she may contract.
PAUL AUSTEN.   Hancock, April 24, 1783.
The Massachusetts Gazette Or The General Advertiser, May 6, 1783; May 13, 1783; May 20, 1783; *The Massachusetts Or The Springfield And Northampton Weekly Advertiser,* May 6, 1783; May 13, 1783; May 20, 1783. See *The Massachusetts Gazette Or The General Advertiser,* August 12, 1783.

WHEREAS *MARY* the Wife of the Subscriber, hath behaved herself in a very unbecoming Manner, and hath eloped from my Bed and Board, these are therefore to forbid all Persons from harbouring or trusting the said Mary on my Account, as I will not pay any Debt of her contracting from the date hereof.
EBENEZER CHILD.   *Sturbridge, April* 25, 1783.
Thomas's Massachusetts Spy Or, American Oracle of Liberty, May 8, 1783; May 16, 1783; May 22, 1783; May 29, 1783; June 5, 1783; June 12, 1783.

WHEREAS a person who called his named WILLIAM TYLER, and said he belongs to Attlebro' in the Commonwealth of Massachusetts, did, on 15th day of March, last, sell and convey to the subscriber, by writing under his hand and seal, the one half of a single share in all prizes that should be captured by the sloop Hancock, John Conkling, commanded, in a cruize of three months, on which cruize the said sloop was then bound, and the said Tyler (so called) received of the subscriber a valuable consideration therefor. And the said Tyler did, about the same day, sell and convey to Joseph Bolles, 3d, of New-London, the one quarter part of a single share in all the prizes that should be captured as aforesaid, for which he received the sum agreed on. And after receiving his reward as aforesaid, the said Tyler absconded, did not go in said sloop, but the town and has not since been seen here. The subscriber therefore, as well to recover his just right from said Tyler, as to make known his character, hereby offers a reward of SIX DOLLARS to any person who will return said fellow to me in New-London. Said Tyler (so called) is about 21 years old, about 6 feet high, well set, light eyes, black hair, and pretty likely; he wore here a strait-bodied, chocolate coloured homespun coat, which he exchanged in town for a blue sailor jacket, which he carried off with him, together with a pair brown tow cloth long trowsers, and an under jacket of the same as above described coat. He went off in company with three others who were guilty of the like crime.
    SAMUEL ROGERS, jun. New-London, April 26, 1783.
The Connecticut Gazette; And The Universal Intelligencer, May 9, 1783; May 16, 1783.

STOLEN out of the Subscribers stable, in Norwich, on the night of the 7th of May instant, a bay English STALLION, about 14 hands high, black mane and tail, is long to his gambrills, a little white in his forehead, long ears, a small bunch on the inside of his ancle on his fore leg, trots and canters, carries himself well. The supposed thief is one CURTISS, he is of a dark complexion, black eyes, black hair, about 5 feet 7 inches high, has a small scar over his left eye, and a scar across the back of one of his hands. Whoever will take up said thief and horse and return them to me or secure them so that I can have them, shall have 12 dollars reward and necessary charges paid, for the Horse only 6 dollars.
    ELIJAH WILLOUGHBY.
              Norwich (Connecticut) May 9, 1783.
The Connecticut Courant And Weekly Intelligencer, May 13, 1783; May 20, 1783; May 27, 1783. See *The New-York Gazetteer or Northern Intelligencer*, May 26, 1783, and *The Massachusetts Gazette Or The General Advertiser*, May 27, 1783.

WHEREAS a false and injurious advertisement appeared in the Connecticut Courant of the 4th of May [sic] last, under the signature of Seth Austin, wherein the said Austin accuses me, Phillip Morrell, of theft, &c. &c. in order to undeceive those who may have been prejudiced against me by said advertisement, I hereby let them know that having been employed as a shoemaker, by said Austin, and not receiving any payment, I endeavoured to bring him to a settlement, which he constantly and industriously avoided, and finding that I could get nothing from him, on the night of the 20th of February I packed up my tools and left him, upon which appeared to above advertisement, in consequence of which I was taken out of bed on the morning of the 22d of February, and brought back thirty miles, but he far from having any thing stole, had nothing in the shop that any person would steal, upon which we came to a settlement, but not being able to agree, upon account of a most exorbitant charge he had against me for a small space of time I was sick and for the advertisement and trouble of bringing me back, we left it to the arbitration of honest and judicious men, who gave it as there opinion that there was no theft proved against me, as their names undersigned will evidence.
    TIMOTHY CADWELL, ADAM THOMPSON,
    ISAAC HALLADAY. Arbitrators.
                Suffield, April 8, 1783.
The Connecticut Courant, And Weekly Intelligencer, May 13, 1783; May 29, 1783. See *The Massachusetts Gazette Or The General Advertiser*, February 25, 1783, and *The Connecticut Courant, And Weekly Intelligencer*, March 4, 1783.

WHEREAS, my wife, AMY, has endeavoured, and has been endeavouring, to run me in debt and ruin my estate, and behaves in an unbecoming manner: These are to forbid all persons trusting her on my account, as I will not pay any debts, of her contracting, from the date hereof: And all persons are forbid harbouring the said Amy, at the peril of the Law.
    JOEL MUNGER, jun.   Litchfield, May 5, 1783.
The Connecticut Journal, May 15, 1783; May 22, 1783; May 29, 1783.

WHEREAS KAZIA, my wife, has eloped from my bed and board, without any just cause or provocation: this is therefore to forbid all persons from harbouring or trusting her, as they will answer it at their peril, for I will not pay any debts of her contracting after this date. And furthermore, I make a free offer to my said wife Kazia, that if she will immediately return to her duty, I will receive her.
    LEMUEL SCOVELL.   Chatham, May 5th, 1783.
The Connecticut Gazette; And The Universal Intelligencer, May 16, 1783; May 23, 1783; May 30, 1783.

241

WHEREAS *SALLY* the wife of the subscriber, has lately eloped from my bed and board, and I am apprehensive that she may endeavour to run me in debt by being trusted on my Account; this is to warn all persons not to harbour or trust her on my account, as I will not pay any debt she may contract from this date.
    ISAAC MORGAN, jun.   *Spencer, May* 20, 1783.
Thomas's Massachusetts Spy Or, American Oracle of Liberty, May 22, 1783; June 5, 1783; June 12, 1783.

RAN-AWAY from her Mistress the tenth instant, a Negro Girl about 16 years of age, named VILOT, speaks good English, and is of short stature—Whoever will take up said Negro, shall be handsomely rewarded, and all charges paid by me
    ELIZABETH SERVICE.   Portsmouth, May 17, 1783.
The New-Hampshire Gazette, And General Advertiser, May 24, 1783; May 31, 1783; June 7, 1783. See *The New-Hampshire Gazette, And General Advertiser*, July 13, 1782.

RAN away, from the Subscriber, on the 23d of March last, a Negro Man named PRINCE, Five Feet Ten Inches high, Thirty-eight Years of Age; his Legs very crooked: Had on when he went away a mill coloured Coat, Leather Breeches, and blue Stockings. Whoever will take up said Negro and return him to me, shall receive FOUR DOLLARS Reward, and all necessary Charges paid, by
    JEFFERY CHAMPLIN, JUN.   Exeter, May 7, 1783.
The Newport Mercury, May 24, 1783.

    Ran away from the Subscriber
last Saturday Evening, a Negro Boy, named FIFE, about 17 Years old, about 5 Feet high, strait Limb'd and well set:—Had on when he went off, a brown mix'd Homemade Cloth Jacket and Trowsers of the same. Whoever will take up said Run away, and secure him, or will convey him to this Master, shall have One Guinea Reward, and all necessary Charges paid, by
    SHUBAEL DOWNS.   Boston, May 26, 1783.
 N. B. He may be well known by being at his Master's, when he kept a House of public Entertainment at Walpole.
 The Boston Gazette, And The Country Journal, May 26, 1783; June 2, 1783; June 9, 1783.

JOHN BREWER, of Sudbury, does hereby forbid any Person trusting his Wife, *Lydia Brewer*, with any Dependance upon his paying any Debt for her after this Date of May the 22d. 1783, as she has absented herself from him and refuses the Duty of a Wife.

The Boston Gazette, And The Country Journal, May 26, 1783; June 2, 1783; June 9, 1783.

TWELVE DOLLARS REWARD.

STOLEN from the Subscriber, in Norwich (State of Connecticut) on the evening of the 7th of May instant, A BAY STALLION, about 14 hands high, 5 years old, three fourths blooded, a little white in the forehead, black mane and tail, has a small bunch on the inside of his left for leg, near the footlock joint, trots and canters, lofty carriage, &c. Said horse was stolen by one *JEPTHA CURTISS*, (a native of New-Jersey) about 24 years of age, middling stature, black hair which he combs back, swarthy complexion, black eyes, a small scar over his left eye, about the circumference of a pea, another scar across the back of one of his hands; pretends to speak Latin scholastically, and Dutch as well as English.—Whoever will take up said thief and horse, and secure the thief, and give information to the subscriber, at Norwich, or JONAS GALUSHA, Esquire, in Shaftsbury (State of Vermont) shall have the above reward, and for the horse only SIX DOLLARS, and all necessary charges, paid by

    ELIJAH WILLOUGHBY.   Norwich, May 10, 1783.

N. B. It is supposed the horse is concealed either in Berkshire or Albany county.

The New-York Gazetteer or Northern Intelligencer, May 26, 1783; June 9, 1783. See *The Connecticut Courant And Weekly Intelligencer*, May 13, 1783, and *The Massachusetts Gazette Or The General Advertiser*, May 27, 1783.

Twelve Dollars Reward.

STOLEN out of the subscriber's stable in Norwich, on the night of the 7th inst. a bay Stallion, English breed, 14 hands high, black main and tail, lofty carriage, a little white in the forehead, trots and canters, a small bunch on the inside of his left fore leg, near the fetter lock-joint. The thief is one Curtis, of middle stature, about 24 years of age, swarthy complexion, black hair combed back, black eyes, a scar over his left eye as big as a pea, also a scar across the back of one of his hands. Whoever will take up said thief and horse and return them to me, or secure them so that I can have them, shall have the above dollars reward and necessary charges paid, for the horse only 6 dollars.

    ELIJAH WILLOUGHBY. Norwich,

           State of Connecticut, May 12, 1783.

The Massachusetts Gazette Or The General Advertiser, May 27, 1783; June 3, 1783; June 10, 1783; *The Massachusetts Or The Springfield And Northampton Weekly Advertiser*, June 3, 1783; June 10, 1783. See *The*

Connecticut Courant And Weekly Intelligencer, May 13, 1783, and *The New-York Gazetteer or Northern Intelligencer*, May 26, 1783.

TEN DOLLARS REWARD.

RAN away from the Subscriber, on the 21st of this Instant, a Negro Man named ZEB, about 30 Years old, about 5 Feet 8 Inches high, had on a duroy Coat snuff Colour, black short Breeches, pair long check'd Overhalls, blue and white mixed rib'd Stockings. Said Negro was bought of Mr. Picket Latimer of New-London. Whoever will apprehend and secure said Negro or bring him to me at South-Kingstown in the State of Rhode-Island, shall have the above Reward, and all Charges paid by
    JOSEPH GORDEN. So. Kingstown, May 28, 1783.
All Masters of Vessels are forbid carrying off said Run-away or concealing him.

The Connecticut Gazette; And The Universal Intelligencer, May 30, 1783; June 6, 1783; June 13, 1783. See *The Independent Chronicle and the Universal Advertiser*, June 12, 1783.

TEN DOLLARS REWARD.

BROKE out of the County Goal in Norwich, on the Night following the 3d Inst. one EDWARD WENTWORTH, thick-set fleshy Man; had on blue Coat, small round Hat, and leather Breeches; confin'd for Debt. Whoever will take up and return the above Debtor, shall have the above Reward, paid by me,   DARIUS PECK, Goaler. Norwich, 4th May, 1783.

The Connecticut Gazette; And The Universal Intelligencer, May 30, 1783; June 6, 1783; June 13, 1783.

STOP RUNAWAY.

RAN away from his Master's service, in the evening of the 28th inst. JONATHAN DAVIS, an indented Apprentice to the Shoemaker's trade: he is in the 20th year of his age, had on a small round hat, a red and white striped outside jacket, and tow-cloth trousers; is about five feet four inches high, of a dark complexion, and brown hair; has been seen in Salem since he absconded. Whoever will apprehend said Davis, and deliver him at the Post-Office, in Boston, shall receive eight dollars reward, and be paid all reasonable charges.   Boston, 30th May, 1783.

The Boston Evening-Post and the General Advertiser, May 31, 1783; June 7, 1783; June 14, 1783; June 21, 1783.

RAN AWAY from his master, the 14th of April, one John Merril, had on a striped waistcoat and breeches, was seventeen years old, and five feet high: Whoever will return said boy shall have *one copper* for this trouble, by
   Joseph Clifford.   Kensington, May 21st, 1783.

The New-Hampshire Gazette And General Advertiser, May 31, 1783; June 7, 1783.

THIRTY DOLLARS REWARD!

RUN away from the Subscriber on the 26th of April last, a Negro MAN servant named SCIP, about 23 years of age, middling stature, well sett, born in the country, speaks good English, and can read tolerable well; had on when he went away and carried with him, one pair of blue broadcloth Breeches, a red Waistcoat, a light mixt coating doublebreasted Jacket, with buttons covered with blue cloth, two striped Shirts, one white do. one pair of blue seemed Stockings, one pair of white do. a white Jacket, a green broadcloth Coat, a pair of brown linen breeches, a small beaver Hat, and one felt do. Whoever will take up and return said servant to me in New-London, north parish, shall have the above reward and all reasonable charges paid.—All masters of vessels and others, are forbid to carry off or harbour said servants.

    WILLIAM PRINCE.   New-London, May 15, 1783.

The Connecticut Courant And Weekly Intelligencer, June 3, 1783; June 10, 1783; June 17, 1783; July 1, 1783. See *The Connecticut Gazette; And The Universal Intelligencer*, May 2, 1783.

State of New-Hampshire.

BROKE out of the public Goal at Amherst, Sam'l Jones of Hillsborough, Joseph Clark of Antrim, and Bildad Soul of Gofftown, on the night following the twenty eigth [sic] day of May, all prisoners for debt.—Samuel Jones is about five feet eight inches high, thick set, light complexion, sandy hair, round shouldered.—Joseph Clark is about the same height and seize, [sic] light complexion, light curled hair, well set, stands pretty upright.—Bildad Soul is a tall slim fellow, light complexion.—Whoever shall take up the said Samuel Jones and return him to Amherst Goal, into my custody, shall have forty dollars reward, and for each of the others returned fifteen dollars reward and all necessary charges paid by

    Moses Kelly, Sheriff.   Amherst, May 31, 1783.

The New-Hampshire Gazette, And Historical Chronicle, June 7, 1783; June 14, 1783; June 21, 1783; *The Independent Chronicle and the Universal Advertiser*, June 12, 1783; June 19, 1783; June 26, 1783; July 3, 1783. Minor differences between the papers.

WHEREAS Lieut. Nehemiah Pratt, jun. of Mansfield in the County of Bristol, Gentleman, about 5 Feet 10 Inches high, being taken by the Subscriber, of said Mansfield, by Virtue of several Writs and Executions, did, on the 31st Day of May last, break and make his Escape from me.—Whoever will take up said Pratt and convey him to me, or commit him in any Goal,

shall have Ten Dollars Reward and all necessary Charges paid by
RICHARD TIDD, Dep. Sheriff. *Mansfield, June* 4, 1783.
The Boston-Gazette, And Country Journal, June 9, 1783; June 16, 1783; June 23, 1783.

RUN AWAY, from me on the Evening of the 6th of May, a certain Woman by the Name of MIMA CARNES, *Wife of the Subscriber, and will not return after repeatedly requesting her; and has at sundry times behaved herself unbecoming a virtuous Wife: This is therefore to forbid* Mary Jenner, *or any other Person or Persons, from Trusting or Harbouring he, as I will not pay on farthing she may Contract on my Account from said Date.—Any Person or Persons presuming to carry said Run-away out of this or any other Town, may depend on being Prosecuted to the utmost rigour of the Law.*
THOMAS JENNER CARNES.
N. B. Notice is hereby given to sundry Married and single Gentlemen, if they don't refrain from her Company, they may depend on having their Names exposed to the Publick.
The Independent Ledger and the American Advertiser, June 9, 1783.
See *The Continental Journal, And Weekly Advertiser,* June 12, 1783.

RUN away from the Subscriber, a Negro Man named SAY, about 21 years of age; had on when he went away a blue Broadcloth Coat edged with white, white flannel Jacket and Breeches, silver buttons on his Jacket, and a number of every day cloaths. Whoever will take up said Negro and return him, or give information where he may be found, shall have Ten Dollars reward, and all charges paid, by
ALEXANDER CATLIN. Litchfield, June 3, 1783.
The Connecticut Courant And Weekly Intelligencer, June 10, 1783; June 17, 1783; July 1, 1783.

RUN away from the Subscriber last Sunday, one EDWARD MERRIT, about 25 years of age, about 5 feet 6 inches high, thick set, black short hair tied up behind, dark eyes a little sunk in his head; had on a red Jacket with sleves, a light coloured short Vest, a pair of large striped Trowsers, a felt Hat bound with ferrit.—Said fellow has broke open and robbed several houses, and concealed the goods, and is a most notorious liar. Whoever will take up and secure said villain, that he may be brought to justice, shall receive a generous reward and charges paid, by
JOHN MERRIAM. Meriden, June 3, 1783.
The Connecticut Courant And Weekly Intelligencer, June 10, 1783; June 17, 1783; June 24, 1783.

THE impartial Public will be pleased to take notice, That the certain Woman by the name of MIME CARNES, wife of THOMAS JENNER CARNES, and published by him in the paper of last Monday, as a run-away—is a poor unfortunate distressed female, who, being seduced by the false promises of the abovenamed Thomas J. Carnes, has been over persuaded to abandon her parents, her friends and her country, and become his wife depending upon him only for her protection, support and happiness, but who, after having repeatedly suffered every species of cruelty and insult that villainy and infidelity to her bed could suggest. and inhumanity could inflict, 'till her very life has been threatned and in danger, has been obliged, in regard to her own personal safety, and to obtain the common necessaries of her existance, to seek for this shelter which he has denied to her, from one of his own relations.

  MIME CARNES.

The Continental Journal, And Weekly Advertiser, June 12, 1783; *The Boston Evening-Post and the General Advertiser*, June 14, 1783; June 21, 1783; *The Independent Ledger and the American Advertiser*, June 16, 1783. The *Ledger* has "Boston, June 16, 1783." at the bottom of the ad. See *The Independent Ledger and the American Advertiser*, June 9, 1783.

TEN DOLLARS REWARD.

RAN away from the subscriber, a negro man named ZEB, about 30 years old, five feet seven or eight inches high, carried off with him a horse, saddle and bridle, very black, full ey'd, had on a brown duroy coat, black short breeches, patch'd, check'd linnen draws over them, blew ribb'd Stockings. Whoever will take up and secure said runaway, and confine him in any of the goal in the United States, so that his master may have him again, shall be intitled to the above Reward, and all necessary charges paid me.

  JOSEPH GORDON.

N. B. Said Negro ran away some time ago, went to Marblehead, and returned again.   South Kingstown, May 30, 1783.

The Independent Chronicle and the Universal Advertiser, June 12, 1783; June 19, 1783; June 26, 1783; July 3, 1783. See *The Connecticut Gazette; And The Universal Intelligencer*, May 30, 1783.

WHEREAS *Mary*, my wife, hath for some time past, behaved herself very ill, by wasting my property, and cohabiting with other men; and as I have determined, if possible, to procured a divorce from matrimonial bond—I hereby give public notice, to all persons, not to trust her on my account, as I shall not pay any debt of her contracting, but such as I shall be compelled to pay by law.

  JEREMIAH HEGERTY.   *Salem, June* 10, 1783.

The Salem Gazette, June 12, 1783; June 19, 1783; June 26, 1783.

Whereas LYDIA, the Wife of
the Subscriber, has eloped from my Bed and Board, and refuses to return:—I hereby declare, that I will not pay any Debt which she may contract on my Account, after the Date hereof.

His
REUBEN X WIXSOM.
Mark.

Dated Yarmouth, May 24, 1783.

The Boston Gazette, And The Country Journal, June 16, 1783; June 23, 1783; June 30, 1783.

RUN away from the Subscriber last night, one STEPHEN YEOMAN, about 19 years of age, about 5 feet 8 inches high, fair complexion, has a scar upon his thigh, short sandy hair, wore away or took with him, a claret coloured Coat, spotted woolen Vest, a suit of black Soldiers Cloaths, buttons marked U S A, chec'k Shirt and Trowsers, a pair of linen Stockings, and a Knapsack. Whoever will take up said fellow, and inform the subscriber where he may be found, shall have a generous reward and charges paid, by

JACOB ROBBINS. Wethersfield, June 16, 1783.

The Connecticut Courant And Weekly Intelligencer, June 17, 1783; June 24, 1783; July 1, 1783.

Whereas Esther, wife to
me the subscriber, did forsake my house, and did elope from me and my children in the month of February last, and tho' often requested to return to her duty, yet she still continues to refuse to return, purely on the account of religious principles and sentiments. I hereby declare and certify, that in case she will return to her duty, notwithstanding her different principles, she shall be treated as a wife, so long as God in his providence continues us man and wife, and otherwise, if she still continues to refuse, I hereby caution all person, or persons against harbouring he or trusting her on my credit, for I will not pay no debt after this date.

DANIEL BACON. Date Buckland, June 12, 1783.

The Massachusetts Gazette Or The General Advertiser, June 17, 1783; June 24, 1783; July 1, 1783; *The Massachusetts Gazette Or The Springfield and Northampton Weekly Advertiser,* June 17, 1783; June 24, 1783; July 1, 1783.

Whereas Mary my wife,
has eloped from me the subscriber, and raised and spread false and slanderous reports of me without excuse. These are therefore to forbid all persons to

tread [sic] with, or trust her on any account of mine, for I will not pay any debt of her contracting for the future.

his
JAMES + HILL
mark

Pelham, May 26, 1783.

The Massachusetts Gazette Or The General Advertiser, June 17, 1783; June 24, 1783; July 1, 1783; *The Massachusetts Gazette Or The Springfield and Northampton Weekly Advertiser*, June 17, 1783; June 24, 1783; July 1, 1783.

WORCESTER, June 19.

About day-light yesterday morning, Mansfield and Huggins, who are to be executed this day, endeavoured to make their escape out of prison. For this purpose they by means of a crow bar (which was left out side the prison door, and which they could reach through a grate in the door) wrenched out the staples which fastened their chains to the floor, broke the casing off the vault, and let themselves into it; they carried the bar with them, but either had not time to effect their escape through the wall, or were not able to make a breach of it. As soon as the prison-keeper got up in the morning, (which was, very early) he missed them, and it being suspected by some that they had entered the vault, the floor of the prison was ripped up, when they soon discovered the prisoners lying near the wall, in a miserable condition.

Thomas's Massachusetts Spy Or, American Oracle of Liberty, June 19, 1783; *The Boston Gazette, And Country Journal*, June 30, 1783. See *The Continental Journal, And Weekly Advertiser*, May 1, 1783.

Ten Dollars Reward.

WHEREAS JARED TUTTLE, of Berkhamsted, being arrested by the subscriber by a special writ from lawful authority, for stabbing a man with a weapon of death on the highway, did, on the evening after the 21st inst. make his escape out of my custody—Said Tuttle is about 23 years of age, dark complexion, freckled in the face, something pitted with the small-pox, dark eyes, black hair, five feet eight or ten inches high; had on when he made his escape, a blue waistcoat, white shirt and trowsers, and an old castor hat.—Whoever will take up said Tuttle, and return him to the subscriber, or secure him, so that he may be brought to justice, shall receive the above reward, and necessary charges paid, by

MOSES SHEPARD, Constable.   Berkhamsted, June 23, 1783.

The Connecticut Courant And Weekly Intelligencer, June 24, 1783; July 8, 1783.

Brimfield, June 24, 1783.

Whereas Rose, the wife

of me the subscriber, has left my house, and carried away her cloaths, which gives me reason to believe she has not thoughts of returning, and to prevent her running me into debt: I do hereby warn all persons, not to trust her on my account, or harbouring here [sic] with any expectation of my paying it, for I will not pay any debt that she shall contract.
                    NATHANIEL DANIELSON.
The Massachusetts Gazette Or the General Advertiser, June 24, 1783; July 8, 1783; *The Massachusetts Gazette Or The Springfield and Northampton Weekly Advertiser*, June 24, 1783.

WHEREAS SARAH the Wife of the Subscriber, has eloped from my Bed and Board without any cause: This is to notify the Public not to trust her on my Account, as I will not pay any Debts that she may contracts from this Date.
           JOHN HOGAN.   Newport, June 24, 1783.
The Newport Mercury, June 28, 1783; July 5, 1783.

WHEREAS ELIZABETH, the Wife of the Subscriber, hath eloped from my Bed and Board, and behaved in a very unbecoming Manner: Therefore all Persons are cautioned against crediting her on my Account, or having any Dealings with her in my Name, as I will not pay any Debts of her contracting after the Date hereof.
           WILLIAM MARTIN.   Providence, June 28, 1783.
The Providence Gazette And Country Journal, June 28, 1783.

RUN away from Levi Booth and Samuel Tudor, of East-Windsor, the evening after the 23d of this instant June, two Negro men, the one belonging to the said Booth, was named HECTOR, about 20 years of age, a pretty well built fellow, pitted a little with the small pox, of a yellow complexion, this country born, talks pretty good English, had on when he went away, a brown linen short Coat, Jacket and Breeches, white Shirt, black Handkerchief, a new Felt Hat with large brims; the other, belonging to the said Tudor, about 20 years of age, 5 feet 10 inches high, named LONDON, this country born, talks pretty good English, yellow complexion, had on when he went away, a light grey ratteen Coat, brown line Jacket and Breeches, white Shirt, red spotted silk Handkerchief, an old felt Hat. Whoever will take up and return said Negroes, shall have five dollars reward for each, and all necessary charges, paid by,
                    LEVI BOOTH, SAMUEL TUDOR.
                                        East-Windsor, June 24, 1783.
The Connecticut Courant, And Weekly Intelligencer, July 1, 1783; July 8, 1783; July 15, 1783.

WHEREAS Elizabeth my wife has, without any just cause or reason, eloped from my bed and board, and, in my absence, has conducted herself very unbecoming a person in the marriage state—these are therefore to forbid all persons harbouring or trusting her on my accompt, as I will not pay any debts or her contracting after this date.
     WILLIAM MERRIT.   Hebron, June 23, 1783.
The Connecticut Courant, And Weekly Intelligencer, July 1, 1783.

STRAYED away from the Subscriber on or about the first of May last, Elizabeth Perry, a servant Girl, about 17 years of age, a shaker by persuasion and practice—these are to forbid all persons from harbouring her at the peril of the law.
     DANIEL WOOD.   Somers, June 23, 1783.
The Connecticut Courant And Weekly Intelligencer, July 1, 1783; July 8, 1783; July 15, 1783.

     PORTSMOUTH, June 28.

Last week one Stinson, a refugee from this State, and who has had the effrontery to return, in hopes of partaking, with use, the sweets of that liberty which they have so perfidiously laboured to destroy, was apprehended by order of justice, and committed to Exeter gaol, for transportation.

As also, a John Yeaton, formerly of this town, who has been a privateering or plundering (his own countrymen) the supporters of our dear-bought freedom, who have been so unfortunate as to fall into his hands during the course of the late war.
The Salem Gazette, July 3, 1783.

RAN AWAY from the Subscriber on the 27th instant, an apprentice boy named PETER CHAPPEL, about 15 years old, slim built, light hair and eyes, and much of a talkative; wore away a striped flannel jacket, white tow-cloth shirt and trowsers, and a small round hat. Whoever will take up said boy and return him to his master, shall have Six Pence reward. All persons are forbid harbouring said apprentice on penalty of the law.
     MICAJAH DAVIS.   New-London, June 30, 1783.
The Connecticut Gazette; And The Universal Intelligencer, July 4, 1783; July 11, 1783; July 18, 1783.

RAN away from the subscriber on the 6th of April last, MARY HUNTLEY, a girl about 13 years of age. Whoever will take up said girl shall have Two Dollars reward.   SAMUEL COULT.
N. B. I forbid all persons harbouring or concealing said girl under the penalty of the law.   Lyme, July 10, 1783.

The Connecticut Gazette; And The Universal Intelligencer, July 11, 1783; July 18, 1783; July 25, 1783.

State of New-Hampshire, Rockingham, *ss.*
WHEREAS *Thankful*, the wife of me the subscriber, hath unnecessarily run me in debt, and threatens further to continue the same injurious practise. Therefore I do hereby forbid all persons trusting her, or giving her any credit on my account, for I will pay no debts whatever by her contracted after this date. MOSES BRADLEY. Plastow, April 21st, 1783.
The New-Hampshire Gazette, And General Advertiser, July 12, 1783; July 26, 1783.

Fifty Dollars Reward!
RUN away from the subscriber the night following the 9th inst. July, a likely well built Negro Man, DICK, about 22 years old, near 5 feet and a half high, clear black, talks pretty good English; had on when he went away, a deep blue Coat, a brown Waistcoat, a pair of brown tow cloth Trowsers, and a pair of linen Beeches [*sic*] under them, a check'd Shirt almost worn out, a large brim'd felt Hat almost new, white yarn Stockings, thick Shoes, large block-tin Buckles, his hair turned back.—Went away with a Negro named POMP, about 23 years old, talks broken, is clear black, about 5 feet and a half high, wore chiefly linen cloaths—Whoever will take up said Negroes, or Dick only, and return him to the subscriber, or secure him in any goal, shall have the above reward, paid by
    ELIZUR TRYON. Glastenbury, July 8, 1783.
The Connecticut Courant And Weekly Intelligencer, July 15, 1783; July 22, 1783; July 29, 1783. See next ad.

FIFTY DOLLARS REWARD.
RAN away from the subscriber the night following the 7th instant, a likely well built NEGRO MAN, named DERY, about 22 years of age, near five feet and a half high, clear black, talks pretty good English; had on when he went away a deep blue coat, brown waistcoat, and brown tow cloth trowsers, with a pair of linen breeches under them, check'd shirt almost worn out, a large broad felt hat, almost new, white yarn stockings, thick shoes, large block-tine shoe buckles, his hair turn'd back, went away with a Negro named Pomp, about 23 years of age, thick set, talks broken, is clear black, about 5 ½ feet high, wore chiefly linen clothes. Whoever will take up said Negroes, or said Negro only, and return him to the subscriber in Glastenbury, shall receive the above reward from
    ELIZUR TRYON. Glastenbury, July 8, 1783.
The Connecticut Journal, July 16, 1783; July 23, 1783; July 30, 1783. See previous ad.

Ran away from the subscriber on the 30th of June inst. an apprentice boy, whose name is *Benjamin Blasdel*, in the 16th year of his age.—All persons are hereby forbid entertaining or employing said apprentice, and requested to send him back again to his master, and for their trouble, they shall have six pence reward, and *no* necessary expences by me
    DANIEL MOODY,   Sailsbury, July 7th, 1783.
The Independent Chronicle and the Universal Advertiser, July 17, 1783; July 24, 1783; July 31, 1783.

WHEREAS *Elizabeth Valentine*, my Wife, has absented herself from my Bed and Table, at Cascobay; and, when I was absent in Prison, married one *Luis*, Native of Ireland, at present in Boston: I hereby forbid any Person whatsoever, to trust her on my Account.
    ATHUR [sic] POLTENGER.
The Independent Chronicle and the Universal Advertiser, July 17, 1783.

One Hundred Dollars Reward.
ESCAPED from the Gaol in Providence, on Thursday Evening the 17th of July, ABRAHAM TOURTELOT, 5 Feet 10 Inches high, thick set, a strong well built Man, was born in Gloucester, as light Eyes, long Hair, walks wide, about 40 Years of Age, has lived at Penobscot, at the Eastward; had on a striped Cotton and Linen Coat of a yellowish Cast, a white under Jacket, striped blue and white Overalls, and round Castor Hat of a middling Size. Also SWEETING TAFT, about 32 Years of Age, 6 Feet 1 Inch high, strait limbed, stands and walks upright, has light Eyes and short Hair, has lived in Uxbridge; had on a long light coloured Coat, somewhat worn, a Jacket of the same, coarse Ozenbrigs Overalls, and a Castor Hat, with a Lace round the Crown.—Whoever will return them or either of them to me, shall be paid FIFTY DOLLARS for each.
    EPHRAIM BOWEN, jun. Sheriff. Providence, July 18, 1783.
The Providence Gazette And Country Journal, July 19, 1783; July 26, 1783; August 2, 1783.

WHEREAS RACHEL, my wife, hath several times left me contrary to my will and without any provocation. This is to forbid any persons harbouring trusting or trading with her on my accompt as I solemnly declare I will not pay one farthing contracted by her on my account, from this day forward.
    SAMUEL PERRY.   Adams, July 11, 1783.
The Connecticut Courant And Weekly Intelligencer, July 22, 1783.

WHEREAS my wife KEZIAH has behaved in a very indecent manner, in trying in every particular to break up all good government in my family and

utterly refusing to live with me as a wife. This is therefore to forbid all persons harbouring or trusting her on my account as I will not pay any debt of her contracting after the date hereof.
DANIEL KETCHUM, in the Goar [sic] in the State of Massachusetts between Adams and New-Stamford.
July 9, 1783.
The Connecticut Courant And Weekly Intelligencer, July 22, 1783; August 5, 1783.

MADE his escape from Goal in this town, on Tuesday evening last, JOHN GLOYD, about 5 feet 9 inches high, round shouldered and carries his head considerably forward. Had on a blue coat, long trowsers and a rusty hat. Whoever will take up said GLOYD, and return him to me shall receive FOUR DOLLARS reward, and all necessary charges paid, by
LEMUEL RICE, Gaoler.   *Worcester, July* 23, 1783.
Thomas's Massachusetts Spy Or, American Oracle of Liberty, July 24, 1783; July 31, 1783.

STOLEN from the subscriber in Ferrisburgh, near New Haven Falls, on the evening of the second of this instant July, one half johannes, one French Guinea, eleven crowns, fourteen Spanish milled dollars, twelve silk handkerchiefs, eight yards and a half of corduroy, twenty five yards of Holland, one cotten shirt, one white shirt ruffled; a quantity of penknives, a fusil with a hack in the stock, with a small pin drove in to hold down the split made by the cut. The said thief is supposed to be Simon Toll, who was taken up in the town of Cornwall, at which time Asa Blodget, living near the creek, drew a sham writ, and signed the same as justice of the peace, & one of his neighbours served on him as constable, by which means said Toll was rescued. Whoever will take up said thief and return him to me, at Ferrisburgh, at the house of Mr. David Brada, or secure him in any of the goals, in the United States, so that the said thief may be dealt with as the law directs, shall have ten dollars reward, and necessary charges paid, by
JOHN GRIGGS.
The Vermont Gazette Or Freemen's Depository, July 24, 1783; August 7, 1783.

Mr. GREEN,
WE think it our duty to inform the public, that last week on application being made to Sir Guy Carleton, he gave an order for apprehending a number of people that were counterfeiting and passing Morris's and Hillegas's notes, several of them being apprehended, viz. William May, formerly a chaplain in the American army, belonging to Brimfield, Massachusetts; Sylvester Lyon, of Woodstock, Connecticut; Lemuel Nichols, of Waterbury,

Connecticut; and upon search, the Printer, whose name was Poor, was taken with his tipes, blanks signed, and paper &c. On apprehending the printer, they found one Ferward, at his office, employed in signing them, (he is a refugee from Windsor, in Connecticut) and two others, one a refugee from Waterbury, named Nichols, the other Dennis Fain, from Sturbridge, Massachusetts. The printer had counterfeit money of every kind, nearly two hogsheads; the greatest part were fifteen dollar notes, poorly executed. General Carlton has promised to send them to General Washington.

A. B. C.

The Connecticut Gazette; And The Universal Intelligencer, July 25, 1783.

RAN AWAY from the subscriber in October last, an indented servant, named Thomas Shaw, about twenty years of age, five feet eight inches high, a remarkable, lazy fellow, wears his own chesnut colour'd hair; carried off with him three suits of cloaths and a bed blanket: whoever will take up said boy and return him to his master free of expence, shall have five shillings reward. All persons are forbid harbouring said boy, if they would avoid the penalty of the law.

THEOPHILUS GILMAN.   Exeter, July 22d, 1783.

The New-Hampshire Gazette, And General Advertiser, July 26, 1783; August 2, 1783; August 9, 1783.

WHEREAS on or about the 10th of April 1783, one Lt. John Gile, of Nottingham, appeared at my house in Warner, and demanded of me twenty-five dollars, without having any just demand upon me to the value of one shilling, he said he had the offer of twenty-five men, to come with him, and if I refused paying him the said sum, when he returned, they would immediately pay me a visit; and out of fear he would return with his associates, as he told me he would, and ruin me in body or estate, in this distress of mind, I signed a note of hand, to the amount of twenty-five dollars, and gave the same to the said Lt. John Gile, in order to get rid of him, immediately upon making the above fact known to my friends and neighbours, and the authority of the county to which I belong they warmly relented the matter, and told me to publish the same immediately. I therefore caution all persons from purchasing said note of hand, as I am determined not to pay the same, unless compelled by law, said note being obtained by fraud.

ALL persons are cautioned against harbouring, or trusting Sarah Morrill, wife of me the subscriber, and she has eloped from my bed and board, and refuses to cohabit with me her lawful husband; as I am determined not to pay any debt she may contract after the date hereof, unless compelled to by law.

EPHRAIM MORRELL. Warner, July 12, 1783.
The New-Hampshire Gazette, And General Advertiser, July 26, 1783; August 2, 1783; August 9, 1783.

WHEREAS Ann, the Wife of me the Subscriber, has eloped from my Bed and Board, and threatens to run me in Debt: I hereby forbid all Persons to credit her on my Account, as I will not pay any Debts of her contracting from the Date hereof.
JAMES MALTMAN. Providence, July 26, 1783.
The Providence Gazette And Country Journal, July 26, 1783; August 2, 1783; August 23, 1783.

Hingham, July 17, 1783.

WHereas *Sarah*, the Wife of me the subscriber, did on the 26th day of March last, elope from my Bed and Board, and has continued absent, notwithstanding my frequent requests for her return—this is to warn any Person or Persons from harbouring or entertaining the said *Sarah*, as I hereby declare I shall discharge no debts of her contracting from the date hereof.
ISAAC BEAL, jun.
The Boston Gazette, And The Country Journal, July 28, 1783; August 4, 1783.

Whereas Daniel Norton is this day charged with the murder of Elisha Brown; and Joseph Hawley Esq; hath issued a warrant of hue and cry to apprehend him, he having fled for it: therefore all constables and others are desired to persue after and apprehend the said Daniel, he is about thirty years old, of a sprightly countenance and of a middling stature, dark brown hair, inclined to curl and darkish complexion, had on when he fled, a check'd shirt and stripped trowsers and white cloth jacket, he also took with him a light coloured great coat a light coloured strait bodied coat, one pair of light coloured cloth breeches; he also probably on the 25th inst. took from the place where he had left them, a pair of shoes, and a pair of round flowered silver buckles he may upon examination be known by the following description, two of his toes next to the great toe on one of his feet, grow together to the end of the toe, on which of his feet not remembered.
SIMON PARSONS, Dept. Sheriff.
Northampton 24*th* July 1783.
The Massachusetts Gazette Or the General Advertiser, July 29, 1783; August 6, 1783; August 12, 1783; *The Massachusetts Gazette Or The Springfield and Northampton Weekly Advertiser*, July 29, 1783; August 6, 1783; August 12, 1783. See *The Boston Gazette, And The Country Journal*, August 4, 1783, *The Massachusetts Gazette Or the General*

Advertiser, August 6, 1783, and *The Vermont Gazette Or Freemen's Depository*, August 7, 1783.

TEN DOLLARS REWARD.

BROKE out of the county goal in Norwich, and made his escape on the night following the 26th inst. one ELISHA MILLER, a short thin man, black eyes and hair; had on black breeches and jacket, and brown coat; confined for debt.—Whoever will take up and secure said Miller to the goal in Norwich, shall have the above reward, and necessary charges paid, by me
          DARIUS PECK, Goaler.   Norwich 17th July, 1783.

The Connecticut Gazette; And The Universal Intelligencer, August 1, 1783; August 8, 1783; August 22, 1783.

EIGHT DOLLARS REWARD.

RUN-AWAY from the Subscriber, whilst in West-Chester County, New-York State, the 23d of July last, a Negro fellow, named JACK, 26 years old, about five feet high, thick set, he can read and write, and has served as a hostler this some time past to take care of the noted horses, *Pastime* and *Goldfinder*; and it is likely he will make towards Rhode-Island, as he formerly came from thence: He had on when he went away, an old white short brown jacket, and a pair of striped trouser; a wool hat, bound with white and cock'd, no shoes nor stockings on. And I desire all Captains of vessels, to beware not to take on or receive such fellow on board; and whoever will take up and secure him, so that the owner may get him again, shall have the above reward and all reasonable charges, per me,
        DEMAS FORD, or   JOSEPH PURDY.
The Royal Gazette, August 2, 1783.

SPRINGFIELD, July 19.

We hear from Northampton, that on Thursday last an affray happened between Mr. Elisha Brown, an inhabitant of that place, and one Norton, late of Long-Island (said to be of that class of people, well known under the denomination of Cow Boys) in which Mr. Brown received several blows from the latter, which instantly put an end to his existence. Several persons happening to see the scuffle, were immediately collected; but too late to afford the unfortunate man effectual aid. In the confusion occasioned by the disaster, Norton made his escape; and though the utmost diligence was used in pursuing him, we have not heard that he has yet been taken. The circumstances which gave rise to this unhappy affair, we have not been able distinctly to learn.

The Boston Gazette, And The Country Journal, August 4, 1783; *The Connecticut Courant, And Weekly Intelligencer*, August 5, 1783; *The*

Connecticut Gazette; And The Universal Intelligencer, August 8, 1783. See *The Massachusetts Gazette Or the General Advertiser*, July 29, 1783, *The Massachusetts Gazette Or the General Advertiser*, August 6, 1783, and *The Vermont Gazette Or Freemen's Depository*, August 7, 1783.

STOLEN from the Subscriber, on the 22d. of this inst. a red roan MARE, red Main and Tail, about five years old, natural pacer, one of her hind feet white, crooked hind legs, small head and red nose: the thief is a short thick-sett fellow; about 40 years of age, pitted with the small-pox, short black hair; called his name ROGER PARKER,—had on a white Felt Hatt, striped linen coat, copperas coloured vest, tow trowsers. Whoever takes up said thief and secures him in Bennington goal, and the MARE leave at Capt. ELIJAH DAWES, Inn-holder in Bennington, so that the owner may have her again, shall have FIVE DOLLARS reward, and necessary charges, or two DOLLARS and half a for each, by me
TITUS SIKES.
Dorset, State of Vermont, August 4.
The New-York Gazetteer or Northern Intelligencer, August 4, 1783.

This is to acquaint the Public,
THAT on Saturday the 26th of July, a negro boy about 20 years of age, who calls his name Jack, came to the subscriber on Rockaway Beach; said he was a free negro, and his last service was with Mr. Vokes, of Boston; but not being clear in his telling the truth, thought proper to advertise him, that in case he is that, or any other, person's property, they proving the same, may have him again, by applying to me at my quarters at New Lots, Long-Island.
JAMES FOREMAN, Ensign Royal Garrison Bat.
N. B. Said negro is about 5 feet high, and his nose much pitted with the small pox.
The New-York Gazette; and the Weekly Mercury, August 4, 1783.

Springfield, August 6.
We hear from Northampton, that on Wednesday evening last, the murderer Norton,—mentioned in our last,—was seen near the house he lately resided at, and finding himself discovered instantly took to the woods; the people of the town were immediately rallied, and went in pursuit of him, but night coming on prevented their taking him.
The Massachusetts Gazette Or the General Advertiser, August 6, 1783. See *The Massachusetts Gazette Or the General Advertiser*, July 29, 1783, and *The Boston Gazette, And The Country Journal*, August 4, 1783.

SPRINGFIELD, July 29.
We hear from Northampton, that on Thursday last an affray happened betwixt Mr. Elisha Brown, an inhabitant of that place and one Norton, late of Long-island (said to be of that class of people well unknown under the denomination of Cow boys) in which Mr. Brown received several blows from the latter, which instantly put an end to his existence. Several persons happening to see the scuffle, were immediately collected—but too late to afford the unfortunate man effectual aid.
The Vermont Gazette Or Freemen's Depository, August 7, 1783. See *The Massachusetts Gazette Or the General Advertiser*, July 29, 1783, *The Massachusetts Gazette Or The Springfield and Northampton Weekly Advertiser*, July 29, 1783, *The Boston Gazette, And The Country Journal*, August 4, 1783, and *The Massachusetts Gazette Or the General Advertiser*, August 6, 1783.

RAN-AWAY from the subscriber, on the night of the 20th of July last, an Apprentice Boy named AMOS WHITMON, about 17 Years old, dark complexion; carried away a large pack of Cloaths. Whoever will take up said Boy and return him to his said Master, shall have THREE PENCE Reward. All persons are forbid harbouring said Apprentice on Penalty of the law.
    JOSEPH MOORE.   Canterbury, August 2, 1783.
The Connecticut Gazette; And The Universal Intelligencer, August 8, 1783; August 15, 1783; August 22, 1783.

RUN away from the Subscriber, on the 30th of July, an apprentice Boy, named Elias Goodrich, 18 years of age, about 5 feet 5 inches high, freckled in the face, short dark hair, had on when he went away, a blue Coat lined with white, blue Vest, a brown great Coat, check'd Shirt, striped Trowsers, and old felt Hat bound with leather, he has worked at shoe-making for some time past.—Whoever will return said boy to the Subscriber, shall have Two Coppers reward.
    ELI BARNS.   Middletown, August 4, 1783.
The Connecticut Courant, And Weekly Intelligencer, August 12, 1783; August 19, 1783.

                Hancock, July 1st. 1783.
Mr. Printer,
      By inserting the following
you will oblige that unhappy and distressed Female, who in your paper not long since the good people were forbid to trust on Paul Austin's account, not because I had (for I never have) run him in debt a single six pence, but because his unreasonable hatred conceived that to be the readiest way to

distress my worthy friends. After a long series of abuse from him for a number of months, and upon his threatning my life, and ordering me away from his house, I went home to my father's, where after a few days, at my father's desire, a number of respectable neighbours met together to hear what was the difficulty between us, and to settle amicably if possible, at which time the principal objection Paul Austin made to my conduct was, my selling without his leave, one yard of tow-cloth to buy a pail to use in the family, though we had but one to use,—cloth that I spun and wove myself. This, with other objections of far less weight appeared so sutile and insignificant to the neighbours present that they all condemned and reprobated his conduct for his inhuman behaviour to me at home, as well as his endeavouring to destroy my character by posting me in the public papers. Upon this he was so ashamed of his behaviour that he to my great joy agreed to take the matter up, and solemnly promised before Samuel Hood, Esquire, the Magistrate of the town, to alter his course of life which (sorry I am to day it) was too much of the vicious kind, and to behave towards me with tenderness and love; but instead of that it is but seven or eight weeks since he made this solemn promise, and he has behaved as bad or worse than before and has obliged me (by his behaviour, as well as by his frequently ordering me to be gone) to seek an asylum in my father's house, and has took my only child from me, an infant of eighteen months old; and such is his hatred that he desires, he says, never to see me again. But alas! too late I may repent my folly in yielding my hand and heart to one, so contrary to the advice and judgment of my parents, whose hearts are ready to burst with grief on my account.

The Massachusetts Gazette Or The General Advertiser, August 12, 1783; August 19, 1783; August 26, 1783; *The Massachusetts Gazette Or The Springfield and Northampton Weekly Advertiser*, August 19, 1783. See *The Massachusetts Gazette Or The General Advertiser*, May 6, 1783.

TWENTY DOLLARS REWARD.

ON the Night of the sixth instant, the shop of the subscribers was broke open, and the following Articles stolen, viz.

Three Pieces dark striped Calico, one Piece striped Pompadore Calico, one Piece black Mode, three black silk Handkerchiefs, four Pullicut Handkerchiefs, about ¾ of a pound of sorted Twist, one Piece striped white Gauze, one Piece black Sattin, Remnant of black Sattin, about three Yards, one Piece Lawn Handkerchiefs. one Piece of black Velvet, and about ten Dollars in small Silver.

Whoever secures the Thief, so that the Owners may recover the Goods, shall be entitled to the above Reward.

VAN HORNE & LOTT,   New-Haven, August 1, 1783.

The Thief is suspected to be a Person who calls himself Henry Hinman, but is likely will change his Name; he is of a middling Size, has light, short brown Hair, said to be a Hessian Deserter, and lately whipt for Theft.
The Connecticut Journal, August 27, 1783.

Run-away from the subscriber a YOUNGSTER, his name EBENEZER PINKHAM, will be Nineteen years old next March, 1783, quite small of his age, Runaway on 31st of October, 1782: Whoever will take up said Pinkham and return him, shall have Half a Dollar Reward and no charges paid by
WILLIAM BURNS.
Bristol (County of Lincoln) November 12, 1782. [sic]
The Continental Journal, And Weekly Advertiser, August 14, 1783; August 21, 1783; August 28, 1783.

RAN AWAY from the subscriber, at Norwich-Landing, a negro woman named ROSE, slave for life, about 26 years old, lusty and fleshy, of a smiling countenance, shows her foreteeth when she laughs, wears a large roll or her hair combed back and a small woman's hat, had on or has with her a striped brocaded callico gown, with apron of the same new, two striped short linnen loose ditto, one red calimanco shirt, one brown ditto, one pair of new sale cotton stockings, one pair of homemade ditto, leather shoes some worn with white rands. Whoever will take up slave, and return her to me the subscriber, shall have Ten Dollars reward, paid by me
ABEL BREWSTER.   August 13th, 1783.
N. B. She is supposed to be trying to get to New-York: All masters of vessels and others are forbid harbouring of carrying away said slave, as they will answer it at the law. A. B.
The Connecticut Gazette; And The Universal Intelligencer, August 15, 1783; August 22, 1783; August 29, 1783.

Whereas Betty, once the
wife of me the subscriber (during my absence to the army) behaved in a most shameful, vile and detestible manner, in not only disregarding the necessary provision of her family, but also gadding and idleness, in wasting and disposing of my substance in a most lavish and prodigal manner; and what is far worse, defiled my bed in violation of the marriage covenant, to her own everlasting disgrace, and the great dishonour of her family and relations, for which weighty reasons I have (without the lease equivocation) denounced, abandoned and entirely dissolved the matrimonial union, and determine never to bed or board with her, and forbid all persons ever trusting her on my account, as I will not pay any debt of her contracting after the date hereof.
Attested, BARNABAS DAVISON.

Greenfield, the 12th of August, 1783.
The Massachusetts Gazette Or The General Advertiser, August 19, 1783; August 26, 1783; September 3, 1783; *The Massachusetts Gazette Or The Springfield and Northampton Weekly Advertiser*, August 19, 1783.

Stolen from the subscriber the night after the first of August, a red roan Mare, about thirteen hands and half high, a natural pacer, supposed to be taken by a transient man, who called his name John Edwards, wore a blue coat, striped trowsers, and boots, he is of a darkish complection, black eyes and hair, about 28 years of age, whoever will take up said Mare and Thief, so that the thief may be brought to justice, and the Mare returned to the subscriber shall receive four dollars reward, or two for either of them, and all necessary charges paid by
RUTH NELSON.   West Springfield, August 9, 1783.

The Massachusetts Gazette Or The General Advertiser, August 18, 1783; August 26, 1783; September 3, 1783. *The Massachusetts Gazette Or The Springfield and Northampton Weekly Advertiser*, August 19, 1783.

10 DOLLARS REWARD.
STOLEN from the subscriber, on the evening of the 18th inst. Thirty Pounds, hard money. The thief calls himself John; he is a foreigner and has resided for some months past in Middletown; he is about 30 years of age, six feet in stature, and has a natural mark on the back side of his left hand; had with him a calico coat, a brown coat with white facings, and a pair of short blue trowsers. Whoever will stop said thief and deliver him to the subscriber in Middletown, shall receive ten dollars reward, and all necessary charges paid
by GERSHOM BIRDSEY.   Middletown, August 19, 1783.

The Connecticut Journal, August 20, 1783; August 27, 1783; September 3, 1783.

STOP THIEF!
EIGHT DOLLARS REWARD.
STOLEN from the Subscriber, on Thursday the 21st Instant, by a person by the name of JAMES DAVIS, the following articles—1 suit blue broad cloth cloaths, partly made, lining blue, with fancy buttons; 1 brown lambskin surtout; a waistcoat of fancy velvet, not made, with sundry other articles, such as shirts, stockings and tailor's trimmings. Whoever will apprehend said thief, so that the goods shall be returned, shall receive a reward of EIGHT DOLLARS from JOHN M'CLURE.

N. B. Said Davis is small of Stature, dark eyes, and talks broad Scotch, had on white waistcoat and breeches and blue and white linnen jacket, and felt hat. Boston, August 22, 1783.
The Boston Evening-Post and the General Advertiser, August 23, 1783; August 30, 1783; September 6, 1783; September 13, 1783.

STOLEN from the Subscriber, the 20 of July, a red rone MARE, about 14 hands high, crooked hind legs, natural pacer, suspected to be stole by one Roger Parker, wore a white Hat, striped linen Coat, otter coloured Vest, Brown Trowsers, and check'd Shirt. Whoever will take up said Mare and supposed thief and secure them so that the owner may have her again, shall have five dollars reward and all charges; and whoever will take up said supposed Thief or Mare shall have 15 shillings reward, paid by
TITUS PIKE. Dorset, State of Vermont.
The Connecticut Courant, And Weekly Intelligencer, August 26, 1783.

SIX PENCE REWARD.

RAN away from the subscriber, on the night of the 17th instant, an Apprentice BOY, named Salmon Parker, in the 17th year, small of his age, light complexion and light hair, by trade a shoe-maker. All persons are forbid trusting said Boy on my account and whoever will return him to me, shall have the above reward.
ISRAEL WOODWARD. Watertown, August, 19, 1783.
The Connecticut Journal, August 27, 1783.

TWO SHILLINGS REWARD.

ABSENTED herself from her Master's service, a MOLATTO GIRL, named Alice Curtis, in her 16th year, pretty large and stout of her age. All persons are forbid to harbour, secret, or employ said Girl, as they will answer the consequences, and whoever returns her to me shall receive the above reward, paid by
SETH MERWIN. Fairfield, Aug. 20, 1783.
The Connecticut Journal, August 27, 1783; September 10, 1783.

SPRINGFIELD, August 19.

Saturday the 9th inst. about two o'clock in the morning, a company of ruffians, to the number of about 20, armed with swords, guns and bayonets, surrounded the house of Capt. Joseph Cook, keeper of the goal in Northampton, and having placed centinels at the doors and windows, broke into the house and assaulted Capt. Cook, his wife and daughter, presenting swords and bayonets threatning them with instant death, demanding the keys of the goal, which Captain Cook absolutely refused to give them; whereupon they most inhumanly beat and bruised him and threw him out of the window—ransacked his house—and robbed him of a small amount of money from his desk:—and being under terrible apprehensions of being all taken they suddenly took to flight, and were soon out of town.

Their principal aim, no doubt, was liberating from the goal, one Samuel Wells, who, at the last Supreme Court, was convicted of PERJURY, and in confined in said goal, suffering the sentence of the law of this Commonwealth, for said offence; but another aim they had, no doubt, was plunder, which they succeeded in. A number of them are known, and no doubt will meet with the punishment such high handed offences merit.

The Connecticut Gazette; And The Universal Intelligencer, August 29, 1783.

WHereas SARAH, the Wife of me the Subscriber, has eloped from my Bed and Board, and threatens to run my in Debt.—I hereby forbid all Persons to credit her on my Account, as I will not pay any Debts of her contracting from the Date hereof.
     JOSEPH HOYLE.   *Providence, Aug.* 30, 1783.
The Providence Gazette; And Country Journal, August 30, 1783; September 6, 1783; September 13, 1783.

TWENTY DOLLARS REWARD.
  On Tuesday evening last, about
11 o'clock, a considerable quantity of Fire was accidentally discovered in the cellar window of the house where the Subscriber resides, which, in a very short time, must have destroyed the House, and probably most of the Family, as they had all retired to bed.—His negro girl Dorothy (commonly called Dot) finding herself suspected of this attrocious design, suddenly slipped out of the house and escaped. She is a short sturdy girl, about sixteen years old.—Twenty Dollars Reward, and the discharge of all necessary expences is hereby promised to any person who shall secure said Negro, so that she may be recovered by the Subscriber.
     SAMUEL DANFORTH.
N. B. It is suspected she is gone to Newport, where she was born.
                Boston, Sept, 1, 1781.
The Independent Ledger and the American Advertiser, September 1, 1783; September 8, 1783.

SALEM, September 4.
  On Tuesday evening last, a man stopt at a public house, about three miles from this town on the Boston road, and after calling for some trifling matters, offered a dollar to be changed; but being told it was a counterfeit one, he took out another, which also being bad he then presented a counterfeit English shilling. His character being now sufficiently manifest, Mr. Timothy

Davis, of Gloucester, who happened to be in the house, demanded his name, and was answered, that his name was John M'Lane, and that he belonged to Chesterfield in the state of New-Hampshire. Mr. Davis intended then to get him secured; but, before it could be effected he made his escape. He is supposed to be about 30 years of age, wore a blue coat with yellow metal buttons, and a blue wrapper. The first which he presented as a dollar, was so badly made as scarcely to resemble one;—the other was well executed and required some attention to distinguish it for a true one.—The several pieces are now in possession of Mr. Davis—and it is hoped that the best look-out will be kept for apprehending the villain, together with his accomplices.

The Salem Gazette, September 4, 1783; *The Independent Ledger and the American Advertiser*, September 8, 1783; *The Providence Gazette; And Country Journal*, September 13, 1783; *The Connecticut Courant, And Weekly Intelligencer*, September 16, 1783.

RAN AWAY from his master, an apprentice boy named John Stannel Gilman, about 18 years of age: Whoever will take up said runaway and return him to his master, free of expence, shall have six pence old tenor, as a reward for their trouble: All persons are forbid harbouring or crediting said boy on his masters account.

           STEPHEN LEE,   Gilmantown, Sept. 4, 1783.

The New-Hampshire Gazette, And General Advertiser, September 6, 1783; October 11, 1783. See *The New-Hampshire Gazette, And General Advertiser*, October 18, 1783.

Broke out of the Goal in Exeter, on the night following the 22d day of August, one John Sears, a Frenchman about 30 years of age, 5 feet 6 inches high, wears his own black hair and speaks broken English. And on the 25th day of August broke out of the same goal, Henry Turffs, about 40 years of age, five feet 10 inches high.—Whoever will return them to the said goal, shall have for the said Sears, 10 dollars reward, and for the said Turffs, 6 dollars, paid

          by JOHN PARKER, *Sheriff.*   Exeter, Sept. 1, 1783.

The New-Hampshire Gazette, And General Advertiser, September 6, 1783; September 13, 1783. See *The New-Hampshire Gazette, And General Advertiser*, December 21, 1782, for Sears.

RUN away from the Subscriber on Saturday night last, a Negro man named TACK, about 25 years of age, midling stature, likely, active, and well made, was born and brought up in this town, he had with him all his cloaths, among which were a white broad cloath Coat turned up with blue made short, a scarlet cassimere Coat, nankeen Vest and Breeches, blue corduroy Breeches, white Shirt, tow cloth Trowsers, check'd homespun Shirt, an old claret coloured Coat and beaver Hat half worn, he plays well on the Flute and

Fife,—and went off in company with a Negro Wench of Mr. Platt's of this town who carried her cloaths and female child, she is about 40 years old, thick and fleshy and pretends to be his wife. Whoever will take up and bring said Fellow to the Subscriber, shall be paid TEN DOLLARS Reward and reasonable Charges.
THOMAS SEYMOUR.   Hartford, September 8, 1783.

The Connecticut Courant, And Weekly Intelligencer, September 9, 1783; September 16, 1783; September 23, 1783; *The Massachusetts Gazette, Or General Advertiser*, September 23, 1783; September 30, 1783; October 7, 1783.

SIXTEEN DOLLARS Reward.
DESERTED from on board the Danish ship THREE SISTERS, commanded by Capt. B. STEYN, a SAILOR, called JEP MADSEN, a Dane born; about the Age of 21, a middle sized Man, well made, healthy Complexion, short curled Hair of a light Colour, speaks no other Language than the Danish:—Had on when he went away, a blue Jacket and a Pair of white Linen Trowsers.

Also, one other Man, by the Name of JURGEN CHRISTENSON, aged 36 Years, of a very pale Color, and strongly pitted with the Small Pox, of a middling Size, brown Hair: Had on when he went away, a blue and white Linen Jacket, and speaks a little English.

Whoever will cause the above named Men to be returned on board said Ship, shall receive the specified Reward; or the Half for one Man, and all reasonable Charges paid.   BOSTON, Sept. 6, 1783.

The Boston Evening-Post and the General Advertiser, September 6, 1783; September 13, 1783; September 20, 1783; September 27, 1783.

RUN away from the subscriber last night, a NEGRO LAD, named FRANK, about nineteen years old, a likely well made fellow, rather short—it is supposed he had on a blue broadcloth Coat, but may change it as he took sundry other Coats and small Cloathing with him—He formerly belonged to Mr. Alexander Hunt, and went off in company with a white Boy, about 16 years old, named George Graves.—Whoever will take up said Negro and return him to the subscriber, shall be paid Ten Dollars, and all reasonable charges.   EBENEZER PLATT.   Hartford, September 10, 1783.

The Connecticut Courant, And Weekly Intelligencer, September 16, 1783; September 23, 1783; October 7, 1783.

WHEREAS JANE, the Wife of me the Subscriber, has for some Time behaved herself very unbecoming the relation she stood to me, and has lately eloped from my Dwelling and Place of Abode: This is to forbid all Persons

whatever from harbouring her, or trusting her at all on my Account, as I will not pay any Debt of her contracting after the Date hereof.
          JONATHAN LIVERMORE.   Northborough, July 21, 1783.
The Independent Chronicle and the Universal Advertiser, September 16, 1783; September 25, 1783; October 2, 1783.

WHEREAS Jemima my wife has without any just cause eloped from my bed and board; these are therefore to warn all persons from harbouring or trusting her on my account, as I shall pay no debts of her contracting after this date.
          WILLIAM ROBINSON.   Sharon, August 29, 1783.
The Connecticut Journal, September 17, 1783; September 24, 1783.

RAN AWAY, on the 9th of August last, from Jacob Hooper, of Manchester, a Negro Woman named Phillis, aged 24 years—she may be known by having a stiff joint in the fore finger of her left hand, her finger bending inward.—A reward of FIVE DOLLARS will be given, and necessary charges paid, to any person who shall return her to the said Hooper, her master.
The Salem Gazette, September 18, 1783; September 25, 1783; October 2, 1783.

RANAWAY last night from the subscriber living in East-Greenwich, a negro man slave named BRISTOL, by trade a shipwright and caulker, brought up in the town of Newport; he is of a yellow complexion, aged about 26 years, 5 feet 9 inches high, with a scar on one of his arms; had on when he went off, a striped flannel jacket and trowsers of black and blue, an old felt hat, bound with white; he carried with him one Holland shirt, one striped tow, and one flannel do. Whoever will apprehend said negro, and confine him so that his master may have him again, shall receive TEN DOLLARS reward, and all reasonable charges paid by
          ROBERT MORY.   State Rhode-Island, Sept. 11, 1783.
The Connecticut Gazette; And The Universal Intelligencer, September 19, 1783; September 26, 1783; October 3, 1783.

RAN away from the Subscriber, living in Tiverton, on the 12th of August last, an Apprentice Boy, named JOHN DUNHAM, about Four Feet Ten Inches high, a little round shoulder'd, has blue Eyes, and sandy coloured Hair cut before; had on when he went away a striped Flannel Jacket, with a blue Patch on one of his Shoulders, striped Tow Trowsers, and Tow and Linen Shirt, was bare-footed and had no Hat. Whoever will take up said Apprentice, and secure him so that I get him again, shall have FOUR DOLLARS Reward, and necessary Charges, paid by
          JOHN SHRIEVE.   September 10, 1783.

The Newport Mercury, September 20, 1783; September 27, 1783; October 4, 1783; October 11, 1783.

RAN away from his Master, the Subscriber, on Monday last, a Mulatto or Mustee Servant Boy, named Pero, about ten Years of Age, cross-eyed, and has black curled Hair resembling that of a Negro; had on, when he went away, a Shirt and Trowsers of Linen. Whoever will take up said Boy, and return him to his Master, shall be handsomely rewarded, and have all necessary Charges paid, by
   AMOS ATWELL.   *Providence, Sept.* 19, 1783.
The Providence Gazette; And Country Journal, September 20, 1783; September 27, 1783.

FORTY DOLLARS REWARD.

WHEREAS a young Man, who called himself FREDERICK HALL, hired of the Subscriber, on Tuesday the 16th instant, a full-blooded light bay MARE, to go to Marshfield, and return the next Day, but has not returned yet, which makes me thing he has run away with said Mare, a new Bridle and Saddle, and a striped Saddle Cloth. Said Mare is a light bay, about 15 Hands high, or better, with the near hind Foot white, a black Mane and Tail, pretty gant, in middling Flesh, and looks much like the running breed, trots & canters remarkable well, and walks exceeding fast; she is nicked but does not carry her Tail very high. Said Hall is about 23 Years of Age, a likely Fellow, about 4 Feet, 7 or 8 inches high: had on when he went away a light Loose-Coat, and a green Body-Coat, a Corduroy Waistcoat and Breeches, a Pair of clouded Hose, and a Pair of Overalls. Whoever takes up said Man and Mare, and secures them for me, shall have the above Reward, and all necessary Charges paid by their humble servant,
   JOHN MAGNER.
N. B. Said Mare had two slight Galls, on the Back, one under the fore Part of the Saddle and one under the hind Part.—Said Hall was brought up in Plympton.   Boston, Sept. 20, 1783.
The Boston Gazette, And The Country Journal, September 22, 1783; September 29, 1783.

WHereas *Mary* the wife of me the subscriber has deserted my bed and board: these are therefore to caution all persons from harbouring my said wife, or trusting her on my account, for I hereby declare that I will not pay one farting of any debt that she shall contract from the date hereof.
   EPHRAIM WETHERBEE. Boxborough, August 27, 1783.
The Boston Gazette, And The Country Journal, September 22, 1783; September 29, 1783.

STOLEN from the Subscriber, last Tuesday night, a bay HORSE, 5 years old, natural trotter, white streak in his face, about 14 hands high, shod before, crooked hind legs. Also, a black COLT, 3 years old, never shod nor docked when taken away, trotter. At the same time were stolen two Saddles and Bridles, two blue broadcloth Coats, one Coat trimmed with white buttons, two fustian Jackets, two pair fustian Breeches, two pair white thread Stockings, one or two caster Hats. The Thieves are supposed to be one JONATHAN CURTIS, of Wethersfield, who passed by the name of JAMES BURTON, about 5 feet 8 inches high, about 23 years of age, thick set, pitted with the small-pox, light eyes, light complexion, and brownish hair—the other is a deserter from the British, an Irishman called himself, M'MULLEN, about 21 years of age, about 5 feet 6 inches high, pitted with the small-pox, thinish nose, brown hair, a very sly look, had on an old red coat faced with blue, royal rib breeches and fustian jacket. Whoever will take up said Thieves, and secure the Horses and articles stolen, shall have Five Dollars Reward, and charges paid, or a proportionable reward for any of the articles.
           paid by   JOSEPH PIERCE.
                 Woodbury (Connecticut) September 24, 1783.
The Connecticut Courant, And Weekly Intelligencer, September 23, 1783; September 30, 1783; October 7, 1783.

                Whereas Thankful the
wife of me the subscriber, hath for some considerable time conducted herself in a manner, perfectly inconsistent with the articles of the marriage covenant, and wholly refusing to live with me at such place as appears most conducive for the benefit and interest of us both.—This is therefore to forbid all persons harbouring or trusting her on my account, as I will not pay any debt of her contracting after the date hereof.
                  his
       VALENTINE ✝ WORTHY.
              mark
                              West Springfield, 8th Sept. 1783.
The Massachusetts Gazette Or The General Advertiser, September 23, 1783; September 30, 1783; October 7, 1783.

RANAWAY from me the Subscriber on the fourth instant, an apprentice Boy, named Henry Guralson, about five feet four inches high, a thickset fellow, light complexion, sandy colour'd hair which he wears short—had on when he went away a suit of brown Fustian Cloaths, white cotton and linen short, and felt hat. Whoever will take up said apprentice and convey him to me free of all charges, shall have one old emission dollar for their trouble.
               SAMUEL MORRILL, jr.   Epping, Sept. 10.

The New-Hampshire Gazette, And General Advertiser, September 27, 1783.

Ran-away from the Subscriber the 17th of last Month, Thomas Hinckley, of Barnstable, a bound Apprentice.—This is to notify all Masters of Vessels, that shall carry off said Apprentice, that I shall demand his Wages.—Half a Copper for his return to his Duty.
      WILLIAM FREELAND.
The Independent Chronicle and the Universal Advertiser, October 2, 1783; October 9, 1783; October 16, 1783.

      Whereas PEGGY, Wife of
the Subscriber, has eloped from my Bed and Board—this is to caution any Person from trusting her, as I will not pay *one Two pence* for her.
    FRANCIS LIBERTY.   Boston, Sept. 1783.
The Independent Chronicle and the Universal Advertiser, October 2, 1783; October 9, 1783; October 16, 1783.

      Broke Goal on the 9th of
Sept. last the following persons.—James Holady, born in Sheffield, committed for Stealing, 6 feet 2 inches high about 50 years old,—Benjamin Towley an Indian, 5 feet 10 inches high, committed for forgery, Daniel Holms about 19 years old, light hair committed for burglary, Josiah Smith, alias Clark, about 30 years old, black short hair, lightish eyes: Whoever takes up the said James Holady Benjamin Towley and Josiah Smith alias Clark, and return them to the common goal in Great Barrington, shall receive 5 dollars and reasonably charges paid by
    EBEN. BEMENT, Deputy Goaler.
            G. Barrington, Sept. 12, 1783.
The Massachusetts Gazette, or General Advertiser, October 7, 1783; October 14, 1783; October 21, 1783; October 28, 1783.

      Whereas Elizabeth the
wife of me, has for some time past behaved herself in a very strange manner.—I forbid all persons trusting her on my account, as I shall not pay any debt contracted by her.
    SETH GILLET.   Simsbury, July 15th, 1783.
The Massachusetts Gazette, or General Advertiser, October 7, 1783; October 14, 1783; October 21, 1783; October 28, 1783.

      NEWPORT, Sept. 27.
  At the Honorable Superior Court, held in this Town last Week, George W. Smith, James H. Lafford, and Samuel S. Hayward, were convicted of

counterfeiting and passing Soldiers Notes, signed by the General Treasurer of this State, and sentenced to stand in the Pillory two Hours, to be branded on each Cheek, with the Letter R, and to have their Ears Cropt; which Sentence was Yesterday executed, before a large Concourse of People.
The Connecticut Journal, October 8, 1783. See *The Newport Mercury*, November 15, 1783.

Deserted from on board
the ship FAMA, Capt. *Bernard Suhm*, from Copenhagen, now lying at Messi'rs *Foster* and Company's Wharf, two seamen; the one the Boatswain, named FRIDERICH SCHIOTH, of about 24 years of age, of common size, broad shoulders, and naturally corpulent: he has very dark hair and eyebrows, and speaks only the Danish language: he had on a pair of long trowsers, a sail-cloth jacket, a small round hatt and a blue surtout.

The other a foremast man, named MICHAEL NORD BERG, of about 23 years of age, a Swede by birth, and speaks a little English: he is of a small size, is well made, and wears his hair, which is of a sandy colour, in queue; he had on a pair of brown Manchester striped Breeches, a sail cloth jacket, and round hatt, besides which he has a blue coat and wears a watch.

Whoever will secure the above-mentioned deserters, or give information of them, so that they may be secured, shall have a generous compensation, by applying to the Captain on board said ship, or to
William Cheever, at his store in State-Street.

Boston, October 7, 1783.
The Continental Journal, And Weekly Advertiser October 9, 1783; October 16, 1783; October 23, 1783. See *Independent Chronicle and the Universal Advertiser*, October 9, 1783.

DESERTED from on board the ship FAMA, Capt. Bernard Suhm, from Copenhagen, now lying at Mess'rs Foster and Co's Wharf—two seamen, one the Boatswain, named Frederick Schioth, of about 24 years of age, of common size, broad shoulders and naturally corpulent, he has very dark hair and eyebrows, and speaks only the Danish language; he had on a pair of long trowsers, a sail-cloth jacket, a small round hat and blue surtuit.—The other a foremast man, named Michael Nord Berg, of about 23 years of age, a Swede by birth, and speaks a little English, he is of a small size, is well made, and wears his hair, which is of a sandy colour, in queu, he had on a pair of brown Manchester strip'd breeches, a sail-cloth jacket, and a round hat, besides which he has a blue coat, and wears a watch.

Whoever will secure the above mentioned deserters, or give information of them, so that they may be secured, shall have a generous compensation, by applying to the Captain on board said ship, or to
William Cheever, at his store in State-Street.

Boston, October 7, 1783.
Independent Chronicle and the Universal Advertiser, October 9, 1783.
See *The Continental Journal, And Weekly Advertiser* October 9, 1783.

My Wife DELIGHT, having left my bed and board without any sufficient cause or provocation; these are to forbid all persons harbouring or trusting her on my account, as I will pay no debts of her contracting after this date.
    GEORGE LAMPHEAR.   Norwich, Octo. 8, 1783.
The Connecticut Gazette; And The Universal Intelligencer, October 10, 1783; October 17, 1783.

STOLEN from the Subscriber, in the Night of the 8th Instant, a Sett of red and white Calico Bed-Curtains, one ruffled Shirt, one Pair of Cotton Stockings, marked J. M. one jean and one Dimity Waistcoat, and one Pair of Corduroy Breeches.—The Thief wore a blue Coat, red Waistcoat, Corduroy Breeches, and white Stockings; he is about 30 Years of Age, and 5 Feet 5 or 6 Inches high. Whoever will take up said Thief, and secure him, so that the Owner may recover his Property, shall have Five Dollars Reward, and all necessary Charges, paid by
    JOSEPH MASURY.
Providence, Oct. 11, 1783.
The Providence Gazette; And Country Journal, October 11, 1783; October 18, 1783; October 25, 1783; November 1, 1783.

Twenty Dollars Reward.
RUNAWAY from the Subscriber, on Thursday the 9th Inst. a NEGRO MAN named SAM, about 24 Years old, but appears by his Countenance to be much old, a tall, stout, well built Fellow, in Colour a dark yellow has a very large Foot, he speaks pretty good English, but with something of the Dutch Accent, which Language he has some little Knowledge of, having been brought up in a Dutch Family on Long-Island; had on an old flap'd Hat, a strip'd blue and white Tow-Cloth Coatee and Vest, a white homespun linen Shirt, a Pair of twill'd Tow-Cloth Trowsers patch'd on the Knees with plain Tow-Cloth, and was bare-foot when he left Home. Whoever will take up said Negro, and secure him, or return him to the Subscriber, shall be entitled to the above Reward, and all necessary Charges.
    JOSIAH BURR.   New-Haven, October 11th, 1783.
The Connecticut Journal, October 15, 1783; October 22, 1783; October 29, 1783.

Whereas ANN FITCH, wife of the subscriber, having so criminally conducted in my absence at sea, as to oblige me to seek the recompence of law; this is to forwarn all persons from trusting her on my account, as I will pay not debt of her contracting.
ABEL FITCH.
Boston, October 11, 1783.
The Independent Chronicle and the Universal Advertiser, October 16, 1783; October 23, 1783; October 30, 1783.

RAN-AWAY, an apprentice boy named *John Stannel Gilman*, about 18 years of age from his master *Stephen Bean*, of *Gilmantown*: Whoever will take up the said run away and return him to his master, free of expence, shall have one Spanish petatoe reward: All persons are forbid crediting said boy on his master account. *Octo.* 12.
The New-Hampshire Gazette, And General Advertiser, October 18, 1783; November 1, 1783. See *The New-Hampshire Gazette, And General Advertiser*, September 6, 1783.

WHEREAS HANNAH, consort of the Subscriber (black Man) has greatly misbehaved herself towards me of late:—This, therefore, it to forbid all and every Person trusting her on my Credit, for I will not pay one Farthing of her contracting from this date.
his
BANTOM X PHILLIPS
Mark.
Boston, Oct. 18, 1783.
The Boston Evening-Post and the General Advertiser, October 18, 1783; October 25, 1783.

RANAWAY from the Subscriber, the 22d inst. a Negro Man, named ASA or AFRICA, aged between 40 and 50 years, about 5 feet 9 or 10 inches high, knock-knee'd, Guinea born, with scars on each side of his face—had on when he went away, a brown coat, pretty much worn, a blueish mix'd cloth jacket, tow trowsers, and a small round castor Hat—he formerly lived in Stonington, in Connecticut, and has been seen on his way towards Stephentown or little Hoosack—he must be very well known, on account of his having attended the ferry between Albany and Green-Bush during 8 or 9 years—Whoever secures said Negro, so that his master can have him again shall receive EIGHT DOLLARS reward, and all reasonable charges paid, by
THOMAS LOTTRIDGE, Albany, October 13.
The New-York Gazetteer or Northern Intelligencer, October 20, 1783; October 27, 1783.

FORTY DOLLARS REWARD.
ON the evening after the 6th of October instant, Litchfield County Goal was broke, and the following Prisoners made their escape, viz. Moses Johnson, Moses Woodburn, Nathan Barnam and John Bates, jun. all sentenced to New-Gate for Burglary, passing Counterfeit money and Horse Stealing—Whoever will apprehend and return said prisoners to said Goal again, shall receive the above reward, or Ten Dollars for either of them.
    LYNDE LORDE, Sheriff. Litchfield, October 7, 1783.
The Connecticut Courant, And Weekly Intelligencer, October 21, 1783; October 28, 1783; November 4, 1783.

WHEREAS my wife Rhoda has (in my absence) been expelled the town in which she resided, for her misbehaviour: these are to warn all persons not to harbour, or trust her on my account, as I will pay no debts of her contracting after this date.
    JARED BLAKSLEE. North-Haven, October 7th, 1713. [*sic*]
The Connecticut Journal, October 22, 1783; October 29, 1783.

WILLIAM DOYLE, about 5 feet 5 inches high, Taylor by trade, light complexion, much pitted with the small pox, light hair untied, wears a round hatt, scarlet coat, nankeen waistcoat and breeches, frequently seen in short dress.— JOSEPH MOUNTANY, Frenchman, dark complexion, black hair, black eyes, much pitted with the small pox, speaks fast and tolerable good English, stout built, about 5 feet 10 inches, wears gold drops in his ears, wore away a dark colour'd surtout coat, large cock'd hatt, cued hair very long.—JOHN CANE, an Irishman, about 5 feet 10 inches high, well sett, light complexion, pitted with the small pox, large grey eyes, long hair with a cue, carried with him a new scarlet cloth coat, an embroider'd waistcoat, and black sattin breeches, often appears in the dress of a sailor. JOHN BURK, alias JOHN GREEN, about 5 feet 11 inches high, light complexion, brown bushy hair—had on when he went away, a round hatt, with a silk ribbon for band, long blue great coat, generally in sailor's dress.
  Those gentlemen were of the late company who took our goods without leaving their names or places of abode—their names we know; if any person will put them in a place of abode, say a goal, so that he may settle this small affair, shall for each person receive five half JOES, from
    WHITE and MOORE. Boston, Oct. 22, 1283. [*sic*]
The Continental Journal, And Weekly Advertiser, October 23, 1783; October 29, 1783; *The Independent Chronicle and the Universal Advertiser*, October 23, 1783; October 30, 1783; November 6, 1783; *The Boston Evening-Post and the General Advertiser*, October 25, 1783; November 1, 1783; November 8, 1783; November 15, 1783. Minor differences between the papers. All the papers except *The*

Continental Journal have "*STOP THIEVES!*" at the top. See *Thomas's Massachusetts Spy Or, American Oracle of Liberty*, October 30, 1783.

WHEREAS I have been informed, that a certain *Reuben Tucker,* now in Boston gaol, pretends that he has in his possession a note of hand for 2500 Spanish milled dollars, which Thomas Saxvilla Tufton gave me, and that the same is by me indorsed; I do hereby caution all persons against the purchasing of such note; and that if said Tucker, or any other person, hath any such note, purporting to be indorsed by me, it is forged.
Witness my hand, October 16, 1783.
Nathan Raymond.
The Independent Chronicle and the Universal Advertiser, October 23, 1783; October 30, 1783; November 6, 1783; *The New-Hampshire Gazette, And General Advertiser*, October 25, 1783; *The Salem Gazette*, October 30, 1783; November 6, 1783. Minor differences between the papers. Both *Gazettes* spell the middle name Saxwillee.

Ten GUINEAS Reward.
ON the Night preceding the 22d of October, 1783, was stolen from JOHN DELATOUR, a Pair of Breeches containing a green Purse, with 8 or 10 Guineas in Gold, a few French Crowns and half Crowns;—his Pocket-Book, containing several letters of Recommendation from Mr. Lemairgre at Philadelphia to his Friends at Providence and Newport, a Gold Watch with a Gold Chain, a turtle-shell Snuff-box, and two Sett of Bills of Exchange drawn on two Gentlemen at Boston, amounting together to two Thousand Dollars, one of the Setts payable to two Days and the other at ten Days Sight; both payable to said John Delatour or Order. The Theft was committed at Mr. Ephraim Miner's House; the Man supposedly guilty of the Crime is of a small Size, dressed with a light blue Coat, red Waistcoat, striped Overhalls, and had Boots on. Whoever will apprehend the above Thief, and secure him in any Goal in the United States and give Information thereof to Mr. EPHRAIM MINER, Innholder in New-London, so that the above Articles may be recovered, shall have the above Reward and all necessary Charges paid.
New-London, October 22d. 1783.
The Connecticut Gazette; And The Universal Intelligencer, October 24, 1783; *The Independent Chronicle and the Universal Advertiser*, October 30, 1783; November 6, 1783.

TEN DOLLARS REWARD.
RAN away from the Subscriber, last Night, a Negro Man, named FREEMAN, about 28 Years of Age, about 5 Feet 6 Inches high, stout and well made; had on a dark great Coat, with Horn Buttons, a grey Kersey Jacket, and took with him a Variety of other Cloathing.—Also a Negro

Wench, his Wife, named VENUS, about 32 Years of Age, tall and likely; took with her a red short Cloak, a black Bonnet, a Cloth coloured Worsted Gown, and plenty of other Cloathing. Whoever will take up and return said NEGROES to their Master, shall have TEN DOLLARS Reward, and all reasonable Charges, paid by
    SAMUEL TOMKINS.   Cranston, Oct. 24, 1783.
The Providence Gazette And Country Journal, October 25, 1783; November 1, 1783; November 8, 1783.

                   Essex, ss.
Broke out of the Commonwealth Goal, in Ipswich, on the night of the 21st inst. one William Richardson, who was indicted for attempting to pass a counterfeit Certificate of this Commonwealth, about 25 years of age, 5 feet 6 inches high, light complexion, short curled hair. Whoever will take up said Richardson, and secure him in any of the goals within this Commonwealth, shall have Fifty Dollars Reward, paid by me,
    MICHAEL FARLEY, Sheriff. Ipswich, October 22, 1783.
The Independent Chronicle and the Universal Advertiser, October 30, 1783; November 6, 1783; November 13, 1783.

 A gang of villains have been detected in Boston, who have lately broken open several stores and houses, and committed robberies; a number of them have been taken up and committed to prison in the metropolis. Six or seven have made their escape, five of whom are advertised in the Boston papers, viz. William Doyle, five feet five inches high, taylor by trade, much pitted with the small pox, light hair, wore a round hat and scarlet coat; but was frequently seen in a short dress.—Joseph Mountany, a Frenchman, dark complexioned, black hair and eyes, pitted with the small-pox, speaks fast, and tolerable good English, about five feet ten inches, stout built; wore gold drops in his ears, a dark coloured surtout coat, large cooked [*sic*] hat.— John Crane, an Irishman, five feet ten inches high, well set, light complexion, pitted with the small pox, has large grey eyes and long hair; had a new scarlet cloth coat, an embroidered waistcoat, black sattin breeches, but often appears in the dress of a sailor. John Burk, who sometimes calls himself John Green, about five feet eleven inches high, light complexion, brown bushy hair, wore a round hat with a silk ribbon, for a band, a long blue great coat, but often a sailor's dress. For the apprehending each or either of the above described persons, Forty Dollars are offered as a reward, by
    Messrs. White and Moore, merchants in Boston.
Thomas's Massachusetts Spy Or, American Oracle of Liberty, October 30, 1783. See *The Continental Journal, And Weekly Advertiser*, October 23, 1783.

These are to acknowledge, publish, and declare to all people, that some time last Spring, I being lost to a sense of duty towards God and my fellow creatures, did, without just provocation, publish the following false and defamatory words. viz. That I saw Mr. Ezekiel Smith, and a young woman named Sibbel Johnson, both of Bennington, in Bennington county, in the State of Vermont, in the act of adultery, for which false report I am sorry, and do hereby ask the forgiveness of God and all people, and the said Ezekiel and the said Sibbel in an especial manner, and further also desire this declaration be published in the Vermont Gazette.
     BENAJAH CLEVELAND. Bennington, October 22d. 1783.
The Vermont Gazette, Or Freemen's Depository, October 30, 1783; November 6, 1783; November 13, 1783.

WHEREAS *MARY*, the wife of the subscriber, has, without any just cause or reason, departed from, and refuses to live with me: this is therefore to forbid all persons whatsoever, from trusting her on my account; for I will pay no debt of her contracting from the date hereof.
     ISAAC WALDEN. New-London, October 27, 1783.
The Connecticut Gazette; And The Universal Intelligencer, October 31, 1783; November 7, 1783; November 14, 1783.

     PORTSMOUTH, November 1.
 We hear from Haverhill, in this State, that the noted Wheeler, at the last Superior Court there, was convicted of Counterfeiting Dollars, and sentenced to stand in the Pillory two Hours, one of his Ears clipped, to be imprisoned two Years, and find Security for his good Behavior for three years after his imprisonment.
   The New-Hampshire Gazette, And General Advertiser, November 1, 1783.

WHEREAS SARAH my wife, has conducted herself very impudently, in running me in debt: These are therefore to warn all persons from trusting her on my account, as I will pay no debt of her +contracting after this date.
     JOSEPH ROWLANDSON. Wethersfield, October 28, 1783.
   The Connecticut Courant, And Weekly Intelligencer, November 4, 1783; November 11, 1783

     FIVE DOLLARS REWARD.
RAN-AWAY from the Subscriber, the 8th of October last, a NECRO [*sic*] BOY, (not a slave) about 13 years of age, well made and active; had on when he went off, an old felt Hat, a homespun out side Jacket, streaked black and white, an under Jacket longer than the out side one, streaked various colours,

streaked flannal Breeches, made long, a streaked tow shirt, old Stockings, and a pair of Shoes half wore.

Whoever will take up said Negro, and secure him so that his Master gets him again, shall have the above reward, and Charges paid by me
EZRA CLARK.   Norwich, Nov. 1783.
The Norwich Packet or, The Chronicle of Freedom, November 6, 1783; November 13, 1783; November 20, 1783. Second and third ads show him as a NEGRO BOY.

WORCESTER, October 23.

At the Supreme Judicial Court held at Great Barrington, within and for the county of Berkshire, on the first Tuesday of October, 1783; Francis Dodge and Jehiel Pease, (father and son-in-law) were indicted for maliciously, wilfully and feloniously setting fire to the barn of Jonathan Smith, of New-Marlborough, in the night of the 26th of November, 1782, whereby the said barn with its contents (consisting of twenty-five tons of hay, one hundred bushels of oats, eighty-seven bushels of rye, six bushels of wheat, two bushels of seed corn, fifteen bushels of flax-seed, five hundred weight of flax, two oxen and one horse) were entirely burnt and consumed. After hearing of 18 hours, Francis Dodge was acquitted; but Jehiel Pease was convicted, and received sentence of death.

At the same Court, one James Wells, a married man, and Moresha Shuck, a single woman, convicted of lascivious cohabitation, were sentenced to be publicly whipped, and the man to stand one hour in the pillory.
The Salem Gazette, November 6, 1783.

RANAWAY from the brig Nancy, Robert Niles, Master, a negro fellow named TOM, about 35 years old, 5 feet 8 inches high, slim built, speaks very good English; had on when he went away, an old blue jacket, a buff cap, and a pair of oznabrig trowsers. Whoever will take up said negro, and return him to the subscriber, or secure him so that he may get him again, shall be handsomely rewarded, and all necessary charges paid.
ROBERT NILES.   New-London, Novem. 2. 1783.
The Connecticut Gazette; And The Universal Intelligencer, November 7, 1783; November 14, 1783; November 21, 1783.

IN the month of July last, one *Luther*, who was delirious, took a canoe from me, and on being pursued and brought back, left a bundle of cloaths in my custody, which he had doubtless stole, some of which were claimed by my neighbours, who took them; the following articles are still in my custody, viz. a man's white holland shirt, two women's tow-cloth shifts, a tow-cloth sheet something worn, and a girl's striped tow wrapper. This notice is given that the owner may come and take them away, paying cost.

ALEXANDER ROGERS, New London, Nov. 5, 1783.
The Connecticut Gazette; And The Universal Intelligencer, November 7, 1783; November 14, 1783; November 21, 1783.

Ran away from the subscriber, in Blanford, on Thursday the 16th inst. a boy 11 years old, had on when he went away, an old felt hat, check wollen frock, striped linen trowsers, short brown hair. Whoever will take up said Boy, secure him, and send me word shall be entitled to 3 shillings reward.—no charges paid.
REUBEN BOIES.
Blanford, October 27.
The Massachusetts Gazette, or the General Advertiser, November 11, 1783; November 18, 1783; November 25, 1783.

Five Dollars Reward.
BROKE from the Gaol in the County of Newport, on the Evening of the 10th Instant, JAMES H. LAFFORD and SAMUEL S. HOWARD, both of them have their Ears cropt, and branded on each Cheek with the letter R, for counterfeiting this State's Notes. Whoever will apprehend and return them to the Gaol in Newport aforesaid, shall receive the above Reward from
WILLIAM DAVIS, Sheriff.
November 12, 1783.
The Newport Mercury, November 15, 1783; November 22, 1783; November 29, 1783. See *The Connecticut Journal*, October 8, 1783.

SOME time since Josiah Olcott, jun. being disordered in his mind, left home.—he is about 30 years of age, middling size and stature, short dark brown hair, his complexion a medium between dark and light; had on plan summer cloaths, an old beaver hat bound with ferrit—he is supposed to be gone westward. Whoever shall have knowledge of him, and will give intelligence to the Subscriber, hall be allowed any necessary expence, and will much oblige their humble servant,
JOSIAH OLCOTT. East-Hartford, November 14, 1783.
The Connecticut Courant, And Weekly Intelligencer, November 18, 1783; November 25, 1783; December 2, 1783.

MY wife *Elizabeth* having left my bed and board, and otherwise behaved wickedly and unlawfully, and being apprehensive she may run me in debt, I hereby caution all persons from trusting her, as I will pay no debts of her contracting, from the date hereof.
Andrew Gage. *Beverly, Nov.* 19, 1783.
The Salem Gazette, November 20, 1783; November 27, 1783.

SHOP-LIFTER and THIEF.
TAKEN up in Douglas, on suspicion of being a thief, and breaking open the store of Col. SETH READ, on the night of the 31st of October last, and carrying off from thence a number of goods, a person who has sometimes has called his name *Elijah Smith*, at other times *Elijah Austin*, and has also gone by the names of *Elijah Pomroy,* alias *James Lynds*, alias *Elijah Wood*, &c. This person is about five feet six inches high, wears his own black hair, something short, and sometimes cued, light complexion, middling well set, and somewhat likely; he had on when taken up, a light coloured broad cloth coat, with a tinsel spangled button, the edges of which were wrought with gold thread; with ribbed olive coloured waistcoat and breeches, and a blue great coat, with a red cloth cape and plain flat yellow buttons. He is said to be the person who stole flour out of a waggon in New-Braintree sometime past, and has travelled the country as a drover, pedlar, &c. He has lately sold in several parts of the country many articles of English goods, particularly five or six yards of red and white narrow striped sattin, suitable for waistcoats; and one piece of white sattin, one piece of changeable lutestring, some calico, &c. which he says he purchased at auction, of Messrs. *Parkman* and *Hinckley*, in *Boston*. He had two HORSES, one a chesnut coloured Mare, supposed to be ten years old, cut mane, shod all round, white a white spot on the off buttock, about 14 hands high; on the mare were a man's old saddle, with an old bridle; also a woman's hunting saddle, with a wash leather seat, the leather wore off both pommels: The other Horse sorrel, about four years old, has a blaze in his face, narrow at the nose, grey mane and tail, two white spots where the tail joins the body; about fourteen and an half hands high, shod all round. If any person or persons have goods or horses, answering the above description, stolen from them, they are requested to apply to Col. SETH READ, *Uxbridge*, who will give them information where they are. The person who is suspected of having stole them is committed to the gaol in Worcester.

Uxbridge, November 15th, 1783.
Thomas's Massachusetts Spy Or, American Oracle of Liberty, November 20, 1783; December 4, 1783. See *The Providence Gazette And Country Journal*, December 6, 1783.

To the PUBLIC.
WE the subscribers are bound in duty and real justice to Mr. *Samuel Ely*, to inform the world that he came to Hardwick in our State, made enquiry after a horse stolen from him—he found where the horse was; Mr. Ely then advertised said horse as our law directs; said horse was then taken up and delivered to Mr. Ely before a number of people, after paying the reward and charges; afterwards one Wheeler, who claimed the horse, pursued Mr. Ely, advertised him for a thief, and brought him back by force; Mr. Ely then stood

trial, beat Wheeler, and recovered his cost; Mr. Wheeler then retrieved his horse in law, proved his property fairly and honestly in open court, recovered his horse, and justified his whole conduct to equity and law, like a candid, honest christian and gentlemen.—Now if the above transaction is horse-stealing, then fair, honest, just law suites for property is stealing.

Signed by each of us who were perfectly knowing to the whole matter.
Samuel Hoskin, Joel Johnson, Theodor Forbes, Stephen Johnson, William Perkins, Job Hoskin, Limuel Hart.
N. B. The above declaration we can give our solemn oath to when called upon.

The Connecticut Gazette; And The Universal Intelligencer, November 21, 1783; November 28, 1783. See *The Providence Gazette; And Country Journal*, June 22, 1782, and *Thomas's Massachusetts Spy Or, American Oracle of Liberty*, September 26, 1782, and *The Connecticut Gazette; And The Universal Intelligencer*, November 21, 1783.

WHEREAS *Mary*, my wife, has behaved in my absents in a very unbecoming manner, by running me in debt, defiling my bed, and wasting my property: I therefore forbid any person or persons trusting her on my account, as I am determined not to pay any debt she may contract from the date hereof.
        Cornelius Diskurel.   Portsmouth, 21 Nov. 1783.

The New-Hampshire Gazette, And General Advertiser, November 22, 1783; November 29, 1783.

MADE their Escape from New-Haven Goal, on the Night of the 8th Instant JOHN BLACKSTON, 3d. and TIMOTHY BLACKSTON, who were committed for a Riot: also JARED PALMER, committed by Order of the Hon. County Court for sundry Crimes. The above Persons belong to Branford in New-Haven County. Whoever shall take up the above Persons, shall have a Reward of Forty Shillings for each of them, if delivered to this or any other Goal within this State, so that they may be bro't to justice.
    STEPHEN MUNSON, Goaler.
                                                        New-Haven, Nov. 24, 1783.

The Connecticut Journal, November 26, 1783; December 3, 1783.

             Whereas LYDIA my wife, has eloped
from my bed and board, these are therefore to forbid all persons harbouring or trusting her on my account, as I will not pay any debt of her contracting after this date.
            SAMUEL HERRICK.   Bennington, November 24.

The Vermont Gazette Or Freemen's Depository, November 27, 1783; December 11, 1783.

MADE his escape from me the Subscriber, on the 12th Day of November Instant, one GEORGE GRINNOLD, of Stonington, who was attached by the Subscriber, at the Suit of John Ellis, 2nd, of Norwich, in New-London County, to appear before the County Court, to be holden at Norwich the fourth Tuesday of November Inst. Whoever will take up the said Grinnold, and deliver him to me the Subscriber, or confine him so that me may be had to appear before said County Court, shall receive FOUR DOLLARS Reward, paid by me,
      ELISHA DENISON, Constable.
The Connecticut Gazette; And The Universal Intelligencer, November 28, 1783; December 5, 1783; December 12, 1783.

STOLEN from New-London Harbour's Mouth, last Saturday night, a SLOOP of about 20 tons, white bottom, and black waste, her upper works new, her main-sail lately new headed, which is narrow. She had on board a house frame. The supposed thief is about 23 years old, of a smallish size, his fore-top comb'd back, and said his name was White. Whoever shall give information, so that the owner recovers his vessel, shall receive a generous reward, & all necessary charges paid by
  JOHN HARRIS.   N. London, Dec. 1.
The Connecticut Journal, December 3, 1783; December 17, 1783. See *The Connecticut Gazette; And The Universal Intelligencer*, December 5, 1783.

WHEREAS the Authority and Selectmen of Waterbury, have appointed the Subscriber Master to Israel Calkins, of said Waterbury; these are therefore to order said Israel Calkins to return to my Service, and to forbid all Persons trading or harbouring him, on Penalty of the Law.
  DAVID HOTCHKISS.   Waterbury, Nov. 27, 1783.
N. B. As said Calkins has called himself a Widower, this may inform the Public, that he has a Wife living at Waterbury. D. H.
The Connecticut Journal, December 3, 1783; December 17, 1783.

      FIVE DOLLARS REWARD.
BROKE out of the county goal in Norwich, on the night of the 26th of November last, and made his escape, one JOHN LAWLOR, an old countryman, five feet ten inches high, handsomely made; had on a brown Coat, blue Jacket and Breeches, and a small round Hat; confined for *Debt*. Whoever will take and return the above Prisoner, to the gaol at Norwich, shall have the above reward, and necessary charges paid, by
  DARIUS PECK, Gaoler.   Norwich, December 4, 1783.

The Norwich Packet or, The Chronicle of Freedom, December 4, 1783; December 10, 1783; December 18, 1783.

FIFTEEN DOLLARS REWARD.

RUN AWAY from the subscriber, the 26th instant, a negro or molatto fellow, named PERO, 19 years of age, about 5 feet 10 inches high, speaks good English, his hair about two inches long, wide cheek bones, full eyed, lame in his right foot; had on when he went away, a new felt hat, a mixed dark coloured great coat, a light mixed coloured waistcoat, striped under waistcoat, striped flanel shirt, striped trowsers, and new shoes; carried away with him a violin.—Whoever will take up said run-away, and return him to the subscriber, or secure him in any gaol in the United States, so that the owner may have him again, shall have the above reward, and necessary charges, paid by me
      NATHAN CRARY. Groton, (New-London County)
                 December 4, 1783.

The Norwich Packet or, The Chronicle of Freedom, December 4, 1783; December 18, 1783; December 25, 1783; January 1, 1784. See *The Massachusetts Gazette, Or General Advertiser*, December 9, 1783.

NEW-LONDON, Dec. 5.

Last Friday Night, a Man who called his Name White, (but his true Name is said to be Ketchum) ran off with a Sloop, which the Evening before had arrived from Connecticut-River, and anchored near the Light House. She belonged to Mr. John Harris, and had the Frame and other Materials for a House on Board. No Person being in the Vessel, the Villain slipped the Cable and went off without any Anchor.

The Connecticut Gazette; And The Universal Intelligencer, December 5, 1783; *The Massachusetts Gazette, Or General Advertiser*, December 16, 1783. See *The Connecticut Journal*, December 3, 1783.

THIRTY DOLLARS REWARD.

LAST Night the Shop of the Subscriber was broke open, and a Quantity of Goods taken therefrom, viz, 7 or 8 Pieces of Irish Linens, 1 Piece of Straw coloured and 1 Piece of changeable Lutestring, 1 Pieces of Green Pelong, 1 Piece of striped Muslin, 1 Piece of Fustian, 1 Piece of Calico, 1 Piece of Sarsnet, 2 Dozen of Threat Hose, several Dozen Pieces of Tapes, 2 or 3 lb. of sewing Silk, 2 lb. of fine Thread, some Womens Fans, Gartering, Shoe and Knee Buckles, &c. Any Person that will give Information of the Thief of Thieves, so that he or they may be brought to Justice, and the Good returned, shall have 30 Dollars Reward.
      SETH REED.

N. B. Said Reed has apprehended, and committed to Worcester Gaol, a Person who calls himself Elijah Austin Smith, but he has gone by several other Names, such as Pumroy, James Lines, Elijah Wood, James Potter, &c. A considerable Quantity of Goods are secured, which said Smith had left in small Parcels, and in obscure Parts of different Towns, which Goods were doubtless stolen. There were also take with him a bay Horse, Saddle and Bridle, and a small brown Mare, with a Woman's Saddle. He is about 38 Years of Age, about 5 Feet 6 Inches high, of a ruddy Complexion, and has dark Hair. *Uxbridge, Nov. 27, 1783.*

The Providence Gazette And Country Journal, December 6, 1783; December 13, 1783; December 20, 1783. See *Thomas's Massachusetts Spy Or, American Oracle of Liberty*, November 20, 1783.

TAKEN from a transient person who calls his name John Jones, five pieces of women's wear, viz. one piece 6 yards black and blue plain cloth, one piece of blue ditto 4 yards and 3 quarters, one piece brown worsted of nine yards, one piece of blue ditto of 4 yards and a half, one piece of 7 yards and a half with white selvage, one piece of men's wear dark brown fulled cloth of one yard and a half, and one large sugar box, with some powder, said cloth may be found at
    JOEL MINER's. Hartland,   November 20, 1783.
The Connecticut Courant, And Weekly Intelligencer, December 9, 1783; December 16, 1783; December 23, 1783.

    Ran Away from the subscriber,
a Negro Man, called Pero, 19 years of age, speaks good English, about 5 feet 10 inches high, wide cheek bones, large eyes, wide shoulders, lame in his right foot.—had on when he went away, a mixt dark coloured great coat, a light coloured gray waistcoat, a striped kersey under waistcoat and trowsers, a striped flannel shirt, white stockings, new shoes, new felt hat, a holland short. Whoever will take up said Negro, and return him, or secure him in any goal, so that the owner may have him again, shall have fifteen dollars reward and necessary charges, paid by me
    NATHAN CRARY.   Groton, N. London County, Nov. 26.
The Massachusetts Gazette, or General Advertiser, December 9, 1783 January 16, 1783; December 23, 1783. See *The Norwich Packet or, The Chronicle of Freedom*, December 4, 1783.

PROVIDENCE, Nov. 22.
  At the Superior Court, held by adjournment at East-Greenwich on the second Wednesday of November inst. Francis Perkins, of Coventry, for Horse stealing, was sentenced to be whipped, at the Tail of a Cart, 39 Stripes on three several Days, to forfeit his Estate, to be banished from this State,

and not to return within the same, on Penalty of suffering the Pains of Death.—William Bunting was also convicted of Horse-stealing, and received a like Sentence.—The said Bunting; convicted likewise of setting Fire to the Gaol in this Town, was sentenced to stand in the Pillory at East-Greenwich for the space of two Hours, and to be branded with the Letter A on each Cheek.

The Providence Gazette; And Country Journal, November 22, 1783; *The Connecticut And The Universal Intelligencer*, November 28, 1783; *The Massachusetts Gazette, or General Advertiser*, December 9, 1783; *The Salem Gazette*, December 25, 1783. Minor differences between the papers.

TWENTY DOLLARS REWARD.

STOLEN out of the stable of the subscriber, the night following the 4th instant, a large black HORSE, seven years old, about 15 hands high, loft carriage, a natural trotter, shod all round, cork'd behind, cracks on his hoofs before, a very small tail, part of it having been pull'd out, a grey spot near his right hip bone.—A transient person, that had on a furr cap and overalls, is suspected to be the thief, he is very tall and slim: a saddle with a hog-skin seat, and housing trimmed with white, was stolen the same night, and is supposed to be carried off with the horse. Whoever will take up and return said horse, with the thief, to the subscriber, shall have the above reward; for the horse only, Ten Dollars, and necessary charges paid by

   AZARIAH LATHROP. Norwich, December 6, 1783.

The Norwich Packet or, The Chronicle of Freedom, December 10, 1783; December 18, 1783; December 25, 1783; January 1, 1784; *The Independent Chronicle and the Universal Advertiser*, December 18, 1783; December 25, 1783; January 1, 1784. Minor differences between the papers.

WHEREAS ESTHER, a young Woman, whom People call my Wife, because a few Years since the marriage Ceremmony was imposed upon us in a fiarcical Manner contrary to both our Inclinations, has entered into Dealings and Contracts without my Privity of Consent; for which I have found myself responsible, and on Consequence my Interested thereby injured:—And whereas there may still be People ready to traffick with and trust the said Esther greatly to my Disadvantage, looking upon me as accountable for the fulfilment of her Engagements and Promises;—I have determined, and hereby make known, and publicate my Determination, henceforward not to hold myself responsible for any Bargains, Contracts, or Negotiations of the said Esther, whom whoever shall hereafter trust with any Commodity or Article whatever let him look to her only, and not to me for Recompence.

   WILLIAM RICE.   Ashford, Nov. 17, A. D. 1783.

The Connecticut Gazette; And The Universal Intelligencer, December 12, 1783; December 19, 1783; December 26, 1783.

Whereas my wife ALSE, has eloped from my bed and board, and otherwise behaved in a very unbecoming manner, this is to caution all persons from trusting her in any respect, as I will not pay one farthing of any debts which she contracts after this date.   CHRISTOPHER MAN. Preston,

State of New-Hampshire, Nov. 25, 1783.

The Independent Chronicle and the Universal Advertiser, December 12, 1783.

RUN-away from the subscriber on the 12th instant, one DAVID COTTON, a young man about 5 feet 10 inches high, round shouldered, stoops forward when he walks, has light coloured eyes, sandy hair; had on when he went away a pair blue breeches, snuff coloured coat and vest, new castor hat, new shoes, white cotton stockings, white metal buckles; his other cloathing he carried with him, viz. a short sailor's jacket, brown breeches, striped linen trowsers, two white shirts, one woolen ditto, two pair woolen stockings. It is supposed he is gone to New-London or some other sea port to go to sea. Whoever will take up said boy and secure him and give notice to the subscriber, shall receive a handsome reward and all necessary charges paid, by WILLIBE LOWEL.

Hartford, December 15, 1783.

N. B. All masters of vessels are forbid harbouring or carrying off said Boy.

The Connecticut Courant, And Weekly Intelligencer, December 16, 1783; December 23, 1783; December 30, 1783.

Ten Dollars Reward!

STOLEN on the evening of the 3d instant, a blue Great Coat, with plain mettle buttons, a small Beaver Hat, a pair of Shoes and silver Shoe Buckles, a silk Handkerchief and other articles; the thief is a large man, very much pitted with the small-pox, has a large crooked nose, his little finger on his right hand cut off, he calls himself by the name of Phillipse wore a red sailor vest, a pair of striped trowsers, and a chcck'd linen shirt. Whoever will take up said thief and return him to me, shall have the above reward and all necessary charges paid.
    JEDIAH NORTON.

Worthington, December 4th, 1783.

The Connecticut Courant, And Weekly Intelligencer, December 16, 1783; December 23, 1783; December 30, 1783; *The Connecticut Journal*, January 7, 1784; January 14, 1784.

Broke prison at Newbury,
in the county of Orange, and State of Vermont, on the night of the 1st of instant December one Jacob Marston, late of Fairlee, in said county, a stout portly fellow, about 30 years of age, light complection, hair, and eyes, his beard bearing a little upon a sandy, speaks with a pretty full voice, and assumes some important airs in his behaviour—was committed for several small, but just debts, and has made his escape to discharge them.

Whoever will take up and secure him, so that the subscriber may have him again, shall receive a generous reward from, and has all necessary charges paid by,
ABNER CHAMBERLAIN, Sheriff.
The Vermont Journal and the Universal Advertiser, December 17, 1783; December 24, 1783.

This forbids any Person
trusting SIBELA, Wife of me the subscriber, as I will pay no Debts of her contracting after this Date.
PHINEHAS CHAMBERLAIN. Chelmsford, Dec. 17, 1783.
The Independent Chronicle and the Universal Advertiser, December 18, 1783.

WHEREAS I the Subscriber did the middle of October last a year ago, leave my late wife HAPPY, then residing in the Town of Plainfield, county of Windham, on consideration of her uneasy, fractious, and quarrelsome disposition, which I considered as a duty Incumbent on me when our mutual happiness could no longer exist, together with her wasting or otherwise parting in an unwarrantable manner with the necessaries provided for the family, which has given me the greatest uneasiness, and as no other remedy could be provided, I must leave it to the consideration of the public and those concerned, forbidding them at the same time to harbour or otherwise trust her on my account after this date, as I am unable and will not pay any debts she may contract after this date.
JOHN-THO'S TRANTUM. County of Albany, Nov. 30, 1783.
The Connecticut Gazette; And The Universal Intelligencer, December 19, 1783; December 26, 1783; January 2, 1784.

RAN-away from the Subscriber, a thick-set Negro Man, named ENOCH, about 23 Years old, born in the Country, about 5 Feet 6 Inches high; had on a blue Great Coat with Buttons under the Arms, a short butternut colour'd Coat, striped linen Jacket with a Belt, old white cloth Breeches, mix'd coloured Stockings, and silver Shoe-Buckles. Whoever will take up said Negro, and return him to the Subscriber, shall have TEN DOLLARS Reward, and necessary Charges paid by JORDAN POST, jun.

N. B. All Masters of Vessels are forbid carrying off said Negro, and all others are forbid harbouring him upon Penalty of the Law.

The Connecticut Gazette; And The Universal Intelligencer, December 19, 1783; December 26, 1783; January 2, 1784. See *The Connecticut Courant, And Weekly Intelligencer*, January 6, 1784.

MY wife LUCY, having eloped from my bed and board; I do inform all persons crediting her on my account, that I will not pay any demands they shall make against me therefor.
          PRINCE HULL.   Hartford, December 20, 1783.

The Connecticut Courant, And Weekly Intelligencer, December 23, 1783; December 30, 1783; January 6, 1784.

WHEREAS MABEL, my wife hath conducted bad, and behaved herself in an unbecoming manner. This is therefore to forbid all persons trusting or harboring on my account, as solemnly declare I will pay no debts of her contraction after this date.
          NATHANIEL TYLER.   Cheshire, December 23, A. D. 1783.

The Connecticut Journal, December 31, 1783; January 7, 1784.

RUN-AWAY from the Subscriber, a Negro servant named ENOCH, had on when he went away from me, a felt Hat; blue great Coat, with a brown velvet cape, buttons under the arms and a flappet with button-holes on the shoulders; a brown Coat, with short folds; a striped linen double breasted Jacket; with a belt; old white cloath Breeches; mixed coloured Stockings; silver Shoe and Knee Buckles. He is about five feet high, thick sett, pretty black, a great whistler, about 23 years old, was born in Norwich. Whoever will take up said Negro and return him me the Subscriber in Hebron (in Connecticut) or secure him in any goal in this State and give information to me shall have TEN DOLLARS REWARD and all charges paid by me, JORDAN POST, jun.
N. B. All masters of vessels are forbid carrying off, or other persons harbouring said Negro, on penalty of the Law.   Hebron, December 29, 1783.

The Connecticut Courant, And Weekly Intelligencer, January 6, 1784; January 13, 1784. See *The Connecticut Gazette; And The Universal Intelligencer*, December 19, 1783.

          WHEREAS my wife HANNAH, has
eloped from my bed and board, without any just reasons and refuseth to come home:—I do hereby forbid all persons trusting her on my account, as I will pay no debts of her contracting, from the date hereof. Any do notify and forbid all persons harbouring the said Hannah, upon the penalty of the law.
          DANIEL FOX. New-Canaan, dated Dec. 27, A. D. 1783.

The Connecticut Journal, January 14, 1784.

INDEX

Abbe, John, 69
Abbe, Sarah, 69
Abel, Frederick, 227
Adams, Daniel, 88, 90, 108
Adams, Perces, 87, 90, 107
Aiden, J., 148
Akerly, Nathaniel, 50
Alden, Ichabod, 19
Algor, Roger, 235
Allen William, 11
Allen, David, Jr., 53
Allen, Hannah, 60
Allen, John, 87, 127
Allen, Jonathan, 147
Allen, Jonathan, Jr., 147
Allen, Martha, 53
Allen, Mrs., 128
Allen, Robert, 114
Allen, Samuel, 60
Alley, John, 122
Allibe, John, 197
Allin, Abigail, 38
Allin, David, 38
Ames, John, 23
Ammidown, Caleb, 134
Andrews, Abraham, 101, 103, 106
Anthony, John, 182
Anthony, Mr., 162
Anthony, William, 127
Anturny, Mele, 14
Anturny, John, 14
Appleton, Francis, 195
Appleton, Sarah, 93
Appleton, William, 93
Armstrong, John, 94
Arnold, Abimilech, 118
Arnold, Alfred, 233
Arnold, Benedict, 15
Arnold, Gideon, 57
Arnold, John, 123, 124

Arnold, Jonathan, 9
Arnold, Martha, 178
Arnold, Seth, 178
Atkinson, John, 128
Atwater, John, 121, 122
Atwell, Amos, 267
Atwell, Nabby, 142
Atwell, Richard, 142
Austin, Caleb, Jr., 109, 113
Austin, Elijah, 279
Austin, Stephen, 110
Austin/Austen, Mrs. Paul, 238, 258
Austin/Austen, Paul, 238, 259
Austin/Auston, Seth, 226, 227, 240
Avery, Samuel, 230
Avery, Thomas, 8
Ayers, John, 233
Babcock, Elisha, 200
Babcock, James, 140
Backus, Ebenezer, 190
Backus, William, 190
Bacon, Abner, 232
Bacon, Broadhurst, 24
Bacon, Daniel, 247
Bacon, Esther, 247
Bacon, Joel, 235
Bacon, Pierpont, 63
Bagnall, Benjamin, 219
Bailey, George, 133
Baird, Thomas, Jr., 6
Baker, John, 50
Baker, Mary, 81
Baker, Moses, 81
Baldwin, David, 67, 71
Baldwin, Heth, 151
Baldwin, Loammi, 132
Baley, Nathan, Jr., 72, 94
Ballard, John, 173
Ballou, Daniel, 156

Ballou, Martha, 156
Bancroft, Samuel, 6
Banister, Mary, 61
Banister, Seth, 149
Barber, Daniel, 75
Barber, David, 27
Barber, John, 116
Barber, Mr., 153
Barker, Enoch, 87
Barnam, Nathan, 273
Barnard, William, 135
Barney, John, Jr., 14, 15, 31, 34
Barns, Eli, 258
Barrell, Nathaniel, 58
Bartlet, Mr., 214
Bartlett, Caleb, 118
Barton, Benjamin, 67, 71
Barton, Timothy, 71
Basford, Abigal/Abigail, 86, 92
Basford, Jacob, 86, 92
Bass, Alden, 2
Basset, Sabarah, 13
Basset, Seth, 13
Bates, Dorcas, 157
Bates, John, 20
Bates, John, Jr., 273
Bates, Silas, 157
Baxter, David, 143
Baxter, Simon, 54, 161
Bayley, Nathan, Jr., 128
Beach, John, 186
Beach, Susanna, 185, 186
Beal, Isaac, Jr., 255
Beal, Sarah, 255
Bean, Stephen, 272
Beard, Grace, 198
Beard, Joseph, 113
Beard, Simon, 198
Beckwith, Jonathan, 235
Beckwith, Rachel, 235
Beebe, Abigail, 132
Beebe, Bazaleel/Bezaleel, 16
Beebe, Daniel, 119

Beebe, David, 210
Beebe, Jeremiah, 132
Beers, Nathan, 70
Belden, John, 174
Belding, Oliver, 158
Belknap, Abraham, 201
Bell, William, 107
Bement, Eben., 269
Bemis, Elizabeth, 107
Bemis, Samuel, 107
Benjamin, John, 42
Bennett, Hosea, 1
Bennett, Patience, 1
Bentley/Bently, Azel, 224
Berry/Barry, William, 86
Beverly, John, 132, 226
Bewell, Joseph, 143
Bidwell, Jonathan, 237
Bill, Allen, 169
Billing, Samuel, 145
Bingham, Elijah, 164
Bingham, Jabez, 229
Bingham, Stephen, 27
Birdsey, Gershom, 261
Bishop, Elizabeth, 97
Bishop, James, 97
Bissel, David, 146
Bissel, Hezekiah, 228
Blackle, Margaret, 92
Blackle, Thomas, 92
Blackman, Mehitabel, 55
Blackman, Nathaniel, 139
Blackman, Samuel, 55
Blackston, John, 3d., 280
Blackston, Timothy, 280
Blague, Joseph, 210
Blake, Increase, 73, 136, 163
Blakseley, Eno., 95
Blakslee, Isaiah, 36
Blakslee, Jared, 273
Blakslee, Rhoda, 273
Blanchard, Sarah, 210
Blanchard, Stephen, 210

Blasdel, Benjamin, 252
Blasdel, Roger, 21
Bleckmen, Elizabeth, 1
Bleckmen, Nehemiah, 1
Bliss, Amos, 116
Bliss, Phoebe, 116
Blodget, Asa, 253
Blood, Isaiah, 134
Blood, John, 134
Boham, Rebecca, 64
Boice, James, 56
Boies, Reuben, 278
Boise, James, 34
Bolles, Joseph, 3d., 239
Bomford, Nathan, 158
Booth, Henry, 231
Booth, Levi, 249
Bostwick, Andrew, 199
Bostwick, Daniel, 6
Bourn, Lemuel, 10
Bourn, Melatiah, 10
Bowen, Ephraim, Jr., 252
Bowen, John, 54
Bowen, Oliver, 173
Bowen, William, 38
Boyd, James, 84
Boyd, Robert, 84
Boylston, Joshua, 92
Brada, David, 253
Bradford, Abigail, 24, 29
Bradford, Henry, 76
Bradford, William, 24, 28
Bradish, Isaac, 97
Bradley, Moses, 251
Bradley, Thankful, 251
Bradly, Joseph, 72
Breck, Mr., 143
Breed, Eben., 163
Brewer, John, 241
Brewer, Lydia, 241
Brewster, Abel, 260
Brian, Patrick, 4
Briges, James, 34

Brimer, Lydia, 91
Brimer, Timothy, 92
Bristol, Edward, 187
Bristol, Simon, 159
Britton, Daniel, 230
Broad, Aaron, 206
Broad, Elizabeth, 205
Broad, Josiah, 206
Brockway, Nathan, 66
Brockway, William, 58
Brooks, Thomas, 173
Brown, Benjamin, 72, 187
Brown, Capt., 131
Brown, Cato, 66
Brown, Elisha, 255, 256, 258
Brown, Elizabeth, 215
Brown, Gershom, Jr., 192
Brown, Henry, 170
Brown, Jane, 64
Brown, John, 114, 154, 155, 215, 230
Brown, Joseph, 42
Brown, Mary, 94
Brown, Mr., 160, 175
Brown, Patience, 187
Brown, Phebe, 42
Brown, Rob., Jr., 94
Brown, Sarah, 155
Browne/Brown, James, 86
Browning, Henry, 200
Brownson, Cornelius, 198
Brownson, Elizabeth, 198
Brush, Lemuel, 194
Buckston, Charles, 113
Budlong, Nathan, 100
Buel, Joseph, 80
Buel, Patience, 80
Buford, Abraham, 125
Bulkley, Capt., 24
Bulkley, Joshua, 32, 33
Bull, Frederick, 80
Bunting, William, 284
Burbage, George, 152

Burbank, Ebenezer, 127
Burbank, Shem, 141, 144
Burdick, James, 8
Burgoyne, Augustus, 145
Burgoyne, John, 19
Burk, John, 10, 273, 275
Burnham, Elizabeth, 204
Burnham, Gordon, 100
Burnham, Joseph, 205
Burns, John, 193
Burns, William, 260
Burr, Hannah, 202, 209
Burr, Josiah, 271
Burr, Mr., 176, 179
Burr, Noadiah/Noahdiah, 207, 209
Burr, Noadiah, Jr., 202, 206
Burrage, George, 185
Burrows, Anna, 73
Burrows, Nathan, 2d., 73
Burton, Abel, 84
Burton, James, 268
Burton, William, 140
Burts, Blnathan, 50
Bush, James, 151
Bush, John, 130
Bush, Jonathan, 210
Butler, John, 107
Butler, Samuel, 90
Cable, Joseph Pine, 139
Calder, George, 141
Caldwell, Timothy, 240
Caldwill/Calwill, William, 46
Calkins, Israel, 281
Calkins, Mrs. Israel, 281
Campbell, James, 204
Cane, John, 273, 275
Cannon, Jeremiah, 97
Care, Abigail, 160
Care, Grace, 150
Care, Phineas, 160
Care, Thomas, 150
Carew, Eliphalet, 85, 97

Carleton/Carlton, Guy, 253
Carncross, David, 221
Carnes, Edward, 91
Carnes, Mima/Mime, 245, 246
Carnes, Thomas Jenner, 222, 245, 246
Carpenter, Andrew, 104, 106
Carpenter, Anthony Willett, 1
Carpenter, Nathan, 101, 103, 106
Carpenter, Nehemiah, 23
Carrol, John, 177
Carter, Joseph, 65, 219
Cartey, John, 135
Cary, Daniel, 197
Cary, George, 46
Cary, Hannah, 197
Case, Abraham, 84
Case, Catharine, 81
Case, Elijah, Jr., 81
Case, Joe, 179
Case, Rufus, 152
Case, Thomas, 156
Cassada, Catherine, 59
Cassidy. Mrs., 156
Caswell, Joseph, 52
Cathcart, John, 195, 219
Catlin, Alexander, 245
Caulkins, Daniel, 99
Chadwick, Asa, 128
Chadwick, Joshua, 43
Chamberlain, Abner, 286
Chamberlain, Phinehas, 286
Chamberlain, Sibela, 286
Chambers, John, 35
Champion, Henry, 172
Champlain, Hannah, 77
Champlain, Silas, 78
Champlin, Elihu, 45
Champlin, James, 128
Champlin, Jeffery, 60
Champlin, Jeffery, Jr., 241
Chandler, Joshua, 106
Chaphey, Joseph, 85

Chaphey, Mable, 85
Chapin, John, 196
Chapin, Margaret, 196
Chapman, Samuel, 119
Chappel, Elijah, Jr., 236
Chappel, Mabel, 236
Chappel, Mr., 87
Chappel, Peter, 250
Chard, Samuel, 155
Chase, John, 68
Chase, Joseph, 9
Cheever, William, 270
Cheevers, Ezekiel, 149
Chesbrough, Amos, 225
Chesbrough, Anna, 225
Chester, Leonard, 231
Child, David, 177
Child, Ebenezer, 238
Child, Mary, 238
Christenson, Jurgen, 265
Clafford, Francis, 89
Clark, Ezra, 277
Clark, George, 56
Clark, John, 129
Clark, Joseph, 244
Clark, Josiah, 269
Clark, Norman, 180
Clark,Caleb, 10
Clarke, George, 102
Clarke, John, 160
Clarke, John, Mrs., 160
Clarkson, James, 31
Cleaveland, Albrow, 76
Cleland, Robert, 64
Cleveland, Benajah, 276
Cleveland, Moses, 58, 134, 155, 168
Cleveland, Samuel, 79
Clifford, Joseph, 243
Clinton, Henry, 125
Coburn, John, 39
Cochran, James, 3d., 11
Cochran, Mary, 11

Coffin, Hannah, 118
Coffin, Samuel T., 118
Coit, Joseph, 230
Cole, Elizabeth, 180
Cole, John, 73, 180
Cole, Phoebe, 73
Coleman, John, 171
Collins, Beulah, 112
Collins, Daniel, 52
Collins, Eleazer, 112
Collins, Isabella, 52
Collins, John, 146, 149
Collins, Syranus, 160
Commins, Benjamin, 13
Commins, Joseph, 13
Comstock, Moses, 20
Cone, George, 141
Conkling, Capt., 24
Conkling, John, 239
Connel, Jeremiah, 10
Cook, Governor, 4
Cook, Joseph, 8, 262
Cook, Thomas, 163
Cooke, John, 201
Cool, Lemuel, 137
Cooms, Richard, 152
Cooper, John, 38
Cooper, Mr., 154
Cooper, Polly, 38
Corbett, John, 114
Corey, Roger, 63
Corey, Temperance, 63
Cornish, Elisha, 179
Cornwell, Nathaniel, 32
Cotton, David, 285
Cotton, William, 103, 104, 125
Coult, Samuel, 250
Coupland, Mr., 54
Cowvin, Francis, 211
Cox, James, 56
Craft, Ebenezer, 181
Craig, Robert, 85
Craige, Andrew, 165

Craige, John, 165
Crandal, Asa, 7
Crane, John, 273, 275
Crary, Nathan, 282, 283
Crawford, William, 212
Creed, William, 173
Crookstone, John, 35
Crosby, Joseph, 177
Cross, John, 211
Crossing, William, 52
Culver, Amos, 161
Culver, Daniel, 20
Culver, Hannah, 20
Culver, James, 59
Culver, Samuel, 155
Curtis, Alice, 262
Curtis, Jonathan, 268
Curtiss/Curtis, Jeptha, 239, 242
Cushing, Joseph, 32
Cuzzins, J., 169
D'Hiseures, Mr., 213
Dagget, James, 214
Daggett, Lydia, 78
Daggett, Nathaniel, 78
Dailey, Elisabeth, 112
Dailey, James, 112
Dalton, Michael, 162
Dan, Elisha, 74
Danforth, Samuel, 263
Daniels, Abagail/Abigail, 60, 63
Daniels, Amy, 112
Daniels, John, 61, 62, 112
Danielson, Nathaniel, 249
Danielson, Rose, 248
Danielson, Samuel, 36
Dansey, William, 126
Dart, James, 220
Daton, John, 193
Davenport, Anthony, 160
Davenport, Barnet/Barnett/Barnard, 95, 96, 109
Davenport, James, 8
Davenport, Nicholas, 95, 109, 113, 151
Davids, Daniel, 109
Davis, Hannah, 78
Davis, Hugh, 122
Davis, Jabez, 78
Davis, James, 261
Davis, John, 62, 125
Davis, Jonathan, 243
Davis, Mary, 100
Davis, Micajah, 250
Davis, Nathan, 42
Davis, Timothy, 264
Davis, William, 153, 278
Davison, Barnabas, 260
Davison, Betty, 260
Dawes, Elijah, 257
Day, Luke, 208
Day, Mary/Marcy, 208
De L'Guille, Le Chevalier, 218
De Spaut, Comte de, 216
Dean, Hampshire, 54
Delatour, John, 274
Delivan, Samuel, 82
Delong, Elias, 109
Delong, Isabel, 109
Denison, Elisha, 281
Denison, John, 82
Dennis, James, 54, 114
Denny, Thomas, 171
Denton, Samuel, 11
Derby, James, 151
Devereux, Cato, 222
Dexter, Benjamin, 185
Dexter, Sarah, 185
Dickerman, Joseph, 166
Dimon, Jonathan, 76
Dingley, John, 70
Dingley, Mary, 70
Diskurel, Cornelius, 280
Diskurel, Mary, 280
Dixon, Hannah, 216
Dixon, Moses, 217

Dockum, Benjamin, 110
Dockum, Elizabeth, 110
Dodge, Francis, 277
Doolittle, Isaac, 133
Doolittle, Samuel, 151
Dorious, Henry, 27
Dorrance/Dorramce, John, 64
Douglass, Capt., 82, 137
Douglass, Mr., 121
Douglass, Thomas, 72
Downs, Shubael, 241
Doyle, William, 273, 275
Dr. Cooper, 156
Draper, Ebenezer, 145
Draper, William, 40
Dresser, Richard, 134
Dunham, John, 266
Dunning, Elias, 119, 208
Durfee, Richard, 212
Durkee, Nathaniel, Jr., 158
Dustin, Paul, 200
Dutch, Stephen, 230
Dutton, Richard, 94
Dyar, John, 113
Dyar, Mary, 112
Dyer, Christopher, 232
Eddy, John, 110
Edes, Eunice, 158
Edes. Isaiah, 159
Edgerton, Nathaniel, 137
Edson, Thomas, 216
Edwards, John, 261
Edwards, Jonathan, 50
Elding/Eldding, Thomas, 41, 44
Elliot, James, 74
Ellis, Abiel, 10
Ellis, John, 44
Ellis, John, 2d., 281
Ely, Joseph, 196
Ely, Marsh, 193
Ely, Samuel, 191, 203, 279
Emerson, Jacob, 164
Emerson, Sarah, 164

Ephraim, Hannah, 174
Ephraim, John, Jr., 175
Eurd, Ebenezer, 143
Everitt, Daniel, 106
Fain, Dennis, 254
Fairbanks, Phineas, 31
Fairchild, Dan, 104
Fairchild, Daniel, 135
Farley, Michael, 74, 157, 275
Farnam/Furnam, Daniel, 15
Fellerton, John, 115
Ferguson, Eleazer, 116
Ferguson, Molly, 115
Ferward, Mr., 254
Filey, Anna Cryrena, 127
Filey, Remembrance, 127
Fingell, Andrew, 223
Finley, Rachel, 216
Finney, Josiah, 185
Fish, Eliakim, 110
Fisher, Jo, 40
Fisher, John, 27
Fisk, Ebenezer, 231
Fisk, Joseph, Jr., 37
Fisk, Samuel, 195
Fitch, Abel, 272
Fitch, Ann, 272
Fitch, Benjamin, 13
Folsom, James, 14
Foot, George, 167
Foot, Josiah, 167
Foot, Mr., 65
Forbes, John, 39
Forbes, Theodor, 280
Ford, Demas, 256
Ford, Ezra, 1
Ford, Sarah, 69, 70
Foreman, Daniel, 15
Foreman, James, 257
Forster, Benjamin, Jr., 168
Forster, Jemima, 168
Forsythe, Mr., 57
Forward, Joseph, 212

Foster, Joel, 128
Foster, John, 82
Foster, Mr., 270
Fostwick, Mr., 192
Fowle, Edmund, 21
Fowler, Christopher, 3
Fowler, Jesse, 177
Fox, Daniel, 287
Fox, Elisha, 13
Fox, Hannah, 287
Fox, Samuel, Jr., 70
Francis, Anthony, 65
Franklin, Abel, 33
Freeland, William, 269
Freeman, James, 5
Freeman, Ned, 130
Freeman, Nomy, 130
French, James, 165
Frost, David, 49
Frost, John, 130
Frost, Mrs. David, 49
Fuller, Ephraim, 22
Fuller, Josiah, 52
Fuller, Mary, 52
Gage, Andrew, 278
Gage, Elizabeth, 278
Gale, John, 48
Gales, Mrs. John, 48
Galusha, Jonas, 242
Gannet, Joseph, 32
Ganter, Peter, 51
Gardette, James, 216
Gardette, Rachel, 215
Gardette/Gardine, James, 215
Gardine, Jaques, 216
Gardiner, Thomas, Jr., 180
Gardner, Anne, 234
Gardner, Benjamin, 224
Gardner, Cato, 137
Gardner, David, 234
Gardner, Ezekiel, 184
Gardner, Israel, 123, 124
Gardner, James, 38

Gardner, Jonathan, 53
Gardner, Joseph, 230
Gardner, Samuel, 152, 156
Gardner, Violet, 137
Gary, Seth, 75
Gates, Horatio, 55
Geer, James, 94
Geer, Mary, 94
Gereld, Gamaliel, 103
Gereld, Lydia, 103
Gibbs, Frederick, 80
Gibbs, Henry, 130
Gibbs, Josiah W., 108
Gibbs, Thomas, 127, 168
Gilbert, Col., 55
Gilbert, Mr., 55
Gile, John, 254
Giles, Mr., 172
Gill, Mr., 97
Gillet, Elizabeth, 269
Gillet, Seth, 269
Gilman, John Stannel, 264, 272
Gilman, Nicholas, 7
Gilman, Theophilus, 254
Glass, James, 212
Glover, Jeremiah, 58
Gloyd, John, 253
Godfrey, Simon, 108
Golden, Peter, 5
Goodrich, Benjamin, 36
Goodrich, Elias, 258
Goodrich, Elizabeth, 36
Goodrich, Mr., 115
Goodrich, Wm., 129
Goodwin, Daniel, 202
Gorden/Gordon, Joseph, 243, 246
Gorton, Othniel, 156
Gould, Daniel, 221
Gourly, Capt., 131
Graham, Lewis, 214
Graham, Samuel, 140
Grant, George, 218
Graves, George, 265

Gray, Lammon, 204
Green, John, 273, 275
Green, Joseph, 87
Green, Mr., 143
Green, Thomas, 152
Green/Greene, Jonathan, 25
Greene, Benjamin, 79
Greenelch, Richard, 184
Greenleaf, William., 61
Greenleaf, Wm., 43
Grenell, John, 45
Gridley, William, 212
Griffin, Ebenezer, 177
Griffin, John, 191
Griffin, Mrs., 124
Griffin, Stephen, 2d., 176
Griggs, John, 253
Grinnold, George, 281
Griswold, Isaac, 96
Griswold, Mathew, 212
Grosvenor, Caleb, 67
Grosvenor, Joseph, 67
Grover, Ebenezer, 4
Gummer, Abigail, 85, 97
Guralson, Henry, 268
Gurnsey, Ebenezer, 208
Haden, Mrs., 156
Hagar, Mr., 150
Haile, Isabel, 50
Haile, Joseph, 50
Hair, Uriah, 11
Hale, Elizabeth, 182
Hale, Enoch, 171
Hale, Noah, Jr., 217
Hale, Samuel, 182
Hall, Elisha, 117
Hall, Frederick, 267
Hall, Jesse, 164, 167
Hall, Sarah, 164, 166
Halladay, Aaron, 35
Halladay, Isaac, 240
Hallet, Enoch, 45, 68
Hallett, Enoch, 17

Halsey, Thomas Lloyd, 51
Halstead, Mathias, 45
Hamilton, James, 3
Hancock, Joseph, 133
Hancock, Susan, 133
Hand, Edward, 149
Handy, Charles, 53
Hannon, William, 177
Harding, Jere., 171
Harris, David, 155
Harris, Ezekiel, 175
Harris, George, 53
Harris, John, 281, 282
Harris, Ruth, 175
Harrison, Thomas, 19
Hart, Dennies, 233
Hart, Limuel, 280
Hart, Major, 82
Hartley, Samuel, 83
Hartley, Sarah, 83
Haskel, Elijah, 235
Haslett, James, 215
Hassard, Samuel, 143
Hathaway, Ebenezer, 151
Hathaway, John, 217
Hathway, Philip, 210
Haughton, James, 229
Haward, Caleb, 66
Hawley, Joseph, 255
Hayden, Daniel, 152
Hayward, Samuel S., 269
Hazen, Moses, 10
Heacock, Jo., 151
Heath, William, 19
Heaverlin, Benjamin, 97
Hebard, Jonathan, 142, 171
Hegerty, Jeremiah, 246
Hegerty, Mary, 246
Heminway, Samuel, 125
Hempsted, Joshua, 209, 211, 230
Henderson, Joseph, 202, 223
Hennels, Elihu, 151
Herbert, John, 88

Herrick, Lydia, 280
Herrick, Samuel, 280
Hessex, David, 236
Hewes, Jonathan, 223
Hewes, Joseph, Jr., 23
Heyward, Edward, 27
Hickox, Benjamin, 102
Hide, Eliakim, 55
Hide, Joseph, 189
Hide, Lois/Louis, 55
Higens, Archibald, 135
Higgins, Joseph, 139
Higgins, Mary, 128
Higgins, Silvanus, 220
Hill, Betty, 228
Hill, James, 248
Hill, Jeremiah, 44, 228
Hill, Mary, 247
Hillegas, Mr., 253
Hillman, Noble, 57
Hills, Hannah, 2, 12
Hills, Moses, 2, 12
Hinckley, Mr., 279
Hinckley, Thomas, 269
Hinckly, Wiat, 100
Hine, Dan., 213
Hine, Ruth, 213
Hinman, Edward, 65, 67
Hinman, Ephraim, 67
Hinman, Henry, 260
Hinman, Noble, 3, 49
Hinsdale, Elijah, 131
Hobb, Capt., 62
Hogan, John, 249
Hogan, Sarah, 249
Hoit, Samuel, 151, 178
Holady, James, 269
Holcomb, Asahel, 212
Holcomb, Caleb, 176, 179
Holcomb, Jesse, 176
Holcomb, Timothy, 175, 176, 178
Holden, Charles, 57
Holdin, James, 163

Holdin, Lowis, 163
Holland, Stephen, 6
Holmes, Benjamin, 199
Holmes, Benjamin, Jr., 198
Holmes, Peggy, 198, 199
Holms, Daniel, 269
Holt, James, 8, 119
Hood, Samuel, 259
Hooker, Benjamin, 142
Hooper, Jacob, 266
Hopkins, Abigail, 138
Hopkins, Benjamin, 138
Hopkins, Joram, 130
Hopkins, Reuben, 53
Hopkins, William, 156
Horton, Amos, 201
Hoskin, Benjamin, 144, 162
Hoskin, Job, 280
Hoskin, Lydia, 144, 162
Hoskin, Samuel, 280
Hotchkiss, Anna, 112
Hotchkiss, David, 281
Hotchkiss, Stephen, 112
Hovey, Paul, 175
Howard, John, 77
Howard, Richard, 61
Howard, Samuel S., 278
Howard, William, 7
Howd, Benjamin, 214
Howell, George, 132
Hoyle, Joseph, 263
Hoyle, Sarah, 263
Hubbell, Abijah, 111
Hubbell, Elijah, 194
Hubbill, Isaac, 11
Hudson, Barz., 51
Huffman, Hannah, 78
Huffman, Simon, 78
Huggins, William, 237, 248
Hughes, Christopher, 76
Hull, Amos, 168
Hull, Lucy, 287
Hull, Prince, 287

Humeston, James, 97
Humphrey, Daniel, 179
Humphry, Jonathan, 179
Humphry, Josiah, Jr., 194
Humphry, Rachel, 194
Hungerford, Green, 169, 170
Hunskum, Mariaba, 233
Hunskum, Uriah, 233
Hunt, Alexander, 265
Hunt, Daniel, 72, 73
Hunt, Joseph, 44
Hunt, Martha, 187
Hunt, Seth, 187
Huntley, Mary, 250
Hurlburt, Joseph, 21
Hurlbut, Reuben, 176, 179
Hurlbut, Reuben, Jr., 176, 178
Hurlbut, Susannah, 138
Hurlbut, Titus, 138
Hussey, Mr., 185
Hustead, Nathaniel, 113
Hutchings, Caleb, 57
Hutchings, Sarah, 57
Hutchinson, James, 221
Hutchinson, Jeremiah, 153
Hutchinson, Stephen, 233
Hyde, Caleb, 75
Indians, Gardner, James, 38; Patience, 98; Phoebe, 213; Towley, Benjamin, 269; unnamed, 202
Ingalls, Elizabeth, 31
Ireland, Robert, 107
Ives, Timothy, 221
Jackson, Col., 74
Jackson, Elisha, 111
Jackson, Hall, 219
Jackson, John, 3d., 114
Jackson, Thomas, 14
Jackson, Walter, 180
Jarreau, Capt., 47
Jebbling, Mary, 150
Jebbling, Paul, 150

Jenkins, John, 137
Jenkins, Seth, 238
Jenner, Mary, 245
Jennings, Joel, 182
Jennings, John, 10
Jepson, Wm., 122
Jewett, Jonathan, 216
Jewett, Stephen, 216
Jewett, Thadeus, 217
John, Peter Little, 185
Johnson, Daniel, 232, 236
Johnson, Enoch, 135
Johnson, Francis, 160
Johnson, Francis, Mrs., 160
Johnson, Hezekiah, 84
Johnson, Jacob, 111
Johnson, Joel, 280
Johnson, John, 193, 224
Johnson, Joseph, 159
Johnson, Moses, 273
Johnson, Sibbel, 276
Johnson, Stephen, 280
Johnson, William, 99
Johnston, Mr., 36
Johnstone, William, 79
Jolly, John, 85
Jones, Abijah, 6
Jones, Edward, 195
Jones, Eleanor, 227
Jones, Ephraim, 122
Jones, Evan, 12
Jones, Isaac, 121
Jones, John, 61, 283
Jones, Mr., 182
Jones, Samuel, 244
Jones, William, 227
Judd, James, 138
Kane, Roger, 87
Kelley, Samuel, 152
Kelly, Moses, 244
Kelly, Patrick, 15
Kelsey, Bridget, 177
Kelsey, James, 177

Kelvin, Thomas, 122
Kemp, James, 43
Kerum, Martin, 26
Ketchum, Daniel, 253
Ketchum, Keziah, 252
Ketchum, Mr., 282
Ketchum/Ketcham, Isaac, 14, 15
Keyes, Salma, 111
Keys, Stephen, 167
Kilborn, Doct., 163
Kilborn, Joseph, 163, 168
King, Charles, 139
King, John, 133, 173
King, Mary, 139, 173
King, Mr., 148
King, Richard, 27
King, Violet, 222
Kinne, Eunice, 49
Kinne, Thomas, 50
Kinyon, David, 19
Kinyon, Thomas, 19, 21
Kirby, Daniel, 85
Knap, Thomas, 94
Knight, Hannah, 200
Knight, Manasseh, 200
Knowles, Isaac, 10
Labatut, Mr., 218
Ladd, Ezekiel, Jr., 83
Ladd, Lemuel, 69
Ladd, Merrium, 69
Ladd, Sebbel, 83
Lafford, James H., 269, 278
Laird, Captain, 49
Lameson, William, 186
Lamphear, Delight, 271
Lamphear, Elijah, 53
Lamphear, George, 271
Lancey, Sarah, 83
Lancey, Thomas, 83
Langdon, Samuel, 62, 63, 147
Larabee/Larabe, Asa, 161, 164
Larkin, Edward, 184
Larkin, Pompey, 6

Larshar, Capt., 160
Lathrop, Azariah, 82, 284
Latimer/Latemore, Picket, 25, 243
Lawlor, John, 281
Lawrence, Mr., 30
Lawton, Christopher, 229
Lawton, Nathaniel, 229
Lawton, Robert, 123, 124
Lay, Elisha, 23
Le Verry, Mr., 219
Leavenworth, Gideon, 55
Ledlie, H., 99
Ledyard, George, 5
Lee, Elizabeth, 42
Lee, Henry, 38
Lee, Jeddiah, 42
Lee, Joseph, 166
Lee, Samuel, 22, 29
Lee, Stephen, 264
Leech, Thomas, 98
Leete/Leet, Gideon, 2d., 195
Legate, Thomas, 27, 148
Lemairgre, Mr., 274
Lenox, John Rowland, 182, 183
Letson, Mary, 92
Letson, Robert, 92
Lewis, James, 201
Lewis, John, 235
Liberty, Francis, 269
Liberty, Peggy, 269
Lincon, Hannah, 12
Lincon, Jonathan, 12
Lithlourn, John, 133
Little John, Peter, 185
Little, John, 160
Livermore, Jane, 265
Livermore, Jonathan, 266
Lloyd, John, Jr., 36
Lobidal, Michael, 168
Logee, Philip, 53
Long, John, 157, 230
Long, Sarah, 230

Lord, Enoch, 100
Lord, James, 100
Lord, Lynde, 95, 113
Lord, Samuel P., 101
Lorde, Lynde, 273
Lott, Mr., 259
Lottridge, Thomas, 272
Lovell, Nathaniel, 76
Luis, Mr., 252
Luther, Mr., 277
Lyman, Daniel, 19
Lyman, Samuel, 126
Lynds/Lines, James, 279, 283
Lyon, Sylvester, 253
MacMullen, James, 168
Madsen, Jep, 265
Magner, John, 41, 267
Malbone, Godfrey, Jr., 191
Malbone, Polly, 191
Mallery, Caleb, 95, 96, 109
Maltman, Ann, 255
Maltman, James, 255
Man, Alse, 285
Man, Chrisopher, 285
Manley, John, 57
Manley, Michael, 19
Mann, Moses, 136
Mann, Ralph, 142
Mansfield, John, 237, 248
Mansfield, Joseph, 37
Marks, Mordecai, 85
Marsh, Solomon, 208
Marston, Jacob, 286
Marston, John, 216
Marston, Nathan, 31
Martin, Elizabeth, 249
Martin, Gideon, 208
Martin, John, 152
Martin, Joseph, 23, 47
Martin, Mr., 56
Martin, Percilla/Precillia, 23, 46
Martin, Peter, 159
Martin, William, 249

Marvell, John, 84
Mason, Anne, 162
Mason, Samuel, 162
Mason, Stuart, 11
Masury, Joseph, 271
Mawny, Cato, 66
Maxson, William, 63
Maxwell, William, 107
May, Eleazer, 4
May, John, 5
May, William, 253
May, Wilson, 234
Maynard, Stephen, 109
McCallam, Malcom, 104
McCarthy, Daniel, 66, 68
McCarty, William, 139
McClure, John, 261
McCollom, Daniel, 59
McConnal, Hugh, 9
McGoth, John, 37
McGoth, Mrs. John, 37
McIntosh, Daniel, 88
McKenzie, James, 47
McKinley, William, 107
McKnoll, Mr., 191
McKown, Hugh, 156
McKown, Nancy, 156
McLane, John 264
McLead, Alexr., 48
McLean, Hugh, 56
McLean, Mary, 128
McLothling, John, 14
McMullen, Mr., 268
Meigs, Col., 45
Meigs, Return Jonathan, 36
Mellon, Simon, 133
Men, unnamed, 47, 57, 67, 69,
   118, 146, 152, 170, 176, 189,
   193, 197, 204, 261, 271, 274,
   278, 284
Merriam, John, 245
Merril, John, 243
Merrit, Edward, 245

Merrit, Elizabeth, 250
Merrit, William, 250
Merwin, Seth, 262
Messervy, Philip, 196
Messervy, Remember, 196
Miles, Miner, 130, 131
Miller, Elisha, 256
Miller, Hugh, 125
Miller, John, 122
Miller, Joseph, 232, 236
Miller, Rufus, 191
Miner, Eph., 49
Miner, Ephraim, 7, 9, 24, 82, 274
Miner, Joel, 283
Mitchel, Seth, 198
Mitchell, Henry, 172
Mitchell, James, 134, 135, 136
Mitchell, Seth, 32
Money, William, 44
Monk, Henry, 231
Monro, George, 193
Monro/Munro, George, 214
Moody, Daniel, 252
Moody, Thomas, 80
Moor, Francis, 6
Moor, Wm., 97
Moore, Boaz, 80
Moore, Isaac, 163
Moore, Joseph, 258
Moore, Mr., 273, 275
Moore, Thomas, 43
Morey, Daniel, 142
Morgan, Isaac, 226
Morgan, Isaac, Jr., 241
Morgan, John, 146, 150
Morgan, Jonathan, 230
Morgan, Phebe, 10
Morgan, Sally, 241
Morgan, William, 139
Morrel/Morrell, Philip, 226, 227, 240
Morrill, John, 50
Morrill, Samuel, Jr., 268

Morrill/Morrell, Ephraim, 255
Morrill/Morrell, Sarah, 254
Morris, Luke, 151
Morris, Mr., 253
Morse, Elizabeth, 51
Morse, Jonas, 232, 236
Morse, Silas, 195
Morse, Stephen, 52
Morton, Eben'r, 5
Mory, Robert, 266
Moseley, Ebenezer, 89
Mosman, William, 42, 73
Motte, Joseph, 85
Moulton, Johnson, 152
Moultrop, Enoch, 90
Mountany, Joseph, 273, 275
Mowet, David, 119
Mowet, James Ryder, 119
Mullens, Joseph, 85
Mullins, Thomas, 2
Mulvaney, Sarah, 59
Mulvany, James, 59
Mumford, Giles, 172
Mumford, Samuel, 3
Munger, Amy, 240
Munger, Joel, Jr., 240
Munger, Jonathan, 126
Munn, Joseph, 168
Munson, Obadiah, 18
Munson, Rachel, 17
Munson, S., 114
Munson, Stephen, 10, 90, 104, 133, 140, 166, 182, 193, 234, 280
Munson, Stephen A., 214
Muray, Francis, 179
Murray, Joel, 50
Murrey/Murry, Michael, 110
Murrin, Joseph, 75
Mustees, Pero, 267; Prince, 204; Toby, 79; unnamed, 217; Watt, Primus, 79
Naler, William, 2

Neal, John, 223
Neates, Henry Thomas, 173
Ned, Judas, 140
Neff, John, 171
Negroes, Africa, 272; Alexander, 118; Anthony, 117; Asa, 272; , Bandon/Baudon, 65, 68; Berry/Barry, William, 86; Bet, 138; Bill, 116; Bill/Bell, 120, 123; Bob, 29; Boham, Rebecca, 64; Boston, 123, 141, 144; Bristol, 185, 266; Brown, Cato, 66; Browning, Henry, 200; Bud, 66, 158; Caesar/Caeser, 18, 22, 26, 29, 40, 56, 100, 102, 113, 189; Cambridge, 224; Negroes, Cash, 226 Negroes, Cato, 39, 49, 57, 72, 73, 91; Negroes, Ceaser/Cesar, 62, 63; 93, 147, 155; Charles, 84; Christopher, 144; Cloe, 234; Crisman, 27; Cuff, 169; Curtis, Alice, 262; , Cyrus, 45; Dan, 210; Darby, 194; Dean, Hampshire, 54; Dennis, James, 114; Derry, 77, 210; Dery/Dick, 251; Devereux, Cato, 222; Dick, 24, 25, 101, 131, 194, 195, 220; Dick/Dery, 251; Dinah, 11, 98, 117; Dorothy/Dot, 263; Dublin, 78; Enoch, 286, 287; Esther, 135; Felix, 172; Fife, 241; Fisher, Jo, 40; Fletus, 180; Fortune, 18, 229; Frank, 76, 208, 265; Freeman, 274; Gad, 159; Garrack, 104, 125; Gilliam, 119; Grig, 208; Guinea, 32, 33; Gummer, Abigail, 85; Hager, 217; Hampton, 159; Hannah, 17; Harry, 121, 214; Hector, 249; Negroes, Hull, Amos, 168; Isaac, 138; Jack, 142, 143, 154, 172, 208, 224, 256, 257; Jack/Zack, 218; James, 34; Jaseinte, 213; Jeffery, 12; Jehu, 45; Jericho, 137; Jim, 121; Jo, 101; Joe, 166, 219; Johnson, John, 224; Juba, 225; Jube, 35; Juos, 98; King, Violet, 222; Kit, 144; groes, Lambo, 212; Lankton, 174; Lettice, 67; Lewis, James, 201; Lively, 55; London, 4, 25, 99, 249; Lucy, 218; Mawny, Cato, 66; Money, William, 44; Moses, 53, 232; Nabby, 66, 158; Nancy, 105; Nat, 53; Ned, 172; Neptune, 33; Nero, 47, 148, 157, 161; Newport, 51; Nirum, 37; Obadiah, 44; Pero, 184, 207, 267, 282, 283; Perow, 58; Peter, 24, 47, 110, 158, 208, 209, 211, 214; Philby, 229; Phillips, Bantom, 272; Phillips, Hannah, 272; Phillis, 34, 266; Phoebe, 213; Pomp, 21, 58, 68, 202, 251; Post, Will, 132; Primus, 79; Prince, 30, 31, 36, 39, 60, 92, 108, 119, 134, 135, 162, 167, 205, 216, 221, 241; Quam, 71; Quommino, Caesar, 161; Quonso, 26; Reuben, 124; Richard, 233; Robert, 1; Robin/Robbin, 134, 135, 136, 184; Rogers, 75; Rose, 260; Sam, 24, 271; Sambo, 40; Sampson, 40; Sanno, Pier, 202; Sansy, 105; Say, 245; Scip, 237, 244; Seheter, Sarah, 198; Selah, 209; Si, 63; Silence, 2; Simon, 51, 238; Squash, 193; Stiles, Will, 132; Tack, 264;

Negroes, Tamor, 189; Tanner, 103; Tite, 74; Titus, 38, 121; Titus, Timothy, 32; Tom, 23, 130, 154, 169, 170, 201, 216, 277; unnamed, 3, 9, 20, 24, 30, 56, 65, 84, 85, 145, 174, 188, 191, 265, 276; Venus, 22, 275; Vilot, 194, 241; Violent, 105; Warren, 116; Warwick, 60, 181; Way, Betty, 168; Way, Fred, 168; Wooder, 89; York, 4, 48; Zack/Jack, 215; Zeb, 243, 246; Zil, 53; Zilpha, 27
Nelson, Ruth, 261
Nesfield, James, 43
Neuville, Jules, 173
Newbury, Roger, 151, 212
Newcomb, James, 204
Newcomb, Submit, 204
Newell, John, 186
Newman, Lydia, 222
Newning, John, 156
Newning, Nancy, 156
Newton, David, 183
Newton, Miriam, 183
Nicholas, Mary, 100
Nicholls, James, 121
Nichols, Benjamin, 76
Nichols, Lemuel, 253
Nichols, Mr., 254
Nickols, Joanna, 33
Nickols, Jonathan, 33
Niles, James, 5
Niles, Robert, 277
Nixon, John, 6
Noble, Francis, 135
Nord Berg/Nordberg, Michael, 270
North, Joseph, 228
Norton, Daniel, 255, 256, 257, 258
Norton, Jedediah, 65
Norton, Jediah, 285

Noxon, Peter, 46
Noyes, Joseph, 192
Noyes, William, 163
Nutter, John, 220
O'Brian, Patrick, 88
Oakman, Elizabeth, 203
Oakman, Isaac, 203
Olcott, Josiah, 278
Olcott, Josiah, Jr., 278
Olmstead, Aaon, 50
Orcutt, Susannah, 110
Orcutt, William, 110
Osgood, Christopher, 225
Otis, J., 14
Otis, Joseph, 37, 43, 47, 54, 85, 93, 114, 115, 120
Otis, Joseph, Jr., 88
Owen, Gideon, 119
Packard, Nath'l, 17
Packard, Oliver, 48, 64
Packard, Relief, 48, 64
Page, Rachel, 17
Pain, John, 147
Pain, Joseph, 147
Pain, Stephen, 147
Paine, John, 114, 119
Paine, Stephen, 114, 119
Palmer, Ephraim, 151
Palmer, Jared, 280
Palmer, Sarah, 133
Palmer, Simeon, 133, 134
Pardy, Josiah, 9
Parish, John, 236
Park, Asa, 28
Parker, Caide, 231
Parker, David, 46, 116
Parker, Doctor, 230
Parker, John, 1, 205, 217, 264
Parker, Nathan, 18
Parker, Roger, 257, 262
Parker, Salmon, 262
Parker, Sarah, 116
Parker, Tabitha, 217

Parkman, Mr., 279
Parks, Daniel, 81, 87
Parks, Lydia, 81
Parmele, Asa, 187
Parmele, Lucy, 187
Parsons, Chadwell, 151
Parsons, Simon, 255
Patten, Nathaniel, 74
Pattin, Amy, 128
Pattin, John, 128
Pattinson, Joseph, 36
Paul, Boston I., 220
Paul, Ruter, 220
Payden, Thomas, 75
Pearce, Benoni, 201
Pearce, Timothy, 234
Pearse, Nath'l, 60
Pearson, Joseph, 159
Pease, Jehiel, 277
Pease, Joseph, 231
Peck, Col., 19
Peck, Darius, 216, 243, 256, 281
Peck, William, 52
Peele, Hannah, 227, 228
Peele, Roger, 228
Peirce, John, 93
Pelham, Elisha, 212
Pelham, Francis, 212
Perkins, Abraham, 140
Perkins, Francis, 283
Perkins, Phebe, 10
Perkins, William, 280
Perry, Eliakim, 6
Perry, Elizabeth, 250
Perry, Rachel, 252
Perry, Sam., Jr., 10
Perry, Samuel, 10, 252
Perry, Seth, 10, 16
Perry, Stephen, 10
Perry, Thos., 10
Persons, Chatwell, 237
Pettibone, Abel, 179
Pettibone, Abraham, 33

Pettibone, Ahijah/Abijah, 123
Pettibone, Dudley, 179
Pettibone, Jonathan, 179
Pettibone/Ahijah/Abijah, 120
Phelpes, Alexander, 48
Phelpes, Mary, 48
Phelps, David, 113, 114, 179
Phelps, John, 130
Phelps, Mr., 162
Phelps, Noah, 179
Philips, John, 35
Philips, Nicholas, 35
Philips, Nicholas, Jr., 35
Phillips, Bantom, 272
Phillips, Desire, 13
Phillips, Hannah, 272
Phillips, John, 13
Phillipse, Mr., 285
Pierce, Ebenezer, 238
Pierce, Freelove, 238
Pierce, Joseph, 268
Pierce, Mr., 56
Pierpoint, Giles, 99
Pierpont, Robert, 3
Pike, Jonathan, 133
Pike, Mr., 48
Pike, Mrs., 48
Pike, Nathaniel, Jr., 133
Pike, Titus, 262
Pinkham, Ebenzer, 260
Piper, Benja., 111
Platt, Ebenezer, 265
Platt, Jeremiah, 116
Platt, Mr., 265
Platt, Zebulon, 177
Plumbe, John, 99
Poltenger, Athur, 252
Poltenger, Elizabeth Valentine 252
Pomroy, Richard, 115
Pomroy/Pumroy, Elijah, 279, 283
Pond, Abigail, 26
Pond, Moses, 136, 142

Poor, Mr., 254
Porter, Col., 203
Post, Jordan, Jr., 286, 287
Post, Will, 132
Potter, James, 283
Potter, John, 164
Potter, Stephen, 98
Powers, Joseph, 91
Powers, Joshua, 89
Powers, Timothy, 73
Pratt, Nehemiah, Jr., 244
Prentice, Stephen, 151
Prentiss, William, 201, 225
Prescott, Benjamin, 151
Prescott, Betiah, 197
Prescott, James, 27
Prescott, Oliver, 197
Preston, Lydia, 70
Prince, Job, 65, 68
Prince, William, 237, 244
Prindle, William, 111, 193
Procter, Samuel, 45, 68
Proctor, Nathaniel, 55
Pulveytaft, Robert, 127
Purdy, Joseph, 256
Purk, Edmund, 130
Quin, Francis, 200
Quommino, Caesar, 161
Ranney, Seth, 90
Ransom, Amasa, 144
Ransom, James, 163
Ransom, Robert, 168
Ray, James, 91
Ray, John, 18, 21
Raymond, Nathan, 274
Raymond, Uriah, 199
Raynolds, Joseph, 184
Read, Mary, 209
Read, Matthew, 209
Read/Reed, Seth, 279, 282
Reed, Ebenezer, 113
Reed/Read, Obadiah, 207
Reiley, Patrick, 11

Remsan, Abraham S., 82
Revere, John, 209
Revere, Lydia, 208
Reynolds, Thomas, 156
Rice, Esther, 284
Rice, John, 218
Rice, Lemuel, 253
Rice, William, 284
Richards, James, 65
Richards, John, 210
Richards, Thomas, 227
Richardson, William, 275
Ricker, Noah, 124
Rider, Caleb, 134
Robbins, Jacob, 247
Robbins, Levi, 200
Robbins, Thomas, 140
Robbins, Wait, 37
Robblee, Hulda, 175
Robblee, Thomas, 175
Robie, John, 38
Robie, Naomi, 38
Robins, Chandler, 216
Robinson, Jemima, 266
Robinson, John, 107
Robinson, Mr., 137
Robinson, Thomas, 231
Robinson, William, 266
Rockwood, Abigail, 63
Rockwood, Asa, 40
Rogers, Alexander, 278
Rogers, D. D., 174
Rogers, Daniel, 76, 77, 220
Rogers, Daniel Dennison, 188
Rogers, Hannah, 76, 77
Rogers, Jeremiah, 8
Rogers, Peter, 234
Rogers, Samuel, Jr., 239
Rogers, Thomas, 7
Rose, Amos, 104
Rose, William, 9
Rowlandson, Joseph, 276
Rowlandson, Sarah, 276

Ruggles, Samuel, 161
Rumrill, Aaron, 212, 213
Rumrill, Elizabeth, 212, 213
Rundle, Phineas, 113
Ryley, John, 133
Safford, Jedediah, 62
Sager, Benjamin, 50
Sampson, Wiliam, 119
Sanborn, Caleb, 108
Sanborn, John Smith, 205
Sanders, M., 143
Sandford/Sanford, Thomas, 122, 125
Sanford, Peleg, 65
Sanford, Philemon, 16
Sanford, Stephen, 70
Sanno, Pier, 202
Saunders, Daniel, Jr., 8
Savage, John, 197
Savanet, Peter, 218
Sawin/Sawen, Benjamin, 232, 236
Sawyer, Aaron, 40
Sayles, William, 177
Sayre/Sayer, Paul, 105
Scarfe/Scarf, M. Wm., 143
Schioth, Friderich/Frederich, 270
Scott, Jonathan, 177
Scovel, John, 110
Scovell, Kazia, 240
Scovell, Lemuel, 240
Scranton, Mr., 87
Scribner, Herekiah, 135
Sealeck, Darling, 135
Sealeck, Nathan, 135
Seare, Silas, 131
Searl, Edward, 12
Sears, John, 219, 264
Sedgwick, Deborah, 80
Sedgwick, Samuel, 80
Seeley, Benjamin, 90
Seeley, Seth, 11
Seheter, Sarah, 198

Selah, John, 158
Sellon, Samuel, 68
Service, Elizabeth, 194, 241
Seymour, Thomas, 265
Shackett, Peter, 151
Shaw, Ben., 131
Shaw, Daniel, 99
Shaw, David, 118
Shaw, Nath'l, 65
Shaw, Neal, 6
Shaw, Thomas, 254
Sheal, David, Jr., 102
Sheal, Elizabeth, 102
Sheffield, George, Jr., 8
Sheffield, James, 7
Sheilds/Shields, Hanah/Hannah, 17, 20
Sheilds/Shields, John, 17, 20
Sheldon, Elisha, 95
Sheldon, Isaac, 220
Sheldon, Mr., 106
Shepard, James, 120
Shepard, John, 213
Shepard, Moses, 248
Shepard, Thomas, 207
Shepard, William, 149
Sherman, Matthew, 11
Sherman, Samuel, 142
Shiels, Edward, 232
Shiels, Elizabeth, 232
Shrieve, John, 266
Shuck, Moresha, 277
Sikes, Titus, 257
Simmons, William, 95
Skidder, Abel, 11
Slate, Joseph, 180
Slate, Sovia, 180
Slate, Thomas, 72
Smith, Anne, 188
Smith, Augustus, 145
Smith, Benejah, 26
Smith, Benjamin, 50
Smith, Cornelius, 160

Smith, David, 99
Smith, Elijah, 178, 279
Smith, Elijah Austin, 283
Smith, Eunice, 99
Smith, Ezekiel, 276
Smith, George, 35, 231
Smith, George W., 269
Smith, Isaac, 214, 216
Smith, Joel, 207
Smith, John, 34
Smith, Jonathan, 43, 277
Smith, Joseph, 195
Smith, Josiah, 269
Smith, Lovice, 50
Smith, Mary, 43
Smith, Nathan, 8, 24, 35
Smith, Reuben, 60
Smith, Robert, 219
Smith, Roswell, 89
Smith, Samuel, 141, 153, 188
Smith, Sarah, 26, 216
Smith, Thankful, 231
Smith, Thomas, 50, 151
Smith, William, 44, 123, 124
Smith, Zilpah, 60
Snow, Mr., 185
Snyder, George, 14, 15
Soul, Bildad, 244
Soule, Jonathan, 16
Soule, Mary, 16
Spalding, Abigal, 129, 145
Spalding, Andrew, 129, 145
Spalding, Edward, 89
Spaulding, Reuben, 150, 152
Spencer, Eliphas, 155
Spencer, Rufus, 156
Sperry, Isaac, 70
Sperry, Uri, 70
Sprague, Nathaniel, 101, 103, 106
Springer, Abraham, 41, 44
Springer, Joana, 23
Springer, Joseph, 23
Stacnon, George, 74

Stafford, Joab, 89
Staggs, Cornelius, 160
Stanton, Joseph, 10
Stark, Nathan, 53
Stearns, Thomas, 2
Stebbins, Joseph, 1
Steel, Joseph, 177
Steel, Samuel, 170, 181
Steel, Sarah, 170
Steel, Thomas, 19
Stevens, Brimsely, 207
Stevens, Simon, 3
Steyn, B., 265
Stiles, Job, 104
Stiles, John, Jr., 211
Stiles, Reuben, 169
Stiles, Samuel, 104
Stiles, Will, 132
Stinson, Mr., 250
Stoddard, James, 157, 162
Stodder, Mortimore, 234
Stoder/Stoddard, Nathan, 126
Stone, Noah, 153
Strong, Judah, 222
Strong/Strorg, John, 117
Sturge, David, 140
Suhm, Bernard, 270
Sullivan, Owen, 93
Sumner, Samuel, 11
Sutherland, William, 35, 79
Swan, Elias, 192
Swan, Jabez, 215, 218
Swane, George, 1
Tabor, Philip, 57
Taft, Isaac, 54, 71, 74, 88
Taft, Sweeting, 252
Talbot, Silas, 117
Tallcott, Elizur, 224
Talpey, Henry, 29
Tarleton, Banistre, 125
Taylor, James, 166
Taylor, John, 39, 70
Taylor, Mr., 32

Taylor, Peggy, 70
Taylor, Wm., 98, 117
Tench, Mr., 54
Tharp, Jesse, 36
Thayer, Simeon, 182
Thelly, William, 168
Thomas, Catharine, 83
Thomas, Catherine, 82
Thomas, Gilbert, 28
Thomas, Lewis, 47, 160
Thomas, Moses, 82, 83
Thomas, Mr., 107
Thompson, Adam, 240
Thompson, Joshua, 139
Thompson, Thomas, 41
Thompson, Thos., 202
Thompson, William, 95
Thomson, Anna, 129
Thomson, Augustus, 145
Thomson, E., 174
Thomson, John, 79, 129
Thomson, William, 113
Thrasher, Samuel, 65
Throop, Dan, 51
Thrusher, Arthur, 22
Thurber, Relief, 9
Thurber, Samuel, 9
Thurston, James, 100
Thurston, John, 230
Tibbals, Nathan, 146
Tibbals, Sarah, 146
Tidd, Richard, 245
Tilden, Calvin, 120
Tilley, James, 105
Tillotson, Abel, 131
Tilton, Daniel, 39
Tisdell, Mr., 4
Titus, Timothy, 32
Todd, Cephas, 141
Toll, Simon, 253
Tom, John, 22
Tomkins, Samuel, 275
Tourtelot, Abraham, 252

Tousson, Louis, 87
Towley, Benjamin, 269
Tracey, Jane, 111
Tracey, Thomas, 112
Tracy, Benajah, 154
Tracy, Lucy, 154
Tracy, Naomi, 224
Trantum, Happy, 286
Trantum, John-Tho's, 286
Trowbridge, Easton, 130, 131
Truman, Henry, 187
Trumball, Richard, 124, 141
Tryon, Elizur, 251
Tuck, W., 189
Tucker, Elisha, 169
Tucker, Mary, 169
Tucker, Reuben, 274
Tucker, Sarah, 152
Tucker, William, 152
Tudor, Samuel, 249
Tufton, Thomas Sackville, 132
Tufton, Thomas Saxvilla/Saxwillee, 274
Tufts, Henry, 205
Tuller, Joseph, 179
Tuman, David, 177
Tupper, Prince, 10
Turffs, Henry, 264
Turner, Ann, 102
Turner, Anne, 90
Turner, Caleb, Jr., 88
Turner, John, 102
Turner, Luther, 195
Turner, Pelatiah, 10, 151
Turner, Peletiah, 88
Turner, Samuel, 88
Turner, Simeon, 90
Tuttle, Jared, 248
Tuttle, Stephen, 4
Tyler, Mabel, 287
Tyler, Moses, 100
Tyler, Nathaniel, 287
Tyler, William, 239

Valentine, Elizabeth, 252
Van Horne, Mr., 259
Varney, Massy, 186
Varney, Moses, 186
Violene, John, 56
Vokes, Mr., 257
Wadey, Humphrey, 193
Wadham, Jonathan, 15
Wadsworth, Fenn, 126
Wadsworth, General, 231
Wait, Benjamin, 46
Wait, Sarah, 45
Walden, Isaac, 276
Walden, Mary, 276
Wales, Eleazer, 126
Walice/Wallice, William, 228
Wallis, Sam., 18
Ward, Thomas, 72
Ware, Oliver, 177
Warner, Jonathan, 205
Warren, Ebenezer, 235
Warren, Ephraim, Jr., 25
Warren, Lydia, 235
Washbourn, David, 165
Washburn, David, 11
Washington, George, 146, 149, 254
Waterhouse, Timothy, 127
Waterman, Elisha, 96
Waterman, Eunice, 21
Waterman, John Olney, 21
Waterman, Thomas, 101, 103, 106
Watson, Abraham, 30
Watson, John, Jr., 218
Watson, Patrick, 142
Watt, Primus, 79
Way, Betty, 168
Way, Fred., 168
Way, Joseph, 154
Way, Nathaniel, 234
Weatherbee, Pelige, 228
Weatherbee, Simon, 228

Webb, James, 223
Webb, Joseph, 183
Webster, John, Jr., 195
Welch, Benjamin, 159
Welch, Charity, 159
Welch, John, 113
Welch, Mr., 160
Welds, Edmund G., 13
Wells, Colonel, 17
Wells, James, 277
Wells, John, 130
Wells, Mr., 154
Wells, Rachel, 17
Wells, Samuel, 263
Wendell, John, 154
Wentworth, Edward, 243
Wescott, Ann, 30
Wescott, Thomas, 30
West, Mary, 212
West, William, 212
Wetherbee, Ephraim, 267
Wetherbee, Mary, 267
Wharton, William, 151
Wheeler, Capt., 109
Wheeler, Moses, 59
Wheeler, Mr., 276, 279
Wheeler, Obadiah, 56, 58, 59
Wheelock, James, 229
Whipple, Eunice, 197
Whipple, Joseph, 51
Whipple, William, 197
Whitcomb, Joseph, 165
White, Aaron, 24
White, Jenkins, 195
White, John, 6, 40
White, Mr., 273, 275, 281, 282
White, Phillips, 147
Whitewell, Samuel, 30
Whiting, Asa, 26
Whiting, Fred. J., 225
Whitmon, Amos, 258
Whittemore, Hannah, 174
Whittemore, Peletiah, 174

Whittey, William, 66
Wight, Potter, 37
Wilcocks/Willcox, Martin, 222
Wilcocks/Willcox, Mary, 223
Wilcox, John, 198
Wilder, James, 155
Willcox, Arnold, 237
Willcox, Susannah, 237
Willcox/Wilcocks, Martin, 221
Willcox/Wilcocks, Mary, 221
Williams, Col., 230
Williams, Converse, 151
Williams, Esther, 150
Williams, Ez'l./Ezek./Ezekiel, 5, 11, 20, 22, 35, 72, 122, 130, 178
Williams, Henry Howell, 34, 48
Williams, John, 45, 119
Williams, John F., 107
Williams, John, Jr., 135
Williams, Joseph, 151, 153
Williams, Stephen, 191
Williams, Thomas, 19
Williams, William, 71
Williams. Ez'l., 102
Willington, Mr., 150
Willis, Margaret, 145
Willis, Samuel, 145
Willoughby, Elijah, 239, 242
Wilmarth, William, 41
Wilson, James, 135
Wiman, Mrs. William, 41
Winslow, Joshua, 140
Winslow, Peleg, 41
Winslow, William, 91, 190

Winter, Jonathan Weeks, 232
Wires, George, 41
Witaker, Abraham, 166
Wixsom, Lydia, 247
Wixsom, Reuben, 247
Wolcott, Caleb, 188
Wolcott, Gerusha, 187
Women, Thebe, 36
Women, unnamed, 97, 136
Wood, Daniel, 250
Wood, Elijah, 279, 283
Wood, Francis, 107
Wood, Harper Howard, 166
Wood, Mr., 80
Woodburn, Moses, 273
Woodruff, Jasper, 81
Woodruff, Tobias, 81
Woodruff, Zebulon, 81
Woodward, Beza., 229
Woodward, Gilbert, 28
Woodward, Israel, 262
Worster, David, 151
Worster, Henry, 151
Worthy, Thankful, 268
Worthy, Valentine, 268
Wright, Josiah, 199
Wright, Richard, 61
Wyatt, William, 191
Wyman, David, 39
Wyman, Lucy, 39
Yeaton, John, 250
Yeoman, Stephen, 247
Young, Jacob, 114
Young, James, 41
Young, William, 151
Zedericks, John Christopher, 13

www.ingramcontent.com/pod-product-compliance
Lightning Source LLC
Chambersburg PA
CBHW061428300426
44114CB00014B/1592